The Bible and Crusade Narrative
in the Twelfth Century

Crusading in Context

Series Editor
William J. Purkis

The crusading movement was a defining feature of the history of Europe, the Mediterranean and the Near East during the central and later Middle Ages. Ideas and practices associated with it touched the lives of people within and beyond Christendom and the Islamicate world, regardless whether they were ever directly engaged in, witnesses to, or victims of acts of crusading violence themselves.

This series aims to situate the medieval experience of the crusades and crusading societies in the broader social, cultural and intellectual contexts of the Middle Ages as a whole. Chronologically, its scope extends from the eleventh to the sixteenth century, and contributions from a range of disciplines are encouraged. Monographs and edited collections are both welcome; critical editions and translations of medieval texts will also be considered.

Proposals and queries should be sent in the first instance to the series editor or to Boydell and Brewer, at the addresses below.

Dr William J. Purkis, School of History and Cultures, University of Birmingham, Edgbaston, Birmingham, B15 2TT
w.j.purkis@bham.ac.uk

Boydell and Brewer Ltd, PO Box 9, Woodbridge, Suffolk, IP12 3DF
editorial@boydell.co.uk

Previously Published

Eyewitness and Crusade Narrative: Perception and Narration in Accounts of the Second, Third and Fourth Crusades, Marcus Bull

Baldric of Bourgueil: 'History of the Jerusalemites': A Translation of the Historia Ierosolimitana, translated by Susan B. Edgington, with an introduction by Steven J. Biddlecombe

The Miraculous and the Writing of Crusade Narrative, Beth C. Spacey

The Bible and Crusade Narrative in the Twelfth Century

Katherine Allen Smith

THE BOYDELL PRESS

© Katherine Allen Smith 2020

All Rights Reserved. Except as permitted under current legislation no part of this work may be photocopied, stored in a retrieval system, published, performed in public, adapted, broadcast, transmitted, recorded or reproduced in any form or by any means, without the prior permission of the copyright owner

The right of Katherine Allen Smith to be identified as the author of this work has been asserted in accordance with sections 77 and 78 of the Copyright, Designs and Patents Act 1988

First published 2020
The Boydell Press, Woodbridge
Paperback edition 2023

ISBN 978 1 78327 523 6 hardback
978 1 83765 072 9 paperback

The Boydell Press is an imprint of Boydell & Brewer Ltd
PO Box 9, Woodbridge, Suffolk IP12 3DF, UK
and of Boydell & Brewer Inc.
668 Mt Hope Avenue, Rochester, NY 14620–2731, USA
website: www.boydellandbrewer.com

A CIP catalogue record for this book is available
from the British Library

The publisher has no responsibility for the continued existence or accuracy of URLs for external or third-party internet websites referred to in this book, and does not guarantee that any content on such websites is, or will remain, accurate or appropriate

Contents

Acknowledgements	vii
List of Abbreviations	ix
Introduction	1
Chapter 1. History and Biblical Exegesis in the Latin West	15
The Educational Context	17
Exegesis, History, and Ideology	26
Glossing the Norman Conquest	38
Conclusion	47
Chapter 2. The Bible in the Chronicles of the First Crusade	49
Larger Trends	54
Exegetical Strategies: From Clermont to Jerusalem	68
Glossing Kerbogha's Mother	81
Conclusion	90
Chapter 3. Into the Promised Land	93
Sacred Geographies	98
Crusaders as New Israelites	112
Muslims as Biblical Polytheists	128
Crusade History as Polemic	136
Conclusion	151
Chapter 4. Babylon and Jerusalem	155
Crusading, the City of God, and the Apostolic Ideal	160
A New Babylon in the East	171
The Conquest of Jerusalem and Christ's Cleansing of the Temple	188
Conclusion	207
Conclusion	211

Contents

Appendix 1: Tables and Charts of Biblical References	215
Appendix 2: List of Biblical References in the Texts	219
Bibliography	255
Index	287

Acknowledgements

This project had several beginnings. The wonderful teaching of Michael Lower introduced me, as an undergraduate, to the crusading movement, and a graduate seminar with the extraordinary Jill Claster deepened my interest. Years later, an impulsive decision to teach a class on the crusades led to fourteen years (and counting) of close engagement with some of the texts I have written about in this book. My students' engagement has enriched my scholarship and made this a favorite class to teach. This work with students first got me thinking about the biblical material in crusade chronicles, and a summer stipend from the National Endowment for the Humanities helped me to see how this topic could become the basis for a book.

For a monastic historian trained by monastic historians, entering the world of crusades studies was a daunting prospect, one made immeasurably easier by the kindness of many colleagues. Nervous as I am about inadvertent omissions, I wish to thank the following scholars for sharing expertise, ideas, and work-in-progress, and saving me from errors: Steve Biddlecombe, Scott Bruce, Marcus Bull, Megan Cassidy-Welch, Niall Christie, John Cotts, Jay Diehl, Fiona Griffiths, Elizabeth Lapina, Thomas Lecaque, Anne Lester, Thomas McCarthy, Nic Morton, Martha Newman, John Ott, Nick Paul, Eyal Poleg, Jay Rubenstein, Luigi Russo, Kristin Skottki, Michael Staunton, Georg Strack, Heather Tanner, Stefan van der Elst, Scott Wells, and Brett Whalen. Penny Johnson's pride in my work has meant a good deal, as has the fellowship of Susan Wade, Wendy Schor-Haim, and Paulina Koryakin. The late Jill Claster's unfailing kindness and confidence in my work helped me over many moments of self-doubt; I miss her enormously. Finally, special thanks are due Jessalynn Bird, Cecilia Gaposchkin, and Matt Phillips for timely and incisive feedback on individual chapters, and to Matt Gabriele, who heroically read the whole first draft and offered many valuable suggestions. At Boydell & Brewer, Caroline Palmer and series editor William Purkis have been unflaggingly supportive, while Rebecca Cribb and Elizabeth McDonald have patiently fielded queries large and small. I am grateful, as well, to the press's anonymous readers for their engagement with my work. Any shortcomings that remain in the finished work are mine alone.

Closer to home, my colleagues at the University of Puget Sound have been a terrific source of support. The History Department has provided a congenial and intellectually vibrant academic home, while fellow medievalists Greta Austin, Denise Despres, Kriszta Kotsis, and the late, much-missed Michael Curley provided encouragement and feedback as the project evolved. James Bernhard and David Chiu from the Department of Math and Computer Science helped me find new ways to search medieval Latin texts. I am thankful to the university,

Acknowledgements

too, for a timely course release, summer research support, and a year-long Lantz Senior Sabbatical Fellowship that allowed me to complete the first draft.

Closest of all, my family has patiently borne my interest in events that most sane people regard as incomprehensible, and tolerated frequent oversharing about historical minutiae, Latin etymology, and medieval manuscripts. The Slips family helps keep things in perspective, while my parents never stop being interested. Michael, who makes everything possible, has now logged close to twenty years, while Peter, who makes everything old seem new again, has lived his whole life with this book. It seems like a small gesture to dedicate it to them.

An earlier version of parts of Chapter 2 appeared as "Glossing the Holy War: Exegetical Constructions of the First Crusade, c. 1099–c. 1146," in *Studies in Medieval and Renaissance History*, 3rd series, vol. 10 (2013): 1–39; and an earlier version of the last subsection of Chapter 4 was published as "The Crusader Conquest of Jerusalem and Christ's Cleansing of the Temple," in *The Uses of the Bible in Crusader Sources*, ed. Elizabeth Lapina and Nicholas Morton (Leiden, 2017), 19–41. I gratefully acknowledge permission to reprint this material.

Abbreviations

AA	Albert of Aachen. *Historia Ierosolimitana: History of the Journey to Jerusalem.* Ed. and trans. Susan Edgington. Oxford, 2007.
BB	*The Historia Ierosolimitana of Baldric of Bourgueil.* Ed. Steven Biddlecombe. Woodbridge, 2014.
CCCM	*Corpus christianorum, continuatio mediaevalis.* Turnhout, 1967–.
CCSL	*Corpus christianorum, series latina.* Turnhout, 1947–.
CJ	"The Capture of Jerusalem in the Ripoll Manuscript, Bibliothèque nationale (latin) 5132." Ed. John France. *English Historical Review* 103 (1988): 640–57.
CP	Contributions by the *'Charleville Poet'* to the *Historia vie Hierosolimitane of Gilo of Paris and a Second Anonymous Poet.* Ed. and trans. C. W. Grocock and Elizabeth Siberry. Oxford, 1997.
EP	*Epistulae et chartae ad historiam primi belli sacri spectantes: Die Kreuzzugsbriefe aus den Jahren, 1088–1100: Quellensammlung zur Geschichte des ersten Kruezzuges.* Ed. Heinrich Hagenmeyer. Innsbruck, 1901. Partial trans. Malcolm Barber and Keith Bate as *Letters from the East: Crusaders, Pilgrims and Settlers in the Twelfth and Thirteenth Centuries.* Aldershot, 2013.
FC	Fulcher of Chartres. *Historia Iherosolymitana (1095–1127).* Ed. Heinrich Hagenmeyer. Heidelberg, 1913. Book 1 trans. Martha E. McGinty in *The First Crusade: The Chronicle of Fulcher of Chartres and Other Materials*, 2nd edn, ed. Edward Peters, 47–101. Philadelphia, 1998.
FE	*Frutolfs und Ekkehards Chroniken und die anonyme Kaiserchronik.* Ed. F.-J. Schmale and I. Schmale-Ott. Ausgewählte Quellen zur deutschen Geschichte des Mittelalters 15. Darmstadt, 1972. Trans. T. J. H. McCarthy in *Chronicles of the Investiture Contest: Frutolf of Michelsberg and His Continuators*, 142–59 and 254–60. Manchester, 2014.
GF	*Gesta Francorum et aliorum Hierosolimitanorum.* Ed. and trans. Rosalind Hill. Oxford, 1962.
GN	Guibert of Nogent. *Dei gesta per Francos.* In *Dei gesta per Francos et cinq autres textes*, ed. R. B. C. Huygens. CCCM 127A. Turnhout, 1996. Trans. Robert Levine as *The Deeds of God through the Franks.* Woodbridge, 1997.

List of Abbreviations

GP	Contributions by Gilo of Paris to the *Historia vie Hierosolimitane of Gilo of Paris and a Second Anonymous Poet*. Ed. and trans. C. W. Grocock and Elizabeth Siberry. Oxford, 1997.
HH	Henry of Huntingdon. *Historia Anglorum*. Ed. and trans. Diana E. Greenway. Oxford, 1996.
MC	*Hystoria de via et recuperatione Antiochiae atque Ierusolymarum (olim Tudebodus imitatus et continuatus)*. Ed. Edoardo D'Angelo. Florence, 2009.
MGH	*Monumenta Germaniae Historica*
MGH Lib. de lite	*Monumenta Germaniae Historica, Libelli de lite imperatorum et pontificum*. Ed. Ernst Dümmler, Lothar von Heinemann, Freidrich Thaner, and Ernst Sackur. 3 vols. Hannover, 1891–97.
OV	*The Ecclesiastical History of Orderic Vitalis*. Ed. and trans. Marjorie Chibnall. 6 vols. Oxford, 1969–80.
PL	*Patrologiae cursus completus, series latina*, ed. J.-P. Migne. 221 vols. Paris, 1844–65.
PT	Peter Tudebode. *Historia de Hierosolimitano itinere*. Ed. John Hugh Hill and Laurita Lyttleton Hill. Documents relatifs à histoire des croisades. Paris, 1977. Trans. John Hugh Hill and Laurita Lyttleton Hill. Philadelphia, 1974.
RA	Raymond of Aguilers. *Historia francorum qui ceperint Jerusalem*. Ed. John Hugh Hill and Laurita Lyttleton Hill as *Le 'liber' de Raymond d'Aguilers*. Documents relatifs à histoire des croisades. Paris, 1969. Trans. John Hugh Hill and Laurita Lyttleton Hill. Philadelphia, 1968.
RC	Ralph of Caen. *Tancredus*. Ed. Edoardo D'Angelo. CCCM 231. Turnhout, 2011. Trans. Bernard S. Bachrach and David S. Bachrach as *The Gesta Tancredi: A History of the Normans on the First Crusade*. Aldershot, 2005.
RHC Oc.	*Recueil des historiens des croisades: historiens occidentaux*. 5 vols. Paris, 1844–95.
RR	Robert of Reims. *Historia Iherosolimitana*. Ed. Damien Kempf and Marcus G. Bull. Woodbridge, 2013. Trans. Carol Sweetenham as *Robert the Monk's History of the First Crusade*. Aldershot, 2005.
SF	"Un sermon commémoratif de la prise de Jérusalem par les croisés attribué à Foucher de Chartres." Ed. Charles Kohler. *Revue de l'Orient latin* 8 (1900–01): 158–64.

List of Abbreviations

WM   William of Malmesbury. *Gesta regum Anglorum*. Ed. and trans. R. A. B. Mynors, R. M. Thomson, and Michael Winterbottom. 2 vols. Oxford, 1998–99.

NOTE: Biblical citations follow the Dumbarton Oaks Medieval Library edition of the Vulgate, ed. Swift Edgar and Angela M. Kinney, 6 vols. (Cambridge, MA: Harvard University Press, 2010–13), with translations based on the Douay-Rheims version.

Introduction

> The world is our great book; what I read as promised in the book of God, I read in the world as fulfilled.
>
> — Augustine of Hippo[1]

There is much about medieval histories that most modern historians cannot bring themselves to admire. Partly this reflects an understandable desire to discover what is probably, or at least possibly, true, and thus of obvious historical value in our sources, a desire that leads us, in turn, to disregard much that we consciously or unconsciously judge extraneous to the reconstruction of the past. In the words of Nancy Partner, "We have simply lost contact ... with everything that could allow us to approach medieval histories naturally and directly." Noting that "modern historians have failed to appreciate much of what medieval readers admired in these works," she suggests that "All medieval histories contain more that is valuable to us than scraps of verifiable information, although what that 'more' is, exactly, varies from book to book and is difficult to describe."[2] In histories written in the Latin West before c. 1150 – that is, histories written in Latin by clerics – a great deal of this elusive "more" consists of biblical allusions and exegetical commentary, material which learned medieval readers would have noticed and appreciated but which most modern readers overlook. Nowhere is this truer than in the unprecedented outpouring of historical writing related to the endeavor we call the First Crusade, which inspired over a dozen substantial chronicles and numerous shorter texts in the period between the fall of Jerusalem in 1099 and the preaching of the Second Crusade in 1146 alone. Considered as

---

[1] *Sancti Aurelii Augustini Epistulae I–LV*, 43.25, CCSL 31, ed. Klaus-Detlef Daur (Turnhout, 2004), 185: "maior liber noster orbis terrarum est; in eo lego completum, quod in libro Dei lego promissum."

[2] Nancy F. Partner, *Serious Entertainments: The Writing of History in Twelfth-Century England* (Chicago, 1977), 4–5. Scholarly interest in medieval historiography has grown enormously since this pronouncement, and many studies have attempted to read medieval historians on their own terms, in the context of distinctly medieval visions of history. As a more recent evaluation by Robert M. Stein suggests, while historians' approaches to medieval texts have changed in key ways since the 'linguistic turn,' scholars still tend to "look *through*" rather than "look *at*" texts, in the process overlooking much of what seems dubiously factual; see "Literary Criticism and the Evidence for History," in *Writing Medieval History*, ed. Nancy Partner (London, 2005), 67–86.

a group, these histories contain a staggering amount of biblical material: 1,408 identifiable scriptural references across some 1,300 modern printed pages.³ The Bible appears at every turn, its imagery encroaching on the landscape of the East and adorning epic battle scenes, its words peppering the victory speeches of the crusade's leaders and forcing their Muslim adversaries to predict their own defeat. These works are a powerful reminder of the omnipresence of biblical imagery and language in the Latin West, and of how readily medieval Christians connected their own experiences and concerns to the Scriptures.⁴ They are also suggestive of how the First Crusade forced a rethinking of the traditional relationship between the biblical then and the medieval now, between the promised land of the Scriptures and the crusading home front.

Although modern scholars have long been accustomed to refer to these narratives as works of history, this label is somewhat misleading. Whether judged by medieval or modern standards, the twelfth-century narratives of the First Crusade are much more and much less than histories. Their authors were certainly doing historical work, judging by the well-known medieval definition of the historian as someone concerned with *historiae*, or "things which really have been done."⁵ But the crusade's narrators also concerned themselves with things that had not yet happened, as well as things that had taken place long, long before their narrative framework. Their story's climax was the conquest of a place, the holy city of Jerusalem, that existed at once within and beyond human time. And the crusade's cast of characters included not only heroes of living memory but the warriors of ancient Israel, the apostles, and Christ. Even as they claimed for the first crusaders a place of importance within the *longue durée* of political history, chroniclers were anxious to define the crusade's place within the even longer (and, to them, altogether more significant) arc of salvation history, and were confident that an analysis of recent events could shed new light on the past and future workings of divine providence. To draw out these layers of meaning, chroniclers were obliged to look beyond the historian's rather limited toolbox for models and methods. They found the interpretive aids they required in the Scriptures and their interpretive traditions, as well as in the working methods of biblical exegesis, a sophisticated art which enjoyed a great revival in the decades around 1100. Indeed, it is a central contention of this book that medieval

---

³ See Appendices 1 and 2 for a breakdown of this number, and Ch. 2 for analysis.
⁴ As Eyal Poleg has written, in the Middle Ages "the Bible was made all things to all people," through creative interpretation that "made that its narratives present for medieval society." See *Approaching the Bible in Medieval England* (Manchester, 2013), 2.
⁵ This definition is Isidore of Seville's from the *Etymologiae*, 1.44.5, ed. W. M. Lindsay (Oxford, 1911), n.p.; similar definitions were offered by the eleventh-century grammarian Papias in his *Elementariam* (Venice, 1491), 150; and the early twelfth-century theologian Hugh of St. Victor in his *De sacramentis*, Prol., PL 176: 185.

Introduction

Christians could not have made sense of the First Crusade *without* the sacred texts. Put another way, the advent of holy war inspired new, deeply exegetical ways of thinking and writing about history in medieval Christendom.

A passage from the *Historia Ierosolimitana* of Albert of Aachen (d. aft. 1119) illustrates the centrality of the Bible and exegetical methods within early crusading narratives. Among the hoard of stories Albert amassed in his researches were a series of tales that situated Duke Godfrey of Bouillon (d. 1100), first ruler of the Latin Kingdom of Jerusalem, within sacred history.[6] As Albert heard it, Godfrey had initially kept his desire to undertake the Jerusalem journey secret, revealing his intentions only to a few attendants, including a certain Stabelo. One night this Stabelo received a vision of "a golden ladder (*scala aurea*), extremely long, stretching all the way from heaven to earth," which he began to climb, along with his master and Rothard, the duke's steward. While a broken rung and a temperamental lamp forced Rothard to turn back at the ladder's midpoint, Godfrey made the ascent successfully, as did Stabelo himself. Their climb complete, Godfrey and Stabelo entered "the court of heaven," where they found a table "with all kinds of heaped up sweetness of delicious things," at which a number of the elect (*electi*) were dining. As Stabelo looked on, the duke joined the holy company and "shared in all the sweetness that was there." Here Albert paused in his tale and, like the good monastic exegete he was, put to his reader the question all medieval students of the sacred page were trained to ask: "What is signified (*quid ... significatur*)" by all this? Mining Stabelo's vision for allegorical and moral meaning, Albert unpacked the significance of the ladder's material (gold, signifying purity of heart), the failure of Rothard's lamp (foreshadowing his later desertion from the crusade), the table of delicacies (a symbol of the Holy Sepulcher), and heaven (the city of Jerusalem). Albert's purposeful deployment of scriptural language and tropes adds nuance to his gloss: the heavenly *"table prepared for them"* is the table of Psalm 22:5 which God set for believers amidst their enemies (an apt image for crusaders); Rothard is said to "return to the plough of affliction," recalling the prophecy of Isaiah 17:9 and linking this fair-weather crusader with the inconstant people of the biblical Damascus; and, of course, the typological precedent for the ladder connecting heaven to earth is Jacob's ladder (Gen. 28:12). Cumulatively, Albert's exegetical choices align Godfrey with an appropriate Old Testament precedent, specifically the patriarch Jacob, whose ladder Christian exegetes were accustomed to read allegorically as Christ, or anagogically as a glimpse of "the future fellowship between men and angels through the cross of Christ."[7] At the turn of the twelfth century, when

---

[6] The following discussion is based on AA, 436–38.
[7] E.g., Augustine, *Contra Faustum Manichaeum*, 12.26, ed. J. Zycha, Corpus Scriptorum Ecclesiasticorum Latinum 25/1 (Vienna, 1891), 354–55; Ambrose, *De excessu fratris*

Albert wrote, some Christians hoped that such a fellowship would be realized through the mediation of a saintly ruler of a reconquered Jerusalem, the city of God come down to earth.[8]

Albert's explication of this story is typical of contemporary clerical narrators' hermeneutical approach to the First Crusade as a text with multiple registers of meaning. Historically, they accorded the crusade a place among the epic wars of the ancient world and the more recent past. Typologically, numerous past figures and events foreshadowed the Jerusalemites' journey; thus Jacob could be read as a "type" of Godfrey of Bouillon, or the Exodus narrative as a proto-crusade. Morally, the events of 1095–99 offered an abundance of spiritual exemplars, as well as anti-models; crusaders like Duke Godfrey were presented as paragons of apostolic charity and humility, who opposed Muslim enemies infected (like some of Godfrey's less virtuous fellow crusaders) with the sins of pride and avarice. Mystically, the crusade's place on the timeline of sacred history was hinted at in the Jerusalemites' fulfillment of prophecies from the Old and New Testaments. While individual chroniclers discerned different meanings in the crusade text, they all found the Scriptures and related methods of textual criticism to be essential interpretive tools. Equally importantly, the crusade created opportunities for twelfth-century writers to engage patristic and Carolingian theologians and exegetes in conversation, in the process adding to, and sometimes challenging, their predecessors' readings.

While it has long been noted that the crusading movement drew inspiration from earlier textual traditions, including the Scriptures, patristic and early medieval theology, and the literature of ecclesiastical reform, much work remains to be done if we hope to understand early crusading narratives within their original intellectual and spiritual contexts. Although the chronicles and related works which are the main sources for this study comprise one of the most intensively studied groups of texts from the entire medieval period, until recently scholars tended to mine these works for data useful for reconstructing the chronology and logistics of the First Crusade. The two decades since 2000 have seen a dramatic reconsideration of this agenda, as more historians have begun, in Damien Kempf's words, "to move away from a static conception of [crusade texts] as data, and consider them instead in their dynamic function as literary

---

sui Satyri, 2.100, PL 16: 1342; trans. H. De Romestin et al., *Ambrose: Selected Works and Letters* (Edinburgh, 1986), 90.

[8] Albert and his contemporaries certainly pinned high hopes on Godfrey, a larger-than-life figure who proved tragically short lived. For the legends surrounding Godfrey, some of which may have originated on the expedition to the East, see Jay Rubenstein, "Godfrey of Bouillon versus Raymond of Saint-Gilles: How Carolingian Kingship Trumped Millennarianism at the End of the First Crusade," in *The Legend of Charlemagne in the Middle Ages: Power, Faith, and Crusade*, ed. Matthew Gabriele and Jace Stuckey (New York, 2008), 59–76, esp. 64–65.

works, shaped by their intersection with specific actors at different times."[9] As a result, we now know much more than we did at the turn of the century about the institutional, political, spiritual, and familial contexts of crusading, and exciting new work on the commemoration and materiality of the expeditions to the East, as well as the crusading home front, is further expanding the boundaries of crusades studies.[10]

However, the complex role played by the Bible in the early crusading movement remains relatively unexplored. Pioneering studies by Paul Alphandéry in 1929 and Paul Rousset in 1945 raised important questions about the respective roles of the Old and New Testament in crusade historiography, and probed the chroniclers' eschatological expectations.[11] While few twentieth-century scholars took up these issues, important work by Penny J. Cole on crusade preaching and by Jonathan Riley-Smith on the "theological refinement" of the holy war idea called attention to the Scriptures' importance in the thought world of twelfth-century crusaders and chroniclers.[12] In the twenty-first century, historians have become increasingly interested in the ways in which biblical models shaped the crusade idea and the self-image of crusaders, and indeed the body of scholarship produced on these topics since 2000 greatly exceeds that produced in the

---

[9] Damien Kempf, "Towards a Textual Archaeology of the First Crusade," in *Writing the Early Crusades: Text, Transmission, and Memory*, ed. Marcus Bull and Damien Kempf (Woodbridge, 2014), 116–26 (at 116).

[10] Important recent works that shed light on these aspects of crusading include: James Naus, *Constructing Kingship: The Capetian Kings of France and the Early Crusades* (Manchester, 2016); William J. Purkis, *Crusading Spirituality in the Holy Land and Iberia, c. 1095–c. 1187* (Woodbridge, 2008); Jochen Schenk, *Templar Families: Landowning Families and the Order of the Temple in France, c. 1120–1307* (Cambridge, 2012); Nicholas Paul, *To Follow in Their Footsteps: The Crusades and Family Memory in the High Middle Ages* (Ithaca, NY, 2012); Ann E. Lester, "What Remains: Women, Relics, and Remembrance in the Aftermath of the Fourth Crusade," *Journal of Medieval History* 40, no. 3 (2014): 311–28; and the essays in *Remembering the Crusades and Crusading*, ed. Megan Cassidy-Welch (London, 2016).

[11] Paul Alphandéry, "Les citations bibliques chez les historiens de la première croisade," *Revue de l'histoire des religions* 99 (1929): 139–57; Paul Rousset, *Les origines et les caractères de la première croisade* (Neuchâtel, 1945), 89–100, 185–92. See also Rousset's later "L'idée de croisade chez les chroniqueurs d'Occident," in *Storia del medioevo: Relazioni del X congresso internazionale di scienze storiche iii* (Florence, 1955), 547–63.

[12] See Penny J. Cole, "'O God, the Heathens Have Come into Your Inheritance' (Ps. 78:1): The Theme of Religious Pollution in Crusade Documents, 1095–1188," in *Crusaders and Muslims in Twelfth-Century Syria*, ed. Maya Shatzmiller (Leiden, 1993), 84–111; eadem, *The Preaching of the Crusades to the Holy Land, 1095–1270* (Cambridge, MA, 1991); Jonathan Riley-Smith, *The First Crusade and the Idea of Crusading* (London, 1986; 2nd edn. Philadelphia, 2009), esp. ch. 6; and idem, "Crusading as an Act of Love," *History* 65 (1980): 177–92; repr. in *The Crusades: Essential Readings*, ed. Thomas Madden (Malden, MA, 2002), 32–50.

entire previous century. This work has included quantitative studies[13] as well as in-depth examinations of individual crusading narratives[14] and explorations of the role played by particular biblical books or figures in the definition of the crusade idea.[15] Scholars have also become increasingly attuned to the ways in which the Bible mediated the theology and liturgy of holy war, the experiences of crusaders, and the expectations of chroniclers.[16] But our understanding of the ways in which the Bible informed crusading agendas and experiences, as Elizabeth Lapina and Nicholas Morton recently observed, "has remained in its infancy," and likewise, historians have only begun to consider how the medieval practices of scriptural exegesis shaped the reception of the crusade project.[17] Indeed, as the wide-ranging contributions to the 2017 volume dedicated to *The Uses of the Bible in Crusader Sources* show, scholars have barely scratched this topic's surface. The time is ripe, then, for a reappraisal of the role of the Bible and exegetical thinking in the early crusading movement. Such a reappraisal must build upon the ongoing renaissance in crusades studies, as well as the growing body of scholarship dedicated to exposing the vitality and originality of medieval biblical exegesis.

As the crusading movement has become recognized as a major shaping force in the history of medieval European society and its spirituality, rather than a footnote in the Latin Church's history,[18] much attention has been paid

---

[13] Henri Bresc, "Les historiens de la croisade: Guerre sainte, justice et paix," *Mélanges de l'Ecole française de Rome, Moyen Age* 115 (2003): 727–53.

[14] For example, see Alan V. Murray, "Biblical Quotations and Formulaic Language in the Chronicle of William of Tyre," in *Deeds Done Beyond the Sea: Essays on William of Tyre, Cyprus, and the Military Orders Presented to Peter Edbury*, ed. Susan B. Edgington and Helen J. Nicholson (Farnham, 2014), 25–34; and the essays gathered in *The Uses of the Bible in Crusader Sources*, ed. Elizabeth Lapina and Nicholas Morton (Leiden, 2017).

[15] These include: M. Cecilia Gaposchkin, "Louis IX, Crusade, and the Promise of Joshua in the Holy Land," *Journal of Medieval History* 34 (2008): 245–74; Elizabeth Lapina, "The Maccabees and the Battle of Antioch," in *Dying for the Faith, Killing for the Faith: Old-Testament Faith-Warriors (Maccabees 1 and 2) in Cultural Perspective*, ed. Gabriela Signori (Leiden, 2012), 147–59; and Nicholas Morton, "The Defence of the Holy Land and the Memory of the Maccabees," *Journal of Medieval History* 36 (2010): 275–93. For the use of scriptural exemplars by contemporary Muslim writers, see Yehoshua Frenkel, "Crusaders, Muslims and Biblical Stories: Saladin and Joseph," in *The Crusader World*, ed. Adrian Boas (London, 2016), 362–77.

[16] Exemplary in this regard are Jay Rubenstein, *Armies of Heaven: The First Crusade and the Quest for Apocalypse* (New York, 2011); and Cecilia Gaposchkin, *Invisible Weapons: Liturgy and the Making of Crusade Ideology* (Ithaca, NY, 2017).

[17] Elizabeth Lapina and Nicholas Morton, Introduction to *The Uses of the Bible in Crusader Sources*, 1–16 (quoting 2).

[18] Important treatments of the spiritual dimensions of the crusading movement include: Elizabeth Lapina, *Warfare and the Miraculous im the Chronicles of*

Introduction

to the medieval historiography of the First Crusade. Scholars have been especially concerned with assessing the relative value of individual sources and determining the relationships between the earliest accounts.[19] Until the early 2000s, texts attributed to eyewitnesses were judged to be far and away the most valuable sources for the First Crusade, while the many accounts written by armchair historians were given short shrift. Close analysis of early crusading narratives and their manuscript traditions has, however, made modern scholars less trusting of what purport to be eyewitness accounts.[20] Equally importantly, as Elizabeth Lapina and Marcus Bull have argued, such a hierarchy of sources made little sense from a twelfth-century perspective, as medieval writers did not value eyewitness testimony for its own sake. Insofar as God was the author of history – and, indirectly, of written histories – theologically sophisticated writers who undertook to describe God's hand at work in the world witnessed the events they described with spiritual rather than bodily eyes.[21] In the spirit of the twelfth century, this study encompasses accounts of the First Crusade written by witnesses, maybe-witnesses, and non-witnesses, and includes later works written up to the preaching of the Second Crusade in 1146, whose authors believed their accounts to equal (or exceed) earlier ones in value.

---

the First Crusade (University Park, PA, 2015); Purkis, *Crusading Spirituality*; Sylvia Schein, *Gateway to the Heavenly City: Crusader Jerusalem and the Catholic West (1099–1187)* (Aldershot, 2005); Colin Morris, *The Sepulchre of Christ and the Medieval West: From the Beginning to 1600* (Oxford, 2005), ch. 5–8; Marcus Bull, *Knightly Piety and the Lay Response to the First Crusade: The Limousin and Gascony, c. 970–c. 1130* (Oxford, 1993); Riley-Smith, *The First Crusade*; Bernard McGinn, "*Iter Sancti Sepulchri*: The Piety of the First Crusaders," in *Essays on Medieval Civilization: The Walter Prescott Webb Memorial Lectures*, ed. Bede Karl Lackner and Kenneth Roy Philp (Austin, 1978), 33–71; and A. Dupront, "La spiritualité des croisés et des pèlerins d'après les sources de la première croisade," in *Pellegrinaggi e culto del santi in Europa fino alla Ia crociata*, Convegni del centro di studi sulla spiritualità medievale 4 (Todi, 1963), 449–83.

[19] For a historiographical overview and additional bibliography, see Jean Flori, *Chroniqeurs et propagandistes: Introduction critique aux sources de la Première Croisade* (Geneva, 2010).

[20] For representative examples, see Jay Rubenstein, "What is the *Gesta Francorum*, and Who Was Peter Tudebode?" *Revue Mabillon* n.s. 16 (2005): 179–204; Thomas W. Smith, "First Crusade Letters and Medieval Monastic Scribal Cultures," *Journal of Ecclesiastical History* (forthcoming); and Simon Parsons, "The Letters of Stephen of Blois Reconsidered," *Crusades* 17 (2018): 1–28.

[21] Elizabeth Lapina, "The Problem of Eyewitnesses in the Chronicles of the First Crusade," *Viator* 38 (2007): 117–39; Marcus Bull, *Eyewitness and Crusade Narrative: Perception and Narration in Accounts of the Second, Third, and Fourth Crusades* (Woodbridge, 2018).

This study seeks to contextualize the First Crusade's early narratives within the practices of medieval historiography and exegesis, thereby grounding them more firmly in the intellectual and spiritual world of the late eleventh and early twelfth centuries. While some landmark studies of medieval historiography have ignored these works,[22] other scholars have suggested that they were markedly different, in their focus and presentation of events, from the annals and chronicles characteristic of earlier medieval centuries.[23] But such pronouncements generally fail to pin down what, exactly, was new or different (or not) about the crusade's early histories. Scholars working on specific chronicles, or families of texts, have proposed more satisfying answers. For example, Jay Rubenstein has observed that the early chronicles of the First Crusade are among the earliest single-event histories written in the Latin West, while Samu Niskansen has shown that their authors creatively blended existing genres – including hagiography, pilgrimage itinerary, and chronicle – to create a distinctive new way of recording the past.[24] Equally importantly, the narratological approach favored by Marcus Bull asks scholars to foreground issues of reader response and to appreciate individual crusade narratives as "creative, expressive acts," packed with imaginative leaps, and as concerned with style as with content.[25] Building on this growing body of work that seeks to approach crusades sources on their own terms, with an appreciation of authorial working methods and goals, this study calls attention to the ways in which early crusading sources reflect medieval practices of quotation, a little-studied subject that is nevertheless essential to understanding medieval historiography.[26] For the First Crusade's narrators, like their peers who wrote hagiography, genealogy, and exegesis, were unapologetic borrowers of earlier authors' ideas and language. Some were connoisseurs of ancient Roman history and poetry, and indeed the crusade chroniclers' interest in classical models remains a rich, largely untapped vein of inquiry.[27] It is clear, however, that the Bible was the most important structural, linguistic, and hermeneutic influence on

---

[22] E.g., Bernard Guenée, *Histoire et culture historique dans l'Occident médiéval* (Paris, 1980); and Janet Coleman, *Ancient and Medieval Memories: Studies in the Reconstruction of the Past* (Cambridge, 1992).

[23] See, for example, Beryl Smalley, *Historians in the Middle Ages* (London, 1974), 131–45.

[24] Rubenstein, "What is the *Gesta Francorum*," 180; Samu Niskansen, "The Origins of the *Gesta Francorum* and Two Related Texts: Their Textual and Literary Character," *Sacris Erudiri* 51 (2012): 287–316.

[25] Marcus Bull, "Robert the Monk and His Source(s)," in *Writing the Early Crusades*, ed. Bull and Kempf, 127–39 (quoting 128). For a fuller discussion of his methodology, see Bull's *Eyewitness and Crusade Narrative*, 1–71.

[26] The fullest discussion to date is Jeanette Beer, *In Their Own Words: Practices of Quotation in Early Medieval History-Writing* (Toronto, 2014). Beer devotes a chapter to the *Gesta Francorum* but deals only in passing with practices of biblical quotation.

[27] As suggested by Steven Biddlecombe's Introduction to BB, xxxiv–xxxvii.

Introduction

the crusade's early twelfth-century narrators, an insight which should encourage us to think more deeply about the biblical underpinnings of the holy war concept, as well as the Bible's influence on medieval historiography more broadly.[28]

While an analysis that privileges the scriptural material in crusading narratives may not help us to reconstruct the historical trajectory of the First Crusade in greater detail, such an approach promises to enrich our understanding of the events of 1095–99 in numerous other ways, not least by allowing for a better appreciation of what the crusade meant to contemporaries – or, rather, of the process by which they pondered, debated, and finally decided what it meant to them. Within the context of the First Crusade and its historiography, this study sheds new light on the process by which this momentous series of events passed from memory into written record; on the intellectual and spiritual underpinnings of early historical interpretations of the crusade; and on the relationships between individual works, thereby contributing to the growing body of scholarship on the historical and ritual commemoration of the crusades in the medieval West.[29] It also adds to an emerging strand of historiography on crusading memory,[30] since, as will become clear, twelfth-century Christians' memories of the First Crusade were shaped as much through a dialogue with the biblical past as through commemoration of the crusaders' recent exploits.

Focusing on the chronicles' biblical material and exegetical dimensions also allows us to appreciate this important group of texts as products of a particular way of reading and thinking associated with monastic and cathedral schools in the last decades of the eleventh century and the first decades of the twelfth. These schools, many located in Capetian France, were focal points in a revival of biblical scholarship whose scale is only now beginning to be appreciated.[31] This exegetical revival coincided with contemporary ecclesiastical reform movements, and membership in these two intellectual communities overlapped to a significant degree. As works that blended history with biblical interpretation and promoted

---

[28] On this last topic, see Benoît Lacroix, *L'Historien au moyen âge* (Montreal, 1971), esp. 58–68; Karl Morrison, *History as a Visual Art in the Twelfth-Century Renaissance* (Princeton, NJ, 1990); and Gabrielle M. Spiegel, *The Past as Text: The Theory and Practice of Medieval Historiography* (Baltimore, 1997).

[29] For an orientation to this literature, see Marcus Bull and Damien Kempf, Introduction to *Writing the Early Crusades*, ed. Bull and Kempf, 1–8; and Gaposchkin, *Invisible Weapons*, 1–15.

[30] For example, see Paul, *To Follow in Their Footsteps*; the essays in the special edition of *The Journal of Medieval History* 40 (2014), ed. Megan Cassidy-Welch and Anne E. Lester; and *Remembering the Crusades and Crusading*, ed. Cassidy-Welch.

[31] Guy Lobrichon writes that in the second half of the eleventh century scholars at these schools "inaugurat[ed] a profound transformation in the way the Bible was used throughout the West." See "The Early Schools, c. 900–1100," in *The New Cambridge History of the Bible, Vol. 2: From 600 to 1450*, ed. Richard Marsden and E. Anna Matter (Cambridge, 2012), 536–54 (quoting 537).

a new devotional activity closely linked to reformist agendas, the First Crusade chronicles should be linked to this exegetical renaissance as well as to contemporary reform movements.[32] Restoring these works more fully to their original intellectual context can also allow us to read them in a way that approximates how their original twelfth-century audience would have done, and to appreciate their authors' purposeful manipulation of biblical models and language as an integral part of their narratives, rather than mere window-dressing. To do this, however, modern readers must be willing to put aside their expectations about history – that it should be balanced, linear, based on primary sources – and embrace a medieval model of historical writing that is unabashedly partisan, discursive, and creative in its use of sources. Further, we must be open to the possibility that sometimes the portions of medieval texts that consist of borrowed material can, paradoxically, be sites of great authorial creativity and originality.

Methodologically, this study brings together the interpretive models and tools developed by historians of the crusades and scholars of biblical exegesis, two subfields that have had little to do with one another. The forty years since about 1980 have seen a remarkable amount of innovation within the study of biblical exegesis. Recent studies have revised our picture of eleventh-century intellectual culture, which is no longer regarded as a mere prelude to a "twelfth-century renaissance" but as a time of great exegetical sophistication and theological dynamism in its own right.[33] Scholars like Gilbert Dahan have also given us a more finely tuned understanding of medieval biblical hermeneutics, which centered on the complex relationship between the literal and spiritual meaning of the sacred page.[34] Careful examination of the work of individual exegetes has also shown that the decades immediately after 1100, when the historiography of the First Crusade took shape, saw a reevaluation of the relationship between the

---

[32] The relationship between the early crusading movement and ecclesiastical reform has, of course, interested scholars since the publication of Carl Erdmann's *Die Enstehung des Kreuzzugsgedanken* (Stuttgart, 1935); trans. Marshall W. Baldwin and Walter Goffart as *The Origin of the Idea of Crusade* (Princeton, NJ, 1977), whose interpretations continue to be debated. For an analysis of the First Crusade in light of earlier reform movements, see H. E. J. Cowdrey, "New Dimensions of Reform: War as a Path to Salvation," in *Jerusalem the Golden: The Origins and Impact of the First Crusade*, ed. Susan B. Edgington and Luis García-Guijarro Ramos (Turnhout, 2014), 11–24.

[33] For example, see Ann Collins's case study, *Teacher in Faith and Virtue: Lanfranc of Bec's Commentary on Saint Paul* (Leiden, 2014), esp. ch. 3; and G. R. Evans' *Anselm and a New Generation* (Oxford, 1980), esp. ch. 1, which shows the indebtedness of twelfth-century thinkers to methodological changes implemented in the study of Scripture in the eleventh century. Still valuable is Beryl Smalley's classic "Quelques prédécesseurs d'Anselm de Laon," *Recherches de théologie ancienne et médiévale* 9 (1937): 365–401.

[34] See Dahan's *L'Exégèse chrétienne de la Bible en Occident médiévale, XIIe–XIVe siècles* (Paris, 1999) for an excellent introduction to his methodology.

Introduction

literal and spiritual levels of meaning, a relationship that greatly interested the crusade's narrators.[35] Another strand of scholarship has demonstrated exegetes' active engagement with contemporary social and political developments, revising an older picture of medieval exegesis as backward looking and static.[36] Other studies, straddling the border of theology and social history, have combined the best of both approaches.[37] As a result, we now know much more than we did a century ago about how the Bible was edited, interpreted, and manipulated for various ideological ends in the medieval West. But many crusades historians remain unfamiliar with this body of work, and few studies have bridged both fields.[38] Medieval historians have much to gain from a closer acquaintance with exegetical sources, which comprise the largest body of surviving (and still

---

[35] For example, see Wanda Zemler-Cizewski, "The Literal Sense of Scripture According to Rupert of Deutz," in *The Multiple Meanings of Scripture: The Role of Exegesis in Early Christian and Medieval Culture*, ed. Ineke van 't Spijker (Leiden, 2009), 203–24.

[36] Representative of more 'historical' innovative studies of exegesis are Theresa Tinkle, "Subversive Feminine Voices: The Reception of 1 Timothy 2 from Jerome to Chaucer," ch. 2 in her *Gender and Power in Medieval Exegesis* (New York, 2010); Suzanne M. Yeager, "*The Siege of Jerusalem* and Biblical Exegesis: Writing About Romans in Fourteenth-Century England," *The Chaucer Review* 39 (2004): 70–102; Felice Lifshitz, "Gender and Exemplarity East of the Middle Rhine: Jesus, Mary and the Saints in Manuscript Context," *Early Medieval Europe* 9 (2000): 325–44; and Philippe Buc, *L'ambiguïté du livre. Prince, pouvoir et peuple dans les commentaires de la Bible au Moyen Age* (Paris, 1994).

[37] Good examples are Philippe Buc, *Holy War, Martyrdom, and Terror: Christianity, Violence, and the West* (Philadelphia, 2015); Emmanuel Bain, "Les marchands chassés du Temple, entre commentaires et usages sociaux," *Médiévales* 55 (2008): 53–74; and Jeremy Cohen, *"Be Fertile and Increase, Fill the Earth and Master It": The Ancient and Medieval Career of a Biblical Text* (Ithaca, 1989), esp. ch. 5.

[38] Important exceptions relevant to this study are: Cole, "'O God, the Heathens Have Come into Your Inheritance'"; Philippe Buc, "La vengeance de Dieu: De l'exégèse patristique à la Réforme ecclésiastique et à la première croisade," in *La vengeance, 400–1200*, ed. Dominique Barthélemy, François Bougard and Régine Le Jan (Rome, 2006), 451–86; Elizabeth Lapina, "Anti-Jewish Rhetoric in Guibert of Nogent's *Dei gesta per Francos*," *Journal of Medieval History* 35 (2009): 239–53; and Matthew Gabriele, "From Prophecy to Apocalypse: The Verb Tenses of Jerusalem in Robert the Monk's *Historia* of the First Crusade," *Journal of Medieval History* 42 (2016): 304–16. A handful of studies have considered the exegetical function of images, particularly in illuminated manuscripts, linked to crusading: see Gil Fishof, "The Role and Meanings of the Image of St. Peter in the Crusader Sculpture of Nazareth: A New Reading," and Esther Dehoux, "'If I Forget You, O Jerusalem … ': King Philip the Fair, Saint George, and Crusade," both in *The Crusades and Visual Culture*, ed. Elizabeth Lapina, Susanna Throop (Farnham, 2015), 35–56 and 105–116; Gaposchkin, "Louis IX, Crusade, and the Promise of Joshua"; and Daniel H. Weiss, "Biblical History and Medieval Historiography: Rationalizing Strategies in Crusader Art," *Modern Language Notes* 108 (1993): 710–37.

largely unedited) medieval texts, and their modern scholarship. This is particularly true for historians of crusading, a movement that defined itself in terms of biblical precedents and gained adherents through biblically informed propaganda campaigns, and whose chroniclers used biblical models to situate contemporary holy wars within the arc of salvation history stretching backward to the world's creation and forward to the end of time.

Beginning with an introduction to the chroniclers' intellectual context, this study then considers how Latin writers, as a group, used the Scriptures to make sense of the holy war, before bringing specific exegetical trends into sharper focus. Chapter 1 demonstrates the centrality of the Scriptures and biblical exegesis within the educational institutions of the Latin West between c. 1050 and c. 1150, in order to show how natural it was for the crusade's narrators to turn to the sacred page in their quest to explain the momentous events of the late 1090s. At the same time, a comparative examination of the scriptural material in the contemporary narratives of another profoundly important event, the Norman Conquest of England, suggests that medieval writers believed the First Crusade called for a different, more explicitly exegetical mode of historical writing. Chapter 2 undertakes a systematic analysis of the massive amount of biblical material contained in Latin narratives of the crusade composed in the fifty years between the Council of Clermont and the preaching of the Second Crusade. Such a quantitative approach yields a number of significant discoveries concerning the relative importance of particular biblical books to the crusade's narrators and the changing biblical reception of crusading in the first decades of the twelfth century. A comparison of different authors' use of the Scriptures to frame their accounts of the holy war's two bookends, the speech of Pope Urban II (d. 1099) at Clermont and the crusader conquest of Jerusalem, serves to highlight individual writers' exegetical originality.

The last two chapters turn to the chroniclers' use of specific biblical themes and exegetical strategies, illustrating the different ways in which the Old Testament and New Testament and their commentary traditions were pressed into the service of the holy war. Chapter 3 explores the chroniclers' use of scriptural references to situate the crusaders within the sacred geography of the East, as well as their reliance upon typology to forge new identities for the Jerusalemites and their Muslim opponents. Casting the crusaders as new Israelites battling foes who recalled the polytheist tribes of the Old Testament, chroniclers justified the holy war as a continuation of an age-old struggle against unbelief. Even while selectively identifying the crusading armies with the heroes of ancient Israel, however, Latin writers' christological readings of the Old Testament put their work into conversation with anti-Jewish polemic. Finally, Chapter 4 examines the conceptual roles of Jerusalem and Babylon (with which Latin Christians identified Fatimid Egypt) in early crusade narratives, arguing that the chroniclers viewed these sites as embodiments of the Augustinian two cities: the city of God

Introduction

and the terrestrial city ruled by the devil. The crusaders' worthiness to inhabit the city of God – Jerusalem – was expressed in terms of their imitation of Christ and his apostles, which included the reenactment of Gospel scenes: captive crusaders were credited with moving a mountain through prayer, in fulfillment of Christ's promise in Matthew 17:19, while the conquest of Jerusalem was rendered as a second cleansing of the Temple (Mat. 21, Mk. 11, Lk. 19, Jn. 2).

Throughout the chapters that follow, I have aimed to treat the First Crusade's medieval chroniclers as whole people, and to situate them within living intellectual traditions. While we know a good deal about a few of these men, a little bit about several of them, and virtually nothing about the remainder, what *is* certain is that they were not crusade chroniclers, *tout court*. They were monks, canons, and priests, exegetes, theologians, and hagiographers, scribes and liturgists, pilgrims and comrades-in-arms. They arrived at the problem of the crusade having already completed years of training in how to read and interpret Scripture, and with well-established personal relationships to the sacred texts forged through communal reading, meditative prayer, and liturgical performance. They brought all of this to bear on the crusade and, in the process, were led to affirm and, in some cases, reevaluate the categories and interpretations that formed the bedrock of their intellectual and spiritual lives. Rereading early crusading narratives from the twin vantage points of exegesis and theology, then, not only offers insights into the reception of the First Crusade, but allows us to better appreciate the intellectual and spiritual world of the early twelfth-century West in all of its exuberant creativity, and to affirm the crusading movement's inseparability from this context.

Chapter 1

History and Biblical Exegesis in the Latin West

In about 1107, before Baldric of Bourgueil (d. 1130) began to circulate his history of the First Crusade, he sent a draft to his friend Peter, abbot of Saint-Pierre, Maillezais, for the latter to read and amend. If Baldric was truly looking for an editor, Peter was a natural choice; while Baldric was an armchair historian, Peter was a well-known crusade preacher and veteran of the expedition to Jerusalem.[1] It may be more surprising to modern readers that Baldric framed his request in terms not only of deference to Peter's personal experience of the holy war, but also admiration of his friend's abilities as a biblical exegete and their shared interest in scriptural study.[2] He reminds Peter how "recently, in your room, you showed me some expository glosses (*glossulas exposituras*) on the Pentateuch ... whose author you did not name. This work pleases me, because it explains the meaning of the [biblical] words, and makes clear anything that might seem obscure."[3] Baldric went on to beg Peter (who was probably the modest 'anonymous' author of the glosses) to have this text copied for him, and offered in exchange the "little book (*libellum*) which [he] had composed on the journey to Jerusalem to be amended" at Peter's discretion.[4] The implication is that Peter's fitness to evaluate Baldric's history depended as much, or more, on his skill at deciphering the mysteries of the sacred page as on his personal experience of the expedition to Jerusalem. More broadly, the exchange Baldric proposes – a work of history for a work of biblical exegesis – reminds us that both kinds of texts shared the goal of clarifying the often obscure workings of divine providence. It also indicates that

---

[1] Peter of Maillezais (d. c. 1117), whom Baldric salutes as an "oratorem et viatorem Ierosolimitanum" (BB, 121), may have participated in the crusade of 1096–99 or accompanied Duke William IX of Aquitaine on crusade in 1101–02, as suggested by Lucien-Jean Bord, *Maillezais: Histoire d'une abbaye et d'un évêché* (Paris, 2007), 74–76. It is unclear how widely this epistolary exchange circulated, as Steven Biddlecombe has noted that only one of the twenty-four extant manuscripts of Baldric's history contains a complete copy of both letters, while another contains a summary; see BB, xxiv–xxv n., xcvii.

[2] Following Elizabeth Lapina ("The Problem of Eyewitnesses," *passim*), it is worth noting that Baldric never hinted that his lack of personal experience of crusading compromised his authority as a chronicler of the expedition.

[3] BB, 122: "Glossulas exposituras mihi super nuper Moysis *Pentateuchum* in camera tua ostendisti ... auctorem vero indicare uel nuncupare non nosti. Complacuere michi, quia et verborum connexionem exprimebant; et siquid erat caliginosum elucidabant."

[4] BB, 122: "Libellum quem de Ierosolimitano itinere quo quomodo composui, ad castigandum tibi transmisi ... "

medieval readers admired many of the same qualities in both genres; in his reply to Baldric, Peter praised his friend's history for the "sweetness" and "elegance" of its language, as well as its "wisdom," echoing Baldric's evaluation of the glosses as "neat," "elegant," and "enlightening."[5] Finally, this exchange suggests that in the early twelfth-century Latin West there was considerable overlap between the readers and practitioners of exegesis and history, who would have been unlikely to distinguish between these genres as neatly as modern scholars do.

For the learned men who wrote the histories of the First Crusade, history, theology, and biblical exegesis were not neatly separable disciplines. Works of history rested companionably next to theological treatises and scriptural commentaries on library shelves, to be taken up, chewed over, and commented upon by the same readers. Many medieval scholars whom we label 'historians' – including at least two historians of the First Crusade[6] – also wrote works of exegesis, and would hardly have seen the callings of historian and biblical commentator as incompatible. On the contrary, within the study of Scripture, history was accorded a level of meaning all its own, while medieval chroniclers often judged the deeds of great men with the same interpretive tools used to discern God's will in the sacred texts, and placed contemporary events on a narrative continuum that encompassed the biblical past. The biblical canon not only contained valuable information about the past but offered a prophetic vision of the future, as well as typological parallels which made the present more comprehensible. As Orderic Vitalis (d. c. 1142) observed, "many things in divine Scripture ... if they are subtly accommodated, appear similar to the happenings of our own time."[7] Moreover, even as a new, less allegorical historicism emerged in some quarters in the twelfth century, history continued to be regarded as a close relative of theology, while exegetical methodologies exerted a strong influence over historical inquiry.[8] This chapter introduces the intellectual contexts in which history and biblical exegesis were practiced in Europe in the decades around

---

[5] BB, 122 and 124.

[6] Guibert of Nogent wrote a moral commentary on Genesis (edited in PL 156:19–337) as well as a series of commentaries on the Prophets (partially edited in PL 156: 341–488), while William of Malmesbury wrote a commentary on Lamentations which remains unedited; on the latter work, see Hugh Farmer, "William of Malmesbury's Commentary on Lamentations," *Studia monastica* 4 (1962): 283–311.

[7] OV, 4:228: "multa intueor in diuina pagina quae subtiliter coaptata nostri temporis euentui uidentur similia." Cited and trans. by Elisabeth Mégier, "Divina Pagina and the Narration of History in Orderic Vitalis' *Historia Ecclesiastica*," *Revue Bénédictine* 110 (2000): 106–23 (at 108).

[8] On approaches to history in the twelfth century, see Coleman, *Ancient and Medieval Memories*, ch. 14; the essays by G. Evans, "St Anselm and Sacred History," Valerie Flint, "World History in the Early Twelfth Century: The '*Imago Mundi*' of Honorius Augustodunensis," and Margaret Gibson, "History at Bec in the Twelfth Century," all in *The Writing of History in the Middle Ages: Essays Presented to Richard W. Southern*,

1100, highlighting the ways in which these two disciplines intersected in theory and practice in the decades when the First Crusade's historiography took shape. Finally, it presents a case study of biblical references in the near-contemporary narratives of another momentous event, the Norman Conquest of England, in order to lay the groundwork for a fuller appreciation of the innovative nature of early crusade historiography.

The Educational Context

In the monastic and cathedral schools of our period the study of the *artes* was bookended by the Bible. The Psalter was the traditional primer for beginning Latinists, and those destined to become monks, canons, or priests committed its verses to memory as the basis for the Divine Office.[9] Thereafter students began a course of study that encompassed the *trivium* and, for some, the more advanced subjects of the *quadrivium*. Although these curricula might take students in directions far removed from the Scriptures, the liberal arts were thought to provide a necessary foundation for the *sacra disciplina* of the most challenging text of all, the study of which promised the greatest challenges, but also the greatest rewards.[10] Indeed, a tradition dating from Late Antiquity encouraged the study of the 'profane sciences,' including history, as preparation for biblical studies, and many prominent theologians of the eleventh and twelfth centuries championed this approach. Great biblical scholars like Anselm of Laon (d. 1117) and Bruno of Cologne (d. 1101) further broke down the educational and disciplinary division between sacred and profane studies by insisting that rhetoric, ethics, natural philosophy, and logic could be learned from study of the Scriptures.[11]

In contemporary debates about the hierarchy of various branches of knowledge, formal biblical study was often described as the province of masters, and renowned scholars were known to abandon the *artes* to dedicate themselves to

---

ed. R. H. C. Davis and J. M. Wallace-Hadrill (Oxford, 1981). For medieval historians' interest in precedents and patterns, see Guenée, *Histoire et culture historique*, 346–50.

[9] Pierre Riché, "Le psautier, livre de lecture elementaire d'après les vies des saints mérovingiens," in *Études mérovingiennes: Actes des Journées de Poitiers* (Paris, 1953), 253–56.

[10] G. R. Evans, *Old Arts and New Theology: The Beginnings of Theology as an Academic Discipline* (Oxford, 1980), 53–79; Pierre Riché, *Les écoles et l'enseignement dans l'Occident chrétien de la fin du Ve siècle au milieu du XIe siècle* (Paris, 1979), 281–82; Jean Châtillon, "Les écoles au XIIe siècle," in *Le Moyen Age et la Bible*, ed. Pierre Riché and Guy Lobrichon (Paris, 1984), 167–68.

[11] This argument was made by some patristic authors; see Alastair J. Minnis, *Medieval Theory of Authorship: Scholastic Literary Attitudes in the Later Middle Ages*, 2nd edn (Aldershot, 1988), 26–35; and Collins, *Teacher in Faith and Virtue*, 75–77.

the 'higher' calling of Scripture.[12] But for individual clerics, and those preparing to take higher orders, informal opportunities for studying Scripture and cultivating an exegetical mindset abounded. For monks and regular canons (and those educated by them), scriptural education was imbedded in daily routine; the sacred texts were read by the master in the *schola*, studied privately during appointed times for *lectio divina*, chanted in the church during the offices and during lectors at mealtimes. It is no wonder, then, that the Bible's language profoundly shaped the syntax of those educated in such a setting.[13] But Scriptural education had a loftier goal; it aimed to remake the self into a model of discipline and discernment, by schooling the mind to make the linguistic and symbolic connections that unlocked the many meanings of the sacred books, and nurturing the spirit through the cultivation of contemplative habits and prolonged immersion in the biblical texts.[14]

The Scriptures, as encountered in medieval educational and devotional contexts, "were clothed in the heavy garments of tradition and weighed down with the burden of commentary."[15] The process of scriptural education entailed not only, or even primarily, reading and hearing the Latin texts but pondering over earlier exegetes' interpretations. In the early twelfth century this rich inherited body of commentaries and sermons arguably played a more important role in the transmission of biblical texts than did actual copies of the Scriptures. Such deference to authority was believed to be in keeping with God's will, as expressed in the injunction of Proverbs 22:28 ("Do not cross the ancient boundaries set in place by your fathers"), which early medieval exegetes widely interpreted as a command to heed earlier commentary traditions.[16] Respect for the *instituta*

---

[12] Two famous examples are Lanfranc of Bec (d. 1089) and Manegold of Lautenbach (d. 1103). See Margaret T. Gibson, "The Place of the *Glossa Ordinaria* in Medieval Exegesis," in *Ad Litteram: Authoritative Texts and Their Medieval Readers*, ed. Mark D. Jordan and Kent Emery, Jr. (Notre Dame, IN, 1992), 12–14.

[13] Diane J. Reilly, "The Bible as Bellwether: Manuscript Bibles in the Context of Spiritual, Liturgical and Educational Reform, 1000–1200," in *Form and Function in the Late Medieval Bible*, ed. Diane Reilly (Leiden, 2013), 11–12; Isabelle Cochelin, "When Monks Were the Book: The Bible and Monasticism (6th–11th Centuries)," in *The Practice of the Bible in the Middle Ages*, ed. Susan Boynton and Diane J. Reilly (New York, 2011), 62–70.

[14] See William L. North, "St. Anselm's Forgotten Student: Richard of Préaux and the Interpretation of Scripture in Early Twelfth-Century Normandy," in *Teaching and Learning in Northern Europe, 1000–1200*, ed. Sally N. Vaughn and Jay Rubenstein (Turnhout, 2006), 171–215; and Jehangir Yezdi Malegam, *The Sleep of Behemoth: Disputing Peace nd Violence in Medieval Europe, 1000–1200* (Ithaca, NY, 2013), ch. 5.

[15] Matthew Gabriele, "The Last Carolingian Exegete: Pope Urban II, the Weight of Tradition, and Christian Reconquest," *Church History* 81 (2012): 797.

[16] Edward Peters, "Transgressing the Limits Set by the Fathers: Authority and Impious

patrum, 'the precepts of the fathers,' was further reinforced by scribal practices; before the advent of Bibles with interlinear glosses, it could be difficult for medieval readers of commentaries to distinguish between the original words of the Scriptures and those of later exegetes, and so text and commentary might be taken in together as a single linguistic stream without any conscious navigation between multiple texts on a single page.[17] Even biblical manuscripts copied without extensive commentary customarily included patristic prologues and prefaces as well as *argumenta* – summaries meant to facilitate readers' understanding.[18] As we will see in the following chapters, the crusade's chroniclers actively displayed their knowledge of, and desire to contribute to, the hermeneutical work of earlier generations, though they – like other exegetes of their generation – were sometimes willing to forge new paths through the sacred page.

Unlike students of history, who had little in the way of theoretical treatises to draw upon prior to the mid-twelfth century, those seeking to master biblical exegesis could draw on a substantial body of patristic works that laid out clear interpretive principles. Influential theoretical discussions could be found in Augustine's *De doctrina christiana*, Cassiodorus' *Institutiones*, Isidore's *Etymologiae*, and Gregory I's *Moralia in Job*, to name just a few foundational texts found in most well-stocked monastic and episcopal libraries.[19] Given the saintly status of the Fathers, studying such exemplars was a devotional practice in itself. Within religious communities there were also many opportunities to learn exegetical techniques aurally, by listening to sermons and expositions of particular biblical verses or themes in which abbots or elders modeled approved interpretive practices.[20] Through reading and listening to learned expositions, clerical readers learned simultaneously what the Scriptures said and what previous readers had believed they meant, so that each biblical verse was secured

---

Exegesis in Medieval Thought," in *Christendom and Its Discontents: Exclusion, Persecution, and Rebellion, 1000–1500*, ed. Scott L. Waugh and Peter D. Diehl (Cambridge, 1996), 338–62.

[17] Christopher de Hamel, *The Book: A History of the Bible* (London, 2001), 95–106. For an assessment of how interlinear glosses changed the experience of biblical reading, see David A. Salomon, *An Introduction to the* Glossa Ordinaria *as Medieval Hypertext* (Cardiff, 2012).

[18] Pierre-Maurice Bogaert, "The Latin Bible, c. 600 to c. 900," in *The Cambridge History of the Bible, Vol. 2: From 600 to 1450*, ed. Richard Marsden and E. Ann Matter (Cambridge, 2012), 91–92.

[19] Riché, *Les écoles*, 282–84.

[20] The conception of biblical exegesis, teaching, and preaching as closely related activities stretches back to Gregory I; see Beryl Smalley, *The Study of the Bible in the Middle Ages* (New York, 1941; paperback edn, Notre Dame, IN, 1964), 35. For a thoughtful discussion of how Urban II drew upon older traditions of monastic and papal preaching, see Georg Strack, "The Sermon of Urban II in Clermont and the Tradition of Papal Oratory," *Medieval Sermon Studies* 56 (2012): 30–45.

in the memory by a *catena*, a chain of interpretive associations that might include linked scriptural references as well as snippets of commentary.[21] Thus it is hardly surprising to find, alongside the myriad of biblical allusions in the chronicles of the First Crusade, numerous references to the exegetical works of Ambrose (d. 397), Jerome (d. 420), Augustine (d. 430), Cassiodorus (d. c. 585), and Gregory I (d. 604), as well as to Carolingian commentators like Hrabanus Maurus (d. 856).[22] These references indicate that complex associative chains, forged through their authors' ongoing conversations with past commentators, lie just beneath the surface of early crusade narratives.

The crusade's chroniclers also inherited a long tradition which informed medieval readers' differing approaches to the Old and New Testaments, as well as their perception of the relationship between these. "The incorporation of the Hebrew Bible within the Christian canon," as Deeana Copeland Klepper writes, "effectively bound biblical exegesis with polemic" in the Latin West, and in the decades around 1100 Christian exegetes engaged both contemporary Judaism and its scriptural underpinnings with increased urgency.[23] For some, this entailed closer attention to the Old Testament as a historical and hortatory work which might be read literally; for others, the Hebrew texts' significance for Christians could be grasped only via allegorical readings.[24] While both approaches could be traced to patristic biblical criticism, they took on new significance in the cultural landscape of c. 1100, in which Jews and Christians were exchanging ideas and debating sensitive matters of belief more eagerly and openly than at any previous point in the Middle Ages.[25] The ambivalence of medieval Christians' attitudes towards flesh-and-blood Jews was echoed in their approach to the Hebrew Scriptures; these books held enormous historical and moral significance for Christians, but described a revelation and a law believed to have been superseded

---

[21] On the concept of the *catena*, see Jean Leclercq, *The Love of Learning and Desire for God*, trans. C. Misrahi (New York, 1961), 76–77.

[22] For a fuller discussion of these references, see Chapter 2.

[23] Deeana Copeland Klepper, *The Insight of Unbelievers: Nicholas of Lyra and Christian Reading of Jewish Text in the Later Middle Ages* (Philadelphia, 2007), 13.

[24] John Van Engen, "Ralph of Flaix: The Book of Leviticus Interpreted as Christian Community," in *Jews and Christians in Twelfth-Century Europe*, ed. Michael A. Signer and John Van Engen (Notre Dame, IN, 2001), 150–70, esp. 157–61. For the movement towards historical interpretation in the early twelfth century, see the classic overview by Smalley, *Study of the Bible*, 83–106.

[25] A helpful overview is Anna Sapir Abulafia, "Jewish-Christian Disputations and the Twelfth-Century Renaissance," in her *Christians and Jews in Dispute* (Aldershot, 1998), 105–25; on exchanges between Jews and Christians in the exegetical realm specifically, see Gilbert Dahan, *Lire la Bible au Moyen Âge: Essais d'herméneutique médiévale* (Geneva, 2009), 34–46; and Constant J. Mews and Micha J. Perry, "Peter Abelard, Heloise, and Jewish Biblical Exesis in the Twelfth Century," *Journal of Ecclesiastical History* 62 (2011): 3–19.

by the Incarnation.[26] Indeed, the main value of these biblical texts for Christian scholars lay in what they identified as christological prophecies, messages which bound together the Old and New Testaments with innumerable typological threads, so that Eve prefigured Mary, the sacrifice of Isaac foreshadowed the Crucifixion, and so on.[27] This relationship is neatly summed up in the medieval axiom "*Novum in veteri latet, Vetus in novo patet*" (the New lies in the old, the Old unfolds in the new).[28] Thus it should not surprise us that, as Chapter 3 shows, early crusade chroniclers took a lively interest in those portions of the Old Testament which their fellow Christians used to attack Judaism.

The New Testament played a quite different role in communities of learning in the Latin West. Read from a historical perspective, this compendium documented the life of Christ and the development of the Church in its earliest and most perfect age. Containing as they did the teachings of Christ and his disciples, the New Testament books also had an exemplary spiritual value that defied strictly historical readings; though set in a long-ago world, these texts were the ultimate moral guide for all Christians in every time. Perhaps most importantly, Latin Christians saw the New Testament as deeply relevant to the institutions and debates of their own day; and indeed, unlike the Old Testament, whose histories and prophecies belonged to past ages of human time, the events described in the New Testament were believed by medieval readers to be part of their own age.[29] Whereas the Old Testament was to be approached typologically, mined for *figurae* from earlier ages that presaged the Incarnation and subsequent revelations of the world's sixth age, the New Testament described beliefs and institutions that were believed to have survived, albeit in altered forms, into the present. While patristic commentators had focused their attention on the books of the Old Testament, the exegetical revival that took hold in European monasteries and cathedral schools in the early twelfth century brought with it a new interest in glossing the New Testament, especially the Gospels.[30] Beryl Smalley tentatively linked this devel-

---

[26] Anna Sapir Abulafia, "The Testimony of the Hebrew Bible," in her *Christians and Jews in the Twelfth-Century Renaissance* (London, 1995), 94–106.

[27] Jean Daniélou, Introduction to *The Bible and the Liturgy*, trans. Anon. (Ann Arbor, MI, 1956).

[28] M.-D. Chenu, "The Old Testament in Twelfth-Century Theology," in his *Nature, Man, and Society in the Twelfth-Century*, ed. and trans. Jerome Taylor and Lester Little (Chicago, 1968), 146–61.

[29] On the Augustinian model of the *aetates mundi* and its propagation by later writers, see Amos Funkenstein, *Theology and the Scientific Imagination from the Middle Ages to the Seventeenth Century* (Princeton, NJ, 1986), 260–61; and Dahan, *L'exégèse chrétienne*, 68–70.

[30] For this exegetical revival, see Gilbert Dahan, *Lire la Bible*, 321–22; van Liere, "Biblical Exegesis through the Twelfth Century," in *The Practice of the Bible*, ed. Boynton and Reilly, 167–69; and Jean Leclercq, "The Exposition and Exegesis of Scripture: From Gregory the Great to Saint Bernard," in *The Cambridge History of*

opment to the movement usually known as the Gregorian Reform,[31] a movement whose leaders relied heavily on biblical interpretation to develop and promulgate their ideas.[32] This same keen interest in the Gospels is visible throughout early crusading narratives, which, as we will see in Chapter 4, present the holy war as an opportunity to walk in the footsteps of the first apostles.

As much as medieval exegetes valued *auctoritas* and tradition, theirs was no hidebound thought-world; scholarship since the turn of the century has shown scriptural exegesis to be a dynamic area of medieval intellectual life.[33] Moreover, the First Crusade's chroniclers lived in an age of exegetical revival and experimentation, ushered in by the development of innovative methodologies and textual formats.[34] The century or so after 1050 saw a number of developments that delighted students of the *sacra pagina*, such as the division of biblical books into chapters with Arabic numerals, the proliferation of Bibles with planned marginal commentaries, as well as the creation of new biblical genres, such as exegetical poetry and glosses.[35] Equally significant was the application to

---

the Bible, Vol. 2: The West from the Fathers to the Reformation, ed. G. W. H. Lampe (Cambridge, 1969), 190–92. Exegetes' heightened level of interest in the Gospels is documented by Beryl Smalley, *The Gospels in the Schools, c. 1100–1280* (London, 1985).

[31] Smalley, *Gospels in the Schools*, 33–34.

[32] On the use of exegesis in the service of reform, see Jean Leclercq, "Usage et abus de la Bible au temps de la réforme grégorienne," in *The Bible and Medieval Culture*, ed. W. Lourdaux and D. Verhelst (Leuven, 1979), 89–108; I. S. Robinson, "'Political Allegory' in the Biblical Exegesis of Bruno of Segni," *Recherches de Théologie ancienne et médiévale* 50 (1983): 69–98; idem, *Authority and Resistance in the Investiture Contest* (Manchester, 1978), esp. ch. 1 and 4; and William North, "Polemic, Apathy, and Authorial Initiative in Gregorian Rome," *Haskins Society Journal* 10 (2001): 113–25. Additionally, Guy Lobrichon has shown that the editorial project of establishing authoritative biblical texts was a key concern of the eleventh-century papacy; "Riforma ecclesiastica e testo della Bibbia," *Le Bibbie atlantiche. Il libro delle Scritture tra monumentalità e rappresentazione*, ed. Marilena Maniaci and Giulia Orofino (Milan, 2000), 15–26.

[33] As Gilbert Dahan writes, "l'exégèse chrétienne de la Bible se situe constamment dans une tradition, mais qu'elle est vouée à l'innovation, du fait même des présupposés herméneutiques qui la gouvernement." See "Innovation et tradition dans l'exégèse chrétienne de la Bible en occident (XIIe–XIVe siècle)," in *Auctor et Auctoritas: invention et conformisme dans l'écriture médiévale: actes du colloque tenu à l'Université de Versailles-Saint-Quentin-en-Yvelines (14–16 juin 1999)*, ed. Michel Zimmerman (Paris, 2001), 255.

[34] Lobrichon, "The Early Schools," 536–54; Dahan, *Lire la Bible*, 321–22; van Liere, "Biblical Exegesis through the Twelfth Century," 167–69; and Leclercq, "The Exposition and Exegesis of Scripture," 190–92.

[35] See William J. Courtenay, "The Bible in Medieval Universities," in *The New Cambridge History of the Bible, Vol. 2*, ed. Marsden and Matter, 562; Francesco Stella, "La trasmissione nella letteratura: la poesia," in *La bibbia nel medioevo*, ed.

the Scriptures of new, sometimes controversial, logic-driven modes of textual criticism. Practitioners of these methods opened up new ways of thinking about the Bible – of "going beyond the Fathers," as Rupert of Deutz (d. 1129) put it[36] – as a collection of texts grounded in a historical past as well as a continuous arc of salvific history, of analyzing their dialectical structures and unpacking their allegories.[37] Even as they attempted to resolve the tensions and contradictions inherent in much earlier Christian biblical exegesis, these intellectuals developed new readings of the sacred texts that reflected changing social and political realities, and new interpretive agendas that supported ecclesiastical reform.[38] Whether we regard the exegetes of the late eleventh century as forerunners of a 'renaissance' or fulfillers of an intellectual tradition that stretched back into the Carolingian period,[39] their accomplishments are undeniably impressive.

Much of this innovative exegetical work centered on the cathedral schools of Capetian France, where a new kind of academic culture was born in the last decades of the eleventh century. Though it has rarely been remarked upon, a striking number of the crusade's early historians were associated with these schools, where, as in contemporary religious communities, pupils and masters dedicated themselves to the study of the sacred page. Fulcher of Chartres (d. aft. 1128) is thought to have received his education at the cathedral school in that city during the tenure of the great Ivo (d. 1115).[40] The French Benedictine chroniclers Guibert of Nogent (d. 1124) and Robert of Reims (aka 'Robert the Monk,' d. c. 1122) were associated with, respectively, the schools of Laon

---

Giovanni Cremascoli and Claudio Leonardi (Bologna, 1996), 47–63 (esp. 57–59); and Guy Lobrichon, "Une nouveauté: les gloses de la Bible," in *Le Moyen Age et la Bible*, ed. Pierre Riché and G. Lobrichon (Paris, 1984), 95–114.

[36] John Van Engen, *Rupert of Deutz* (Berkeley, CA, 1983), 71.

[37] Margaret T. Gibson, "The *Artes* in the Eleventh Century," in *Arts libéraux et philosophie au moyen âge* (Montreal, 1967), 125; Irven M. Resnick, "Attitudes towards Philosophy and Dialectic during the Gregorian Reform," *The Journal of Religious History* 16 (1990): 115–25 (esp. 120–25).

[38] As demonstrated by Buc, *L'Ambiguïté du livre*, whose insights about the schools of Northern France from c. 1100 on seem to me to ring true for the later eleventh century as well. On the relationship of textual innovations and reform movements, see Guy Lobrichon, "La Bible de la réforme ecclésiastique: Aspects textuels," in *La Bible au Moyen Age*, ed. Guy Lobrichon (Paris, 2003), 94–108.

[39] For this debate, see C. Stephen Jaeger, "Pessimism in the Twelfth Century Renaissance," *Speculum* 78 (2003): 1151–83 (esp. 1181–83). For a thoughtful discussion of the influence of one Carolingian exegete, Haimo of Auxerre, on later medieval thinkers, see Sumi Shimahara, "Exégèse et politique dans l'oeuvre d'Haymon d'Auxerre," *Revue de l'histoire des religions* 225 (2008): 471–86 (esp. 478, 482–84).

[40] On Fulcher's personal and education background, see Veronica Epp, *Fulcher von Chartres* (Düsseldorf, 1990), 24–25; and Marcus Bull, "Fulcher of Chartres," in *Christian–Muslim Relations, 600–1500*, ed. David Thomas (Leiden, 2010), accessed May 2, 2019, http://dx.doi.org/10.1163/1877-8054_cmri_COM_24025.

and Soissons, and Reims, while their peer Baldric of Bourgueil, a self-proclaimed autodidact, may have been an informal student of Marbod of Rennes (d. 1123).[41] Ralph of Caen (d. aft. 1130) is thought to have been educated for the priesthood at the cathedral school of Caen under Arnulf of Chocques (d. 1118), who was himself a pupil of Lanfranc (d. 1089),[42] and Gilo of Paris (d. 1142) studied in the Capetian capital before making his profession at Cluny.[43] The anonymous continuator of Gilo of Paris' *Historia*, known simply as the 'Charleville Poet' (d. aft. 1118), may have been a teacher at a Northern French school.[44] The canon Raymond of Aguilers (d. aft. 1101) presumably trained at Le Puy, one of the most respected cathedral schools in Southern France.[45] Even the English crusade chroniclers William of Malmesbury (d. c. 1143) and Henry of Huntingdon (d. c. 1157) had indirect intellectual ties to leading Continental schools via their connections with Canterbury and Lincoln.[46] Students at these schools were exposed to the cutting edge of exegetical theory and practice, and learned to approach the study of the Scriptures and their interpretive history in a highly focused and systematic way, closely engaging with the literal-historical sense of the text.[47] Given the propensity of the First Crusade's narrators for reading key scriptural passages *ad litteram*, we should ask whether this

---

[41] For Guibert, see Jay Rubenstein, *Guibert of Nogent: Portrait of a Medieval Mind* (New York, 2002), 111–16; for Robert, whose identity (though not his association with Reims) remains uncertain, see RR, xix–xxxi; and for Baldric, see F. J. E. Raby, *A History of Secular Latin Poetry in the Middle Ages* (repr. edn, Oxford, 1967), 1:337–338; and BB, xv–xviii.

[42] Bernard S. Bachrach and David Stewart Bachrach, Introduction to *The* Gesta Tancredi *of Ralph of Caen* (Burlington, 2005), 1–2.

[43] C. W. Grocock and Elizabeth Siberry, Introduction to the *Historia vie Hierosolimitane* (Oxford, 1997), xviii–xiv.

[44] Grocock and Siberry, Introduction to the *Historia vie Hierosolimitane*, xxii–xxiii.

[45] Raymond identifies himself as "Raimundus canonicus Podiensis"; see RA, 35, and for commentary, 10. For the episcopal school at Puy in Raymond's time, see Emile Lesne, *Les Écoles de la fin du VIIIe siècle à la fin du XIIe*, vol. 5 of his *Histoire propriété ecclésiastique en France* (Lille, 1940), 49–50; and for the library of Le Puy in this period, see Thomas Lecaque, "Reading Raymond: The Bible of Le Puy, the Cathedral Library and the Literary Background of Raymond of Aguilers," in *The Uses of the Bible in Crusader Sources*, ed. Elizabeth Lapina and Nicholas Morton (Leiden, 2017), 105–32.

[46] Rodney M. Thomson, *William of Malmesbury* (Woodbridge, 1987), 5; Diana Greenaway, Introduction to HH, ixxx–xxi, xxxii–xxxiii.

[47] G. R. Evans, *The Language and Logic of the Bible: The Earlier Middle Ages* (Cambridge, 1984), 27–36. It is worth noting that eleventh-century writers like Lanfranc were quite interested in the historical sense of scriptural texts well before the better-known 'historical turn' of the twelfth century; see Collins, *Teacher in Faith and Virtue*, 84–88. In light of the recent reconsideration of some of the manuscripts traditionally associated with Lanfranc, such concerns might be pushed back even earlier, to the later tenth century, as discussed by Lobrichon, "The Early Schools," 500 and n. 56.

tendency reflects these authors' exegetical training, or whether the crusade's seemingly literal fulfillment of biblical prophecies may have further encouraged medieval readers' interest in the literal sense of the Scriptures.

Several other chroniclers were educated, so far as we know, entirely at monastic schools. This number includes Albert of Aachen, Ekkehard of Aura and Frutolf of Michelsberg's anonymous continuator, Orderic Vitalis, and William of Malmesbury, as well as the Monte Cassino Anonymous (fl. c. 1130), who is thought to have been a monk of that abbey.[48] These men were immersed in the study of the sacred texts simply by virtue of their monastic profession, and would have encountered the great works of the patristic and Carolingian commentary traditions in the course of their programs of spiritual and intellectual formation. And they would have cultivated exegetical habits that were, generally speaking, more deeply rooted in personal spiritual meditation and, as a result, more discursive than the biblical commentary then emerging in the urban schools. Insofar as we can define 'monastic exegesis' in this period, it tended to be anthological, strongly emphasizing the commentator's place at the end of a long line of readers of the Scriptures, and to privilege the moral meaning of the text.[49] But we should be wary of flattening out the diversity of monastic approaches to the Bible; consider, for example, that the ninth-century Benedictines Haimo of Auxerre (d. c. 865) and Hrabanus Maurus – the two most-copied exegetes in the eleventh-century West – took quite different approaches to the glossing of the *sacra pagina*.[50] Nor should we overstate the differences between the brands of

---

[48] On Albert, see Susan Edgington, Introduction to AA, xxiii–xxiv; for an important reevaluation of the authorship of the Michelsberg Chronicle's continuations, and the contributions and biography of Ekkehard of Aura, see T. J. H. McCarthy, Introduction to *Chronicles of the Investiture Contest: Frutolf of Michelsberg and His Continuators* (Manchester, 2014), 46–48, 73–74, and idem, *The Continuations of Frutolf of Michelsberg's Chronicle* (Wiesbaden, 2018), 39–80. For Orderic, see Marjorie Chibnall, *The World of Orderic Vitalis* (Oxford, 1984), 86–87; for William, see Thomson, *William of Malmesbury*, 4–5; and for the Monte Cassino Anonymous, see Edoardo D'Angelo, Introduction to MC, xv–xvi.

[49] Gilbert Dahan has defined 'monastic exegesis' as a particular way of approaching the scriptural text, rather than as the body of exegetical work produced by monks; "Genres, Forms and Various Methods in Christian Exegesis of the Middle Ages," in *Hebrew Bible, Old Testament: The History of Its Interpretation*, 2 vols., ed. Magne Saebo (Göttingen), 1: 201–2. Derek A. Olsen's *Reading Matthew with Monks: Liturgical Interpretation in Anglo-Saxon England* (Collegeville, MN, 2015), offers a thoughtful meditation on the mutual impact of monastic educational practices, liturgical training, and exegesis.

[50] For these exegetes' methods and long-term influence, see John J. Contreni, "The Patristic Legacy to c. 1000," in *The New Cambridge History of the Bible*, ed. Marsden and Matter, 527–32. My thanks to Matt Gabriele for suggesting the examples of Haimo and Hrabanus to illustrate this point. Further, Ambrogio M. Piazzoni has, for example, discerned differences in how members of the 'old' and 'new' monastic orders of the

scriptural education practiced in monastic communities and cathedral schools, especially not prior to 1150. Examples abound in this period of men who studied at urban centers of learning before taking religious orders; such was the case with the crusade's official initiator Urban II, who was a disciple of Bruno of Cologne at Reims before taking the habit as a monk at Cluny; and Baldric of Bourgueil and Gilo of Paris followed similar trajectories.[51] Moreover, the careers of men like Guibert of Nogent show that membership in a monastic order hardly precluded participation in the fluid intellectual communities that gathered around urban school masters. Whatever their individual educational paths, these men shared in common intensive training in the arts of the *sacra pagina*, a training visible on virtually every page of the crusade's early twelfth-century historiography.

Exegesis, History, and Ideology

Our period's historical narratives have attracted so much modern scholarly attention that we tend to forget that history was at best a minor art in the eleventh and early twelfth centuries, occupying a marginal and unofficial place within the curricula of medieval schools, and practiced – and, judging from surviving numbers of manuscripts, read – by relatively few people.[52] While a minority of religious houses might be termed centers of historiographical production, many communities still had not acquired their own written histories, let alone in-house historians, by 1100 (or even by 1200).[53] Histories of recent events were rare before the twelfth century, since, as Marcus Bull writes, "historiography was not some predominant or automatic reflex among the educated classes of

---

Central Middle Ages approached the Bible; see "L'esegesi neomonastica," in *La bibbia nel medioeveo*, ed. Cremascoli and Leonardi, 217–37.

[51] Alfons Becker, *Papst Urban II (1088–1099)*, MGH, Schriften 19, 1–3 (Stuttgart, 1964–2012), 1:33–51.

[52] Points made by James M. Powell in the context of the First Crusade's early historiography in "Myth, Legend, Propaganda, History: The First Crusade, 1140–ca. 1300," in *Autour de la Première Croisade*, ed. Michel Balard (Paris, 1996), 127–41, esp. 127–28 and nn. 1–2.

[53] A fine example is the community of canons at Reims, documented by Michael E. Moore, "Prologue: Teaching and Learning History in the School of Reims, c. 800–950," in *Teaching and Learning*, ed. Vaughn and Rubenstein, 19–49. On the dearth of historical writing produced by most religious houses, see Steven Vanderputten, "Benedictine Local Historiography From the Middle Ages and Its Written Sources: Some Structural Observations," *Revue Mabillon*, n.s. 15 (2004): 107–29. This hardly means that monastic communities were uninterested in history, of course; indeed, historical thinking pervades the most common genres produced in monastic *scriptoria* in this period, such as hagiography, institutional foundation legends, and charters.

late eleventh-century Europe."[54] Biblical exegesis, by contrast, was, without question, *the* most popular intellectual pursuit in this period. Eleventh- and early twelfth-century practitioners generated a vast number of original commentaries, prologues, and *florilegia* (as well as countless copies of patristic and Carolingian exegetical works), most of which remain unedited.[55] While very few exegetes would have received specialized training in the historian's craft, virtually every twelfth-century cleric who wrote history would have learned at least the rudiments of biblical interpretation. In an age that "drew faint lines between history, liturgy, hagiography, exegesis, preaching, and poetry,"[56] the methodologies and aims of these two disciplines intersected with and influenced one another at a number of points, shaping the development of both genres.

Like contemporary biblical exegetes, medieval historians were seekers after truth, following in the footsteps of Moses, who was regarded as the first historian.[57] The historian dealt not in *fabulae* (fables or fictional narratives) but *historiae*, "things which really have been done." So declared Isidore of Seville (d. 636) in the first book of his *Etymologiae*, and writers of the eleventh and twelfth centuries concurred.[58] Whether one recorded past events in the form of a chronicle (*cronica*) or a didactic history (*historia*), as Gervase of Canterbury (d. c. 1210) declared, it was necessary, above all, to "heed the truth (*veritati intendit*)."[59] Indeed, the explication of the truth, as revealed by God through earthly institutions and human actions, was a central task of early medieval historiography.[60] Scriptural study, too, involved the separation of truth from untruth, through the discernment of God's hand at work in the world in the past and present. Thus, exegetes could not help but concern themselves with history.

---

[54] Marcus Bull, "The Historiographical Construction of a Northern French First Crusade," *Haskins Society Journal* 25 (2013): 35–56 (quoting 38).
[55] de Hamel, *The Book*, 94–95.
[56] Roger D. Ray, "Medieval Historiography through the Twelfth Century: Problems and Progress of Research," *Viator* 5 (1974): 33–60 (quoting 35).
[57] Isidore of Seville, *Etymologiae*, 1.42.1, ed. Lindsay, 1: n.p.
[58] Isidore of Seville, *Etymologiae*, 1.44.5, ed. Lindsay, 1: n.p.: "Nam historiae sunt res verae quae factae sunt ... ." Cf. the definitions of history by mid-eleventh-century grammarian Papias (as the "narratio rei gestae") in his *Elementariam*, 150; and by the early twelfth-century theologian Hugh of St. Victor (as "rerum gestarum narratio") in his *De sacramentis*, Prol., PL 176:185.
[59] Gervase of Canterbury, *Chronica*, prol., in *The Historical Works, Vol. I*, ed. William Stubbs (repr. edn., Cambridge, 2012), 87. A commitment to 'truth,' in this sense, meant not only (or even primarily) that a narrator would tell a factually accurate account, but that he or she would use historical events to reveal universal moral truths. See Chris Given-Wilson, *Chronicles: The Writing of History in Medieval England* (London, 2004), ch. 1.
[60] Robert W. Hanning, *The Vision of History in Early Britain from Gildas to Geoffrey of Monmouth* (New York, 1966), esp. ch. 1–3.

Much of the Bible was obviously of historical value, and presented in chronological order. Medieval Latin writers used the term *historia* to refer to these parts of Scripture, and sometimes to the sacred texts as a whole.⁶¹ It was necessary, furthermore, to grasp the historical, or literal, sense (*sensus*) of a biblical passage before one could unlock its allegorical and moral meanings.⁶² While some early Christian commentators had downplayed the Bible's historicity, many of the most enduringly influential manuals and exemplars of patristic exegesis were deeply historically minded. In his *De doctrina christiana*, for instance, Augustine cautioned readers lest they overlook the Scriptures' language and history, and influentially defined history not as a secular subject, nor even as a "human institution," but as part of "the order of time (*ordo temporum*), whose creator and administrator is God."⁶³

It is true that early medieval exegetes tended to privilege the allegorical and moral meanings of Scripture. If the Bible's *littera*, its literal or historical sense, was its body, such a reading had an inescapably 'fleshly' quality; the allegorical and moral senses were, by comparison, spiritual, even ascetic, allowing the reader to transcend his or her own physical body as well as the 'body' of the text.⁶⁴ But the exegetical revival of the early twelfth century spurred a renewed interest in the sacred texts' historical meaning. For some commentators, this interest in the literal-historical sense grew out of a new engagement with the unique linguistic challenges of the Scriptures.⁶⁵ For others it seemed clear that the *sensus litteralis* and the *sensus historicus* could be separated and the latter analyzed on its own terms, using techniques borrowed from the historian's toolbox.⁶⁶ Rupert of Deutz, a contemporary of many of the First Crusade's narrators, rebuked commentators who impatiently leapt over the historical sense of the text "as if the visible and corporal things [described there] did not exist" in their rush to reach the spiritual meaning, and whose forgetfulness of scriptural history he regarded as impiety.⁶⁷

---

[61] Ray, "Medieval Historiography," 36; Mayke de Jong, "Old Law and New-Found Power: Hrabanus Maurus and the Old Testament," in *Centres of Learning: Learning and Location in Pre-Modern Europe and the Near East*, ed. Hendrick Jan van Drijvers and Alastair A. MacDonald (Leiden, 1995), 161–76 (at 166–67); M. Duchet-Suchaux and Y. Lefèvre, "Les noms de la Bible," in *Le Moyen Age et la Bible*, ed. Riché and Lobrichon, 13–23.

[62] The classic work on the 'senses' of Scripture is Henri de Lubac, *Medieval Exegesis: The Four Senses of Scripture*, 3 vols., trans. Mark Sebanc and E. M. Macierowski (Grand Rapids, MI, 1998–2009).

[63] Augustine, *On Christian Doctrine*, 2.28, trans. D. W. Robertson (New York, 1958), 64.

[64] For this metaphor and a discussion of reading *carnaliter* vs. *spiritualiter*, see Smalley, *Study of the Bible*, 1–2.

[65] Dahan, *Lire la Bible*, 210–14.

[66] Evans, *Language and Logic*, 67–71.

[67] Rupert of Deutz, *Se Sancta Trinitate, In Genesim*, 2.24, ed. Hrabanus Haacke, CCCM 21 (Turnhout, 1971), 212: "Nam alii spiritualem omnino sequentes intelligentiam

A generation later, Anselm of Havelberg (d. 1158) and Hugh of Saint Victor (d. 1141) took Rupert's critique further, forging new interpretive models in which the historical sense of Scripture played an essential role.[68]

If exegetes could not do without history, no more could medieval chroniclers make sense of history – as the story of God's hand at work in the world in the past, present, and future – without the Scriptures. As Benoît Lacroix has written, the Latin Bible was the first and foremost source for Christian historians, who perceived their enterprise as a continuation of the work of Moses.[69] Biblical history offered early medieval Christians a shared past that gave coherence and meaning to disparate ethnic groups and fledgling political communities, and informed the emerging concept of Christendom with its spiritual hierarchy.[70] Following the example set by earlier historians like Eusebius (d. c. 339) (and his Latin translator, Jerome) and Orosius, who approached the study of history as part of the larger challenge of interpreting God's plan for humanity, medieval world chronicles ranged biblical history and later history along a single continuum.[71] After all, the traditional Augustinian schema posited no clear break between biblical and post-biblical historical time; according to this view, the Scriptures described the entirety of the first five ages of the world and the first part of the sixth, in which medieval Christians believed themselves to be still living.[72] Such an approach endowed world histories with a timelessness that encouraged anachronism and elided important elements of difference between historical cultures, but also created a feeling of closeness and kinship with the biblical past.[73] While not all early medieval historians were equally enamored of Scriptural models and

---

narrationem sacrae huius Scripturae neglexisse uidentur historicam, tamquam uisibilia illa et corporalia non fuerint ... ." Quoted and discussed in Jay Terry Lees, *Anselm of Havelberg: Deeds into Words in the Twelfth Century* (Leiden, 1998), 135.

[68] Lees, *Anselm of Havelberg*, 136–38; Franklin T. Harkins, *History and the Work of Restoration: History and Scripture in the Theology of Hugh of St Victor* (Toronto, 2009), ch.3.

[69] Lacroix, *L'Historien au moyen âge*, 58–59.

[70] Jennifer A. Harris, "The Bible and the Meaning of History in the Middle Ages," in *The Practice of the Bible*, ed. Boynton and Reilly, 84–104.

[71] Michael I. Allen, "Universal History, 300–1000: Origins and Western Developments," in *Medieval Historiography*, ed. Deborah Mauskopf Deliyannis (Leiden, 2003), 17–42; and, for the long-term influence of these early Christian writers on medieval historical practices, see Guenée, *Histoire et culture*, 301–3.

[72] For Augustine's six ages theory and its medieval reception (which was often creative and idiosyncratic), see Jay Rubenstein, *Nebuchadnezzar's Dream: The Crusades, Apocalyptic Prophecy, and the End of History* (Oxford, 2019), 25–29.

[73] Hans-Werner Goetz, "The Concept of Time in the Historiography of the Eleventh and Twelfth Centuries," in *Medieval Concepts of the Past: Ritual, Memory, Historiography*, ed. Gerd Althoff, Johannes Fried and Patrick J. Geary (Cambridge, 2002), 139–65 (at 155–56); Giles Constable, "A Living Past: The Historical Environment in the Middle Ages," *Harvard Library Bulletin*, n.s. 1, no. 3 (1990): 49–70 (at 49–51); and Peter

the Vulgate's Latin style, even those writers who preferred to emulate Roman pagan historical writing typically included biblical references in their work.[74] Indeed, given the Bible's centrality in medieval education and spirituality, they could hardly help doing so.

Medieval historiographical traditions not only built upon the past events described in the Scriptures, but also liberally borrowed from the biblical exegete's repertoire.[75] Early medieval historians like Bede (d. 735) emulated the Latin style of the Hebrew Bible's historical books and presented their narratives of the more recent past in the form of spiritual allegories.[76] Later medieval chroniclers also shared with contemporary exegetes a propensity for elaborate allegory and moralizing commentary. Finally, the art of typological interpretation, a foundational element of biblical exegesis, helped chroniclers like Gregory of Tours (d. 594) to make sense of the miracles and villainies of their own ages by linking these to scriptural precedents.[77] Typology continued to be a prominent feature of chronicles in the Central Middle Ages,[78] and early twelfth-century clerical narrators found typology an indispensable tool for contextualizing and justifying the first crusaders' actions.

The didactic purposes of history and scriptural study were also similarly defined in the medieval West. The study of history, like the study of the Bible, promised the attentive reader enhanced self-understanding as well as opportunities for personal growth: the former by drawing one out of oneself into a wider world of action, the latter by promoting inwardly directed reflection and,

---

Darby, "The World Ages Framework," in *Bede and the End of Time* (London, 2012), 17–91.

[74] On the range of early medieval historians' interest in using biblical models and language, see Mauro Donnini, "Bibbia e storiografia," in *La bibbia nel medioevo*, 313–26 (esp. 314–19); and Beryl Smalley, "L'Exégèse biblique dans la littérature latine," in *La Bibbia nell'Alto Medioevo*, no ed., Settimane di studio del Centra Italiano di Studi sull'Alto Medioevo 10 (Spoleto, 1963), 631–55. Smalley notes (ibid., 649) that the most commonly cited biblical books in early medieval histories were Psalms, the Gospels and Epistles, and the four Books of Kings.

[75] Hans-Werner Goetz, "Die 'Geschichte' im Wissenschaftssystem des Mittelalters," in Franz-Josef Schmale, *Funktion und Formen mittelalterlicher Geschichtsschreibung: eine Einführung* (Darmstadt, 1985), 165–213 (esp. 194–208).

[76] Dominic James, "The World and its Past as Christian Allegory in the Early Middle Ages," in *The Uses of the Past in the Early Middle Ages*, ed. Yitzhak Hen and Matthew Innes (Cambridge, 2000), 102–13; Roger D. Ray, "Bede, the Exegete, as Historian," in *Famulus Christi: Essays in Commemoration of the Thirteenth Centenary of the Birth of the Venerable Bede*, ed. Gerald Bonner (London, 1976), 125–40 (esp. 133–35); Hanning, *Vision of History*, ch. 3.

[77] Walter Goffart, *The Narrators of Barbarian History (A. D. 550–800): Jordanes, Gregory of Tours, Bede, and Paul the Deacon* (Princeton, NJ, 1988), 149.

[78] See, for example, the analysis of the political implications of typology in the chronicle tradition of the abbey of Saint-Denis, see Spiegel, *The Past as Text*, ch.5.

indirectly, spiritual growth. Contemporaries referred to both history and the Scriptures as *speculi*, mirrors, which reflected exemplars of virtue and piety, as well as abundant anti-models, for the viewer-reader's edification.[79] This essentially Augustinian vision of history was familiar to the learned narrators of the early crusading movement, and they believed it would appeal to both clerical and lay audiences. Thus, the collection of First Crusade histories that the knightly Jerusalemite W. Grassegals presented to King Louis VII (r. 1137–80) around 1146 invited the royal crusader to "look in this book with the eye of reason as if in a mirror at the image of your ancestors ... and you might follow their footsteps on the path of virtue."[80]

The study of history and of the Scriptures were twin paths leading not only to self-knowledge but to an understanding of God's plan for humanity.[81] This was a plan grounded in history, insofar as it always had and would unfold in time; medieval thinkers equated the fulfillment of scriptural prophecy with the fulfillment of history, when the cycle of typology would be broken and the divine plan fully revealed.[82] As Brett Whalen has shown, the definition of Christendom that emerged in the Central Middle Ages depended on a complex Latin "theology of history" that blended historical knowledge, biblical prophecy and its exegesis, and eschatology.[83] The dramatic suffering and triumphs that accompanied the First Crusade offered an ideal whetstone upon which contemporary theologians and historians could sharpen their theories about what Christendom's future might hold. At least some contemporary historians invested the events of 1099 with apocalyptic significance, developing eschatological interpretations that blended the accounts of eyewitnesses with the prophecies of Israel's ancient prophets, using the interpretive tools of biblical exegesis to bring the two groups into dialogue across the gulf of centuries.[84]

---

[79] On the Scriptures as *speculum*, see John A. Alford, "The Scriptural Self," in *The Bible in the Middle Ages: Its Influence on Literature and Art*, ed. Bernard S. Levy (Binghamton, NY, 1992), 1–21 (esp. 11–13); for this view of history, see Guenée, *Histoire et culture*, 211.

[80] Jay Rubenstein, "Putting History to Use: Three Crusade Chronicles in Context," *Viator* 35 (2004): 131–68 (quoting 134).

[81] E.g., Cassiodorus comments in *Institutions* 1.17.1 that Christian history is distinguished from pagan history by its insistence that "nothing happens by chance," and Christian historians' task is "to attach all events to the providential guidance of the creator"; trans. James W. Halporn (Liverpool, 2004), 149. For the twelfth-century view, see Gabrielle M. Spiegel, "History as Enlightenment," in *Abbot Suger and Saint-Denis*, ed. Paula Gerson (New York, 1986), 151–58.

[82] Spiegel, *Past as Text*, 91–92.

[83] See Brett Whalen, *Dominion of God: Christendom and Apocalypse in the Middle Ages* (Cambridge, MA, 2009), esp. ch. 2 on the early twelfth century.

[84] This topic has been thoroughly studied by Jay Rubenstein; see especially his *Armies of Heaven*, passim; and idem, *Nebuchadnezzar's Dream*, ch. 2–5.

The crusade's early narrators came of age at a moment when traditional historiographical methodologies were undergoing a reappraisal. But while it is commonplace to identify the late eleventh and, especially, twelfth centuries with the rise of new kinds of historical writing, historians have not agreed on precisely what was new about the 'new history' of this period. One view suggests that Augustinian monastic models of historical analysis were giving way to less allegorical, more logic-driven approaches.[85] On the other hand, Bernard Guenée has identified an *increasing* level of historical engagement with the Scriptures, which he linked to monastic reform, the rise of urban schools, and the advent of the crusading movement.[86] Gillian Evans has suggested that we should regard history "as a branch of the new enlarged theology" of this period, whose practitioners, like Saint Anselm, brought theological methodologies to bear on historical problems.[87] Given the variety of historiographical approaches current in the twelfth century, these readings need not be mutually exclusive. A survey of historical sources created in the decades around 1100 reveals important continuities with earlier medieval traditions, but also demonstrates that the field of historical inquiry, like biblical exegesis, was growing in new directions as practitioners experimented with new genres, (vernacular) languages, and methodologies.[88] As a particularly knotty historical problem, the crusade inspired contemporaries to experiment with all of these emerging tools.

Scholars of medieval historiography have been reticent to treat early crusading histories as part of this great flowering of the historical discipline, with the result that these works have often been artificially separated from the mainstream of contemporary history writing.[89] While in some ways these texts are quite distinctive, such an approach prevents us from appreciating crusading narratives as products of particular intellectual contexts. Recontextualized, it is clear that the histories of the First Crusade exemplify what might be termed the 'in betweenness' of early twelfth-century historiography, which

---

[85] Coleman, *Ancient and Medieval Memories*, 286–90.
[86] Guenée, *Histoire et culture*, 30–32; M.-D. Chenu, "Theology and the New Awareness of History" in his *Man, Nature, and Society in the Twelfth Century*, trans. Taylor and Little, 162–201.
[87] G. R. Evans, "St Anselm and Sacred History," in *The Writing of History in the Middle Ages*, ed. Davis and Wallace-Hadrill, 187–210 (quoting 191–92).
[88] As suggested by the case studies in Peter Classen, "*Res gestae*, Universal History, Apocalypse: Visions of Past and Future," in *Renaissance and Renewal in the Twelfth Century*, ed. Robert L. Benson and Giles Constable (Cambridge, MA, 1982), 386–417.
[89] For example, consider the absence of any extended analysis of crusade histories by Bernard Guenée in his *Histoire et culture* (although he briefly acknowledges their importance at p. 360), and Peter Classen's explanation of his omission of these sources in "*Res gestae*," 414.

in hindsight seems caught between earlier Eusebian–Augustinian traditions and the proto-humanist chronicles of the later Middle Ages. The crusade's historians were as eager as earlier historians – if not more so – to frame their narratives in terms of divine providence, and their works' hagiographical and homiletic dimensions declare their kinship with monastic *vitae* and house-histories, as well as pilgrimage guides.[90] Likewise, accounts of the Jerusalem journey share some narratological assumptions with earlier universal histories, which, as Stephen Nichols has shown, drew inspiration from scriptural models and emphasized their subjects' privileged place within the order of revelation.[91] At the same time, accounts of the First Crusade reflect twelfth-century historians' willingness to experiment with form and genre. We see this, for example, in the decision to narrate and interpret a single chain of events, thereby adopting a narrow focus unprecedented in the annals of earlier medieval historiography,[92] as well as in some chroniclers' awareness of the emerging genre of the *chanson de geste*.[93]

If the narratives of the First Crusade have largely been studied outside the context of medieval historiography, they have likewise been divorced from the context of exegesis as it was practiced in the late eleventh and early twelfth centuries. As texts which marshaled biblical support for a particular ideological position, early crusading narratives can be linked to what I. S. Robinson termed "political allegory," an interpretive tradition rooted in the eleventh-century disputes over ecclesiastical reform.[94] Sacred texts served as ammunition in heated debates over the best models and truest meanings of Christian life, and the concomitant exegetical revival was surely linked, in ways not yet fully understood, to the wars of words that accompanied the drive for reform. In the eleventh and early twelfth centuries, reformers fitted out many biblical passages with new layers of interpretive dress, creating distinct exegetical traditions that served the purposes of their partisans, be they members of the Gregorian curia, the imperial Salian court, or new monastic orders. The apologists of the early

---

[90] On the influence of pilgrimage guides and hagiography on the earliest crusade histories, see Niskansen, "The Character and Origin of the *Gesta Francorum*," 299–309.

[91] Stephen G. Nichols, *Romanesque Signs: Early Medieval Narrative and Iconography* (New Haven, 1983), 1–16.

[92] Rubenstein, "What is the *Gesta Francorum*?" 180–81.

[93] Stefan van der Elst, *The Knight, the Cross, and the Song: Crusade Propaganda and Chivalric Literature, 1100–1400* (Philadelphia, 2017), ch. 1–4; Susan B. Edgington, "Albert of Aachen and the *chansons de geste*," *The Crusades and Their Sources: Essays Presented to Bernard Hamilton*, ed. John France and William G. Zajac (Aldershot, 1998), 23–28; and Matthew Bennett, "First Crusaders' Images of Muslims: The Influence of Vernacular Poetry?" *Forum for Modern Language Studies* 22 (1986): 101–22.

[94] Robinson, "'Political Allegory.'"

crusading movement, most of whom came of age during the culture wars of the late eleventh century, were quite familiar with the ideological baggage carried by particular biblical themes and verses.

Pressing biblical exegesis into the service of theological and political agendas was not, of course, new in the eleventh century. Principles of scriptural interpretation had been developed in Late Antiquity to serve well-defined ideological ends: the articulation of a model of Christian *imperium*, the degradation of Judaism along with its laws and rituals, and the distinction between worldly and spiritual service. Elizabeth Clark has emphasized patristic commentators' desire to "provide exegetical solutions to real-life problems," and proposed that much of the commentary we read as "personal interpretive resolutions to textual problems" is better understood as work "informed by the religious, ecclesiastical, and moral (not to speak of social and material) circumstances of the interpreters."[95] Patristic methodologies that survived the end of the Western Roman Empire helpfully supplied Germanic rulers with impeccable biblical credentials and, a few centuries later, helped to create the myth of the Franks as a 'New Israel,' overseen by a Carolingian dynasty that identified itself with the House of David and its bishops with the prophetic traditions of the Hebrew Bible.[96] Similarly, the Roman pontiff's claims to universal primacy were articulated via biblical exegesis in a centuries-long process that accelerated in the eleventh century.[97]

Engagement with this-worldly concerns remained a prominent characteristic of biblical commentary in the decades leading up to the First Crusade. Guy Lobrichon has identified five main thematic strands of eleventh-century exegesis: the problem of how to integrate new peoples into Christendom; the visibility of the Church, its sacred structures, congregations, and sacramental life; the nature of the original apostolic life and strategies for its revival; universal salvation; and eschatology.[98] We might add to this list growing concerns with heretics and Jews (groups often derided as literalists who failed to grasp the allegorical and moral nuances of the Scriptures), the nature of Christian kingship, and the basis for papal power and clerical authority more broadly.[99] The early crusading project

---

[95] Elizabeth Clark, *Reading Renunciation: Asceticism and Scripture in Early Christianity* (Princeton, NJ, 1999), 328–29; see also Gerard E. Caspary, *Politics and Exegesis: Origen and the Two Swords* (Berkeley, CA, 1979), ch. 4.

[96] Pierre Riché, "La Bible et la vie politique dans le haut Moyen Age," in *Le Moyen Age et la Bible*, ed. Riché and Lobrichon, 385–400; Mary Garrison, "The Franks as the New Israel?" in *The Uses of the Past in the Early Middle Ages*, ed. Hen and Innes, 114–61.

[97] Karlfried Froehlich, "Saint Peter, Papacy Primacy, and the Exegetical Tradition, 1150–1300," in *The Religious Role of the Papacy: Ideals and Realities*, ed. Christopher Ryan (Toronto, 1989), 3–44.

[98] Lobrichon, "The Early Schools," 552–54.

[99] For heretics, see Michel Lauwers, "Usages de la Bible et institution du sens dans l'Occident médiéval," *Médiévales* 55 (2008): 5–18 (esp. 5–6); for Jews, see David

grew out of and intersected with all of these concerns, and its exegetically savvy chroniclers contributed to these ongoing debates.

The eleventh-century monastic and papal reform movements, whose relationship to the First Crusade continues to be debated, were deeply rooted in the Scriptures and fully engaged with their interpretive challenges. To begin, reformers at the Roman curia tackled the daunting editorial project of establishing authoritative biblical texts, thus providing a firm foundation for programs of *reformatio*.[100] The 'giant bibles' that appeared around 1050 are particularly impressive symbols of reformers' desire to affirm the scriptural basis of the Latin Church's authority.[101] Throughout the Latin West at this time, monastic scriptoria invested in the production of new biblical manuscripts, reflecting their commitment to the communal scriptural reading that was a hallmark of reform.[102] Reform-minded bishops and abbots exhorted the unrepentant and defended the righteous using biblical language, and ridiculed as ignorant (*indocti*) clerics lacking a ready command of the divine word.[103] During the dramatic unfolding of the Investiture Contest in the 1070s through 1090s, clerical polemicists ransacked the Scriptures and their commentary traditions to support their visions of properly reordered worlds, which they subsequently promoted in a flood of polemic, hagiography, and history.[104] According to the monastic chronicler Lambert of Hersefeld (d. 1088), the Salian rulers Henry IV (r. 1056–1105) and Henry V (r. 1099–1125) employed scholars whose sole task it was to churn out historical treatises supporting the imperial side.[105] Likewise, under Gregory VII (r. 1073–85) the papal curia became "a scriptorium of reform," generating great

---

Timmer, "Biblical Exegesis and the Jewish-Christian Controversy in the Early Twelfth Century," *Church History* 58 (1989): 309–21; for kingship, see Buc, *L'Ambiguïté du livre*, and idem, "David's Adultery with Bathsheba and the Healing Power of the Capetian Kings," *Viator* 24 (1993): 101–20; and for papal power, see Giuseppe Fornasari, "L'esegesi gregoriana," in *La bibbia nel medioevo*, 199–214.

[100] Lobrichon, "Riforma ecclesiastica e testo della Bibbia," 15–26.

[101] Lila Yawn, "The Italian Giant Bibles," in *The Practice of the Bible*, ed. Boynton and Reilly, 126–56; Diane J. Reilly, *The Art of Reform in Eleventh-Century Flanders: Gerard of Cambrai, Richard of Saint-Vanne and the Saint-Vaast Bible* (Leiden, 2006); Robert Timothy Chasson, "Prophetic Imagery and Lections at Passiontide: The Jeremiah Illustrations in a Tuscan Romanesque Bible," *Gesta* 42 (2003): 89–114; and Ovidio Capitani, "La Riforma gregoriana," in *Le Bibbie atlantiche*, ed. Maniaci and Orofino, 7–14.

[102] Walter Cahn, *Romanesque Bible Illumination* (Ithaca, NY. 1982), 95–119.

[103] Leclercq, "Usage et abus de la Bible," 92–93.

[104] On exegesis in the service of reform, see, in addition to Leclercq, "Usage et abus," Robinson, "Political Allegory", and idem, *Authority and Resistance*.

[105] Cited by Ernst Breisach, *Historiography: Ancient, Medieval & Modern* (Chicago, 1983), 123.

quantities of textual support for ecclesiastical authority.[106] Writers on both sides shared the conviction that recent history, like biblical history, was subject to interpretation on literal, allegorical, and moral levels, and used the methods of biblical commentary to draw out these layers of meaning from the rich 'text' of worldly happenings.[107] This strategy set a precedent that the crusade chroniclers of the next generation would emulate.

Not surprisingly, given the close connections between biblical commentaries and contemporary reformist treatises,[108] the eleventh- and twelfth-century polemical literature of reform abounds in biblical references. The *Libelli de lite*, which take up just over 2,000 large-format pages in the *Monumenta Germaniae Historica*, contain over 700 scriptural citations, divided roughly equally between the Old and New Testaments.[109] (This number does not include nearly 300 references to patristic and Carolingian biblical commentaries, which show that the venerable Fathers were posthumously dragooned into exegetical service on both sides of the Church–State contest.[110]) The register of Gregory VII, with well over 600 biblical references as well as numerous citations of patristic exegetical works, offers a fascinating case study of how exegesis might be deployed in the service of reform.[111] Some two-thirds of Gregory's biblical allusions (417 out of 634) are from the New Testament, especially the Epistles (224) and Gospels (183), with the most-cited books being the Gospel of Matthew (73), Psalms (64),

---

[106] The phrase is from North, "Polemic, Apathy, and Authorial Initiative," 120; though North also cautions (p. 122) "against assuming that Gregory VII ... viewed his curia as salaried propagandists."

[107] Sverre Bagge, *Kings, Politics, and the Right Order of the World in German Historiography, c. 950–1150* (Leiden, 2009), esp. ch. 4–5.

[108] I. S. Robinson, "The Bible in the Investiture Contest: The South German Gregorian Circle," in *The Bible in the Medieval World: Essays in Memory of Beryl Smalley*, ed. Katherine Walsh and Diana Wood (Oxford, 1985), 61–84 (at 71–72). See also Florian Hartmann, "'*Quid nobis cum allegoria?*' The Literal Reading of the Bible in the Era of the Investiture Conflict," in *Reading the Bible in the Middle Ages*, ed. Jinty Nelson and Damien Kempf (London, 2015), 101–18.

[109] Leclercq, "Usage et abus," 98–99.

[110] My count is based on the references in the *indices auctoritatum: scriptores ecclesiastici* at the end of each volume of the MGH Lib. de lite compiled by Ernst Sackur (1: 655–61), Julius Dieterich (2: 731–36), and Heinrich Boehmer (3: 765–69), and includes only biblical commentaries.

[111] H. E. J. Cowdrey has shown that Gregory was extraordinarily careful in his use of biblical proof-texts; for examples, see *Pope Gregory VII, 1073–1085* (Oxford, 1998), 468, 509 and 617 n. 35. Against viewing the Register as a collection of impersonal documents, H. E. J. Cowdrey argues that "many [of the letters] bear the marks of Gregory's own composition or dictation," citing internal evidence including the habitual citation of particular biblical texts. See Cowdrey, Introduction to *The Register of Pope Gregory VII, 1073–1085* (Oxford, 2002), xv.

the Gospel of John (46), Romans and 1 Corinthians (40 each).[112] Besides having a clear predilection for certain books, Gregory returned again and again to biblical narratives or injunctions which resonated with his vision of papal authority, such as the prophet Samuel's rebuke of King Saul (1 Kgs. 15:23)[113] and Christ's declaration that Peter would be the 'rock' of his church (Mat. 16:18–19),[114] and to hortatory verses which held personal meaning for him (e.g., Eph. 6:10, Phil. 2:21).[115] On its surface, Gregory's register reads like the archive of a propaganda war, but the patterns of biblical references across his letters reflect the pope's habits of *lectio divina* and the personal relationship with the Scriptures which he had developed in the cloister.[116]

It should not surprise us that Gregory and his reform-minded contemporaries, most of them from monastic backgrounds, viewed contemporary events through a scriptural lens and turned to a stable fund of biblical metaphors and typological comparisons to make sense of a world in which the unthinkable had become commonplace: the pope was driven from Rome and an anti-pope (or Antichrist?) installed on Saint Peter's throne; throngs of priests' wives rioted in the streets; the most powerful ruler in Christendom groveled, excommunicate, at the pope's feet on a snowy mountaintop. Thus Anselm of Lucca (d. 1086) could allegorize the Church as the "ship of Peter," tossed on a sea of conflict that recalled the storm on the sea of Galilee (Mat. 8:24–28), with the important difference that the present-day 'Peter' (i.e., Gregory VII) showed greater fortitude than his apostolic predecessors.[117] Even as reformers continued to approach the Scriptures through earlier commentaries, they were also willing to reassess the meaning of key biblical passages in light of quarrels over issues like simony, clerical celibacy, and the limits of papal power, which had not greatly concerned the Fathers. In light of debates about episcopal celibacy, general injunctions against fornication and adultery in the Epistles (e.g., 1 Cor. 6:15, Rom. 7:3) were reinterpreted to show

---

[112] *Das Register Gregors VII*, MGH Epistolae selectae 2.1–2.2, ed. Erich Caspar (Berlin, 1920–23) contains an index of biblical references in 2:644–48 and of patristic works at 2:649–50; but I have used the more complete indices in Cowdrey, *Register of Gregory VII*, 451–55 (biblical references) and 455–56 (patristic and conciliar references).

[113] See Ep. 2.45, 2.75, 4.1, 4.2, 4.11, 4.23, 4.24, 6.10, 6.11, 7.14a (bis), 7.16, 7.24, 8.15, 9.20, and 9.35. That these letters span the period from 1075 to 1083 shows Gregory's consistent use of a particular biblical pericope within his reforming rhetoric. Note, too, the appearance of the same biblical text in consecutive letters, suggesting Gregory may have been pondering and discussing its interpretations with advisors during these periods.

[114] See Ep. 2.70, 2.72, 3.6, 3.10, 3.10a, 4.2, 4.28, 5.10, 6.28, 7.6, 7.14, and 8.20.

[115] See Ep. 1.25, 1.26, 1.49, 2.5, 3.15, 4.7, 6.14, 8.9 (Eph. 6:10); and 1.42, 2.14, 2.31, 3.3, 4.24, 6.11, and 8.21 (Phil. 2:21).

[116] On Gregory's monastic training, see Cowdrey, *Pope Gregory VII*, 27–30.

[117] Cited by I. S. Robinson, "Church and Papacy," in *The Cambridge History of Medieval Political Thought, c. 350–1450*, ed. J. H. Burns (Cambridge, 1988), 256–57 and n. 32.

Paul's disapproval of married or otherwise unchaste bishops, who were exhorted to be faithful to a single 'spouse,' the Church.[118] The story of how Christ drove the moneychangers from the Temple (Mat. 21:12–13, Mk. 11:15–17, Lk. 19:45–46, Jn. 2:13–17) was retrofitted as a pericope to justify the Church's persecution of simoniacal clergy and the use of force against the pope's enemies.[119] And, in an exegetical shift of particular importance in the history of holy war, Gregory VII used the spiritual "soldier of Christ" of the Epistles (2 Tim. 2:3–4) as the basis for a *militia Sancti Petri* that defended the papacy's primacy in return for spiritual rewards.[120]

In seeking to assess the impact of these strands of thought on early crusade narratives, we must remember that our chroniclers would have encountered the great ideological contest over reform as a set of living debates. Even if tempers had cooled somewhat by the time of the First Crusade, many of the most pressing issues remained unresolved, and debates over the limits of ecclesiastical authority, the meaning of apostolic life, and the roles of laypeople in the Church loom large in the background of early twelfth-century crusade historiography. As we shall see in Chapters 3 and 4, contemporary observers eager to decode the dramatic events of the 1090s were as willing as reformist exegetes to reconsider traditional biblical interpretations, bending the scriptural pericopes in ways that promoted the holy war or explained the Jerusalemites' startling successes in the East.

Glossing the Norman Conquest

As histories and as works of exegesis, early crusading narratives were very much of their twelfth-century moment in some respects; we see this, for example, in their authors' foregrounding of the deeds of great men, as well as their close attention to allegory and typology. At the same time, chronicles of the First Crusade fuse historical and exegetical methodologies to a degree that sets them apart from the mainstream of contemporary historiography. Comparing the chronicles with another body of texts, the Norman and Anglo-Norman histories of the conquest of England in 1066, brings the distinctiveness of early crusade narrative into sharper focus. Accounts of the Norman Conquest make for a

---

[118] Megan McLaughlin, "The Bishop as Bridegroom: Marital Imagery and Clerical Celibacy in the Eleventh and Twelfth Centuries," in *Medieval Purity and Piety: Essays on Clerical Celibacy and Religious Reform*, ed. Michael Frassetto (New York, 1998), 209–37 (at 223 and 225); for a series of rich analyses of reformers' use of biblical texts and imagery related to marriage, family, and gender roles see eadem, *Sex, Gender, and Episcopal Authority in an Age of Reform, 1000–1222* (Cambridge, 2010).

[119] Bain, "Les marchands chassés du Temple," 25–32.

[120] I. S. Robinson, "Gregory VII and the Soldiers of Christ," *History* 58 (1973): 169–92 (esp. 177–78).

promising comparison for several reasons. Like the First Crusade, the Conquest was widely recognized by Latin observers as a major event which cried out for commemoration and analysis; indeed, for some contemporaries, the two events seemed to be connected links on the chain of history.[121] Significantly, this view was shared by some first crusaders who were descended from veterans of 1066.[122] The series of events leading from the death of Edward the Confessor to the coronation of Duke William II of Normandy as king of England inspired monastic and clerical authors to compose chronicles, biographies, and martial epics, works that echo early crusading narratives in their wide range of Latin styles. As was the case with the First Crusade, too, the Norman Conquest's historiography began to take shape in its immediate aftermath, but continued to attract historical interest for decades as later writers amended and expanded upon their predecessors' work.[123] Perhaps most significantly for our purposes, modern scholars have often read the narratives of the Conquest as evidence that, three decades before the Council of Clermont, Norman partisans viewed the endeavor as something akin to a crusade.[124]

Duke William II certainly went to great lengths to justify his invasion of England in ideological terms, and was as outwardly concerned with spiritual preparations as with military and diplomatic matters in the months leading up to his fleet's departure. These preparations were calculated to boost political support for William and underscore the justness of his cause. In the spring of 1066 the duke received crucial backing from the Roman church in the form of a "banner of Saint Peter" (*vexillum sancti Petri*) dispatched from Pope Alexander

---

[121] For coverage of 1066 by the "international press," see Elisabeth van Houts, "The Norman Conquest through European Eyes," *English Historical Review* 110, no. 438 (1995): 832–53. Albert Derolez has suggested that Lambert of Saint-Omer regarded the conquests of 1066 and 1099 as related events within a sacral historical framework; see *The Autograph Manuscript of the* Liber Floridus: *A Key to the Encyclopedia of Lambert of Saint-Omer*, Corpus Christianorum, Autographa Medii Aevi 4 (Turnhout, 1998), 181.

[122] Lars Kjær, "Conquests, Family Traditions and the First Crusade," *The Journal of Medieval History* 45 (2019): 553–79.

[123] For the development of the medieval historiography of 1066, see Marjorie Chibnall, *The Debate on the Norman Conquest* (Manchester, 1999), 9–27; and for the ways in which personal allegiance and distance from the events shaped contemporaries' assessments, see Elisabeth van Houts, "The Memory of 1066 in Written and Oral Traditions," *Anglo-Norman Studies* 19 (1996): 169–79.

[124] See Erdmann, *The Origin of the Idea*, 155; David C. Douglas, *The Norman Achievement* (Berkeley, CA, 1969), 89f.; R. Allen Brown, *The Normans and the Norman Conquest*, 2nd edn (Dover, NH, 1994), 128–29; and Matthew Bennett, *The Campaigns of the Norman Conquest* (London, 2001), 23. The Norman conquest of Southern Italy and Sicily has also been interpreted in this way, most recently by Paul Chevedden, "A Crusade from the First: The Norman Conquest of Islamic Sicily, 1060–1091," *Al-Masāq: Journal of the Medieval Mediterranean* 22 (2010): 191–225.

II (r. 1061–73), a powerful symbol which seems to have helped William to rally support.[125] Although evidence for the banner is admittedly murky, its existence – and the alliance between the Normans and the reforming papacy which it implied – is generally accepted.[126] Alexander II's bestowal of a banner on Duke William was a remarkable break with the diplomatic practices of earlier and later reformist popes, including Urban II, who usually reserved such signs of approval for recipients fighting directly under the aegis of the papacy, generally against non-Christians.[127] Public displays of piety also helped to bolster William's claims that the invasion was a just war. The dedication in June 1066 of the abbey of La Trinité at Caen, less than a day's ride from the Norman ships gathering at the estuary of the Dives, was a carefully calibrated public expression of William's religiosity, underscored by the gift of his seven-year-old daughter, Cecilia, to the abbey as an *oblata*.[128] In the final days before disembarkation, as William awaited a favorable wind, he organized and participated in a procession of the relics of a local saint, Valéry, to whom he promised a grant of land in return for the saint's favorable intercession.[129] As a final touch, William of Poitiers tells us, the duke "hung around his neck in humility the relics whose protection [King] Harold

---

[125] The only near-contemporary source to mention the banner is William of Poitiers, *Gesta Guillelmi Gesta ducis Normannorum et regis Anglorum*, 2.3, ed. and trans. R. H. C. Davis and Marjorie Chibnall (Oxford, 1998), 104. Among the later historians, Orderic Vitalis frames William's overture to the pope as a means of reassuring the duke's reluctant followers (OV, 2:142), while William of Malmesbury indicates that the arrival of the banner was a recruiting boon for William (WM, 1:448). For an overview of William's alliance with the papacy and its implications, see H. E. J. Cowdrey, "Pope Gregory VII and the Anglo-Norman Church and Kingdom," *Studia Gratiana* 9 (1972): 79–114; repr. in *Popes, Monks, and Crusaders* (London, 1984), IX.79–114 (at 83–85).

[126] Though generally rejected, Catherine Morton's claims that the banner was an invention of the Norman propaganda machine, and that William received papal approval for the invasion only retroactively, in c. 1070, have prompted a valuable reexamination of the evidence. See Morton, "Pope Alexander II and the Norman Conquest," *Latomus* 34 (1975): 362–82; and, for responses, David Bates, *William the Conqueror* (New Haven, 2017), 220–21; R. H. C. Davis, *From Alfred the Great to Stephen* (London, 1991), 85 n. 4; David S. Bachrach, *Religion and the Conduct of War, c. 300–1215* (Woodbridge, 2003), 66–67.

[127] See Erdmann, *The Origin of the Idea*, 43–53 (for the prevalence of such banners in the later eleventh century) and 185–86 (for the presence of a *vexillum Sancti Petri* on the First Crusade).

[128] Bates, *William the Conqueror*, 226–27; and Jean Dunbabin, "Geoffrey of Chaumont, Thibaud of Blois and William the Conqueror," *Anglo-Norman Studies* 16 (1993): 101–16 (at 111).

[129] William of Poitiers, *Gesta Guillelmi*, 2.5, ed. and trans. Davis and Chibnall, 108–10; *Carmen de Hastingae proelio of Guy, Bishop of Amiens*, ll. 56–57, 98–99, ed. Frank Barlow (Oxford, 1999), 6–8; OV, book 3, 2:168–70; and for commentary, Bachrach, *Religion and the Conduct of War*, 83–84.

had forfeited by breaking the oath that he had sworn on them," in a gesture that advertised his own submission to God as well as his rival's alleged sacrilege.[130]

It is clear, then, that Duke William and his supporters sought to justify the invasion of England in religious terms as an undertaking which enjoyed papal – and thus divine – approval. If not explicitly a holy war, the conquest was presented as a *bellum publicum*, which eleventh-century canonists defined as "violence in a just cause at the order of a legitimate ruler against a tyrant seeking to subvert Christian peace."[131] Norman churchmen further defended the Conquest as a means of bringing the English church into line with Rome's reform agenda, and made much of the simony, nicolaitism, and pluralism of their English counterparts.[132] Given these circumstances, as well as the fact that the Norman and Anglo-Norman narrators of 1066 were churchmen steeped in the study of the Scriptures and exegetical methods described earlier in this chapter, we might understandably expect the Conquest's histories to be very similar to those of the First Crusade. That the two groups of texts are, in fact, extremely different should give us pause, and prompt us to look more closely at how contemporaries interpreted both events.

The accounts of the Conquest and the First Crusade have considerable thematic overlap: both groups of authors give considerable attention to larger-than-life martial heroics, the challenges of military logistics and leadership, and the construction of worthy adversaries. But the hermeneutic framework is different, as becomes apparent when we pay closer attention to their authors' use of metaphors and quotations. One cannot read the crusade narratives without noticing the persistent, often elaborate, incorporation of scriptural language and comparisons; indeed, this would have been one of the most obvious features of these texts to medieval readers. By contrast, the seven accounts of the Norman Conquest produced between c. 1067 and c. 1135 rarely employ biblical language or draw parallels between the events of 1066 and the biblical past.[133] The

---

[130] William of Poitiers, *Gesta Guillelmi*, 2.14, ed. and trans. Davis and Chibnall, 124: "Appendit etiam humili collo suo reliquias, quarum fauorem Heraldus abalienauerat sibi, uiolata fide quam super eas iurando sanxerat."

[131] George Garnett, *Conquered England: Kingship, Succession, and Tenure, 1066–1166* (Oxford, 2007), 9.

[132] Hugh M. Thomas, *The Norman Conquest: England after William the Conqueror* (Lanham, MD, 2008), 122–23. Antonia Gransden has argued that the post-conquest reform of monasticism has been exaggerated; see "Traditionalism and Continuity during the Last Century of Anglo-Saxon Monasticism," in her *Legends, Traditions, and History in Medieval England* (London, 2004), 31–79. Even the most notorious of English clerics, the archbishop of Canterbury Stigand, has been rehabilitated, by Mary Frances Smith; see "Archbishop Stigand and the Eye of the Needle," *Anglo-Norman Studies* 16 (1994): 199–220.

[133] My analysis is based on the following accounts of the Conquest, ordered chronologically: *The Carmen de Hastingae proelio* (c. 1067), ed. Barlow; William of Jumièges'

Conquest's medieval historiography is admittedly relatively brief, as compared to that of the First Crusade, consisting of some 106 pages in the Oxford Medieval Texts series[134] (versus some 1,300 pages' worth of material in the *Recueil des historiens des croisades* dealing with the First Crusade, produced between c. 1095 and c. 1146). While the Conquest's corpus contains just 19 biblical references,[135] or roughly one reference every six pages, the crusading narratives contain a total of 1,408 references, or a little more than one reference per page.[136] Behind these numbers lie two divergent approaches to recounting and interpreting history, and two events that contemporaries perceived to be hugely significant, but also fundamentally different.

This becomes apparent when we examine the work of four authors who wrote accounts of both the Conquest and the Crusade: the French Benedictine Baldric of Bourgueil, who included a description of the Norman invasion in a long poem written for the Conqueror's daughter, Countess Adela of Blois; and the Anglo-Norman chroniclers Henry of Huntingdon, Orderic Vitalis, and William of Malmesbury, all of whom dealt with 1066 and its aftermath within their longer histories. The earliest of these texts, Baldric's ekphrastic poem *Adelae Comitissae* (bef. 1102), has most interested scholars for its description of what purports to

---

account of the Conquest in the *Gesta Normannorum Ducum* (c. 1070), 7.13(31)–20(41), ed. and trans. Elisabeth M. C. van Houts, 2 vols (Oxford, 1995), 2:158–82; William of Poitiers, *Gesta Guillelmi* (c. 1071–77), 2.1–33, ed. and trans. Davis and Chibnall, 100–160; Baldric of Bourgueil, *Adelae Comitissae* (bef. 1102), no. 134 in *Baldricus Burgulianus Carmina*, ed. K. Hilbert, Editiones Heidelbergenses 19 (Heidelberg, 1979), 149–89 (with the relevant section at 155–64, ll. 243–560); Henry of Huntingdon, *Historia Anglorum* (c. 1129), 6.26–39, HH, 384–406; Orderic Vitalis, *Historia ecclesiastica* (c. 1135), book 3, 2:142–44, 168–86; and William of Malmesbury, *Gesta regum* (c. 1135), 3.238–48, WM, 1:592–612, 620–22, 628–54.

[134] Where accounts of the Conquest are included within larger works, as in the *Gesta Normannorum ducum*, and the histories of Orderic Vitalis, William of Malmesbury, and Henry of Huntingdon, my count includes only relevant sections (as specified in n. 133).

[135] These are as follows: *The Carmen de Hastingae proelio* (10 references), ed. Barlow: Ps. 32:20 (l. 55, p. 6), Ps. 72:28 (l. 64, p. 6), Is. 40:12 (l. 66, p. 6), Mat. 14:29 (l. 69, p. 6), Ps. 103:32 (l. 94, p. 8), Gen. 9:2 (ll. 94–95, p. 8), Gen. 4:8 (ll. 137–38, p. 10), Jud. 8:9 (l. 678, p. 40), Hebr. 10:1 (l. 733, p. 42), Rev. 21:19–20 (l. 764ff, pp. 44–46); William of Poitiers, *Gesta Guillelmi* (3 references), ed. Davis and Chibnall: Ecclus./Sirach 43:37, p. 102; Gen. 16:5, p. 122; Ps. 71:10 (cf. Ps. 71:15), p. 154; HH (2 references): Tob. 8:3, p. 390; Ps. 76:11, p. 395; Orderic Vitalis (3 references), OV, book 3: Mat. 9:4, 2:160; Ps. 67:3 (cf. Wis. 5:15), 2:170; Ps. 13:3, 2:178; and William of Malmesbury, *Gesta Regum* (1 reference), WM, 3.245: Mat. 7:14 (1:458). I have not identifed any biblical references in these portions of William of Jumièges or Baldric of Bourgueil's texts.

[136] For a breakdown of this number, see Chapter 2 and Appendices 1 and 2.

be a tapestry depicting the Norman invasion,[137] but also makes for an intriguing comparison with the *Historia Ierosolimitana* which Baldric wrote perhaps five or ten years later. An ardent admirer of ancient poetry, Baldric presents the events of 1066 in a classical mode, dazzling the reader's senses with "the splendor of Phoebus" and "the trumpets of Mars," and likening the Norman enterprise to Xerxes's invasion of Greece and the assault on Troy.[138] The battle of Hastings itself becomes a classical set-piece, in which Duke William channels both Hector and Achilles while the Fates race to keep up with the carnage, speed-cutting the threads of men's lives and dispatching them to the "subterranean kingdoms."[139] Baldric's presentation echoes earlier works, notably those of William of Poitiers (d. 1090) and Guy of Amiens (d. 1075), which cast the Conquest in a classical guise for a courtly audience, though he seems not to have worked from these directly; at any rate, his work fits into what was, by 1100, a well-established interpretive tradition.[140] By contrast, the *Historia Ierosolimitana* has been identified with a process of what Jonathan Riley-Smith called the "theological refinement" of the crusade idea in the early twelfth century, and Baldric's engagement with biblical exegesis, as well as moral theology and canon law, is apparent throughout this work.[141] Like the *Adelae Comitissae*, the *Historia* is composed in elegant Latin and incorporates references to Roman history and literature, but with a crucial difference: in the *Historia* Baldric uses classical texts to fill in basic information about the Holy Land or simply to embellish his prose. The classics are not used to create an entire narrative universe for the crusaders to inhabit, as Baldric had done in his account of the Norman Conquest; instead, like other early narrators of the First Crusade, for this purpose he used the Scriptures – references to which outnumber those to classical texts by four to one in the *Historia*.[142] This is a reminder that, as suggested at the start of this chapter, biblical study was very much on Baldric's mind when he composed and revised the *Historia*.

Like Baldric, his successors Henry of Huntingdon, Orderic Vitalis, and William of Malmesbury were well-educated churchmen capable of applying a

---

[137] Shirley Ann Brown and Michael W. Herren, "The '*Adelae Comitissae*' of Baudri of Bourgueil and the Bayeux Tapestry," *Anglo-Norman Studies* 16 (1993): 55–73.

[138] Baldric of Bourgueil, *Adelae Comitissae*, ll. 232, 298, 349–50, 365–70, 397, ed. Hilbert, 155, 157, 158–59.

[139] Baldric of Bourgueil, *Adelae Comitissae*, ll. 445–46, 455–58, ed. Hilbert, 160–61.

[140] Neither Guy's nor William's work circulated widely; see Barlow, Introduction to *The Carmen Hastingae Proelio*, xix–xxi; and Davis and Chibnall, Introduction to the *Gesta Guillelmi*, xliii–xlv.

[141] Riley-Smith, *The Idea of Crusading*, 135–52; and Steven Biddlecombe, "Baldric of Bourgueil and the *Familia Christi*," in *Writing the Early Crusades: Text, Transmission, and Memory*, ed. Bull and Kempf, 9–23.

[142] For example, see BB, 5 (ref. to Josephus, *De bello Judaico*), 22, and 28 (decorative echoes of Virgil's *Aeneid*).

variety of interpretive strategies to a complex historical event like the Conquest (or the Crusade).[143] None of them applied heroic classical imagery to the Norman invasion, though Henry and William of Malmesbury in particular were generally fond of classical references; nor did they set the story of 1066 within a biblical framework; a total of just six biblical allusions adorn their accounts of the Conquest.[144] Notwithstanding their differences of emphasis, these works are predominantly political histories, concerned with what Henry, Orderic, and William – all of them the bilingual sons of English mothers and Norman fathers – recognized as the great watershed moment in England's history.[145] While they had little choice but to accept the outcome of 1066 as God's will, however, they were not inclined toward extravagant praise of the Conqueror. Indeed, their ambivalence towards the terrible violence that accompanied the Norman victory may have made them recoil against the classically inspired glorification of the Normans seen in the work of earlier writers.[146]

Henry, Orderic, and William of Malmesbury thus rejected the possibility of recounting the Norman Conquest in a biblical mode, despite their deep familiarity with the Scriptures and interest in contemporary exegetical methodology.[147] By contrast, these writers regarded the inclusion of scriptural material as appropriate, indeed integral, to their narratives of the Crusade. While they were more restrained in their use of biblical language than earlier crusade chroniclers like Guibert of Nogent, Robert of Reims, and Raymond of Aguilers, the Anglo-Norman writers included a total of sixty-three biblical citations in their accounts of the Crusade, citing the Scriptures three times more often in these portions of their chronicles than in the portions dedicated to the Conquest.[148] These citations appear not only

---

[143] For these men's educational background, see above, 24–25.

[144] These collectively fill 45 printed pages in the Oxford Medieval Texts series, as cited in n. 133.

[145] On Henry's background, see Diana Greenway's Introduction to the *Historia Anglorum*, xxix–xl; on William, see Thomson, *William of Malmesbury*, 3–13; and for Orderic, see Chibnall, *The World of Orderic Vitalis*, 3–16.

[146] Roger Ray makes this argument with regard to Orderic's rejection of William of Poitiers' work; see "Orderic Vitalis and William of Poitiers: A Monastic Reinterpretation of William the Conqueror," *Revue belge de philologie et d'histoire* 50, fasc. 4 (1972): 1116–27. Lars Kjær ("Conquests, Family Traditions, and the First Crusade," 573) argues that first crusaders descended from Norman conquerors of England may have seen their forefathers' deeds "as religiously and morally problematic," while Emily Albu discerns an ambivalence towards the Normans more generally on the part of their historians, including Orderic and William; see *The Normans in their Histories: Propaganda, Myth, and Subversion* (Woodbridge, 2001).

[147] For William's exegetical output, see n. 6 above; for Henry's engagement with biblical studies, see Greenway's Introduction to the *Historia Anglorum*, xxxiii–xxxiv, xxxviii; and for Orderic see Smalley, *Gospels in the Schools*, 15 and 35 n.

[148] See Appendix 1, Table 3. While the material on the crusade (which covers 134 pages

in predictable contexts, like Orderic and William of Malmesbury's accounts of Urban II's speech at Clermont, but throughout each narrative, and, as in Baldric's *Historia*, are used to comment on the spiritual value of the crusading enterprise and to situate the crusaders within sacred time. For instance, Henry, Orderic, and William of Malmesbury all describe the Jerusalemites' sacrifice of home, family, and patrimony in the language of Christ's injunction in the Gospel of Matthew 19:29: "And everyone that hath left house or brethren or sisters or father or mother or wife or children or lands for my name's sake shall receive a hundredfold, and shall possess life everlasting."[149] Biblical language also allowed the Anglo-Norman writers to hint at the eschatological significance of the crusade. This was a conflict, Henry wrote, which pitted *"the children of God against the children of the Devil"* (1 Jn. 3:10),[150] while William of Malmesbury borrowed from Revelation 8:4 to describe the aftermath of the conquest of Jerusalem, an event "more easily imagined than described" (*cogitetur ... potius quam dicatur*).[151] Moreover, the Anglo-Norman chroniclers use the Scriptures in distinctive ways; while Henry cited the Old Testament more frequently, Orderic and William preferred the New. They also treated their source material differently. While Henry and William borrowed their basic narratives of the Crusade from, respectively, the *Gesta Francorum* (or, rather, a text very like the extant *Gesta Francorum*) and Fulcher of Chartres's *Historia Hierosolymitana*, they preferred to replace the abundant scriptural allusions in these texts with new ones; thus only three of Henry's twelve biblical citations appear in the *Gesta*, while none of William of Malmesbury's fourteen citations derives from Fulcher.[152] Orderic, who

---

in the Oxford Medieval Texts editions) in their three chronicles is three times longer than the material on the Norman Conquest (which covers 45 pages in these editions), the proportion of biblical references in the accounts of the crusade (at one per 2.1 pages of text) is significantly greater than that in the accounts of the Conquest (at one per 7.5 pages of text).

[149] HH, 422; WM, 1:608; OV, 5:16, 34. See Chapter 4 for a fuller discussion of the relevance of Mat. 19:29 within early crusading narratives.

[150] HH, 436.

[151] WM, 1:650. William uses language from Rev. 8:4, where the prayers of the saints rise to heaven, to evoke the crusaders' first visit to the Holy Sepulcher: "Quot ibi precum thurificatione caelum incenderint, quot lacrimis deum in gratiam reuocauerint ... ."

[152] For Henry's use of the *Gesta*, see Greenway's Introduction to the *Historia Angelorum*, xcviii–xcix. Henry's borrowed citations all appear in a single section of the *Historia*; see HH, 436 (Rev. 10:1 and Joel 2:20), and 438 (Mal. 3:7). Cf. GF, 58, 62. William acknowledged his debt to Fulcher with a back-handed compliment (WM, 1:660; also see Thomson, *William of Malmesbury*, 179–81). While William of Malmesbury does cite one verse, Mat. 19:29, in common with Fulcher, the locations of the citation in each work, the precise wording each author uses, and the omnipresence of this text in early crusade narratives suggest that this was not a direct borrowing. Cf. WM, 1:608; and FC, 115.

greatly admired his main source, the *Historia* of his friend Baldric of Bourgueil, took over half of his thirty-seven biblical references from Baldric, though it is equally noteworthy that he declined to include most of Baldric's references (seventy-two out of ninety-six).[153] Clearly, the Anglo-Norman chroniclers were selective and purposeful in their integration of scriptural allusions into their accounts of the crusade.

Why did medieval chroniclers adapt such different approaches to narrating the Norman Conquest and the First Crusade? Writers who tackled both events clearly saw them as important in different ways. As an event of major significance within human history, the Conquest sparked a renaissance of historical writing by clerical authors, some bent on glorifying the Norman achievement and others concerned to defend ancient rights under the new regime.[154] The events of 1066 could be comprehended through a comparison with earlier conflicts over lands and titles, and here the epic pagan past supplied abundant source material. By contrast, the Crusade was perceived as a watershed in sacred history, whose meaning was to be sought not only through comparison with past human actions but in dialogue with the divine admonitions and prophecies of the Scriptures. Indeed, the crusade called for a different way of writing history, one that more fully integrated the methods of biblical exegesis and prominently featured biblical imagery. Henry of Huntingdon evokes this challenge when, at the start of his crusade narrative, he calls attention to "the magnitude of this event" and protests that "it would be impossible to keep silent about the *wonderful* and mighty *works of God*."[155] If modern readers have missed Henry's allusion to Acts 2:11, the moment when Christ's disciples are filled with the Holy Spirit and their many languages become mutually intelligible, we can be sure that Henry's twelfth-century readers did not. Like Henry, learned writers across Christendom who found the ordinary language of men inadequate to describe the Jerusalemites' accomplishment turned for inspiration to the sacred texts familiar from the liturgy and the schoolroom.

---

[153] For Orderic's use of Baldric's work, see Chibnall's comments in OV, 5: xiii–xv. Orderic and Baldric's scriptural references are listed in Appendix 2. In his study of the commentary tradition on the Book of Revelation, Guy Lobrichon notes that such authorial silences can be quite meaningful; see "Stalking the Signs: The Apocalyptic Commentaries," in *The Apocalyptic Year 1000: Religious Expectation and Social Change, 950–1050*, ed. Richard Landes, Andrew Gow, and David C. van Meter (Oxford, 2003), 69.

[154] See R. W. Southern, "Aspects of the European Tradition of Historical Writing: 4. The Sense of the Past," *Transactions of the Royal Historical Society* 23 (1973): 243–63, esp. 246–56.

[155] HH, 422: "Ob cuius rei magnitudinem digrediendi ueniam a lectore postulo, nec enim si uoluero tam miranda *Dei magnalia* tacere ... ."

Conclusion

This chapter has attempted to restore early crusade historiography to its original intellectual context, a context in which the concerns of history and theology were inextricably linked and the techniques of scriptural interpretation were essential elements of the historian's toolbox. As products of the vibrant monastic and urban schools of the late eleventh and early twelfth centuries, the First Crusade's chroniclers inherited the rich legacy of patristic and Carolingian biblical exegesis, as well as the new methods of textual criticism pioneered in the decades around 1100. As will become apparent in subsequent chapters, the crusade's early narrators were also steeped in the ideological debates around ecclesiastical reform, which shaped their reading of the Scriptures and, in turn, of the crusade 'text' itself. For, whatever else the crusade was – an act of love or vengeance, a new chapter of ecclesiastical reform, or a radical reappraisal of spiritual hierarchies – for the learned men who wrote its history, the crusade was a text.[156] A complex and contradictory text, it shared many attributes with the Scriptures; it urgently demanded to be decoded, and held out the promise of shedding light on God's plan for the world, but required sophisticated interpretive techniques to unlock its layers of meaning. Thus, we should not be surprised that the twelfth-century narratives of the First Crusade resemble the clerical propaganda of the *Libelli de lite* as much as they do contemporary histories of the Norman Conquest; indeed, when we follow the lead of the crusade's chroniclers and privilege biblical analogies and theological concerns, their works' affinity with several genres modern scholars tend to think of as completely different – biblical commentary, theology, pilgrimage narratives, and hagiography – becomes apparent. As we shall see in the next chapter, scriptural language and themes permeate the narratives of the First Crusade so thoroughly that there is good reason to privilege this material; indeed, doing so can yield new insights into some of our most pressing questions about the reception of holy war in the early twelfth century.

---

[156] Here I am indebted to Gabrielle M. Spiegel's reading of medieval historical narrative; see *The Past as Text*, esp. ch. 5–8.

Chapter 2

The Bible in the Chronicles of the First Crusade

I cannot tell you all of the things we did ... for there is in this land neither cleric nor layman who could describe or write down the whole of it.

— *Gesta Francorum et aliorum Hierosolimitanorum*[1]

But there are also many other things Jesus did which, if they were all written down, the world itself, I think, would not be able to contain the books that should be written.

— Gospel of John 21:25[2]

Even as it taxed the descriptive and interpretive powers of chroniclers across Christendom, the First Crusade inspired a greater outpouring of historical writing than any other event of the Middle Ages. In the decades after 1099, numerous chroniclers, preachers, liturgists, and poets tackled the job of making sense of events widely regarded as incredible and unprecedented, in so doing building up a mythology of the first crusaders' deeds that ultimately inspired thousands to join the Second Crusade.[3] The Scriptures had a central role to play within this ambitious commemorative project. At every stage of the process by which the crusade passed from event to living memory to written record, biblical texts and exegetical techniques smoothed the way, allowing Christians to find historical and spiritual meaning in the holy war.

As modern historians have often noted, the words of the Scriptures came readily to the minds of Christian narrators of the events of 1095–99.[4] This is hardly surprising, in light of the close relationship between history and biblical exegesis traced in Chapter 1, and considering that the crusade's early historians were almost exclusively monks, canons, and priests well versed in the sacred texts and trained in at least the rudiments of exegetical methods. Indeed, the learned men

---

[1] GF, 44: "Omnia quae egimus ... nequeo enarrare, quia nemo est in his partibus siue clericus siue laicus qui omnino possit scribere uel narrare, sicut res gesta est." Cf. the similar statement by PT, 82.
[2] The Vulgate text reads: "sunt autem et alia multa quae fecit Iesus quae si scribantur per singula nec ipsum arbitror mundum capere eos qui scribendi sunt libros."
[3] Jonathan Phillips, *The Second Crusade: Extending the Frontiers of Christendom* (New Haven, CT, 2007), 17–36. On the resonance of the First Crusade within aristocratic family traditions, see Paul, *To Follow in Their Footsteps*, ch.1.
[4] For example, Norman Housley, *Fighting for the Cross* (New Haven, CT, 2008), 181–82; and Riley-Smith, *The Idea of Crusading*, 91–92.

who narrated the holy war's history would have had far more formal instruction in the art of biblical exegesis than in the writing of history. This is not mere conjecture; the crusade histories contain clear evidence of their authors' interest in scriptural study, in the form of citations from patristic and Carolingian works of exegesis. Collectively, the crusade's chroniclers demonstrate knowledge of an impressive array of biblical scholarship, including works by Ambrose, Jerome, Augustine, Cassiodorus, Gregory the Great, Bede, and Hrabanus Maurus that were staples of eleventh- and twelfth-century libraries.[5] Additional references throughout the chronicles demonstrate their authors' familiarity with foundational works of salvation history and Christian ethics, such as Ambrose's *De officiis*, Augustine's *De civitate Dei*, Orosius's *Historia adversum paganos*, and Gregory the Great's *Dialogi*.[6] The issue of genre is further complicated by the internal organization of some of the chronicles, which suggests that they may have originally served a homiletic purpose. The *Gesta Francorum*, as Jay Rubenstein has argued, may have begun as a collection of *exempla* or short sermons, while Raymond of Aguilers's modern editors proposed that his chronicle was organized in the manner of a lectionary, from which short liturgical readings might be excerpted.[7] The manuscript traditions of the First Crusade's early histories also show that they were often copied or bound with theological and exegetical works, or with Holy Land guidebooks.[8] There is considerable evidence, then, that neither the crusade's early narrators nor their medieval audiences saw their interpretive endeavor in strictly historical terms; rather, their work grew out of, and deepened, a longstanding dialogue between the practice of history, biblical commentary, and theology.

To be sure, not all events comprising human history were fit subjects for *expositio*; Augustine's crucial distinction between ordinary worldly happenings (what we might call 'secular history') and events concerned with the story of mankind's redemption exercised a powerful influence on medieval thinkers.[9]

---

[5] For references to Ambrose, *Expositio psalmorum*, see MC, 109; and RA, 36 n. 4 and 91 n. 2. For Jerome, *Commentariorum in Hiezechielem libri XIV*, see OV, 5:136. For Augustine, *Enarrationes in psalmos*, see GN, 79. For Cassiodorus, *Expositio psalmorum*, see GN, 81. For Gregory the Great, *Homiliae in evangelia*, see GN, 94; and FE, 330 (identified by McCarthy, *Chronicles of the Investiture Contest*, 257 n. 307). For Bede, *In Lucam*, see GN, 293. For Hrabanus Maurus, *De universo*, see PT, 91 n. 42 and 92 n. 50.

[6] For Ambrose, see RA, 37 n. 2 and 6; and PT, 33, n. 25; for Augustine, *De civitate Dei*, see Ray, trans. 55 n. 9 and GP, 244; for Orosius, see CP, 150–52; for Gregory's *Dialogues*, see MC, 137.

[7] Rubenstein, "What is the *Gesta Francorum*?" 197–98. For Raymond, see RA, 28–29; and for a recent reassessment of Raymond's biblical inflections, see Lecaque, "Reading Raymond," 105–32.

[8] For several examples with discussion, see Chapter 3.

[9] R. A. Markus, *Saeculum: History and Society in the Theology of St. Augustine*

But the crusade, an event which contemporaries regarded as the unambiguous work of divine providence, belonged to the privileged category of sacred history. As such it was as open to multi-layered interpretations as were the *historia sacra* of ancient Israel and the accounts of Christ's life in the Gospels. Other factors doubtless encouraged twelfth-century writers to look to the Bible and its commentary traditions for inspiration. The experience of hearing the crusade preached, which many of our chroniclers would have shared, further reinforced the idea that the holy war was to be 'glossed,' since preachers presented the journey east in biblical terms, whether as a new form of *imitatio Christi*, a revival of the apostolic life, or a renewal of the wars of ancient Israel.[10] We must also remember that the crusading enterprise's novelty obliged early twelfth-century writers not only to record but to defend the Jerusalemites; in this context, enlisting the aid of the Scriptures was a shrewd way of lending *auctoritas* to their position.[11] Finally, and perhaps most importantly, the First Crusade posed descriptive and interpretive challenges because it broke the historical mold.[12] The suffering of its participants, the brutality of its battles and sieges, and the glory of its victories, above all the conquest of Jerusalem, sent would-be historians scrambling for interpretive cover.[13] Surveying the entire history of human achievement, they found that even the greatest human accomplishments – the siege of Troy, the conquests of Alexander the Great, and the wars of the Maccabees – paled in comparison.[14] Robert of Reims famously declared the crusade the greatest miracle since the world's creation, barring only Christ's incarnation and resurrection.[15] If the First Crusade was, as was widely agreed in the early twelfth century, "unheard of and greatly to be wondered at" (*inaudita et plurimum admiranda*),[16] then perhaps what was needed to describe it was not the ordinary language of men, but the words of God.

(Cambridge, 1970), ch. 1.

[10] On the use of biblical references in accounts of Clermont, see Cole, *The Preaching of the Crusades*, 14–19 and 23–27.

[11] For this point, see T. J. H. McCarthy, "Scriptural Allusion in the Crusading Accounts of Frutolf of Michelsberg and His Continuators," in *The Uses of the Bible*, ed. Lapina and Morton, 161, 168.

[12] As Benoît Lacroix (*L'Historien au moyen age*, 26–27) wrote, "Un événement pourtant dépasse tout, autant l'histoire des rois que celle des monastères, sauf évidemment Jésus au temps d'Auguste. C'est une guerre, la plus extraordinaire guerre qui soit arrivée à l'humanité, aventure telle que ni Israel, ni 'les autres siècles n'en ont jamais connue de pareille': la croisade."

[13] For twelfth-century understandings of the First Crusade as history on an epic scale, see Steven Biddlecombe, "Baudri of Bourgeuil and the Flawed Hero," *Anglo-Norman Studies* 35 (2014): 83–84.

[14] RC, 107, 114; GN, 85–86; RA, 53.

[15] RR, 4.

[16] AA, 2.

The Bible and Crusade Narrative in the Twelfth Century

In the Scriptures the crusade's participants, historians, and homilists found a rich trove of sacred language, in the form of prayer, prophecy, and history, which helped them to meet the challenge of explaining the events of the 1090s. Equally importantly, the interpretive difficulties posed by the crusade could be met with the aid of traditional methods of biblical exegesis. Viewed with an exegete's well-trained eye, the crusade became a kind of sacred text, one that offered skilled readers insights into God's plan for humanity and was, like the Scriptures themselves, subject to interpretation on historical, typological, moral, and mystical levels. This was a two-way exegetical process; the Scriptures offered texts and interpretive tools with which to gloss the crusade, and the holy war in turn prompted readers to reevaluate the meaning of familiar biblical texts. Yet there has never been a systematic analysis of the ways in which the Scriptures function in the First Crusade's medieval historiography, nor have modern scholars acknowledged how deeply indebted these early histories are to traditional methods of biblical exegesis. A reading that privileges the biblical material and exegetical thinking in these narratives offers a new vantage point from which to assess the early reception of the holy war, and helps to clarify the relationships between individual sources.

This chapter offers an overview of how biblical references shape early crusade narratives, highlighting larger trends in twelfth-century authors' use of the Scriptures as an interpretive lens. Here I follow the example of Jean Flori and Henri Bresc, whose studies have shown that a quantitative approach, when combined with case studies of individual themes and texts, can allow us to see the crusade's medieval historiography, and potentially the crusade itself, in a new light.[17] The data presented below derives from the best modern editions of the major epistolary, narrative, and homiletic sources for the First Crusade composed between the Council of Clermont in 1095 and 1146, when preaching of the Second Crusade began in earnest. Although Christian writers by no means lost interest in the First Crusade after 1146, the disastrous Second Crusade changed the balance of power in the Latin East and, more importantly for this study, marked the beginning of a new era in crusade historiography.[18] My analysis includes major narrative sources written within two decades of the crusaders' conquest of Jerusalem in 1099, as well as a small number of chronicles from the 1120s and 1130s, the corpus of letters related to the First Crusade, and a handful of

---

[17] See Jean Flori, *Chroniqueurs et propagandistes*, ch. 1, for an analysis of the mentions of key individuals and places in chronicles of the First Crusade composed up to c. 1110; and Henri Bresc's comments on the biblical material in various sources for the First and Fifth Crusades, "Les historiens de la croisade," 727–53.

[18] See Jonathan Phillips, *Defenders of the Holy Land: Relations between the Latin East and the West, 1119–1187* (Oxford, 1996), esp. ch.3–4; and for a shift in the historiography of crusading after the crusaders' defeat in 1148, idem, *The Second Crusade: Extending the Frontiers of Christendom* (New Haven, CT, 2007), ch. 14.

shorter texts and sermons. While these latter sources have received less scholarly attention, they can greatly enrich our understanding of the crusade's reception, while helping us to appreciate the distinctiveness of the earliest accounts.

A word about methodology is in order. The data discussed below derives from a careful count of the biblical references in modern editions. Cross-referencing editions and, where available, translations of each source and comparing the Latin texts of closely related sources yielded many additional references not identified by earlier scholars, and computer-aided searching turned up still more.[19] The better to compare different authors' glosses of the same events, I have focused on descriptions of the First Crusade itself – from Urban II's preaching at Clermont in 1095 to the Battle of Ascalon in August 1099 – and have omitted the sections of various chronicles which deal with the aftermath of the crusade and the early history of the Latin Kingdom of Jerusalem.[20] The final count of 1,408 references – more than one per page in the modern printed editions – is undoubtedly low. While I am confident that this number includes the obvious biblical references in the chronicles, there are surely many more biblical allusions that remain to be identified by future researchers. Modern critical editions of medieval historical sources tend to omit such subtle references,[21] both because they are more difficult to recognize than direct quotations and because they are generally taken to be less meaningful.[22] One disadvantage of such an approach, practical as it is, is that it obscures the degree to which the Scriptures shaped the language and even the syntax of medieval clerical writers. Taken to an extreme, it can seriously mislead modern readers about a text's authorship.[23] I have included allusions as well as

---

[19] Special thanks are due to Professor James Bernhard, who created a Python-based search engine that allowed me to cross-reference select texts against a digital version of the Vulgate, and to Professor David Chiu, Joshua Nance, and Ray Hermosillo, who helped me refine the text-mining process.

[20] For this reason I have included only the first book of Fulcher of Chartres' *Historia Hierosolymitana* and the first twelve books of Albert of Aachen's chronicle. I have also left out accounts of the Crusade of 1101, sometimes identified (following Riley-Smith, *The Idea of Crusading*, ch.5) as the 'third wave' of the First Crusade, simply because relatively few of our writers describe this campaign in detail.

[21] An exception is R. B. C. Huygens' edition of Guibert of Nogent's *Dei gesta per francos*, which includes over 300 biblical references, the majority of which are *not* direct quotations.

[22] See the insightful comments on this distinction by Damien Kempf and Marcus G. Bull in RR, lx–lxi.

[23] A prime example is Rosalind Hill's 1962 edition of the *Gesta Francorum*, which has formed the basis for scholarly study of this text for several decades. Hill's identification of just fourteen of the many biblical references in the *Gesta*, and her emphasis on the author's 'misquoting' (a problematic judgement, given the lack of a single authoritative edition of the Bible in this period), encouraged readers to assume that the anonymous author must have been a layman, an assumption now being reevaluated. Consider, for example, how Hill's edition has influenced later scholars' encounters with the text;

direct quotations because the line between the two is often blurry, and because a consideration of allusions – which, unlike direct quotations, might unconsciously creep into an author's text– can offer insights into the chains of associative thinking that, in turn, hint at what the twelfth-century writers were thinking as they wrote. While some biblical references are undoubtedly more meaningful than others,[24] even where the use of scriptural language in the chronicles does not serve an obvious interpretive purpose, it helps, as Carole Sweetenham has written, to "create a continuum of expression which tacitly assimilates the crusaders into the world of the Bible."[25]

Larger Trends

An overview of the biblical material in the crusade's early histories demonstrates that their authors were very much in step with contemporary developments in the study of Scripture. Not surprisingly, given what we know of their educational backgrounds and institutional affiliations, our authors shared with contemporary reformers and theologians an interest in particular biblical books and passages. As the following discussion demonstrates, Latin Christians' understanding of the holy war was continually evolving in the years after 1099, as individual writers brought a substantial amount of creativity and originality to the challenge of commemorating and interpreting the crusade. At the same time, larger interpretive patterns emerge, as indicated by the chroniclers' shared interest in certain biblical books and themes. This suggests that these sources were composed against a backdrop of lively discussion and debate about the crusade's historical, allegorical, and eschatological significance. While there was some consensus about the broader features of crusading spirituality and their scriptural pedigree,

---

e.g., Colin Morris has written of the *Gesta* Anonymous, "Nor … does he quote the Scripture all that often, and when he does it is always as part of a speech ascribed to one of his characters," a judgement in need of revision. See "The *Gesta Francorum* as Narrative History," *Reading Medieval Studies* 19 (1993): 55–71 (quoting 57). For an argument in favor of the author's clerical identity, see Jay Rubenstein, "What Is the *Gesta Francorum*?" 181–88; and compare Conor Kostick's view that the author was a knight with earlier training in an ecclesiastical setting, "A Further Discussion on the Authorship of the *Gesta Francorum*," *Reading Medieval Studies* 35 (2009): 1–14.

[24] Alan V. Murray has shown this effectively for William of Tyre; see his "Biblical Quotations and Formulaic Language," 25–34. See also the comments by Yitzak Hen on Merovingian authors' sometimes unconscious use of biblical language; "The Uses of the Bible and the Perception of Kingship in Merovingian Gaul," *Early Medieval Europe* 7 (1998): 277–90 (at 280).

[25] Carole Sweetenham, "Robert the Monk's Use of the Bible in the *Historia Iherosolimitana*," in *The Uses of the Bible in Crusader Sources*, ed. Lapina and Morton, 133–51 (quoting 143).

and about how the crusade was to be interpreted in moral terms, in other respects learned Christians' readings of the crusade differed markedly in their thematic emphases and biblical underpinnings. This is suggestive of the complexity of Christian holy war as a concept subject to multiple interpretations in twelfth-century Christendom.

Most broadly, a quantitative approach allows us to gauge the relative interest of early crusade apologists and historians in the Old and New Testaments. Scholars have long emphasized the prominence of Old Testament texts and metaphors within the First Crusade's medieval historiography, and indeed, the crusaders are often depicted as new Israelites and their armed pilgrimage is typologically linked to the wars and wanderings of the ancient Jews.[26] In fact, a survey of the biblical material in our sources demonstrates a fairly equal distribution of Old and New Testament citations. In the major narrative sources for the period c. 1095–1146, we find that the Old Testament predominates, but not by a very wide margin, accounting for 52% of all references.[27] Grouping the texts by date of composition, moreover, reveals a series of interpretive shifts. In the earliest textual witnesses, those composed between c. 1095 and c. 1101, New Testament citations account for a slight majority – 51% – of the total references, and in fact only one of these earliest witnesses, Raymond of Aguilers's history, demonstrates a marked preference for the Old Testament.[28] Between c. 1102 and c. 1105 the ratio remained well balanced, with 50% of references coming from the New Testament.[29] In the corpus of First Crusade letters, which likely took their present form in monastic scriptoria in the euphoric years immediately after 1099, New Testament references outnumber those to the Old Testament by

---

[26] Highly influential in this regard were the early studies of Alphandéry, "Les citations bibliques," 146–54; and Rousset, *Les origines*, 93–98. Also see Penny Cole, *The Preaching of the Crusades*, 21–30; Riley-Smith, *Idea of Crusading*, 141–45; D. H. Green, *The Millstättter Exodus: A Crusading Epic* (Cambridge, 1966), ch. 8; and for the prominence of the Old Testament in crusade preaching, *Crusade Propaganda and Ideology: Model Sermons for the Preaching of the Cross*, ed. Christoph T. Maier (Cambridge, 2004), 55–56.

[27] See Appendix 1: Chart 1 (739 OT to 630 NT). Note that 39 references, accounting for 3% of the total number, are ambiguous citations that might equally be to the Old or New Testament, reflecting the reuse of Old Testament language in the New. These references are marked with an asterisk (*) in Appendix 2.

[28] Texts from c. 1095–c. 1101: GF, PT, and RA: compare 137 OT references (49%) to 144 NT references (51%). If we omit Raymond from this count, the balance is tipped further in favor of the NT: 65 OT (37%) to 110 NT (63%).

[29] Texts from c. 1102–c. 1105: EP (nos. 2–4, 8–10, 12, 15–23, pp. 136–40, 144–52, 153–55, 156–81), FC, AA, and FE (i.e., the Michelsberg material, including the continuation of Frutolf's chronicle for the years 1095–99 and the '*Hierosolimita*' appendix attributed to Ekkehard of Aura): compare 130 OT references (50%) with 131 NT references (50%).

four to one.[30] It is only with the histories of the Benedictine chroniclers Guibert of Nogent, Baldric of Bourgueil, and Robert of Reims, written between c. 1106 and c. 1110, that we see a dramatic move away from the New Testament, which represents only 36% of these authors' total citations.[31] In the following decades the original textual equilibrium was restored, as the New Testament figures in 53% of the references in histories written between c. 1111 and c. 1125,[32] and 58% of the references in texts dating from c. 1126 to c. 1146.[33] These numbers suggest that the New Testament was conceptually as important as the Old to the reception of the holy war in the Latin West. Further, it is clear that from its inception the crusading ideal was defined and promoted through an active engagement with the Scriptures *as a whole* by contemporaries keenly aware of the utility of both Old and New Testament models and messages for their rhetorical project.

These interpretive shifts bear out recent reevaluations of crusading spirituality. As William Purkis has shown, early crusaders were widely regarded as the immediate heirs of Christ and the apostles, particularly in the period from c. 1095 to c. 1110.[34] This understanding of crusading as a form of *imitatio Christi* and *vita apostolica* may explain why the authors of many of our earliest sources turned more readily to the Gospels and Epistles than to the Hebrew Bible.[35] Even Raymond of Aguilers, who stands out for his marked preference for the Old Testament as an exegetical source, shared this understanding of the crusade as a Christomimetic and apostolic activity.[36] Turning to the later accounts by Guibert of Nogent, Baldric of Bourgueil, and Robert of Reims, we might ask how these authors' forceful reorientation of the holy war's scriptural basis relates to what

---

[30] Compare 30 New Testament citations to 7 Old Testament citations in EP (as cited in n. 29 above). Here I am following the careful reassessments of several letters' manuscript traditions by Thomas W. Smith and Simon Parsons, whose work shows these to be literary-historiographical constructions with a tenuous connection to the actual campaign trail of 1096–99. See especially Smith, "First Crusade Letters and Medieval Monastic Scribal Cultures"; and Parsons, "The Letters of Stephen of Blois Reconsidered."

[31] Compare 334 OT references (64%) with 190 NT references (36%).

[32] Texts from c. 1111–1125: RC, GP, and CP: compare 55 OT references (47%) with 61 NT references (53%).

[33] Texts from c. 1126–1135: HH, MC, WM, and OV: compare 62 OT references (42%) to 85 NT references (58%).

[34] Purkis, *Crusading Spirituality*, ch. 2.

[35] The corpus of first crusaders' letters, for example (EP, as cited in n. 29 above) contain only 7 OT references as compared to 30 from the NT; the *Gesta* includes 32 OT references and 58 NT references; Peter Tudebode includes 33 OT references and 52 NT references.

[36] Compare Raymond's 72 OT references to only 34 from the NT (roughly a reversal of the OT/NT proportions of his contemporary Peter Tudebode). For Raymond's understanding of the crusade in light of the imitation of Christ and the apostles, see RA, 144–45, 151.

Jonathan Riley-Smith dubbed their "theological refinement" of the crusade ideal. Riley-Smith has shown how, in addition to polishing the style of their common source, the *Gesta Francorum*, these writers took pains to represent the crusade as a series of victories made possible by divine intervention, in fulfillment of biblical prophecies, and to show the crusaders as a new chosen people who combined the virtues of monks and martyrs.[37] Considered in light of these chroniclers' exegetical goals, their heavy dependence on the Old Testament makes perfect sense. To develop typological readings of crusader victories (and defeats) it was natural to look back to ancient Hebrew campaigns, as the New Testament offered little of relevance for this particular interpretive undertaking. Similarly, with few exceptions, the prophecies which most interested the chroniclers, those related to the city of Jerusalem, clustered around the Old Testament books of Isaiah, Proverbs, Jeremiah, and Zechariah. But, as I seek to demonstrate below, the French Benedictines' work was not so much a 'refinement' of first-generation narrators' 'raw' work – which was far from unsophisticated – as an attempt to redirect the exegetical conversation.

A quantitative approach also allows us to identify the most frequently cited biblical books. These are as follows: the Gospel of Matthew (187 references), Psalms (177 references), Isaiah (73 references), the Gospel of Luke (65 references), the Acts of the Apostles (54 references), the Gospel of John (54 references), the two Books of Maccabees (49 references), the Epistle to the Romans (45 references), Exodus (41 references), Genesis (37 references), and Revelation (34).[38] Together these account for over half (55%) of the total citations. The remaining references range widely across the Vulgate, representing all but eight of its seventy-three canonical books.[39] This presentation of the data obscures some important points, however. For example, while we might conclude from these numbers that the chroniclers were relatively uninterested in the Epistles, this is far from being the case; the combined references to Pauline texts (218) account for over one-third of the New Testament references.[40] Similarly, these figures might lead us to underestimate the role of the Pentateuch, which accounts for nearly one-fifth of the Old Testament citations in the crusade histories.[41] Finally, given that the significant repetition within the Gospels, especially the three synoptic Gospels, makes it difficult to assign many of these citations to a single one of these biblical books, we

---

[37] See Riley-Smith, *The Idea of Crusading*, ch.6.
[38] See Appendix 1: Chart 2.
[39] The OT books not represented are Baruch, Amos, Obadiah, Nahum, Zephaniah, and Haggai. Like the NT books not represented – Titus and 2 John – these had very sparse early medieval exegetical traditions.
[40] See Appendix 1: Table 2.
[41] See Appendix 1: Table 1.

should be cautious about placing too much weight on the seeming preeminence of Matthew, given that 52% (97 of 187) citations to Matthew have close textual analogues in other Gospels.[42]

The chroniclers' choice of Old Testament citations reflects their desire to present the history of ancient Israel as a prologue to the crusade and the crusaders as new Israelites, a theme explored more fully in Chapter 3. This exegetical strategy is visible both in the clustering of references around particular chapters of Old Testament books and in multiple writers' quotation of individual verses from these books. In some cases, the heroes of ancient Israel were identified as models; thus, references to spiritual exemplars such as Moses, Judith, and Judah Maccabee (e.g., Ex. 3, Jgs. 13, 2 Mac. 15) identify them as types, or *figurae*, whose heroism prefigured that of the Jerusalemites. The crusaders' enemies, too, were assigned typological doubles from the Old Testament's panoply of villains, including the Egyptian pharaoh, Holofernes, and the Canaanites, through the deployment of scriptural references (e.g., Ex. 14, Jgs. 7, Num. 2). More generally, allusions to God's promises to protect, bless, and enrich the ancient Israelites (e.g., Deut. 11:24–25, Pss. 9:10, 32:12, 67 *passim*) were appropriated for the crusaders, who were in turn exhorted to honor and praise their divine benefactor (e.g., Ex. 15, Pss. 32, 73, 106). As these examples suggest, references to Psalms did much of the work of establishing the terms of God's relationship with his new chosen people. The chroniclers also invoked the Scriptures to identify the Muslim enemy with faithlessness and idolatry and explain their defeat as the divine punishment of paganism (e.g., 4 Kgs. 1:10–14, Ps. 78:4, Hos. 13:3), a strategy that we will explore in Chapters 3 and 4. These patterns are in keeping with medieval Christians' view of the Old Testament as a collection of allegories foreshadowing the advent of Christ, and may also reflect the rising interest among early twelfth-century Christian (and Jewish) exegetes in the historical books of the Hebrew Bible.[43]

The Old Testament's prophetic books were also of great interest to the crusade's narrators, as these texts, properly understood, could explain how the events of 1095–99 fit into God's larger plans for humanity and the Holy Land. Although the chroniclers' use of these books was somewhat idiosyncratic, they showed an unmistakeable interest in passages which foretold the fate of the chosen people, especially insofar as these promised that God would

---

[42] See Appendix 2. Given the ascendancy of Matthew in contemporary exegesis of the Gospels (discussed below, at nn. 46–48), where gospel citations are ambiguous, I have assumed this was likely the book in the crusade historians' minds.

[43] Van Liere, "Biblical Exegesis Through the Twelfth Century," 160–61; and Michael Signer, "Peshat, Sensus Literalis, and Sequential Narrative: Jewish Exegesis and the School of St. Victor in the Twelfth Century," in *The Frank Talmage Memorial Volume*, ed. Barry Walfish (Haifa, 1993), 203–16.

reward the faithful and smite their enemies (e.g., Jer. 31:10, Mal. 3 *passim*). Unsurprisingly, passages to which Christian exegetes accorded christological significance (e.g., Is. 60 *passim*, Mic. 5:8) held particular appeal, as did verses which seemed to forecast the advent of the crusaders in the Holy Land (e.g., Is. 11:10, 35:10). In their use of this prophetic material, the crusade's narrators echoed the exegetical practices of monastic writers such as Peter Damian (d. 1072) and Gilbert Crispin (d. 1117), who discerned in Old Testament prophecies proof that Christ was the true Messiah, and actively sought to use the Hebrew prophets' words against living Jews.[44]

Clear trends are also evident in references to the New Testament, which the chroniclers used to interweave the history of the First Crusade with the ur-story of Christianity, namely the life and Passion of Christ, and the subsequent apostolic missions. It is noteworthy that one-third of the New Testament citations (210, or 33%) consist of direct quotations of Christ's words, often put into the mouths of the crusade leaders or used to praise the pilgrims' actions en route to Jerusalem. Behind these citational strategies lay a desire to represent the holy war as a new way of living out the Gospel. It is also instructive to consider that references to the Gospels tend to focus on the teachings and prophecies of Christ more than on his life or Passion. Patterns in these citations suggest that the chroniclers found certain of Christ's injunctions particularly applicable to the crusaders. For example, verses celebrating the virtues of humility and poverty (e.g., Mat. 5:40, 16:26, 19:29, 23:11, Mk. 9:34, 10:29–30, Lk. 1:52–53, 12:23, 18:29), commanding believers to live in peace with their fellow men (e.g., Mat. 22:39, Lk. 6:29, Jn. 14:27), and promising rewards to those willing to suffer for Christ or their brethren (e.g., Mat. 10:38, 16:24, Lk. 9:23, 14:27, Jn. 15:13) appear throughout the histories, as well as in related sermons and letters. It is also clear that, as exegetes, the chroniclers showed a marked preference for Gospel verses that could be read allegorically or typologically, rather than merely historically, and that could be used to support their presentation of the crusade as a legitimate expression of Christ's teachings.

Citations of the Acts of the Apostles and the Epistles similarly cluster around particular themes that contemporary writers found relevant to the holy war. In particular, descriptions of the calling of the disciples in Acts (e.g., 2:1–13, 6:5, 9:15–16) and their subsequent suffering as missionaries (Acts 7 *passim*, 12:19–23, 14:21, 23:10–11) serve to emphasize the crusaders' status as heirs of the apostles and the primitive church. Writers were equally selective in their use of the Epistles, texts originally written for communities that had, like the crusading armies, faced persecution from

---

[44] Rebecca Rist, *Popes and Jews, 1095–1291* (Oxford, 2016), 52; Anna Sapir Abulafia, *Christians and Jews in the Twelfth-Century Renaissance* (London, 1995), 101–2. This point is discussed more fully in the following chapter.

without and dissension from within. The chroniclers used the Epistles much as they did the Gospels, to depict the crusading ideal as a manifestation of the peace and love enjoined on believers by Christ (e.g., Rom. 12:18, 1 Cor. 13:5, Phil. 1:9–11, Heb. 14:12) to praise the crusaders' willingness to suffer and die for Christ (e.g., Rom. 8:17, 12:1, 2 Cor. 4:10, 11:27), and to stress the heavenly rewards awaiting faithful pilgrims (e.g., Rom. 6:8, 2 Cor. 12:2–3, 2 Tim. 4:7–8). As a group, then, our authors used the language of the New Testament to highlight particular aspects of crusading spirituality and to link the crusade to the values of the first Christians, thereby equating the crusaders with other contemporary groups who claimed affiliation with the primitive church.

It is noteworthy that most of the scriptural books that feature prominently in the crusade's early historiography also loomed large in medieval exegesis and spirituality. The prominence of the Gospels in early crusading narratives reflects an early twelfth-century climate in which the traditional interpretive focus on the Psalms and Epistles was giving way to a greater interest in the Gospels.[45] While monumental exegetical traditions, forming canons in their own right, surrounded the Psalms and the Epistles, with the Gospels the crusade's first promoters and early twelfth-century historians found themselves in a less exhaustively mapped interpretive world. Nevertheless, the Gospel of Matthew in particular had played an important role as ammunition in eleventh-century debates over ecclesiastical reform, and was, as we have seen, the biblical centerpiece of Gregory VII's reformist writings.[46] Matthew's primacy among contemporary exegetes, reformers, and crusade historians reflects the longstanding view – propounded by Augustine and Jerome and largely accepted until the advent of modern biblical criticism – that this Gospel offered the earliest and most authoritative account of Jesus's life and teachings.[47] The crusade's historiography took shape at a moment when Matthew was being avidly discussed in episcopal schools, and we know that these discussions moved beyond the schools to influence monastic readers. Orderic Vitalis, for instance, copied and annotated an anonymous early twelfth-century gloss on Matthew for the library at Saint-Evroul quite soon after the original work's composition within the circle

---

[45] A development described by Smalley, *The Gospels in the Schools*, 33–34. It is noteworthy that the chroniclers' relative lack of interest in the Gospel of Mark is mirrored in the exegetical output of contemporary schools; see Lesley Smith, *The Glossa Ordinaria: The Making of a Medieval Bible Commentary* (Leiden, 2009), 2.

[46] E. Delaruelle, "La vie commune des clercs et la spiritualité populaire au XI siècle," in *La vita commune del clero nei secoli XI e XII*, Atti della Settimana di Studio, 2 vols (Milan, 1962), 1:142–85 (at 172). See also Chapter 1, n. 112.

[47] Kevin Madigan, "Nicolas of Lyra on the Gospel of Matthew," in *Nicholas of Lyra: The Senses of Scripture*, ed. Philip D. Krey and Lesley Janette Smith (Leiden, 2000), 200–2.

of Laon.⁴⁸ That Orderic also used several passages from Matthew to gloss his account of the First Crusade is suggestive of the intellectual cross-pollination, born of simultaneous engagement with theology, exegesis, and current events, that underlay the composition of early crusade histories.⁴⁹

The predominance of the Psalms reflects the central place of this biblical book in the intellectual culture and spiritual lives of medieval Christians. Monastic chroniclers learned the Psalter by heart, and performing the weekly cycle of psalmody kept their memories sharp, so they could mnemonically scan its prayers for apt verses.⁵⁰ Priests like Peter Tudebode (fl. c. 1101) and Fulcher of Chartres would have studied the Psalms as part of their grammatical education, and needed to memorize, at the very least, those verses contained in the musical portions of the Mass.⁵¹ Indeed, it is likely that the liturgy is the direct source of many, if not most, of our writers' references to the Psalter. Historically one of the most commented-upon biblical books, Psalms was the subject of great interest in the monastic schools of the eleventh century and, in the decades after 1100, was the subject of innovative new commentaries.⁵² Given this background, we might well expect the Psalms to permeate early crusade historiography to an even *greater* degree; judged simply by the number of citations, our histories evince a lesser engagement with the Psalter than, say, the works of Bernard of Clairvaux (d. 1153), 20% of whose biblical references are to Psalms.⁵³

---

⁴⁸ Smalley, *The Gospels in the Schools*, 15 and 35 n. This commentary is now Alençon, BM ms. 26, ff.91–198v. The incipit reads: "Expositio ex diversis auctoris a domino Ansello [sic] Laudunensi phylosopho exquisitim collecta super evangelium domini nostri Ihesu Christi secundum Mattheum." See Friedrich Stegmüller, *Repertorium Biblicum Medii Aevi*, 11 vols (Madrid, 1950–80), no. 1359, accessed October 23, 2017, at http://www.repbib.uni-trier.de.

⁴⁹ See OV 5: 16 and 34 (Mat. 19:29), 168 (Mat. 27:22–23), 186 (Mat. 22:29).

⁵⁰ For overviews of the place of the Psalms in monastic culture, see Joseph Dyer, "The Psalms in Monastic Prayer," in *The Place of the Psalms in the Intellectual Culture of the Middle Ages*, ed. Nancy Van Deusen (Albany, NY, 1999), 59–89; and Susan Boynton, "Prayer as Liturgical Performance in Eleventh- and Twelfth-Century Medieval Psalters," *Speculum* 82 (2007): 896–931.

⁵¹ Nancy Van Deusen and Marcia L. Colish, "*Ex utroque et in utroque: Promissa mundo gaudia, Electrum*, and the Sequence," in *The Place of the Psalms*, ed. Van Deusen, 105–38 (at 106).

⁵² Lobrichon, "Une nouveauté," in *Le Moyen Age et la Bible*, ed. Riché and Lobrichon, 99; Theresa Gross–Diaz, "From *Lectio Divina* to the Lecture Room: The Psalm Commentary of Gilbert of Poitiers," in *Place of the Psalms*, ed. Van Deusen, 91–104. The gloss on Psalms was also the first to be completed in the *Glossa ordinaria* project; see Smith, *Glossa Ordinaria*, 56.

⁵³ J. Figuet, "La Bible de Saint Bernard: Données et ouvertures," in *Bernard de Clairvaux: Histoire, mentalités, spiritualité: colloque de Lyon-Cîteaux-Dijon*, SC 380 (Paris, 1992), 237–69 (at 238–39, table 11).

Here again we come up against a limitation of quantitative analysis, which does not allow us to appreciate the degree to which the Psalter informed our authors' Latin syntax and style, as well as their very patterns of thought.[54]

More than any other biblical book, the crusade's historians used Isaiah to explain the holy war as a fulfillment of ancient prophecy. Jeremiah, Ezekiel, Daniel, and Zechariah were also mined for clues about the crusade's significance within providential history, but Isaiah's precedence over these other prophets likely reflects its status as an honorary 'fifth Gospel.'[55] Frequent allusions to Isaiah throughout the New Testament encouraged typological readings of its contents by patristic writers, who credited the prophet with foretelling the Incarnation and Passion, as well as describing the sacraments of baptism and the Eucharist.[56] Given the widely held sentiment that Isaiah was an honorary Christian martyr, as well as (in the words of Jerome) "an evangelist and apostle" who had foretold "all the sacred mysteries of the Lord," his words occupied a unique intermediate position between the Old and New Testaments.[57] This special status is demonstrated by Anselm of Canterbury's decision to give the book pride of place in his *Prologion*, in which Isaiah 7:9 served as the basis for his famous maxim "*fides quaerens intellectum.*"[58] Our authors' familiarity with Isaiah would also have been encouraged by its prominence within the liturgy, and by the incorporation of the 'Canticles of Isaiah' into many Psalters.[59] Isaiah offered the chroniclers a means of understanding the Jerusalem expedition as a fulfillment of biblical prophecies concerning the chosen people and the city of Jerusalem.

Modern scholars have drawn attention to the ways in which the Maccabees feature in twelfth-century crusade chronicles, and the large number of references to 1 and 2 Maccabees affirms that the ancient Jewish warriors and martyrs were regarded as proto-crusaders.[60] While early medieval exegetes tended to present the Maccabean warriors, their worldly combats safely allegorized, as models

---

[54] For a more in-depth exploration of the role of the Psalms in the chronicles, see Chapter 3.

[55] On readings of Jeremiah in light of the crusade, see Chasson, "Prophetic Imagery and Lections," 97; and for Daniel, see Rubenstein, *Nebuchadnezzar's Dream*, ch. 2–4. A useful overview of Christian interpretation of Isaiah is provided by John F. A. Sawyer, *The Fifth Gospel: Isaiah in the History of Christianity* (Cambridge, 1996), esp. ch. 2–5.

[56] J. David Cassel, "Patristic Interpretation of Isaiah," in *'As Those who are Taught': The Reception of Isaiah from the LXX to the SBL*, ed. Claire Matthews McGinnis and Patricia K. Tull (Atlanta, 2006), 145–70.

[57] Cassel, "Patristic Interpretation," 146.

[58] Anselm read the last phrase of the verse, "si non credideritis non permanebitis," to mean "if you will not believe, you will not understand."

[59] Sawyer, *The Fifth Gospel*, 56–58.

[60] On the role of the Maccabees in the preaching of the First Crusade, see Cole, *Preaching of the Crusades*, 24–32; and for references to the Maccabees in the First Crusade chronicles, see Lapina, "The Maccabees and the Battle of Antioch," 147–59.

for monks,[61] in the half-century before the First Crusade the Maccabees were subject to significant exegetical revisions. Oliver Münsch has traced their uses in eleventh-century reformist propaganda, in which Gregorian clerics associated their party with the Maccabean martyrs and glossed the pope's lay defenders as Maccabean warriors.[62] Unlike the references to Psalms and Matthew, which are spread evenly across the chronicles, those to 1 and 2 Maccabees cluster around a handful of texts, especially the chronicles of Guibert of Nogent, Raymond of Aguilers, the Monte Cassino Anonymous, Peter Tudebode, and Albert of Aachen, and many writers never reference these books. Elizabeth Lapina has explained Guibert's particular interest in the Maccabean warriors in terms of anxiety about the 'Judaizing' of contemporary Christians and his desire to exalt the crusaders at the expense of the holy warriors of the Old Testament.[63] The pattern of references in our sources suggests some disagreement among Guibert's contemporaries about whether the Maccabees should be regarded as models for crusaders, and ambivalence may have led some chroniclers to ignore them.

The chroniclers' interest in the Acts of the Apostles, a book with a fairly thin exegetical history of formal exegesis prior to the twelfth century,[64] reflects the book's connection to the ideal of the *vita apostolica*. Cassian (d. 435) had identified monks as the heirs to the primitive apostolic church in his *Conferences*, and the *Rule of Augustine* made the same claim for regular canons.[65] These were very much living texts in medieval religious communities, and debates over the truest form of the apostolic life resonated throughout the literature of reform, institutional histories, and hagiography.[66] Applying models and metaphors from Acts to the first crusaders was one way

---

[61] Lapina, "Anti-Jewish Rhetoric," 241.

[62] Oliver Münsch, "Hate Preachers and Religious Warriors: Violence in the *Libelli de Lite* of the Late Eleventh Century," in *Dying for the Faith*. ed. Signori, 161–76 (esp. 164–74).

[63] Lapina, "Anti-Jewish Rhetoric," *passim*.

[64] In the absence of patristic Latin commentaries, Hrabanus Maurus and Remigius of Auxerre, the only Carolingian commentators known to have tackled Acts, relied (like the later compilers of the *Glossa Ordinaria*) heavily on Bede's *Expositio Actuum Apostolorum* and his *Retractatio in Actus Apostolorum*; see E. Ann Matter, "The Church Fathers and the *Glossa Ordinaria*," in *The Reception of the Church Fathers in the West*, ed. Irena Dorota Backus (Leiden, 1997), 106–7. It should also be noted that readings from Acts (as well as Epistles and Revelation) were incorporated into the celebration of Mass, which would have kept the book's words fresh in medieval clerics' minds.

[65] Cassian, *Collationes*, 18.5, ed. Eugène Pichery as *Conférences*, SC 64 (Paris, 1959), 14–16; trans. Boniface Ramsey (New York, 1987); and *The Rule of Saint Augustine*, 1.2–3, 8, ed. Tarsicius J. Van Bavel and trans. Raymond Canning, CS 138 (Kalamazoo, MI, 1996), 11, 13.

[66] Giles Constable, *The Reformation of the Twelfth Century* (Cambridge, 1996), 156–57.

by which the chroniclers glossed the holy war as a quasi-monastic activity and a new form of *imitatio Christi* and apostolic life.[67] Practically speaking, Acts also proved useful as a geographical orientation as chroniclers set out to map the first crusaders' journey onto a biblical landscape. The routes of the crusading armies took them through sacred lands where Christ and the apostles had preached, and, as we will see in Chapter 3, Acts allowed them to connect many sites that they visited with the primitive church, thereby lending scriptural support to Christian campaigns of conquest.

The chroniclers' strong interest in the Pauline Epistles reflects their primacy as sources of theological instruction, as well as the heightened interest in these books in the contexts of ecclesiastical reform and early scholastic theology. Along with the Psalms, the Epistles had been the most intensively studied part of the Scriptures in the early Middle Ages, and continued to be a major focus of masters in monastic and cathedral schools in the decades around 1100. The complete glosses of the Epistles compiled at Reims in the circle of Bruno of Cologne, by Lanfranc at Bec, and by Anselm at Laon between the 1070s and 1120 attest that early scholastics debated theological issues of grace and sacramental agency through the Epistles and their patristic and Carolingian commentaries.[68] In the Eucharistic Controversy, still in living memory at the time of the First Crusade, Berengar of Tours (d. 1088) and Lanfranc of Bec and their successors looked to the Epistles for support, and their vitriolic exchanges were inflected with Paul's denunciations of opponents.[69] Gregory VII repeatedly cited a handful of passages from the Epistles to present himself as a Pauline *defensor ecclesiae*, and to comfort those suffering persecution at the hands of the Church's enemies, including the Seljuk Turks.[70] The Epistles also supplied many of the pericopes in debates over the ritual purity of the clergy after c. 1000.[71] As we shall see, the crusade's narrators followed earlier theologians' example, relying on the Epistles to bolster the holy war's theological underpinnings.

---

[67] See Purkis, *Crusading Spirituality*, 52–57.

[68] Smith, *Glossa Ordinaria*, 22 and n. 17; Artur Michael Landgraf, *Introduction à l'histoire de la littérature théologique de la scolastique naissante* (Montréal, 1973), 47–48; and Ann Collins, "Eleventh-Century Commentary on the Epistles of St. Paul," in *A Companion to St. Paul in the Middle Ages*, ed. Steven Cartwright (Leiden, 2013), 175–204 (at 176–78). Other eleventh-century teachers, such as Drogo of Notre-Dame, Paris, Berengar of Tours, and Manegold of Lautenbach, glossed the Epistles, but their work survives only in fragments.

[69] As observed by Collins, "Eleventh-Century Commentary," 178–79 and 200–3.

[70] Ken Grant, "St. Paul in the Register of Pope Gregory VII and the Collection in Seventy-Four Titles," in *A Companion to St. Paul*, ed. Cartwright, 297–323 (esp. 298–308).

[71] C. Colt Anderson, "St. Paul and Reform Rhetoric in the High Middle Ages," in *A Companion to St. Paul*, ed. Cartwright, 325–48 (esp. 326–29).

The chroniclers' numerous references to Genesis and Exodus reflect these books' importance within medieval historiography, cosmogony, and theology. Genesis provided medieval Christians with a starting point for historical narratives *ab orbe condita*, and explained the origins of humanity and human sinfulness. Early scholastic thinkers based their explanations of humans as *imagines Dei* on Genesis and its long interpretive tradition, and in the twelfth century Genesis furnished proof-texts for theological discussions of man's natural dignity.[72] Like Genesis, Exodus was a natural touchstone for chroniclers and homilists who viewed the crusaders as a new chosen people, typologically bound to the ancient Israelites by their renewal of the earlier people's wars against unbelievers, their status as exile-pilgrims, and their final reconquest of the land once promised to Abraham and Moses.

Finally, our authors' interest in the Book of Revelation is especially noteworthy in light of ongoing scholarly conversations about the First Crusade's apocalyptic significance for medieval Christians.[73] A quantitative approach may lead us to underrate the value of this biblical book within the crusade's historiography,[74] and indeed it is striking that some of the chroniclers' most dramatic images – of white-robed ghostly armies, horses wading through bloody streets, and fire descending from heaven – are inspired by descriptions of the End Times.[75] Revelation had consistently drawn the interest of early medieval commentators, though they generally eschewed literal interpretations, instead seeking the text's spiritual meaning, which they often defined in ecclesiological terms.[76] While Joachim of Fiore (d. 1202) is often credited with the bold revision of this

---

[72] Brigitte Miriam Bedos-Rezak, *When Ego Was Imago: Signs of Identity in the Middle Ages* (Leiden, 2010), 147; Constable, *Reformation of the Twelfth Century*, 285.

[73] For the view that contemporaries saw the crusade as an event of major apocalyptic significance, see Jay Rubenstein, "Lambert of Saint-Omer and the Apocalyptic First Crusade," in *Remembering the Crusades: Myth, Image, and Identity*, ed. Nicholas Paul and Suzanne Yeager (Baltimore, 2012), 69–95; idem, *Armies of Heaven*; idem, *Nebuchadnezzar's Dream*, esp. ch. 2–4; and Buc, *Holy War. Martyrdom and Terror*, ch. 2.

[74] The majority of authors – 13 out of the 15 included in Appendix 2– cite Revelation at least once. Further, if we take into consideration references that could be to Revelation *or* to virtually identical passages in other books, the total number of citations of Revelation rises from 34 to 41.

[75] See RA, 150 (referencing Rev. 14:20); BB, 81, and OV, 5:112 (both referencing Rev. 19:14); FE, 132 (citing Rev. 13:13).

[76] Kevin Poole, "The Western Apocalypse Commentary Tradition of the Early Middle Ages," in *A Companion to the Premodern Apocalypse*, ed. Michael A. Ryan (Leiden, 2016), 103–43; E. Ann Matter, "The Apocalypse in Early Medieval Exegesis," in *The Apocalypse in the Middle Ages*, ed. Richard K. Emmerson and Bernard McGinn (Ithaca, 1992), 38–50. As Matter notes (49–50), a parallel, future-oriented exegetical tradition anticipated the coming of the Antichrist, variously described in Revelation as a beast or false prophet (Rev. 13:11, 16:13–14, 19:19–20, 20:10); however, much of the

hermeneutic tradition, already in the eleventh century the proliferation of eschatological works on the 'Last Emperor' and the fate of the Holy Land signaled a new willingness to read Revelation (and related prophetic books like Daniel) differently, as blueprints, however blurry, for the future.[77] In the decades following the First Crusade, theologians like Rupert of Deutz and Honorius Augustodunensis (d. c. 1140) increasingly looked to Revelation for clues to highly anticipated future events, such as the conversion of Jews, Saracens, and pagans.[78] Like these writers, the crusade's chroniclers were largely trained in reformist monastic milieux where such ideas were in the air.

Although these biblical books loom large in our sources as a group, when the letters, chronicles, and sermons are examined individually it becomes clear that each text has a distinct exegetical fingerprint, composed of a unique collection of biblical references that resonated for its author. This individuality is reflected in the references to the most-cited biblical books, the Gospel of Matthew and Psalms.[79] The 177 references to the Psalter represent 152 different verses from eighty-five psalms, and 70% (or 124) are verses cited by only one author. Interestingly, the proportion of repeated references is much higher among the citations to the Gospel of Matthew,[80] accounting for over half of the total number (108 out of 188), but again a large proportion of the biblical text is represented; citations from Matthew span 115 different verses from twenty-seven of the Gospel's twenty-eight chapters. Across the sources, biblical references repeated by more than one author account for just 37% (or 519) of the total number.[81] Significantly, there is substantially more repetition among the references to the New Testament (which is, after all, much shorter); only 53% (or 332) of these are original citations found in a single text, as compared with 72% (or 534) of Old Testament references.[82]

Both original citations and references repeated by multiple authors should be of interest to crusade historians, as well as scholars interested in the authorial practices of medieval historians and biblical exegetes more generally. Building on recent scholarly efforts to clarify the relationships between various narrative sources for the First Crusade and gauge the relative originality of individual

---

early medieval concern with Antichrist was mediated less by exegesis of Revelation than by commentary on related passages in Daniel and 2 Thessalonians.

[77] Matthew Gabriele, *An Empire of Memory: The Legend of Charlemagne, the Franks, and Jerusalem before the First Crusade* (Oxford, 2011), 97–128.

[78] Whalen, *Dominion of God*, 93–99.

[79] In calculating percentages of references in Matthew and Psalms, I have omitted ambiguous references.

[80] This must reflect, at least in part, the respective lengths of these books. Given that Psalms is more than five times the length of Matthew, there is much more scope to quote from the Psalter without repetition.

[81] This figure includes the 39 ambiguous references.

[82] These numbers omit the 39 ambiguous references.

textual witnesses, this data offers a new, hitherto untried, method of gauging what is original and what is derivative in various texts (even as it should be acknowledged that medieval and modern expectations about 'originality' often differ significantly). It is noteworthy that most of the repeated citations are found in a handful of closely related sources. Biblical references original to the *Gesta Francorum* and repeated in the *Gesta*'s reworkings by Peter Tudebode and/or the Monte Cassino Anonymous account for just under half (or 211) of the 519 repeated references. If we omit these from the total number of repeated references, we can better appreciate the originality of the remaining texts, among which fully 78% of the biblical references appear in just one source. Shared biblical emphases are equally worthy of consideration. A handful of verses, such as Matthew 19:29, Luke 6:1, and John 19:34 are cited by several chroniclers, including writers not known to have used one another's work. Authors' use of these verses may reflect their awareness of common exegetical traditions, while also offering insight into the ways in which the original crusade idea was defined and transmitted in Christendom. For example, in the absence of a body of sermons used to preach the First Crusade, these verses might provide clues to how crusade preachers bolstered their message with scriptural authority. They may also hint at now-lost popular textual traditions that, as Carol Symes has argued, flourished in the decades after 1099.[83]

We have seen that, as a group, the crusade's early historians shared an interest in many of the same biblical books that featured prominently in the exegetical production and ideological debates of the late eleventh and early twelfth centuries. Considered individually, however, each narrative – even those that on the surface seem to be no more than different versions of the same text – reveals a distinct, indeed unique, exegetical fingerprint that reflects its author's educational background, spiritual training, and reading practices. The chroniclers' individual relationship with the Scriptures – relationships developed through years of liturgical performance and devotional reading and, for some, formal or informal study of exegetical technique – are hinted at in their patterns of citation. Some authors have a clear predilection for the Old Testament over the New (or vice versa).[84] Compare, for instance, the *Historia* of Robert of Reims, in which only 26% of the citations are from the New Testament, with the chronicle of Peter Tudebode, in which the New Testament provides 59% of the total. Patterns of references, especially in the longer narratives, also suggest that each author's gloss of the crusade privileged a handful of biblical books. Some authors' preferences are quite pronounced. For instance, nearly one-third of Raymond of Aguilers's biblical references, and more than one-quarter of those

---

[83] Carol Symes, "Popular Literacies and the First Historians of the First Crusade," *Past & Present* 235 (2017): 37–67.

[84] The following discussion depends on Appendix 1: Table 3.

in Robert of Reims' *Historia*, are to the Psalter.[85] By contrast, the language of the Psalms is far less visible in other works, like Ralph of Caen's *Gesta Tancredi* and Albert of Aachen's *Historia*.[86] Since all of these writers presumably had formal training in psalmody, and thus could have called to mind the words of the psalmist with ease, the most likely explanation is not that Ralph and Albert did not know the Psalms well but, rather, that they sought explanations for the crusade elsewhere in the Bible. If some writers were particularly inclined to use the Psalter as an interpretive lens, others sought to discover the crusade's meaning through meditation on the Gospels. For instance, the Gospels play a particularly important role in the composite *Historia Vie Hierosolimitane* (where they account for 37% of the total references).[87] The *Gesta Francorum* also contains a large proportion of Gospels references – thirty-five out of ninety-three, or 38% – and, as they edited and expanded the *Gesta*, Peter Tudebode and the Monte Cassino Anonymous continued to feature Gospel references prominently.[88] Finally, chroniclers identified individual biblical books as hermeneutical touchstones in their glosses of particular themes or events. Robert of Reims, for instance, borrowed the language of Deuteronomy to emphasize the crusade's status as a divinely sanctioned enterprise, while Guibert of Nogent built his lengthy disquisition on the conquest of Jerusalem around a gloss of Zechariah.[89] Close comparisons of the use of biblical material in various authors' accounts of the two momentous events that bookended the crusade, Urban II's call to arms at Clermont and the crusaders' conquest of Jerusalem over three years later, allow for an even better appreciation of the chronicles' exegetical diversity and a reassessment of individual narrators' originality and sophistication.

Exegetical Strategies: From Clermont to Jerusalem

The chroniclers' distinctive readings of the Scriptures and wide-ranging exegetical strategies are on prominent display in their accounts of Pope Urban II's speech at Clermont.[90] Historians have scrutinized these texts – especially

---

[85] The Psalms account for 30 of Raymond's 108 references, as compared with 32 of Robert's 128 total references.

[86] The Psalms account for 12 of Ralph's 69 references, and 12 of Albert's 118 references.

[87] In the sections attributed to Gilo of Paris, 5 of 22 references are to the Gospels, and in the sections by the anonymous Charleville Poet, 14 of 30 are to the Gospels.

[88] Peter Tudebode includes 26 Gospel references out of a total of 88, for 30%; the Monte Cassino Anonymous includes 26 Gospel references out of a total of 90, for 29%.

[89] RR, 61–63; GN, 301–7.

[90] The versions are: GF, 1–2; PT, 31–32; MC, 12–13; RR, 5–7; FC, 130–38; GN, 111–17; BB, 6–10; CP, 8–10; WM, 1:598–606, and OV, 5:14–18. Note that three of the early historians of the crusade, Raymond of Aguilers, Albert of Aachen, and Ralph of

those believed to be the work of eyewitnesses – as evidence for the pope's original crusading vision,[91] but they also offer insight into how the holy war's narrators developed their highly individualistic glosses of the venture. As is well known, the extant versions of Urban's speech differ widely, not only in their length and thematic emphases but also in their modes of presentation; some depict Urban's call as a pastiche of biblical references, others as a typical synodal sermon, and still others as a rousing call to arms.[92] What these accounts have in common is that – with a few exceptions[93] –they incorporate a substantial amount of biblical material. The majority of the Scriptural references – sixty-one out of eighty-nine, or 69% – derive from the New Testament, though the Old Testament is also well represented. A survey of these citations reinforces the preceding discussion of larger trends in the chroniclers' scriptural usage: the Gospel of Matthew is the most frequently cited book, followed by the Epistle to Romans, Acts of the Apostles, and Psalms.[94]

In the surviving accounts of Clermont, the pope appears in many guises: as a reformer, he alludes to the Gregorian agenda and the peace movement; as a diplomat, he calls upon his audience to aid Byzantine Christians; and as an aristocrat, he exhorts fellow Franks to emulate the glorious deeds of their ancestors. But Urban also speaks through the chroniclers as an exegete, a role the real pope had thoroughly rehearsed at Reims and Cluny, and which he embraced in his letters.[95] As an exegete, the pope calls upon his audiences (that is, both the audience at Clermont and the audience of the chronicles) to meditate on the meaning of key scriptural passages, and models a variety

---

Caen, did not include accounts of Urban's speech, while the Michelsberg Continuator summarizes it in a single sentence.

[91] Dana Carleton Munro pioneered the technique of cross-referencing the various accounts to arrive at a 'true' core narrative; see "The Speech of Urban II at Clermont, 1095," *The American Historical Review* 11 (1906): 231–42. Subsequent studies of Clermont have focused to a much greater extent on the differences between accounts of Urban's speech, and have compared these with representations of the crusade in contemporary charters and letters: for example, H. E. J. Cowdrey, "Pope Urban II's Preaching of the First Crusade," *History* 55 (1970): 177–88; Cole, *Preaching the Crusades*, 1–36; Riley-Smith, *Idea of Crusading*, ch. 1; and John O. Ward, "Some Principles of Rhetorical Historiography in the Twelfth Century," in *Classical Rhetoric and Medieval Historiography*, ed. Ernst Breisach (Kalamazoo, MI, 1985), 127–48.

[92] For a recent reassessment of the issue of genre in these accounts, see Strack, "The Sermon of Urban II," 30–45.

[93] The accounts of Clermont by Orderic Vitalis and the Michelsberg Continuator include only one citation each, to Gal. 4:25–26 and Mat. 10:38, respectively, but it should be noted that these accounts are brief, as compared to most other chroniclers' versions.

[94] Eighteen references are from Matthew (accounting for the majority of the 24 Gospel references), 9 from Romans (out of 29 total references to the Epistles), 8 from Acts, and 7 from Psalms.

[95] Gabriele, "Last Carolingian Exegete," *passim*.

of interpretive approaches to the sacred texts. Urban's exegesis takes quite different forms in the various accounts, however. In the *Gesta Francorum* and its later redactions, the call to crusade is presented as a litany of biblical pericopes:

> When the time approached which the Lord daily points out to his faithful, especially in the Gospel, saying, "*If any man will come after me, let him deny himself and take up his cross and follow me* (Mat. 16:24)," therefore a wave of religious fervor swept through all the regions of Gaul, so that anyone of pure heart and mind who wished to follow him and to bear his cross did not hesitate, but hurried to make the journey to the Holy Sepulcher. Then the Pope hurried over the Alps ... and began to speak eloquently and preach ... And the lord pope said, "Brothers, *you must suffer greatly for the sake of Christ's name* (cf. Acts 9:16, 5:41); that is, in misery, poverty, *nakedness, persecution, want, sickness, hunger, thirst and other sorts of tribulation* (cf. Rom. 8:35), just as the Lord said to his disciples: '*You must suffer greatly for my name's sake*,' (Acts 9:16) and '*Be not ashamed* to speak in the presence of men (cf. 2 Tim. 1:8),' for '*I shall give you a mouth and eloquence* (Lk. 21:15),' and then: '*You will receive a great reward* (cf. Lk. 14:14).'"[96]

Due to its brevity and simple rhetorical structure, the *Gesta*'s account is often overlooked in discussions of Clermont.[97] But the *Gesta* presents the call to crusade in a form that would have been familiar to medieval readers, who, as Robert Worth Frank, Jr. reminds us, "experienced Scripture through pericopes," and were accustomed to a homiletic style of preaching that was associative and episodic, and which modern readers often find fragmented and incoherent.[98]

---

[96] GF, 1–2: Cum iam appropinquasset ille terminus quem dominus Iesus cotidie suis demonstrat fidelibus, specialiter in euangelio dicens: "*Si quis uult post me uenire, abneget semetipsum et tollat crucem suam et sequatur me*" (Mat. 16:24) facta est igitur motio ualida per uniuersas Galliarum regiones, ut si aliquis Deum studiose puroque corde et mente sequi desideraret, atque post ipsum crucem fideliter baiulare uellet, non pigritaretur Sancti Sepulchri uiam celerius arripere. Apostolicus namque Romanae sedis ultra montanas partes quantocius profectus est ... coepitque subtiliter sermocinari et predicare [...] Ait namque domnus apostolicus, "Fratres, *uos oportet multa pati pro nomine Christi* (cf. Mat. 8:22), uidelicet *miserias, paupertates, nuditates, persecutiones, egestates, infirmitates, fames, sites* (cf. Rom. 8:35) et alia huiusmodi, sicuti Dominus ait suis discipulis: '*Oportet uos pati multa pro nomine meo*' (cf. Mat. 8:22), et: '*Nolite erubescere loqui ante facies hominum* (cf. 2 Tim. 1:8); *ego uero dabo uobis os et eloquium*' (Lk. 21:15), ac deinceps: '*Persequetur uos larga retribution*' (cf. Lk. 14:14)."

[97] For instance, it receives no consideration in Riley-Smith, *Idea of Crusading*, ch. 1 ("Pope Urban's Message"), and is dealt with very briefly by Cole, *Preaching of the Crusades*, 9–10.

[98] Robert Worth Frank, Jr., "*Meditationes Vitae Christi:* The Logistics of Access to

Moreover, the *Gesta*'s version of Urban's speech functions as a gloss on two levels. First, it justifies the crusading enterprise as a fulfillment of Christ's injunctions in the Gospels (and Paul's later interpretations of these), and identifies would-be crusaders as imitators of Christ, the apostles, and martyrs. Here the author is engaging with two levels of the crusade-text's meaning: the typological and moral. Second, the *Gesta* offers up this collection of biblical citations as commentary on a popular movement underway in France *before* Clermont.[99] The anonymous author develops a reading of this spiritual revival – itself sanctioned by a reinterpretation of Matthew 16:24 as a call to Jerusalem pilgrimage – by treating this biblical passage as a medieval preacher would a Gospel lesson, putting it into dialogue with other New Testament verses that provide additional justification or add new elements, such as the exhortation to preach the Gospel and the promise of a reward for those who suffer en route to the holy city. Seen in this light, the opening of the *Gesta* seems less like an unsophisticated mishmash and more like a short homily (or an excerpt of a longer homily) of the sort that could be preached either on the journey east or in the crusade's immediate aftermath.[100]

While the account of Urban's sermon by Fulcher of Chartres, who was likely present at Clermont, is longer and more detailed than the *Gesta Francorum*'s, its use of the Scriptures is much more understated. This is typical of Fulcher, who, though he knew the Bible well and likely had formal exegetical training, quoted the Scriptures less frequently than most other early historians of the crusade.[101] Rather than adopting a homiletic structure like the *Gesta* Anonymous, Fulcher summarizes Urban's speech in the form of a *reportatio*,[102] using biblical language to describe the crusaders as "sons of God, who maintain peace among yourselves," echoing the Sermon on the Mount (Mat. 5:9),[103] and *milites Christi* (2 Tim.

Divinity," in *Hermeneutics and Medieval Culture*, ed. Patrick J. Gallagher and Helen Damico (Albany, NY, 1989), 33.

[99] Baldric of Bourgueil, who used the *Gesta* as a source, presents a similar chronology, in which Urban is not the instigator of the crusade but, rather, responds to a popular movement; for commentary on this issue, see Jay Rubenstein, "How, or How Much, to Reevaluate Peter the Hermit?" in *The Medieval Crusade*, ed. Susan J. Ridyard (Woodbridge, 2004), 53–70.

[100] This would support the argument of Rubenstein, "What is the *Gesta Francorum*?"

[101] For example, the first book of Fulcher's *Historia* contains roughly the same number of total citations as the work of the Charleville Poet, which is about half as long. It should also be noted that Fulcher's modern editors and translators have overlooked some of the biblical references in his chronicle, including most of the New Testament references in his account of Clermont discussed here.

[102] For commentary on Fulcher's presentation, see Cole, *Preaching of the Crusades*, 12–13.

[103] Compare the Gospel verse: "beati pacifici quoniam filii Dei vocabuntur" with FC, 132:

2:3).¹⁰⁴ As Urban urges those "who formerly fought against their brothers and kinsmen" to take arms instead against the "barbarians" who "are devastating the kingdom of God (*regnum Dei uastando*)" we hear echoes of 1 Corinthians 6:6–10, which warns that the unjust shall not possess God's kingdom.¹⁰⁵ While a twelfth-century reader could have readily identified the Muslim enemy – described by Fulcher as "a people ... enslaved by demons" (*daemonibus ancilla*) – with the "slaves of idols" barred from heaven by the apostle Paul (1 Cor. 6:9), the pope also reminds Latin Christians that they themselves had indulged in theft, greed, and fratricide, and had been saved from damnation by "divine correction" only so that they might serve the Church.¹⁰⁶ Fulcher's gloss of Clermont is, above all, a moral commentary, which justifies the enterprise of holy war by emphasizing the ideal of Christian brotherhood and associating the Muslim enemy with barbarity, idolatry, and pollution. Moreover, Fulcher's biblical rhetoric bears the hallmarks of ecclesiastical reform. As Fulcher would have known, in the eleventh century 1 Corinthians 6 had become a proof-text in discussions of the excommunication of simoniac and nicolaitist clergy,¹⁰⁷ as well as new articulations of the *familia Christi*,¹⁰⁸ and its message of brotherhood echoed that of the contemporary peace movement.

While the accounts of Urban's Clermont speech by Fulcher and the *Gesta* Anonymous have received poor marks from modern scholars, those by Robert of Reims, Baldric of Bourgueil, and Guibert of Nogent have been judged more favorably, as they are assumed to convey a better sense of the pope's persuasiveness and sophistication as an orator, even if they are not reliable guides to his actual words.¹⁰⁹ Though their versions vary considerably in their emphases, all three writers use the pope's speech to highlight the holy war's typological, moral, and eschatological registers of meaning. These readings operate on several levels, linking the crusaders to the ancient Israelites and the original apostles, and identifying biblical prophecies that foreshadowed their pilgrimage to Jerusalem.

"o filii Dei, si pacem apud uos tenendam ... ." Cf. 1 Jn. 3:2 for another reference to the faithful as "filii Dei."

¹⁰⁴ FC, 136.
¹⁰⁵ FC, 136, 134.
¹⁰⁶ FC, 135–36: "gentem omnipotentis Dei fide praeditum et Christi nomine fulgidam sic superaverit!"
¹⁰⁷ For example, see Bernold of Constance, *De damnatione scismaticorum*, ed. Friedrich Thaner, MGH Lib. de lite 2:41; and the anonymous *Epistola de vitanda missa uxoratorum sacerdotum*, c.2, ed. Ernst Sackur, MGH Lib. de lite 3:4.
¹⁰⁸ For example, Bruno of Cologne, *Expositio in Epistolas Pauli: Epistola ad Corinthios prima*, c.9, PL 153:150–51. The concept of the *familia Christi* is also central to Baldric of Bourgueil's reading of the crusade, as demonstrated by Biddlecombe, "Baldric of Bourgueil and the *Familia Christi*," 9–23.
¹⁰⁹ Cole, *Preaching of the Crusades*, 15–27.

In the first place, Urban reminds the Franks of their status as a new chosen people, a *gens electa* whose faith is even now being tested, just as God had once tested that of the Jews. In Robert's version, the crusaders are the new sons of Israel, and the heirs to the "land that floweth with milk and honey" (Ex. 3:8, 17, Num. 13:28) promised to Abraham and his heirs.[110] To claim their birthright, they must "humiliate *the hairy scalp*" of the enemy (Ps. 67:22), a people *"that set not their heart aright, and whose spirit was not steadfast with God"* (Ps. 77:8).[111] Like Robert, Baldric cites the Psalms to cast the Franks as the spiritual heirs of ancient Israel, who have, in Urban's words, *"become a reproach to our neighbors"* (Ps. 79:7) now that *"the nations are come into [God's] inheritance and [His] holy temple"* (cf. Ps. 78:1).[112] Following in the footsteps of "the children of Israel ... who prefigured (*prefigurauerunt*) [them]" in their wars against the Jebusites, the Franks must renew the battle against unbelief by fighting the Turks, whom Baldric identifies with the Amalekites, pagan enemies of ancient Israel.[113] For his part, Guibert suggests the Maccabean warriors as 'types' for the crusaders, even as he insists on the latter group's spiritual superiority.[114]

In Baldric and Robert's accounts especially, Urban not only presents the crusaders as new Israelites but also invites them to make the sacrifices – of wealth, status, family ties, even life itself – that will verify their apostolic status. Baldric emphasizes that in making the Jerusalem pilgrimage the crusaders are retracing the steps of the apostles, and glosses Urban's promise of salvation to those who die en route with the parable of the laborers in the vineyard (Mat. 20:1–16), in which Christ reminded his disciples, *"so shall the last be first, and the first last."*[115] In his account of Clermont, Robert draws more extensively on the Gospel of Matthew to present the crusade as a literal fulfillment of Christ's commands to abandon worldly ties (Mat. 10:37, 19:29) and take up one's cross (Mat. 10:38).[116]

Each of the French Benedictines uses scriptural aids to expose the crusade's moral level of meaning. While Robert and Baldric employ different biblical imagery, they nonetheless offer similar moral readings. In light of the plight of the eastern Christians and Jerusalem pilgrims, whose ill-treatment at the hands of the

---

[110] RR, 6: "Terra illa filiis Israel a Deo in possessionem data fuit, sicut Scriptura dicit *que lacte et melle fluit*." Trans. 81.
[111] RR, 6; trans. 79–80.
[112] BB, 8.
[113] BB, 8, 10. The implications of identifying Muslims with Old Testament polytheists are discussed in Chapter 3.
[114] GN, 112–13.
[115] BB, 9. Compare Baldric's "Deus ejusdem denarii est retributor, prima et hora undecima" with Mat. 20:9–10.
[116] RR, 6–8.

Muslims is a prominent theme of virtually all accounts of Clermont,[117] heeding the crusading call is a moral imperative: it is a stark choice between the soldiery of the world and the *militia Christi*,[118] and he who chooses rightly makes of himself "*a living sacrifice, holy, pleasing unto God*" (Rom. 12:1).[119] The crusade's moral message is also a message about divine justice; those who take part in the holy war not only win salvation but also become instruments of divine vengeance, led into battle by the warrior God of the Psalms, his *sword girded upon [His] thigh* (Ps. 44:4).[120] Robert and Baldric ground the crusade's moral significance in the spiritual urgency of the present day, in which eastern Christians are threatened and the fate of Jerusalem hangs in the balance, while countless Christian knights waver on the brink of Hell. Guibert, by contrast, weights his moral exegesis of the crusade with greater eschatological significance. While he emphasizes the same themes – the suffering of Christians in the Holy Land, the moral turpitude of their brethren in the West who are embroiled in private wars – as Baldric and Robert, Guibert presents the crusade as the fulfillment of biblical prophecy. For him, the issue of the crusaders' individual salvation is less pressing than the crusade's role in the larger drama of salvation history that is rapidly drawing to a close. The Jerusalem pilgrimage, for Guibert, was a sign that "*the times of the nations*" that Christ had foretold in Luke (21:24) was at hand, when there would be a "*falling away from faith*" and the Antichrist would openly preach (2 Thes. 2:3–4).[121] Finally, following an epic contest between the wicked and the righteous – who would, following the prediction of Isaiah (43:5), come from the West – Jerusalem would be restored to Christian hands and the Lord's tomb would be glorified (Is. 11:10).[122]

Robert, Baldric, and Guibert's versions of Clermont bear precious little resemblance to the account of Urban's speech found in the *Gesta*, the text they reworked and expanded, even as they used its basic narrative framework. A comparison of the accounts of Clermont by the second-generation chroniclers Orderic Vitalis and William of Malmesbury with the corresponding sections of their acknowledged sources, Baldric of Bourgueil and Fulcher of Chartres,

---

[117] On this theme, see Cole, "The Theme of Religious Pollution," 84–111.

[118] BB, 8.

[119] RR, 7.

[120] BB, 9. The concept of crusading vengeance has been thoroughly discussed by Susanna A. Throop, *Crusading as an Act of Vengeance, 1095–1216* (Farnham, 2011); see esp. ch. 2 for the First Crusade material.

[121] GN, 114–15.

[122] GN, 115, 112. Guibert's use of this reference is quite different from Robert of Reims's evocation of the same verse in his commentary on the fall of Jerusalem, as shown by Matthew Gabriele; see "From Prophecy to Apocalypse," 309–16. Guibert's juxtaposition of east and west is also thoughtfully dissected in Lapina, *Warfare and the Miraculous*, 132–36.

demonstrates that chroniclers who liberally borrowed historical material from earlier writers might be more circumspect when it came to copying biblical references.[123] As mentioned in Chapter 1, Orderic relied on Baldric's *Historia* for much of his information about the crusade, but in fact omitted the majority of the latter's numerous biblical allusions, and his account of Urban's speech at Clermont is noteworthy for its dearth of biblical allusions.[124] William of Malmesbury seems not to have taken a single scriptural citation from his main source, Fulcher of Chartres,[125] and, though his account of Urban's speech – the longest of any twelfth-century source – echoes some of the same themes, William's presentation is quite different than Fulcher's. William's thoughtful deployment of biblical pericopes and accompanying glosses remind us that he was a respected exegete. In William's version, Urban begins by warning his audience of the spiritual perils of worldly life before shifting into a homily punctuated by biblical references, which recalls the *Gesta Francorum*'s opening lines:

> Do but compare the energy you have expended on criminal practices and what will be demanded by the journey I am recommending to you. Many are the terrors that spring from adulterous and murderous thoughts, for, as Solomon says, "*Nothing is more timorous than wickedness*" (Wis. 17:10); many the toils (for what is more toilsome than injustice?). But "*he that walketh upright, walketh surely*" (Prov. 10:9). Of these toils and these terrors the outcome was sin: "*the wages of sin is death*," and the deaths of sinners are the worst of all. Now "*no greater are the toil and fear you seek, but higher the reward*" (Lucan 1.242). The motive force of your toils will be charity,

---

[123] This holds true for some earlier writers as well; consider that Gilo of Paris, who directly used Robert of Reims's *Historia* as a major source (as shown by Bull, "Robert the Monk and His Source(s)," 127–39), did not copy any of Robert's numerous scriptural references. See Appendix 2 for a full list of the references in each text.

[124] For Orderic's reliance on Baldric, see 45–46. Marjorie Chibnall's useful overview of the relationship between these two accounts of the crusade (introduction to OV, 5: xiii–xv) is supplemented by Daniel Roach, "Orderic Vitalis and the First Crusade," *Journal of Medieval History* 42 (2016): 177–201, who shows that Orderic's interventions in Baldric's narrative were designed to connect the monastic community of Saint-Evroul to the heroes and wonders of the crusade. The only biblical allusion in Orderic's account of Clermont is to Gal. 4:25–26; see OV, 5:18.

[125] For William's use of Fulcher's work, see Rodney Thomson, "William of Malmesbury, Historian of Crusade," *Reading Medieval Studies* 23 (1997): 121–23. While William does cite one verse, Mat. 19:29, in common with Fulcher, the locations of the citation in each work, the precise biblical wording each author uses, and the omnipresence of this text in early crusade narratives all suggest that this was not a direct borrowing. Cf. WM, 1:608; and FC, 115. William and Orderic are thought to have read one another's histories, and they do include two biblical references in common, both of which were, however, cited by multiple authors in various contexts: the aforementioned Mat. 19:29 (WM, 1:609; OV 5:16, 34) and Jn. 5:13 (WM, 1:600, 604; OV, 5:56).

that following the Lord's commands you may *lay down your life for your brethren; the reward of charity will be God's favor* (cf. Jn. 15:13), and God's favor will be followed by eternal life.[126]

From here, William goes on to offer an extended account of the Seljuk conquests and enumerate the spiritual rewards of crusading, before concluding with a final homiletic section which develops an extended gloss on Matthew 7:14 ("*How narrow is the gate and strait is the way that leadeth to life*"), which verse crusaders are encouraged, in the best monastic meditative tradition, to "set before their hearts" (*proponite animis*).[127] William's choice of this extract of the Sermon on the Mount as a proof-text frames the crusade as a new kind of *vita apostolica*, an association that he underscores through the addition of other New Testament passages that amplify its meaning. Like the first apostles, the crusaders will "*through many tribulations enter into the kingdom of God*" (Acts 14:21), but need not fear the death of the body, for "*the sufferings of this present time are not worthy to be compared with the glory to come that shall be revealed*" (Rom. 8:18). The soul's liberation from its bodily prison – another very monastic image – is to be welcomed, rather than feared, nor should crusaders hesitate to liberate themselves from the burden of worldly ties and follow the injunction of Matthew 19:29.[128]

When considered thematically, there is significant overlap between the various early twelfth-century accounts of Clermont, as indeed historians have long recognized. But each writer buttressed his interpretation of Clermont with a distinctive collection of scriptural references, and the lack of repetition in the biblical material in the various accounts is striking. While the biblical citations attributed to Urban II span an impressive twenty-four biblical books, only fourteen of these are referenced by multiple authors.[129] Unsurprisingly, the *Gesta Francorum* and the redactions by Peter Tudebode and the Monte Cassino Anonymous contain almost identical collections of biblical references,[130] but there is remarkably little overlap between the remaining seven accounts.

---

[126] WM, 1:598–601: "Comparate nos labores quos in scelerum exercitio habuistis, et eos quos in itinere quod precipio habituri estis. Plures uel adulterii uel homicidii meditatio dat timores (*nichil enim timidius nequitia*, ut ait Salomon [Wis. 17:7]), multos labores (*quid enim laboriosius iniustitia* [Prov. 10:9]); *qui autem ambulat simpliciter, ambulat confidenter*. Horum laborum, horum timorum exitus erat peccatum; *stipendium autem peccati mors*, mors uero peccatorum pessima. Nunc a uobis 'par labor atque metus pretio meliore petuntur' (Lucan 1.242). Horum laborum erit causa caritas ut, precepto Dominico ammoniti, *animas pro fratribus ponatis*; *caritas stipendium erit Dei gratia* (cf. Jn. 15:13); Dei gratiam sequetur uita aeterna."

[127] WM, 1:602–7.

[128] WM, 1:606.

[129] These are: Exodus, Psalms, Wisdom, Matthew, Luke, John, Acts, Romans, Galatians, Colossians, and 1 Peter.

[130] The accounts of Clermont in GF, 1–2 and PT, 31–32 contain identical collections of

In fact, only four biblical passages (comprising a total of nine citations) recur in multiple accounts of Urban II's speech at Clermont. The first of these, Matthew 21:13 (cf. Mk. 11:17, Lk. 19:46), from the narrative of the "Cleansing of the Temple," is cited by Baldric of Bourgueil, the Charleville Poet, and William of Malmesbury to affect a typological comparison between the present-day Muslim rulers of Jerusalem and the temple-merchants, whom the Gospels label "thieves" (*latrones*).[131] The second citation, to Matthew 19:29 (cf. Mk. 10:29–30, Lk. 18:29–30), a reference to Christ's promise of a hundredfold reward (*centuplum*) to those who abandoned home, family, and property to follow Him, is used by Robert of Reims and William of Malmesbury to underscore the crusaders' apostolicity.[132] As we shall see in Chapter 4, both verses were important touchstones in the twelfth-century glossing of the holy war. The third instance of repetition, found in Robert of Reims and Orderic Vitalis, evokes Galatians 4:25–26 to present Jerusalem as a "mother" in need of aid from her "sons," the crusaders.[133] The final biblical text cited by multiple authors is a scrap of 1 Peter 5:4 ("*et cum apparuerit princeps pastorum percipietis inmarcescibilem gloriae coronam*"), attributed to Urban II in the histories of Robert of Reims and Baldric of Bourgueil. A closer look at the verse's context in these two texts illustrates that chroniclers who cited the same verses were not necessarily 'copying' one another. Consider how Robert and Baldric use the epistle's words:

Robert: So seize on this road to obtain the remission of your sins, sure in the unfading glory of the heavenly kingdom. [Arripite igitur viam hanc in remissionem peccatorum vestrorum, securi de *immarcescibili gloria* regni coelorum.][134]

Baldric: The way is short and the labor slight that will, nevertheless, reward you with a crown that never fades. [Via brevis est, labor permodicus est qui tamen *immarcescibilem* vobis rependent *coronam*.][135]

---

biblical references (some of the sources of which I have identified differently than the texts' modern editors): Mat. 8:22, Rom. 8:35, Mat. 8:22, 2 Tim. 1:8, Lk. 21:15, Lk. 14:14, and 1 Pet. 2:21. MC, 3.1–8, pp. 12–13 also contains all but the very last of these references (to 1 Pet. 2:21).

[131] BB, 5; CP, 8; and WM, 1:604. For a discussion of the trope of Muslims as the "thieves" of the Gospel narrative, see 201–07.
[132] RR, 6; WM, 1:606.
[133] RR, 6–7; OV, 5:18. This theme is fully explored by David Morris, "The Servile Mother: Jerusalem as Woman in the Era of the Crusades," in *Remembering the Crusades: Myth, Image, and Identity*, ed. Nicholas Paul and Suzanne Yeager (Baltimore, 2012), 174–94.
[134] RR, 7. Trans. Sweetenham, 81.
[135] BB, 9.

Both writers remain true to the sense of the original biblical verse, which promises that "when the prince of pastors shall appear" (that is, when Christ returns to earth), believers "shall receive a never-fading crown of glory," and both use the citation to the same interpretive end, to emphasize that those who take the cross will earn salvation. Notably, earlier exegetes associated this text with martyrdom.[136] But the contexts in which Robert and Baldric use the citation are quite different; Robert places it at the end of a disquisition on the unique status of Jerusalem, the "navel of the world" and goal of the crusade, while Baldric uses the citation to complement his discussion of the many rewards – worldly and material as well as spiritual – to be gained by heeding the pope's call. In other words, neither Baldric nor Robert simply duplicated the other's gloss. Did Baldric and Robert, both of whom are thought to have been present at Clermont, hear Urban quote 1 Peter 5:4, and recall this years later, as they composed their *Historiae*? The pope did cite the verse in his correspondence, though not, so far as we know, in connection with the crusade.[137] Could Baldric and Robert have been inspired by a common earlier text – a now-lost history, sermon collection, or letter – which cited this verse? Or did they, as learned monks well versed in the language of the Bible, their minds strung with common associative *catenae* from the Scriptures and Fathers, spontaneously call to mind the same phrase in the process of writing? Perhaps a better question is why there is *so little* overlap between the scriptural verses cited in the accounts of Clermont, and, indeed, throughout the chronicles of the First Crusade more generally.

As another way of highlighting the diversity of exegetical thinking in our sources, we can compare how various authors used the Scriptures as a lens through which to understand the culminating event of the crusade, the siege and sack of Jerusalem in July 1099. The thirteen narratives of this event composed before 1146[138] reference an impressive thirty books of the Bible, reflecting the chroniclers' desire to frame this momentous victory as fully as possible within scriptural history and prophecy. At the same time, it is clear that a handful of biblical books – the Psalms, the prophecies of Isaiah and Ezekiel, and the Gospels of Matthew and Luke – were seen as particularly relevant to this undertaking.[139]

---

[136] E.g., Augustine, Sermon 309 (*In natali Cypriani martyris*), c. 4, PL 38: 1411.

[137] Urban II, *Epistolae*, 240, PL 151: 508. This is a bull from July 1098 confirming the archbishop of Salerno's authority over the sees of Conza and Acerenza.

[138] The versions are those in GF, 87–93; PT, 134–43; RA, 143–53; RR, 96–101; FC, 293–306; GN, 270–85, 301–7; BB, 103–112; AA, 400–46; RC, 84–112; CJ, 643–53; SF, 160–62; OV, 5:156–74; and WM, 1:646–50. The composite *Historia vie Hierosolimitane* does not include an account of the conquest of Jerusalem, and the Michelsberg Continuator summarizes the siege and sack in three sentences.

[139] Kaspar Elm has noted the importance of Old Testament models in contemporary and near-contemporary accounts of the sack of Jerusalem; see "Die Eroberung Jerusalems im Jahre 1099: Ihre Darstellung, Beurteilung und Deutung in den Quellen

The Bible in the Chronicles of the First Crusade

As in the accounts of Clermont, individual narrators showed themselves capable of considerable originality in their use of the Scriptures; among a total of 130 biblical references, only five biblical verses are repeated by multiple authors (and the number drops to three if we discount Peter Tudebode's repetitions of the *Gesta Francorum*'s citations).[140] Whereas the chroniclers' commentaries on Clermont privileged the New Testament, accounts of the conquest of Jerusalem mined the Old Testament to a much greater degree; out of 130 citations, eighty (or 62%) derive from the Old Testament. As in their glosses of Clermont, the chroniclers present historical, typological, moral, and anagogical readings of the crusaders' victory, but, once again, individual authors differ both in their actual interpretations and in their relative interest in each level of meaning.

To begin with, the Scriptures offered detailed information about the history of Jerusalem and its holy sites that allowed chroniclers to situate the 1099 conquest within a much longer historical narrative. Sylvia Schein has shown that Jerusalem's Latin settlers were extremely interested in the city's biblical past, including its Old Testament history,[141] and this historical consciousness permeates the chronicles. The 1099 conquest prompted comparisons with earlier sacks of the city by the Babylonian king Nebuchadnezzar, the Greek ruler Antiochus, and the Roman general Titus,[142] and the city's new Latin masters were given a place on a timeline of political and spiritual rulers that included the Hebrew kings Saul and David, as well as the apostle James.[143] Even if Jerusalem was, in a sense, a city out of time, as Ralph of Caen reminded readers, its sacred status was rooted in the events of a sacred past whose literal truth could not be doubted; the Temple Mount, as he wrote, was "a place unique on earth, most like the heavens" of any earthly place, but also the site of Jacob's dream, the youthful Christ's teaching, and the adult Christ's expulsion of the moneychangers.[144]

While all of the crusade's historians recognized the conquest's historical significance, most went further, as medieval exegetes were trained to do, identifying biblical passages that seemed to foreshadow the crusaders' victory. Building upon the kind of typological thinking that had long accustomed Christian readers

---

des Ersten Kreuzzugs," in *Jerusalem im Hoch- und Spätmittelalter: Konflikte und Konfliktbewältigung – Vorstellungen und Vergegenwärtigungen*, ed. Dieter R. Bauer and Nikolas Jaspert (Frankfurt, 2001), 31–54; and more recently, Buc, *Holy War*, 264f.

[140] The repeated verses are: Ps. 32:3 (conflated with Ps. 95:1), cited by RA, 151 and FC, 305; Ez. 12:2, cited by GF, 96 and PT, 146; Mat. 24:2 (conflated with Mk. 13:2 and Lk. 19:44), cited by AA, 432, and CJ, 644; Lk. 10:4, cited by GF, 96 and PT, 147; and Gal. 4:26, cited by BB, 103, AA, 410, and SF, 161.

[141] Schein, *Gateway to the Heavenly City*, 96–97.

[142] AA, 432. For Nebuchadnezzar, see 4 Kgs. 24–25; for Antiochus, see 1 Macc. 2:20–40.

[143] BB, 112. An early Christian tradition identified James as the first bishop of Jerusalem.

[144] RC, 112–13: "huic, inquam, unico in terris, si quid terra celis simile habet, celorum simillimo." Trans. Bachrach and Bachrach, 149–50.

to seek precedents for New Testament events in the Old, Latin chroniclers claimed that the crusade's events were prefigured by numerous passages in both Testaments. It is clear that typology was being used to make sense of the crusaders' accomplishments very soon after 1099, if not actually on the march.[145] In the years to come, chroniclers sought out additional typological links in the Old Testament, reflecting a widespread view of the victorious crusaders as new Israelites. To cite just a few examples, the crusaders' piety and purity of heart was likened to that of Moses and Joshua, and the breaching of the city's walls to the parting of the Red Sea.[146] But the chroniclers generally agreed that the "wonderful things he did in the sight of the fathers, in Egypt" for the Israelites – this is Guibert of Nogent, citing Psalms 77:12[147] – paled in comparison with the miracle that God had worked for the crusaders, his new chosen people, in granting them possession of Jerusalem.

Finally, the conquest had moral and anagogical dimensions which contemporaries were determined to unravel. The obvious moral message for medieval Christians concerned God's just judgment on the faithless or sinful (that is, Jerusalem's Fatimid defenders) and his rewarding of the pure and steadfast (that is, those crusaders who remained with the army to the bitter end, or died before reaching Jerusalem). The chroniclers found the key to this moral level of meaning in the Psalter, whose promises and warnings seemed particularly well suited to explain the events of 1099. God was the crusaders' *"helper in tribulation,"* who *"turned [their] mourning into joy," "taught [their] hands to fight and their fingers to make war,"* and *"broke [their enemies] in pieces like a potter's vessel."*[148] This pastiche of Psalms references from Guibert of Nogent, Raymond of Aguilers, and Robert of Reims is suggestive of how individual authors used different verses to present a unified moral interpretation of the conquest of Jerusalem.

Moving from the moral to the anagogical level, the conquest became much trickier to interpret. On the one hand, contemporaries agreed that the crusaders had literally fulfilled a number of biblical prophecies concerning Jerusalem's bondage and deliverance, and that the Scriptures held the key to understanding the crusade's significance for the future. On the other hand, they debated the precise nature of this significance. Fulcher of Chartres and Raymond of Aguilers agreed that the conquest had ushered in *"a new day"* and its celebration called for *"a new canticle to the Lord"* (Ps. 32:3; cf. Ps. 95:1).[149] Surrounded by mountains

---

[145] A letter purportedly dispatched west by the crusaders in 1099, for instance, recalled that the army's spiritual leaders had likened their arrival outside the walls of Jerusalem to Christ's entry into the holy city. EP, no. 18, p. 170.

[146] CJ, 648; RC, 104 (citing Ps. 135:13–14).

[147] GN, 305.

[148] GN, 307 (Ps. 9:10); RA, 149 (Ps. 29:12); RR, 98 (Ps. 143:1); and GN, 307 (Ps. 2:9).

[149] RA, 151; FC, 305.

of corpses in a city they had made a charnel house, the crusaders could hardly doubt this was *a* day of judgment, if not Judgment Day itself. Robert of Reims saw the conquest in terms of an epic confrontation between good and evil, pride and humility, Christ and the Devil, and identified the crusaders as the remnant of Israel whom Ezekiel (11:19) had prophesied would be saved by the Lord to do his work.[150] Robert's contemporaries identified biblical prophecies in Isaiah, Ezekiel, Zechariah, Lamentations, Matthew, and Galatians that seemed to have literally come true in 1099, but the chroniclers emphasized different prophecies and invested them with apocalyptic significance to varying degrees. Whether they viewed conquest as an apocalyptic event or merely a miraculous victory, the chroniclers agreed that the crusaders, as instruments of God's will, had brought humanity one step closer to the Last Days and the end of history.[151]

As this comparison of the early twelfth-century accounts of the Council of Clermont and the conquest of Jerusalem has shown, early narrators agreed upon the main features of crusading spirituality, and about the usefulness of the Scriptures as a source for understanding and describing this new form of devotion. But, in making sense of the crusade, each forged a unique path through the Scriptures. Several factors encouraged our authors to develop original readings of the events at Clermont and Jerusalem. First, the process of glossing the crusade was a highly personal one, in that authors searched for the holy war's meaning in those biblical books that seemed to them most likely to offer satisfying answers, and were likely to turn to those parts of the Scriptures with which they were most familiar. In addition, individual writers were interested to varying degrees in excavating different levels of meaning within the crusade narrative, perhaps reflecting their prior exposure to different exegetical methodologies in monastic or cathedral schools. In other words, it is possible to discern in early crusading narratives both a broad hermeneutic reflecting our authors' shared clerical identity and similar training, and a collection of individual hermeneutics shaped by each individual's habits of mind. The following section explores this dynamic further through a comparison of several accounts of a single curious incident set at the siege of Antioch.

Glossing Kerbogha's Mother

In June 1098 the crusaders finally captured Antioch, only to be besieged in turn by troops under the command of Kerbogha, Atabeg of Mosul. Within the city walls, the Christians' sufferings were punctuated by wonders, as heavenly visitations and miraculous discoveries assured them of God's continued favor. It is at

---
[150] RR, 96 and 100.
[151] A point emphasized by Rubenstein, *Armies of Heaven*, ch.18–19.

this point that several Latin writers tell the curious story of how the Atabeg's aged mother paid a surprise visit to the Muslim encampment. Kerbogha's mother, who remains unnamed in the Christian chronicles, is said to have come to warn her proud son of the futility of doing battle with the Latins, whose God watched over them and guaranteed them victory over all adversaries. Despite her dire predictions that he would lose his power, lands, and life within the year if he persisted in defying the crusaders, the story goes that Kerbogha arrogantly rejected his mother's advice and she returned, sorrowing, to her home in Aleppo.

The exchange between Kerbogha and his mother appears in several Latin chronicles: the *Gesta Francorum*, Peter Tudebode, and the anonymous Monte Cassino chronicle provide virtually identical accounts; each of the three northern French Benedictines, Robert of Reims, Guibert of Nogent, and Baldric of Bourgueil, offers a distinctive version; and Orderic Vitalis briefly mentions the incident.[152] Either because they had not heard the story, or perhaps because it was unverifiable, the other chroniclers omitted the episode.[153] Earlier generations of scholars speculated that this "highly fanciful interview" derived from a "camp story" current among Norman knights at Antioch, or else was the wholesale invention of an anonymous clerical editor of the *Gesta*; in any event, they dismissed it as a fabrication unhelpful for reconstructing the course of the First Crusade.[154] More recently, Susan Edgington has argued for the episode's historiographical significance, while Natasha Hodgson has called attention to its value as a source for twelfth-century attitudes towards women, motherhood, and non-Christians.[155] In his reassessment of the Jerusalemites' encounter with the

---

[152] GF, 53–56; PT, 93–96; MC, 71–75; RR, 61–65; GN, 212–16; BB, 64–65; OV, 5:96.

[153] Albert of Aachen (AA, 250–58) includes a similar story in which Kerbogha is warned against fighting the Franks not by his mother but by the sultan Suleiman, the latter fresh from his defeat by the crusaders at Dorylaeum. The story's magical and prophetic elements also appealed to the imaginations of authors of later crusading *chansons de geste*, such as the *Chanson d'Antioche* and *Enfances Godefroi*, in which Kerbogha's mother features as a two-hundred-year-old sorceress who foresees the entire course of the First, Second, and Third Crusades. See Susan B. Edgington, "Romance and Reality in the Sources for the Sieges of Antioch, 1097–1098," in *Porphyrogenita: Essays on the History and Literature of Byzantium and the Latin East in Honour of Julian Chrysostomides*, ed. Charalambos Dendrinos et al. (Aldershot, 2003), 33–45 (esp. 42–44).

[154] Quoting August C. Krey, "A Neglected Passage in the *Gesta* and its Bearing on the Literature of the First Crusade," in *The Crusades and Other Historical Essays Presented to Dana C. Munro*, ed. Louis J. Paetow (Freeport, NY, 1928), 78; also see Louis Bréhier's introduction to his edition of the *Gesta Francorum*, *Histoire anonyme de la première croisade* (Paris, 1924), vi.

[155] Edgington, "Romance and Reality," 37; Natasha R. Hodgson, "The Role of Kerbogha's Mother in the *Gesta Francorum* and Selected Chronicles of the First Crusade," in *Gendering the Crusades*, eds. Susan B. Edgington and Sarah Lambert (New York, 2002), 163–76.

Islamic world, Nicholas Morton identifies the tale as "a component in a much wider polemical narrative ... which describes a dawning awareness among the Turks that God was fighting for the crusaders."[156] Kerbogha's conversation with his mother also makes an ideal case study of how scriptural exegesis informs narratives of the First Crusade. A close comparison of different chroniclers' treatment of this episode reveals the medieval exegetical imagination at work, and prompts us to consider how the inclusion (or exclusion) of scriptural language might shape a historical narrative by serving as authorial commentary.

The *Gesta Francorum*'s account of Kerbogha's meeting with his mother is the earliest extant version, and is usually taken to be the inspiration for other versions. It is not difficult to imagine the compiler of the *Gesta* plucking the story from a collection of *exempla*, with the aim of enlivening his account of the long siege of Antioch.[157] Here, as in other redactions of the tale, Kerbogha's mother quotes the Scriptures extensively, crafting a powerful warning that falls on her son's deaf ears. The central lessons of her impromptu sermon concern the power of the Christian God and his special protection of the crusaders, themes frequently developed in the chronicles through the use of carefully chosen biblical references. In the *Gesta*, Kerbogha's mother freely borrows metaphors from the Old Testament, evoking an image of God "watching over [the crusaders] *just as a shepherd keeps his flock*" (Jer. 31:10)[158] and citing the Psalms to warn her son of God's wrath: he will "*scatter the nations that delight in wars*" (Ps. 67:31) and "*pour out [his] wrath upon those who have not known [him], and upon the kingdoms that have not called [his] name*" (Ps. 78:6).[159] She also employs phrases from the Epistles, describing the Christians as "*sons of adoption and promise*" (cf. Rom. 9:8, Gal. 4:5) and "*heirs of Christ*" (Rom. 8:17), and even glosses these titles for her son, explaining that the "inheritance" in question is nothing other than the Turks' lands, as promised in various Old Testament passages: "From the rising of the sun to its going down shall be your bounds, and no man shall stand against you" (cf. Pss. 49:1, 112:3, Deut. 11:24–25, Josh. 1:4–5).[160] Yet, even while she speaks in the words of holy writ, the reader is reminded that Kerbogha's mother is not one of the chosen people; she includes herself in the prophecy of the defeat of the Turks, whom she refers to as "pagans,"[161] and begs her son to heed her words "by the names of the gods" (*deorum nomina*), a phrase found

---

[156] Morton, moreover, makes a compelling case that the story may have been inspired by real events. See *Encountering Islam on the First Crusade* (Cambridge, 2016), 24.

[157] This line of thinking follows Jay Rubenstein's argument about the *Gesta* compiler's working methods; "What is the *Gesta Francorum*?" 197.

[158] The *Gesta* substitutes "vigilat" for the Vulgate's "custodiet," but this is otherwise an exact quotation (not noted by Hill, GF, 53). Cf. Ez. 34:12 for similar imagery.

[159] GF, 54.

[160] GF, 54: "A solis ortu usque ad occasum erunt termini vestri, et nemo stabit contra vos."

[161] GF, 54: "inventum est in nostra pagina et in gentilium voluminibus, quoniam gens

in Old Testament prohibitions against the ancient Jews worshipping the gods of their neighbors.[162] The overall effect of Kerbogha's mother's speech in the *Gesta* is to legitimize the crusading enterprise by recourse to scriptural authority, and one might read this passage as a crusading sermon or *exemplum* in which an unbeliever is made to testify to the truth of Christian revelation.

In light of current debates concerning the identity of the *Gesta*'s author or editor, the text's incorporation of no less than eight biblical allusions within such a short space is particularly interesting.[163] What is more, the use of this language is more sophisticated than has often been acknowledged, as may be seen through a comparison of how Peter Tudebode and the Monte Cassino Anonymous describe this episode in their adaptations of the *Gesta*.[164] Following the line of reasoning that the *Gesta* represents a raw, theologically unsophisticated eyewitness account,[165] we would expect later clerical redactors to correct scriptural misquotations and add layers of learned exegetical commentary to the episode described above, but this is not what we find when we read the three texts side-by-side. In the first place, *pace* Rosalind Hill, it should be noted that the *Gesta* is hardly full of egregious scriptural misquotations, either in this section or elsewhere.[166] Second, the later authors neglected to add new biblical allusions, contenting themselves with those supplied in the *Gesta*. Confronted with the

---

Christiana super nos foret ventura, et nos ubique victura, ac super paganos regnatura ... ."

[162] GF, 53; cf. Ex. 23:13, Deut. 18:20, Josh. 23:7, and 1 Kgs. 18:24.

[163] The only other point at which the *Gesta* makes such rapid-fire use of scriptural language is in its opening account of Clermont; see n. 96 above.

[164] Jay Rubenstein ("What is the *Gesta Francorum*?" 201–2) suggests the Monte Cassino chronicler had before him two early crusading narratives, one of which was the basis for the now-extant *Gesta* and one of which was the text we refer to as the *Historia* of Peter Tudebode.

[165] Rosalind Hill's edition of the *Gesta* makes much of the author's "misquoting" of Scripture as evidence that he was "a devout layman" reliant on a faulty memory (*passim*; quoting 54), an interpretation challenged by Rubenstein, "What is the *Gesta Francorum*?" 187–88. As the examples at n. 158 and 166 suggest, few of the scriptural passages are misquoted as egregiously as Hill implies; at any rate, a large number of the biblical quotations found throughout the crusade chronicles written by clerics have similar minor errors, which may simply reflect the lack of a single, standardized Latin Bible.

[166] While these writers may have had access to other versions of the biblical texts, I have judged scriptural 'accuracy' by comparison with modern editions of the Latin Vulgate. For example, depending on which edition of the Vulgate one consults, the passages from Psalms 67:31 and 78:6 included in the *Gesta* may appear to have minor errors of wording, but these do not alter the sense of the original text. Moreover, the *Gesta*'s wording is actually identical to the text of the Psalter as given in the Dumbarton Oaks edition, ed. Edgar and Kinney (Cambridge, MA, 2011), 326, 364. GF, 54 reads: "'*Dissipa gentes quae bella volunt*' (Ps. 67:31). Et alibi: '*Effunde iram tuam in gentes quae te non noverunt, et in regna quae nomen tuum non invocaverunt*' (Ps. 78:6)."

Gesta's gloss, which, as we saw above, utilized passages from Psalms 67:31 and 78:6, Peter Tudebode simply combined parts of both quotations to create a new passage – "*Dissipa gentes quae nomen tuum non invocaverunt*" – that preserved the biblical verses' basic meaning but obscured their source.[167] The Monte Cassino Anonymous took a different tack, omitting the *Gesta*'s citation of Psalm 67:31 altogether, perhaps because it seemed extraneous (or was absent from the version of the *Gesta* available to the chronicler).[168] In addition, both Peter Tudebode and the Monte Cassino chronicler made only minor alterations to the *Gesta*'s composite quotation from Psalms, Deuteronomy, and Joshua that failed to bring it any closer to the Vulgate texts.[169] Clearly, this is not a case of later clerical chroniclers reworking and embellishing a rough patchwork of biblical misquotations; on the contrary, we find that the *Gesta*'s gloss passed muster with at least two discerning later writers, one of whom was a monk with a renowned library at his disposal.

The story of Kerbogha's mother also made its way into the histories of Robert of Reims, Guibert of Nogent, and Baldric of Bourgueil. Each of these men prefaced his chronicle with a declaration of dissatisfaction with an earlier history of the First Crusade (presumably the *Gesta*), the style of which was judged "uncertain and unsophisticated" and "too rustic" to do justice to the "wonderful sequence of events" of 1095–99.[170] In their attempts to improve on this rough *libellus*, these authors produced works of acknowledged literary merit, historical vision, and theological sophistication.[171] As we have seen, these chronicles collectively stand out among the histories of the First Crusade for their exegetical richness, and each features a wealth of clearly identifiable scriptural quotations.[172] While it has been suggested that these writers broadly agreed upon the crusade's theological significance,[173] a comparison of how they glossed the

---

[167] PT, 94. Since the omission consists of sixteen consecutive words found in the *Gesta*, this may well be the result of scribal error rather than a deliberate revision.

[168] MC, 72: "Effundam iram meam in gentes quae te non noverunt, et in regna quae nomen tuum non invocaverunt" (a direct quotation of Ps. 78:6).

[169] Compare the *Gesta* (GF, 54): "A solis ortu usque ad occasum erunt termini vestri, et nemo stabit contra vos" with the Vulgate: "ab ortu solis usque ad occasum" (Ps. 49:1 / Ps. 112:3); "usque ad mare occidentale erunt termini vestri, nullus stabit contra vos" (Deut. 11:24–25); "contra solis occasum erit terminus vester" (Josh. 1:4–5). Both Peter Tudebode (PT, 94) and the Monte Cassino chronicle (MC, 73) have: "A solis ortu usque in occidentem erunt termini vestri, ita quod nemo audax stabit contra vos."

[170] GN, 79; RR, 3; BB, 4.

[171] On these works as a group, see Riley-Smith, *Idea of Crusading*, 135–52; for a close comparison of how Robert, Guibert, and Baldric treat the fall of Antioch, see Robert Levine, "The Pious Traitor: Rhetorical Reinventions of the Fall of Antioch," *Mittellateinisches Jahrbuch* 33 (1998): 59–80 (at 64–74).

[172] See Appendix 1, Table 3.

[173] Riley-Smith, *Idea of Crusading*, 152.

story of Kerbogha's mother demonstrates the creativity that each author brought to smaller-scale exegetical challenges.

While retaining the basic narrative elements of the story as found in the *Gesta* and its later redactions, Robert of Reims renovated the tale's exegetical structure by replacing nearly all of the scriptural references in Kerbogha's mother's speech. Once again, the ancient seeress refers to the Christians' God in the words of the Old Testament (as the "*Deus deorum*" of Deuteronomy 10:17), and warns her son that he will smite all who oppose the crusaders, just as he had long ago destroyed the ancient Israelites' enemies.[174] But, compared with the earlier versions of the tale, Robert's text bears a much stronger resemblance to the formal glosses found in contemporary biblical commentaries and monastic sermons.[175] Again and again, he has Kerbogha's mother gloss scriptural pericopes for her son's (and presumably the reader's) benefit. Consider the following excerpt, in which Robert's "pagan" speaker cites Deuteronomy and then explains the verses' meaning:

> The prophet says of this same invincible God: "*I will kill, and I will make to live, I will strike and I will heal: neither is there any that can deliver out of my hand* (Deut. 32:39). *If I shall whet my sword as the lightning, and my hand take hold on judgment, I will render vengeance to my enemies, and repay them that hate me. I will make mine arrows drunk with blood, and my sword shall devour flesh*" (Deut. 32:41–42). It is terrifying to fight him who knows how to sharpen his sword thus, when sharpened to sate it, and when sated to mince flesh. Who, my son, sank Pharaoh, King of Egypt, into the Red Sea with his whole army (cf. Ex. 14)? Who disinherited Seon, King of the Amorites and Og, the King of Bashan (cf. Ps. 134:11, Deut. 29.7), and all the kingdoms of Canaan and gave it to his own people to inherit? [...] That is the God who is angry with our race (*gens*) ....[176]

Robert signaled the beginning of the original text with the phrase "the prophet

---

[174] RR, 61–63.

[175] For a discussion of similar contemporary exegetical methodologies and their relationship to the *trivium*, see Dahan, *L'Exégèse chrétienne*, 81–86.

[176] RR, 61–62: "De ipso quidem invictissimo Deo dicit propheta: *Ego occidam et ego vivere faciam: percutiam et ego sanabo: et non est qui de manu mea possit eruere* (Deut. 32:39). *Si acuero ut fulgur gladium meum, et arripuerit iudicium manus mea, reddam ultionem hostibus meis, et his qui oderunt me, retribuam. Inebriabo sagittas meas sanguine, et gladius meus devorabit carnes* (Deut. 32:41–42). Formidolosum est contra hunc conflictum inire, qui gladium suum sic novit acuere, acutum inebriare, inebriato carnes macerare. Fili, Pharaonem regem Egypti quis submersit in mari Rubro cum omni exercitu suo? Quis exhereditavit *Seon regem Amorreorum, et Og regem Basan, et omnia regna Canaam, et dedit* suis in *hereditatem*? (cf. Ps. 134:11, Deut. 29:7) Genti nostre iratus est Deus ille ... ." Trans. Sweetenham, 154–55.

says" (*dicit propheta*), rendered the quotations with characteristic fidelity to the Vulgate,[177] and methodically glossed the quoted passages, moving from a literal interpretation (the God of the Franks is a formidable enemy) to a typological one (as the enemies of the new chosen people, the Turks can expect the same sort of harsh treatment once meted out to the ancient polytheists who opposed the Israelites), which represents a departure from earlier exegesis of Deuteronomy 32.[178] In the remainder of the exchange, Kerbogha's mother bolsters this interpretation with additional scriptural quotations from Exodus (23:20–23) and Deuteronomy (32:20) which warn that God's angel leads the crusading army, just as it had led the armies of Israel, and that with divine aid the Franks can defeat even the most powerful enemy. Robert rendered each of these quotations with equal precision and followed them with commentaries that, though, ironically, delivered by a speaker whose reliance on "*soothsayers, magicians, and diviners*" (Dan. 2:27) allies her with Old Testament idolatry,[179] promote the new chosen people's cause. In sum, Robert completely rethought the exegetical component of the scene, choosing to preserve only one of the *Gesta Francorum*'s scriptural quotations, and even here he could not resist tinkering with the wording to personalize the gloss.[180]

Whereas Robert used Kerbogha's mother as a narrative device to reinforce the typological connection between the Israelites and the first crusaders, and developed his commentary entirely through Old Testament references, Guibert of Nogent took a different approach. Like Robert, Guibert left the *Gesta*'s basic narrative intact while selectively revising its scriptural content, and offered formal glosses of direct biblical quotations that serve to guide the reader. But, to a much greater degree than Robert, Guibert's exegesis aims to establish the crusade's privileged place in Christian eschatology. His biblical quotations, drawn primarily from Psalms, were carefully chosen and introduced with this aim in mind, so that Kerbogha's mother is made to preach

---

[177] This is an excerpt from the "Canticle of Moses," often included in the office of Lauds on Saturdays, which Robert (and many of his readers) would have undoubtedly known by heart.

[178] Earlier exegetes had been inclined to read Deut. 32:39–42 as a call to believers to repent so they might merit eternal life, or as an allegory of God's fight with the Devil; see, for example, Gregory the Great, *In Librum Primum Regum Expositionum Libri VI,* 3.93, ed. Pierre-Patrick Verbraken, CCSL 144 (Turnhout, 1963), 251; Rather of Verona, *Sermo 8 (De Ascensione Domini),* c.4, PL 136:739; and Bruno of Segni, *Expositio in Pentateuchum,* c. 32, PL 164: 542.

[179] RR, 63. Albert of Aachen uses the same phrase from Daniel in reference to the Sultan of Babylon; see n. 153 above.

[180] Where the *Gesta* (GF, 54) has "A solis ortu usque ad occasum erunt termini vestri, et nemo stabit contra vos" (cf. Ps. 49:1, Ps. 112:3, Deut. 11:24–25, Josh. 1:4–5), Robert of Reims (RR, 63) inserts a snippet of Ps. 106:3 to make: "A solis ortu et occasu, *ab aquilone et mari* (Ps. 106:3), erunt termini vestri, et nullus stabit contra vos."

the doctrine of the Incarnation and explain the supersession of God's original covenant with the Jews.

Thus, Guibert had Kerbogha's mother introduce Psalm 81:8 – "Arise, O God! Judge you the earth, for you shall inherit among all the nations" – as a prayer "to a God about to rise from the dead" (*deo a mortuis surrecturo*), following an interpretive tradition in which the verse was seen to foreshadow Christ's resurrection.[181] And in two cases where Guibert preserved citations from the *Gesta Francorum* in whole or in part (Pss. 78:6, 49:1), he did not merely have Kerbogha's mother offer these (as the *Gesta* Anonymous had) as prophecies of the crusaders' conquests, but used them as points of departure for an explanation of how divine favor had been successively bestowed upon and withdrawn from various peoples throughout time. An accomplished exegete, Guibert would have been aware that earlier writers had glossed "the nations that have not known thee" of Psalm 78:6 as a reference to the Jews' denial of Christ's divinity and the subsequent transfer of the covenant to the Christians,[182] and his gloss on this verse sets up the possibility for a comparison between the "pagan" Turks, who "hate the name of Christ," and contemporary Jews.[183] Guibert's subsequent commentary on Psalms 49 and 112 further develops this idea with reference to the Epistle to Romans:

> *"From the rising of the sun to its going down the name of God is worthy of praise"* (Pss. 49:1, 112:3–4), for he is said to be exalted not over the Jews, but over all nations, and by the mouth of God himself it was said that the people who had not been his people were now his people and those who had not been loved were now loved (cf. Rom. 9:25), and what had been among the Jews was transferred to all nations by the grace of adoption ... then who except a madman [Kerbogha's mother asks her son] would dare attack the sons of God?[184]

---

[181] GN, 213–14; for this interpretation, see Augustine, *Enarrationes in Psalmos*, 81.7, ed. Eligius Dekkers and Jean Fraipont, CCSL 38–40 (Turnhout, 1956), 2:1140, and the *Glossa Ordinaria, Liber Psalmorum*, 81.8, PL 113:982.

[182] GN, 214; for a representative gloss on this passage, see Cassiodorus, *Expositio psalmorum LXXI–CL*, c. 78, ed. M. Adriaen, CCSL 98 (Turnhout, 1958), 736.

[183] GN, 214; trans. 97. The anti-Jewish bent of Guibert's *Dei gesta* has been recognized by Elizabeth Lapina ("Anti-Jewish Rhetoric"), and his other theological writings embody a similar hostility towards the Jews, as observed by Abulafia, *Christians and Jews*, 110–13.

[184] GN, 214: "Si his prophetico ore promittitur quod *a solis ortu usque ad occasum laudabile nomen domini* (Pss. 49:1, 112:3–4) habeatur, dum non super Iudeos sed *super omnes gentes excelsus* predicatur et dei ipsius ore quae plebs sua non fuerat iam plebs sua et quae non dilecta dilecta vocatur (cf. Rom. 9:25), dum quae extiterat in Iudeis in nationes adoptionis gratia transfertur ... quis nisi demens filios dei impugnare molitur? Trans. 97.

Guibert used Kerbogha's mother's speech to remind his readers that the crusade, by which "pagans will be subjected to the faithful," had been foreordained by God as a means of expanding Christendom, and to identify the holy war as an important milestone on the path to the Last Judgment.[185] This exegetical strategy, which is particularly noteworthy in light of modern scholars' emphasis on Guibert's interest in framing the events of 1095–99 in eschatological terms, suggests that Guibert, perhaps more than most of his learned contemporaries, believed the first crusaders' triumph – a triumph foretold by Kerbogha's mother in the *Dei gesta* – helped to set in motion a chain of events that would lead to the end of history.[186]

After Robert and Guibert's carefully crafted exegeses, Baldric of Bourgueil's treatment of the episode involving Kerbogha's mother takes the reader by surprise; all of the scriptural passages have been excised from the *Gesta* version, leaving most of the story's narrative elements but removing the gloss. In Baldric's version Kerbogha's mother is an aged sorceress who gives a flowery speech about maternal love and filial piety, offering the familiar warnings that if her son fights the Christians and their God he will pay with his life. Her delivery is quite elegant, rhetorically speaking, and liberally studded with Classical flourishes (e.g., "Upon whom will Mars smile?"), but contains only the barest hints of biblical phrasing and could hardly be confused with a sermon or a formal commentary.[187] Since, as we have seen, Baldric was hardly averse to blending exegesis with history, his elimination of the *Gesta*'s gloss must have been a considered decision. Did he find the *Gesta*'s inclusion of a veritable sermon preached by a "pagan" woman faintly blasphemous, or simply implausible? Or did the erudite chronicler perhaps build his version of the story around an as yet unidentified – and, considering Baldric's stylistic tastes, likely Classical – source?[188] Whatever the reason, such a narrative was apparently not in keeping with Baldric's vision of the crusade.

---

[185] GN, 215; trans. 97–98. Cf. Guibert's account of Clermont (GN, 113–14) for a more explicit statement of the apocalyptic significance of the crusade.

[186] See Whalen, *Dominion of God*, 54–55, 71. In *Armies of Heaven*, Rubenstein argues that the First Crusade's victory at Jerusalem was widely interpreted by participants and chroniclers as "an event of apocalyptic proportions, if not the Apocalypse itself" (xiii).

[187] No scriptural allusions are identified in the RHC Oc. edition, but two phrases Baldric has Kerbogha's mother use (BB, 64) are clearly biblical, if not particularly rich in meaning: "Deus omnipotens" is found in Gen. 17:1 and elsewhere; "os meum et caro mea" occurs in Gen. 29:14 and 2 Kgs. 19:12–13.

[188] Neil Wright has documented some of Baldric's Classical borrowings, as well as the effect of these borrowings on the medieval reception of Baldric's *Historia*, in his "Epic and Romance in the Chronicles of Anjou," *Anglo-Norman Studies* 26 (2004): 177–89 (at 180–86).

A comparison of the half-dozen versions of the episode involving Kerbogha's mother reveals how twelfth-century writers used scriptural references to add interpretative layers to their crusade narratives, and highlights the care that went into the construction of such intra-textual glosses. To be sure, some authors took a more active hand than others in reshaping the exegeses they found in earlier histories, and it is as important to recognize interpretive continuities between texts as to note instances of radical reinvention. A comparison of the *Gesta Francorum*'s story of Kerbogha's mother with later versions is particularly instructive in this regard. Some chroniclers found the *Gesta*'s gloss worthy of wholesale replication, while others reshaped the *Gesta* tale in accordance with their distinctive exegetical agendas, but preserved a minority of the *Gesta*'s scriptural references, presumably because they found them theologically sound.[189] While all of these writers, including Baldric of Bourgueil, might be said to have 'copied' the episode's basic narrative from the *Gesta*, a side-by-side comparison of their works reveals the range of interpretive practices that 'copying' might encompass in the early twelfth century,[190] and the degree to which adding (or stripping away) scriptural allusions could shape learned readers' understanding of a historical narrative.

Conclusion

Reflecting on the unique place of the Bible in medieval intellectual culture, Alastair Minnis writes that "as the authoritative text *par excellence*, the 'Book of Life' and the book of books, the Bible was for medieval scholars the most difficult text to describe accurately and adequately."[191] Like the Scriptures, the events of the First Crusade presented formidable descriptive and interpretive challenges to Christian commentators. For the chroniclers who tackled these challenges, as for contemporaries who sought to unravel the meaning of the sacred page, what was at stake was nothing less than an understanding of God's will and humanity's future. History, as usually practiced before the turn of the twelfth century, was not quite up to this challenge. By drawing upon the traditional methods of biblical exegesis, the crusade's early historians pioneered a new way of writing about the recent past, one which treated events as texts capable of yielding multiple levels

---

[189] This conclusion is in keeping with scholarship which has challenged the traditional view of the *Gesta* as a primitive text: see Kenneth Baxter Wolf, "Crusade and Narrative: Bohemond and the *Gesta Francorum*," *Journal of Medieval History* 17 (1991): 207–16; and Morris, "The *Gesta Francorum* as Narrative History."

[190] On the creativity potentially involved in medieval practices of compilation and copying, see Bernard Guenée, "L'Historien par les mots," in *Études sur l'historiographie médiévale* (Paris, 1977), 1–17 (at 13).

[191] Minnis, *Medieval Theory of Authorship*, 4.

of interpretation. The crusade's narrators also carried with them other sorts of interpretive baggage from the intellectual world of scriptural study: their work was shaped by the tension between authority and innovation that defined biblical exegesis, as well as by the associative chains of meaning that linked disparate scriptural passages to one another and to commentary traditions. Moreover, each chronicler approached the project of glossing the crusade as an individual reader who had already cultivated a highly personal relationship with the Bible, whether by honing the techniques of monastic prayer, participating in a liturgical community, or formally studying exegesis (or perhaps all three).

Approaching the crusade's early histories through their biblical elements offers a new vantage point from which to appreciate what is distinctive about each text, and prompts us to reconsider earlier judgments about the relative value of individual sources. In the case of the *Gesta Francorum*, which is often considered unsophisticated by virtue of its workmanlike Latin, highlighting its substantial biblical content and range of exegetical strategies allows us to better appreciate that this work, as twelfth-century readers recognized, offered a theologically sound gloss of the crusade. Authors writing in the second and even third generations after the conquest of Jerusalem, whose work has often been accorded less importance than that of eyewitnesses, can likewise be reevaluated on the basis of their exegetical creativity. Whether written in a 'high' or 'low' style, in the immediate aftermath of the crusade or decades later, each of these works can help us to understand the relationship between scriptural study and history, and the ways in which the Bible mediated memory and lived experience in the medieval Latin West. As we shall see in the following chapter, exegesis of the crusade 'text' also allowed Latin Christians to affirm their collective identity as a new chosen people, and to bolster their claim to the newly conquered lands in the East.

Chapter 3

Into the Promised Land

In the second half of the twelfth century two scribes at the Poitevin abbey of Saint-Pierre, Maillezais undertook a project that would allow their brethren to relive the first crusaders' triumphs and tour the holy sites of the East without leaving the cloister. The product of their efforts, now preserved in Paris, Bibliothèque nationale (BN), ms. latin 4892,[1] opens with an impressive array of excerpts from patristic and Carolingian historical, homiletic, and visionary literature that trace two closely entwined narratives: the rise of Christianity and the deeds of the Roman Church's preeminent defenders, the Franks.[2] In the final sixty-seven folios, the manuscript's creators presented this story's climax, the First Crusade, carefully wrapped in layers of historical, geographical, and devotional context.[3] Most modern readers have treated this assemblage of nine

---

[1] The manuscript is thought to have come from either Maillezais or Saint-Maixent; its contents and known history seem to support the first possibility. On the manuscript's provenance and dating, see Louis Halphen, "Note sur la chronique de Saint-Maixent," *Bibliothèque de l'École des chartes* 69 (1908): 405–11 (at 410); Jean Verdon, *La Chronique de Saint-Maixent* (Paris, 1979), xx–xxvii; and Yves Chauvin and Georges Pon, Introduction to *La fondation de l'abbaye de Maillezais: Récit du moine Pierre* (La Roche-sur-Yon, 2001), 9–12. As Verdon notes, fols. 1r–193v are the work of one scribe, while the remainder of the incomplete ms. (fols. 194r–255v) is in a second hand.

[2] This compendium, detailed by Verdon (*Chronique de Saint-Maixent*, xxii–xxv), reflects the richness of Maillezais's twelfth-century library, confirmed by a contemporary catalogue bound into fol. A of the manuscript. It is edited by Léopold Delisle, *Cabinet des manuscrits de la Bibliothèque nationale*, 4 vols (Paris, 1868–81), 2:506–8; for commentary, see Hervé Genton, "La bibliothèque de Maillezais à la fin du xiie siècle," in *L'Abbaye de Maillezais: des moines du marais aux soldats huguenots*, ed. Mathias Tranchant and Cécile Treffort (Rennes, 2005), 78–97.

[3] These are: the Chronicle of Saint-Maixent, an abbey 30 miles east of Maillezais (fols. 189r–207r); Peter Tudebode's account of the First Crusade, with an accompanying *descriptio* of Jerusalem's holy places (fols. 212r–236v); an excerpt of *De situ Terra Sanctae*, a ninth-century Holy Land itinerary (fols. 236v–239r); a Holy Land geography that draws upon Book 15 of Isidore of Seville's *Etymologies* and Bede's *Nomina regionum atque locorum de Actibus apostolorum* (fols. 239r–243r); *De proprietatibus gentium*, a ninth-century catalogue of the virtues and vices of the world's peoples (fol. 243r); an excerpt from Book 14 of Isidore of Seville's *Etymologies* (fols. 243r–244r); the *Epistola Premonis*, a sixth-century account of the marvels of the East (fols. 244r–245r); an early medieval description of the world's three parts, Asia, Africa, and Europe (fol. 245rv); and finally, a narrative of Maillezais's foundation and subsequent acquisition of Saint Rigomer's relics (fols. 246r–255v).

texts as a grab-bag, considering individual sources without addressing the logic behind what is, in fact, a quite thoughtful commemorative and devotional plan.[4] Reading the collection holistically reveals how geographical knowledge and theology informed the reception of the First Crusade in the twelfth-century West, and reminds us of the importance of restoring early crusade narratives to their original contexts.

Maillezais's monks had every reason to be interested in crusading to the Holy Land in the later twelfth century. An earlier abbot, Peter, had helped preach the First Crusade and subsequently journeyed east, probably in the entourage of his patron, Duke William IX of Aquitaine (r. 1088–1127), with the *iter*'s final wave.[5] Since the abbey's cartulary has been lost, it is impossible to reconstruct its connections to individual crusaders, but, given both Abbot Peter's enthusiasm for the expedition and Maillezais's ties to the dukes of Aquitaine (who were also the counts of Poitou at this time), the community could have served as a recruiting

---

[4] The following texts have been edited separately: The Chronicle of Saint-Maixent (fols. 189r–207r), ed. Verdon, *La Chronique de Saint-Maixent*; Peter Tudebode, *Historia de Hierosolimitano itinere* (fols. 212r–236r), ed. John Hugh Hill and Laurita L. Hill (Paris, 1977); the *Descriptio sanctorum locorum Hierusalem* (fol. 236rv), ed. Jesse Keskiaho, "The Transmission of Peter Tudebode's *De Hierosolymitano itinere* and Related Chronicles, with a Critical Edition of *Descriptio sanctorum locorum Hierusalem*," *Revue d'histoire des textes*, n.s. 10 (2015): 69–102 (at 98–102); *De situ Terra Sanctae* (fols. 236v–243r), ed. J. Gildemeister (Bonn, 1882), 21–30; *De proprietatibus gentium* (fol. 243r), ed. T. Mommsen, MGH Auctores Antiquissimi 11: 389–90; Isidore of Seville's *Etymologiae* (fols. 243r–244r), extracts from book 14.2–5, ed. Lindsay, 2: 14.2–5 (n.p.); *Epistola Premonis regis ad Traianum Imperatorem* (fols. 244r–245r), ed. Patrick Gautier Dalché, "Notes sur la tradition du '*De rebus in oriente mirabilibus*,'" in *Amicorum societas: Mélanges offerts à François Dolbeau*, ed. Jacques Elfassi, Cécile Lanéry, and Anne-Marie Turan-Verkerk (Florence, 2013), 237–70 (at 264–66); the treatise on the tripartite world (fol. 245r–v), ed. Patrick Gautier-Dalché, "Cartes et enseignement de la 'géographie' durant le haut Moyen Âge: l'exemple d'un manuel inédit," in *Du copiste au collectionneur: Mélanges d'histoire des textes et des bibliothèques en l'honneur d'André Vernet*, ed. Donatella Nebbiai-Dalla Guarda and Jean-François Genest (Turnhout, 1998), 49–56 (at 55–56); and the foundation legend of Maillezais (fols. 246r–255v) as Peter of Maillezais, *Qualiter fuit constructum Malliacense monasterium et corpus sancti Rigomeri translatum*, PL 146: 1247–72, and more recently by Chauvin and Pon, *La fondation de l'abbaye de Maillezais*, 90–169.

[5] See above, Chapter 1, n. 1, for Abbot Peter's epistolary exchange with Baldric of Bourgueil. Noting stylistic similarities between the capitals of Maillezais's early eleventh-century abbatial church and the twelfth-century capitals of the Dome of the Ascension (Qubat al M'iraj) at Jerusalem, Bianca Kühnel has suggested that Peter's voyage may have formed the basis for a durable connection between the community and the crusader Kingdom of Jerusalem; see *Crusader Art of the Twelfth Century: A Geographical, an Historical, or an Art Historical Notion* (Berlin, 1994), 37–39.

hub in the Bas-Poitou.⁶ Certainly a large number of Poitevin knights participated in the First Crusade, and continued to fight in defense of Outremer in subsequent decades.⁷ The 1136 marriage of William IX's younger son, Raymond of Poitiers, to Constance, heiress of Antioch, and the participation of sizeable Poitevin contingents in the Second and Third Crusades ensured the ongoing relevance of Levantine affairs to the elite of the Bas-Poitou, and thus for the monasteries they patronized, throughout the twelfth century.⁸ This was the backdrop against which the compendium in BN latin 4892 was planned.

The manuscript's scribes directly confronted pressing questions raised by the first crusaders' success: How did the events of 1095–99 fit into God's plan for humanity? What were their implications for the Church? The monks of Maillezais added a level of specificity to these queries that reflected local concerns: What did the crusade mean for God's chosen people, the Franks, and the nobility of West Francia? These concerns inform the organization of BN latin 4892, which presents a sweeping spiritual biography of the Franks from their origins to the twelfth century, but they become especially apparent when we reach the Chronicle of Saint-Maixent, whose lengthy excursus on the crusade parallels the narrative of the Poitevin priest Peter Tudebode.⁹ The Chronicle attests to the twelfth-century Poitevin clergy's ongoing interest in Levantine affairs; in its coverage of the years 1102 to 1140 (the Chronicle's terminus) every folio makes mention of at least one military engagement, dynastic development, or miracle in the East. Having established the crusade's wider historical context, the scribes then plunged readers into the Jerusalem journey with Tudebode's chronicle, a work which may have resonated at Maillezais because of its concern with the

---

6   Sylvie Refalo, "Les ducs d'Aquitaine and l'abbaye de Maillezais (vers 970–vers 1100)," in *L'Abbaye de Maillezais*, ed. Tranchant and Treffort, 319–42.
7   See the examples in Jonathan Riley-Smith, *The First Crusaders, 1095–1131* (Cambridge, 1997), 104, 137, 139, 140.
8   On Raymond, see most recently Andrew D. Buck, *The Principality of Antioch and its Frontiers in the Twelfth Century* (Woodbridge, 2017), 69–79; some connections between the Poitevin nobility and crusading in the twelfth century are made by Linda Paterson, "Syria, Poitou, and the Reconquista (or Tales of the Undead): Who was the Count in Marcabru's *Vers del Lavador*?" in *The Second Crusade: Scope and Consequences*, ed. Jonathan Phillips and Martin Hoch (Manchester, 2001), 133–49 (at 139–45). Aquitainian clergy also held important ecclesiastical offices in the Antiochene church, as shown by Bernard Hamilton, "The Growth of the Latin Church of Antioch and the Recruitment of Its Clergy," in *East and West in the Medieval Mediterranean, vol. 1: Antioch from the Byzantine Reconquest until the End of the Crusader Principality*, Orientalia Lovaniensia Analecta 147, ed. K. Ciggaar and M. Metcalf (Leuven, 2006), 171–84 (at 180).
9   This section spans fols. 203r–204r in the ms., corresponding to *La Chronique de Saint-Maixent*, ed. Vernon, 154–68; see also ibid., xv–xvi for the chroniclers' use of Tudebode.

exploits of pilgrims from southwestern France.[10] That the scribes placed considerable importance on Tudebode's work is evident from the fact that it is one of only three texts (along with the Chronicle of Saint-Maixent and the account of Maillezais's foundation) copied into the manuscript in full,[11] whereas the majority of items are excerpts comprising just a few folios. Further, given the considerable overlap between the Chronicle of Saint-Maixent and Tudebode's work, it would have been reasonable to omit the latter unless the scribes were particularly interested in the crusade. It is clear that the manuscript's creators wished to situate the crusade within the long arc of sacred history, a history in which the Franks – first as Christian converts, later as defenders of the Church, and finally as holy warriors – played a leading role.

If the crusade prompted Latin Christians to consider historical questions of identity and belonging, it also encouraged them to renegotiate their relationship to God and reassert their entitlement, as a new chosen people, to the Holy Land. These linked interpretive processes are clearly visible in the final folios of BN latin 4892. To begin, it is evident that the Maillezais scribes valued Tudebode's account not only – perhaps not even primarily – as a history but as a guide to the sacred sites of the Holy Land.[12] This is suggested by its title in the manuscript, *De Hierosolymitano itinere*, or "The Jerusalem Journey,"[13] and by the assortment of geographically oriented texts appended to Tudebode's work, which collectively situate the crusade in a long tradition of Jerusalem pilgrimage and vividly evoke the landscapes, shrines, and peoples of the Levant. Immediately following Tudebode's account is the *Descriptio sanctorum locorum Hierusalem* (fol. 236rv), a short text which twelfth-century scribes copied with Tudebode's *Historia* (and with the closely related *Gesta Francorum*, as well as the *Historia*

---

[10] For an overview of Tudebode's text and its authorship, see Marcus Bull, "Peter Tudebode," in *Christian–Muslim Relations, 600–1500*, ed. David Thomas (Leiden, 2010), accessed December 14, 2017, at http://dx.doi.org/10.1163/1877-8054_cmri_COM_24164. The scribes' choice of crusade narrative and obvious concern with matters of local interest hints at how later generations in some regions of the crusading home front reoriented the First Crusade's historiography, which initially focused on Northern French heroes (on which, see Bull, "The Historiographical Construction of a Northern French First Crusade," *passim*.)

[11] While the foundation legend cuts off mid-sentence at the bottom of fol. 255v, given the contents of the surviving folios it is clear that this was the result of damage or rebinding, and not the original scribe's intent.

[12] Bearing in mind that the manuscript was created in the last decades of the twelfth century, when the crusader states were threatened by the resurgency of Saladin and his Ayyubid heirs, the scribes may have been motivated by fear that these sites would no longer be physically accessible to Latin pilgrims.

[13] This was the original title of the work, predating its styling as the "*Gesta Francorum*," as shown by Jesse Keskiako's survey of the text's manuscript tradition; see "On the Transmission of Peter Tudebode's *De Hierosolymitano Itinere*," 74–77.

Into the Promised Land

of Robert of Reims).[14] A reworking of the Late Antique *Itinerarium Burdigalense*, a well-known pilgrimage guide, the *Descriptio* was composed in the immediate aftermath of the First Crusade and circulated widely, offering readers a virtual tour of biblical sites in and around Jerusalem.[15] The following six patristic and early medieval texts distill much of the geographical knowledge about the East that was available in the West at this time, in the form of a detailed topography of Palestine, an itinerary of its shrines, a register of eastern cities' names and histories, and an essay on the earth's tripartite division. The scribes also prized ethnographic information, judging from their inclusion of a list of the characteristics of different *gentes mundi* and reports of the 'wonders of the East' and the monstrous peoples said to inhabit the world's furthest reaches.[16] The assumed relevance of such material to the crusading project reminds us that after 1099 Latin Christians renegotiated their collective identity as God's elect through an affirmation of other groups' alien status.

Far from being a hodgepodge, then, this suite of texts is ideally suited to perform a very specific function, namely to guide monastic readers through a virtual pilgrimage to the holy places before returning them, in the spirit, to the cloister of Maillezais, whose foundation legend completes the manuscript. This was a book that bore the stamp of the cloister, in the sense that it intentionally set out to engage the particular habits of mind cultivated in monastic settings, and reflects the practices of 'scribal crusading' which Thomas W. Smith has traced in other twelfth-century manuscripts.[17] Most importantly for our purposes, the Maillezais scribes' work is suggestive of how the events of the 1090s complicated Latin Christians' relationship with the Holy Land; while the sacred places of the Levant were brought into sharper relief and thus made more real to devotees thousands of miles away, these sites – like the holy war which had returned them to Christian hands – continued to be viewed through an interpretive lens comprised of centuries-old pilgrimage guides and exegetical works, which in turn rested on a solid foundation of biblical narrative.[18]

---

[14] Rosalind Hill included the text in her edition of the *Gesta Francorum* (GF, 98–101), but it is omitted from the Hills' edition of Peter Tudebode.

[15] Keskiaho, "On the Transmission of Peter Tudebode's *De Hierosolymitano Itinere*," 73.

[16] For commentary on this portion of the manuscript, which may have been copied *en bloc* from an earlier compendium, see Patrick Gaultier Dalché, "Cartes et enseignement de la 'géographie' durant le haut Moyen Âge," and idem, "Notes sur la tradition du '*De rebus in oriente mirabilibus*.'"

[17] See Smith, "Scribal Crusading," *passim.* Another interesting comparison might be made with other twelfth-century crusading *compendia*, such as the historical collection in BNF latin 14378, whose contents and intended audience have been reconstructed by Rubenstein, "Putting History to Use," 131–68.

[18] This impression is reinforced by other contemporary crusading compendia, e.g., Rouen, Bibliothèque municipale, ms. 1125 (a twelfth-century manuscript linked to the Norman

As the organization of BN latin 4892 suggests, the reception of the First Crusade entailed a reassessment of Christians' relationship with God, of the spiritual geography of the Levant, and of the status of non-Christian peoples in a world where, in Latin Christian eyes, God's bestowal of victory in the East was an unambiguous sign of his disapproval of Muslims and Jews. These issues were raised in a society already deeply concerned with the integration of non-believers into the expanding dominion of *christianitas*, a problem whose solution lay, clerical thinkers believed, in the proper exposition of the Scriptures.[19] This chapter considers three key aspects of this interpretive process. First, it surveys Latin narrators' efforts to inscribe the crusade onto the landscapes of the Holy Land and to link the crusaders to earlier chosen peoples whose stories had imprinted virtually every inch of the Levant. Next, it examines how a model of spiritual election borrowed from the Old Testament helped Latin Christians to explain the first crusaders' sufferings and triumphs, while simultaneously informing their presentation of the crusaders' Muslim adversaries. Finally, it explores how christological readings of the Old Testament enabled chroniclers to distance the crusaders from contemporary Jews even as they valorized their ancient Israelite ancestors as spiritual exemplars and proto-crusaders. My reconstruction of these strategies highlights not only Latin chroniclers' indebtedness to earlier interpretive traditions and genres, including biblical exegesis and also pilgrimage guides and anti-Jewish polemic, but also their willingness to modify these in light of the crusade.

Sacred Geographies

If, as we saw in Chapter 1, the conceptual line dividing history from exegesis was often blurry in medieval Europe, so too did geography often overlap with theology, exegesis, and history. As Natalia Lozovsky has shown, geographical knowledge was of great interest to medieval exegetes and, equally, "biblical ideas about the world, reflected and explained in exegesis, were bound to influence the perception and description of the earth."[20] Knowledge about the Holy Land's topography and toponyms, often gleaned from works intended for pilgrims, played an essential role in biblical scholarship, in particular the historical

---

abbey of Notre-Dame de Lyre), in which Josephus's world history, the *Antiquitatum Judaicarum epitoma*, and his *De bello Judaico* frame Baldric of Bourgueil's *Historia Ierosolimitana*. For discussion of the manuscript, see Biddlecombe, Introduction to BB, lxxix–lxxx.

[19] Lobrichon, "The Early Schools," 552.
[20] Natalia Lozovsky, *"The Earth is Our Book": Geographical Knowledge in the Latin West, ca. 400–1000* (Ann Arbor, 2000), 33–35 (quoting 35).

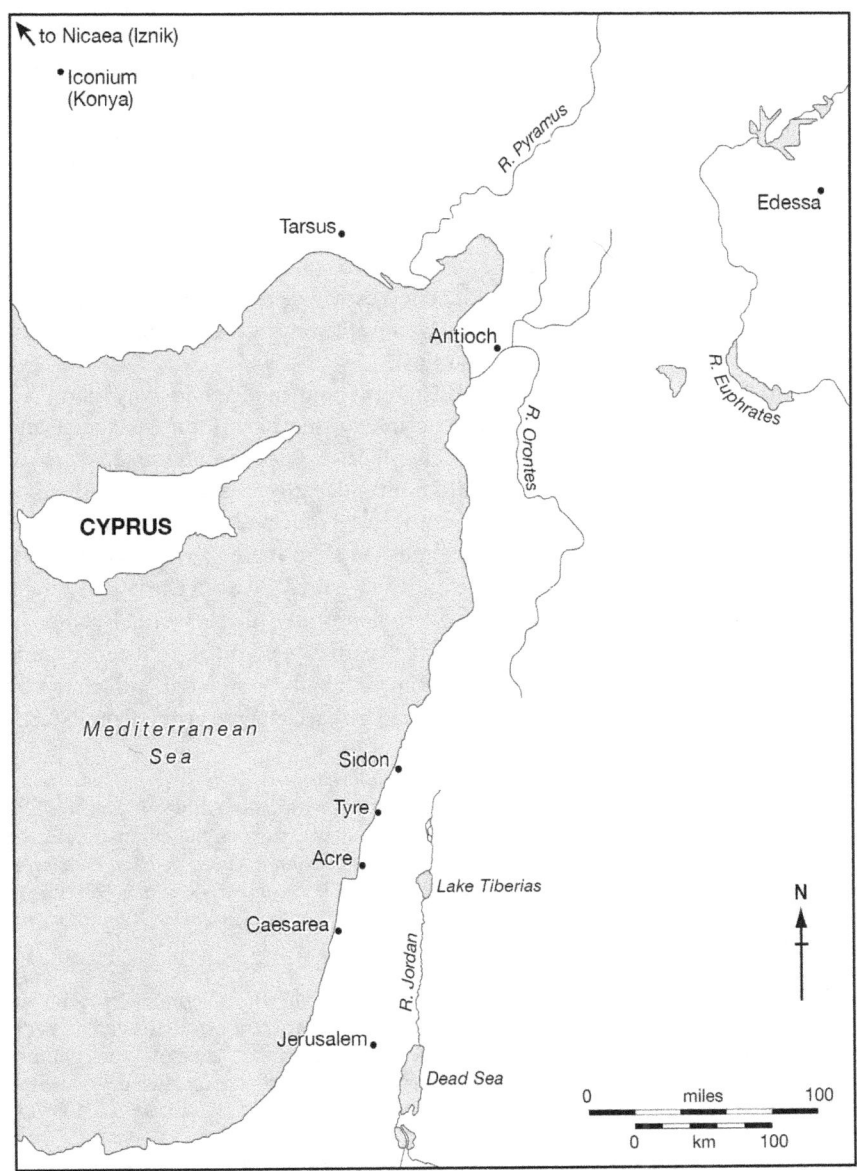

Key places mentioned in early crusade narratives.

readings of Scripture that were becoming more popular in the early twelfth century.[21] These connections strongly inform early crusading narratives, whose authors viewed the landscapes and peoples of the East through a biblical-patristic textual lens, and used the events of 1095–99 as the basis for itineraries that encouraged readers to relive the Jerusalemites' journey. In addition to encouraging personal spiritual reflection on the crusade, such itineraries participated in a larger ideological project: the assertion of the Levant and its sacred sites as rightful Latin patrimony against the competing claims of other faiths. This was hardly a new agenda; from Constantine's day to the eleventh century, the Roman Church had articulated its right to the terrestrial Promised Land, and to Jerusalem itself, via architecture, pilgrimage, relic translations, and biblical commentary.[22] The mapping of the First Crusade onto a biblical landscape, and the typological association of the crusaders with biblical heroes whose actions had sacralized the Levant, directly supported this agenda, even as the crusaders' victories gave new weight to Latin territorial claims in the East.

When the crusaders crossed the Bosphorus and made their way into Asia Minor, they entered a land almost indescribably rich in scriptural associations. In the words of Baldric of Bourgueil, here "there is not even a footstep (*passus*) that the body or spirit of the Savior did not render glorious and blessed; which embraced the holy presence of the mother of God, and the meetings of the apostles, and drank up the blood of the martyrs shed there."[23] The desire to see and touch the holy places was unbearably strong for Latin Christians,[24] and the pilgrimage experience could be overwhelming – these were, Fulcher of Chartres reminded readers, "the very lands" of the "Israelites, Maccabees, and other chosen peoples (*praerogativae*) whom God had illuminated with abundant great miracles."[25] As they retraced the crusaders' two-year journey from Nicaea

---

[21] Lozovsky, "*The Earth is Our Book*," 47–49. Later historical readings of Scripture, of course, drew inspiration from much earlier precedents, such as the commentaries on Genesis by Jerome and Bede; see Jerome, *Hebraicae quaestiones in libro Geneseos*, ed. P. de Lagarde, CCSL 72 (Turnhout: Brepols, 1959); and Bede, *Libri Quatuor in principium Genesim ad Nativitatem Isaac et Eiectionem Ismahelis Adnotationum*, CSEL 118A, ed. C. W. Jones (Turnhout, 1967).

[22] Gabriele, *An Empire of Memory*, 73–93.

[23] This passage comes from Baldric's version of Urban II's Clermont speech; see BB, 8: "Quam terram merito sanctam dixerimus, in qua non est etiam passus pedis quem non illustrauerit et sanctificauerit uel corpus uel umbra saluatoris, uel gloriosa presentia sancte Dei genetricis, uel amplectendus apostolorum comeatus, uel martirum ebibendus sanguis effusus." Trans. Krey, ed. Peters, *The First Crusade*, 31. Cf. GN, 111–12.

[24] An especially poignant illustration is Guibert of Nogent's description of the crusaders' feelings upon finally reaching Jerusalem; see GN, 270.

[25] FC, 116–17: "Licet autem nec Israeliticae plebis nec Machabaeorum aut aliorum praerogativae, quos Deus tam crebris et magnificis miraculis inlustravit … ."

to Jerusalem, twelfth-century narrators used the Scriptures to map the holy war onto the biblical geography of the Near East (a region most of them had never visited), underscoring the status of the crusaders as pilgrims and reinforcing the symbolic connections between their venture and the wanderings, conquests, and miracles which had marked these same sites as sacred long before the Latins' arrival. In so doing, chroniclers laid claim to this long, sacred history and carved out a place for the first crusaders – and, indirectly, for themselves and their imagined readers – within its course.

The chroniclers were well aware of the historical associations of Nicaea – the first target of the crusade – with early Christianity, and of its status for much of its existence as "a most firm stronghold of the Catholic faith (*catholice fidei turrim firmissimam*)."[26] A decade after the city's capture by a Byzantine-crusader force in June 1097, Guibert of Nogent reminded his readers that Nicaea was "famous for the synod of 318 fathers [that is, the Council of Nicaea in 325], but even more famous for the declaration of Homousion, and the condemnation of Arius," through which the early Church had first defined a unified theological front against heresy.[27] Robert of Reims went further, offering a typological comparison between the purging of heresy from the Constantinian church in 325 and the Latins' conquest of the city in 1097. As he wrote, "it was highly appropriate that it should be wrested from the enemies of the Holy Faith, reconciled to God and returned to our Mother Church like a limb being restored."[28] Such interpretations reflect the chroniclers' conviction that the crusading enterprise had a preordained role to play in the longer narrative of Christian history and eschatology, in which struggle for control of the Holy Land was a major theme. Further, it is clear that Robert and his contemporaries regarded the first crusaders' achievements not only as military conquests but as triumphs of orthodoxy over unbelief.[29] In this sense, too, the Jerusalemites were participants in a drama much bigger than themselves.

As the main crusading force made its way across Anatolia, smaller contingents broke off and conquered several towns in Cilicia and Northern Mesopotamia, including important centers of early Christianity. Iconium, which the main army briefly garrisoned in August 1097, was recognized as a site mentioned in the New Testament (2 Tim. 3:11, Acts 14:1–5, 21).[30] Soon after, Norman knights led by

---

[26] FE, 134.
[27] GN, 145; trans. 62. Cf. CP, 38.
[28] RR, 24: "Et ob hoc dignum erat ut inimicis sancte fidei auferetur, et deo reconciliaretur, et sancte matri nostre ecclesie ut membrum suum redintegraretur." Trans. 106–7. This sentiment is echoed by CP, 70.
[29] The spread of orthodoxy entailed, of course, the promotion of the Roman church's interests over those of competing Christian traditions, including the Byzantines. This is evident from the dismay of Latin chroniclers over the cessation of Nicaea to the Greeks; e.g., RA, 44.
[30] RR, 31.

Tancred of Hauteville seized Tarsus, well known to Christians as the birthplace and, in William of Malmesbury's words, "the nurse of the Apostle Paul" (cf. Acts 9:11, 30; 21:39; 22:3).[31] Baldwin of Boulogne's 1098 conquest of Edessa brought under Latin rule a city which had been one of the earliest centers of Christianity and was home to the famed Holy Mandylion, a divinely produced portrait of Christ. In a commentary that expressed the dominant Latin view of all of these victories, Orderic Vitalis wrote that whereas Eastern Christians had lost the city to the Turks "as a penalty for their sins" (*peccatis exigentibus*), under crusader rule "the divine cult was magnificently restored in Edessa and divine compassion worked miraculously in the hearts and deeds of God's people."[32] As with the conquest of Nicaea, the crusaders' subsequent victories could be glossed on multiple levels: as the preordained reclamation of rightfully Christian territory, and as signs of divine approval of the holy war, which was accorded a privileged place within the sacred history of the East.

When the crusaders arrived outside the walls of Antioch in the autumn of 1097 they saw not merely a formidable military target but a holy site rich in associations with the ancient Israelites[33] and early Christianity. This was the city of Saint Peter, widely believed to have been the first bishop of Antioch, who, in the words of Fulcher of Chartres, "sat on the throne here after he had received dominion of the Church and the keys of the Kingdom of Heaven from the Lord Jesus."[34] Here, too, several chronicles noted, the apostles Paul and Barnabas had preached (Acts 13:14–46), and "the sacred name of Christian was first invented" (Acts 11:26).[35] Having captured the city, the victorious crusaders reflected that these past events, which had made Antioch "the first leading city of the Christian name," had also marked the city as their rightful future patrimony, and even invited Pope Urban II to come and take possession of "the place of [his] fatherhood, and as victor of Saint Peter to sit on his throne ... eradicating and destroying all types of heresy."[36] The comment in the *Gesta Francorum* that Christ had "handed over the city to Blessed Peter, prince of the apostles, so that he might recover it for the worship of

---

[31] WM, 1:660.
[32] OV, 5:120 (for the Turkish conquest as divine chastisement), and 126: "Diuinae seruitutis series insigniter Edessae restaurata est et multo plus incomparabiliter quam stilus noster annotare potest, diuina pietas in populo suo mirabiliter intus et exterius operata est."
[33] These (and corresponding Old Testament references) are enumerated by CP, 96.
[34] FC, 217: "Estque in ea basilica una satis veneranda, in honore Petri apostoli dedicata, ubi in episcopum sublimatus sedit in cathedra, postquam a Domino Jesu principatum ecclesiae, clavibus acceptis regni caelestis, suscepit." Trans. 71. Cf. OV, 5:68.
[35] See Acts 11 and 13. WM, 1:632. Cf. BB, 38; RR, 34; and CP, 96.
[36] EP, no. 16, p. 164: "et qui beati Petri es uicarius, in cathedra eius sedeas et nos filios tuos in omnibus recte agendis oboedientes habeas, et omnes haereses, cuiuscumque generis sint, tua auctoritate et nostra uirtute eradices et destruas." Trans. 32–33.

the true faith" is suggestive of the chroniclers' typological understanding of this conquest; just as, with Christ's help, Saint Peter had first won the city for the true faith, so had the crusaders recaptured Antioch in the name of Christ and Peter's direct successor, the pope.[37] Here again, the crusade is envisioned as a means of extending the interests of the Roman church, a project that entailed not only the founding of a network of new Latin bishoprics throughout the Levant[38] but the retroactive 'Latinizing' of biblical figures.

In their final push to reach Jerusalem in the late spring of 1099, the crusading army marched past the great ancient cities of the Mediterranean littoral, including Tripoli, Sidon, Sarepta, Tyre, and Acre, finally reaching Caesarea on Pentecost (29 May). Gilo of Paris noted the significance of the date in a typological aside: as once before "the Lord granted to his disciples the power to do all things, that left the world amazed at the new gifts," now again he had bestowed his favor upon a new generation of disciples.[39] Although in actuality the pilgrims kept up a brisk pace that left little time for religious tourism, crusade chroniclers retrospectively located this region's landmarks within a familiar biblical framework. Fulcher of Chartres described how, early in 1099, the pilgrims reached "the stronghold of Arqa, situated at the foot of Mount Lebanon, which, as we read (*ut legitur*), was founded by Aracaeus, the son of Canaan, the nephew of Noah (Gen. 10:15–17)."[40] Guibert noted that Sarepta, which the crusaders reached in spring, was the site of a miracle performed by the prophet Elijah (1 Kgs. 17:9–24),[41] while other chroniclers (mistakenly) identified Acre as the Philistine city of Ekron,[42] recognized Sidon and Tyre as sites mentioned in the Gospels (Mat. 15:21),[43] and recalled the wonders worked by the apostles Peter, Paul, and Philip at Caesarea (Acts 10, 12, 21).[44]

By the time the crusaders arrived at the outskirts of Jerusalem the holy places had become so plentiful that hardly a hillock or crumbled wall lacked significance. Reaching this point in their narrative, Latin chroniclers breathlessly listed

---

[37] GF, 27: "dominus Iesus Christus tradidit beato Petro apostolorum principi, quatinus eam ad cultum (*culturam* – Monte Cassino) sanctae fidei reuocaret ... ." The comment is repeated verbatim by PT, 62–63 and MC, 37–38.

[38] This process is thoroughly documented by Bernard Hamilton, *The Latin Church in the Crusader States: The Secular Church* (London, 1980).

[39] GP, 234–35: "In quo discipulis Dominus dedit omnia posse, / Vsus iure suo, mundo noua dona stupente."

[40] FC, 268–69.

[41] GN, 269.

[42] The city is mentioned in Josh. 13:2–3, 13, 19:43; 1 Sam. 5:10, 6:1–8, and 2 Kgs. 1:2. For the mis-identification, see AA, 394; for the correction, see FC, 268–69.

[43] FC, 272–74.

[44] RR, 94. In his description of the Genoese siege of Caesarea in 1101, an event in which he participated, Caffaro di Rustico da Caschifellone similarly emphasized the city's status as a cradle of apostolic preaching; see *De liberatione civitatum orientis*, c. 15, RHC Oc. 5:62–63.

all of the sacred sites and their biblical associations.⁴⁵ For these men, even those without firsthand experience of the East, Jerusalem's history was as familiar as those of their own communities, and they eagerly sought to situate the crusade within the city's story. Robert of Reims bookended his précis of Jerusalem's history with two typologically linked events: the city's foundation by the priest-king Melchizedek (Gen. 14:18, 33:18) and the arrival of the crusaders, whom God had "led ... from the ends of the earth with the intention that they should free her [i.e., Jerusalem] from the filthy Gentiles" and re-found the city as a Christian site.⁴⁶ For the crusaders, as for countless generations of Christian pilgrims, Jerusalem was also a stage for the reenactment of Christ's Passion. According to Ralph of Caen, when Tancred de Hauteville first saw the holy city, he "fixed ... his heart on heaven" and meditated on the Passion, resolving to imitate Christ's sacrifice by giving up his own life "if he might be permitted to kiss the base of Calvary."⁴⁷ After camping outside the city walls, Raymond of Aguilers reported, some pilgrims "went down to the plain of Jordan, and gathered palms [traditional pilgrims' souvenirs], and were baptized in the River Jordan," in an unambiguous act of *imitatio Christi*.⁴⁸ In the days before the final assault, the crusaders continued to follow in Christ's footsteps as they processed up the Mount of Olives, the site of the ascension, where a cleric "preached a sermon elaborating on the mercy which God would bestow upon Christians who followed him even to his grave, from which he mounted to heaven."⁴⁹ When describing how the army's contingents erected siege-works at strategic points along the city's walls, chroniclers again took pains to align their actions with Jerusalem's sacred history and geography. Guibert of Nogent described how,

> From the north, Count Robert of Normandy laid siege to it, near the church of the blessed Saint Stephen, who, because he said that he had seen the son of man standing at the right hand of God, was covered with a rain of stones by the Jews (Acts 7). ... From the south, the count of Saint-Gilles laid siege, on the mount

---

⁴⁵ E.g., RA, 138–40.

⁴⁶ RR, 110: "Cum autem ipsi Domino placuit, adduxit Francigenam gentem ab extremis terre, et per eam ab immundis gentilibus liberare illam voluit." Trans. 212–14.

⁴⁷ RC, 95: "Ad haec suspirans, ad haec conquiniscens: illa euum pro luce pasisci cuperet, si quando, cuius prospectabat fastigia, liceat sibi Caluariae osculari uestigia!" Trans. 129–30. For a more skeptical view of Tancred's piety, see RA, 143.

⁴⁸ The baptism of Christ is described in Mat. 3:13–17, Mk. 1:9–11, and Lk. 3:21–22. See RA, 153; and FC, 333–34, for the report that other pilgrims followed suit after the city had been taken.

⁴⁹ PT, 137–38: "Et ibi suum sermonem fecit quidam honestissimus clericus, scilicet Arnulfus, ostendendo misericordiam quam Deus Christianis fecerat, qui secuti sunt eum usque ad lapidem illum ex quo ascendit in celum." Trans. 116. Cf. RA, 145; and AA, 412–14. OV, 5:164 adds the detail of the preachers pointing with their fingers to the locations of different events from the Passion.

of Zion, near the church of the blessed Mary, mother of God, where the Lord is said to have sat at dinner with his disciples on the day before his Passion (Mat. 26, Mk. 14, Lk. 22, Jn. 13).[50]

In the bloody fighting for the city, the crusaders symbolically reenacted the long-ago events of the Passion; as they strove to take the city from its Fatimid defenders, Baldric of Bourgueil wrote, each fighter became another Joseph of Arimathea, taking down Christ's body from the cross.[51] For Guibert of Nogent, the conquest was like an act of communion, a reverent consumption of Christ's body by a new generation of disciples.[52]

In their efforts to orient the crusaders geographically, historically, and typologically, Latin narrators drew heavily on the Scriptures, especially the historical books of the Old Testament, the Gospels, and Acts of the Apostles. But they also found inspiration in scripturally oriented pilgrimage literature, in particular the firsthand pilgrimage accounts (*peregrinationes*) and guidebooks (*itineraria*) to the Holy Land that widely circulated in the eleventh and twelfth centuries.[53] For instance, William of Malmesbury, who never traveled east, professed his reliance on "an abundance of authorities" (*copia scriptorum*), including the well-known Carolingian itinerary of Bernard the Monk, for descriptions of Jerusalem.[54] There are many indications that other narrators of the crusade wrote under the influence of these genres, and that accounts of the Jerusalem journey reminded medieval readers and copyists of traditional pilgrimage narratives – or were even meant to serve, simultaneously, as both histories and itineraries. The monk Ekkehard of Aura offered his *Hierosolimita* as a history-cum-guidebook to Abbot Erkembert of Corvey, who undertook a pilgrimage to the Holy Land in 1117.[55] Other early crusade narratives were copied under titles reflecting their association with pilgrims' handbooks; for example, as Samu

---

[50] GN, 270: "A septentrionali igitur plaga comes eam Robertus obsederat Northmannorum, iuxta eam Beati Stephani aecclesiam, ubi propter Filium hominis, quem a dextris dei se vidisse clamaverat stantem, a Iudeis est obrutus imbre saxorum. ... a meridie obsedit eam comes Sancti Egidii, in Monte videlicet Syon circa aecclesiam Beatae Mariae genitricis domini, ubi dominus cum suis ad cenam pridie quam pateretur fertur discubuisse discipulis." Trans. 126. Cf. RR, 96; BB, 104; and OV, 5:156.
[51] BB, 108.
[52] To make this point, Guibert christologically reframes a quotation from Ps. 23:30: "De qua, sicut de domimici corporis mansoribus legiture quia *comederunt et adoraverunt*, ita de his dici potest: 'adoraverunt eam et expugnaverunt.'" GN, 270.
[53] On the characteristics of these texts and their connections with other medieval genres, see Jean Richard, *Les récits de voyages et de pèlerinages*, Typologie des sources du Moyen Age occidental 38 (Turnhout, 1981), 23–25, 39–40.
[54] WM, 1:640–42.
[55] McCarthy, *The Continuations of Frutolf of Michelsberg's Chronicle*, 2, 241; and see Ekkehard's dedicatory letter to Abbot Erkembert, *Chronica*, prol., ed. G. Waitz, MGH SS 6 (Hannover, 1884), 1–11.

Niskansen observes, what we call the *Gesta Francorum* is in several manuscripts labeled "the Jerusalemites' itinerary" (*Itinerarium Hierosolimitanorum*), a title that "is demonstrably earlier and, therefore, potentially more authentic than the one favored by the *Gesta Francorum*'s modern editors."[56] A similar conclusion may be drawn about Peter Tudebode's closely related work, called "the Jerusalem journey" (*Hierosolymitano itinere*) in several twelfth-century manuscripts.[57] The titles of other chronicles signaled their geographical orientation through their incorporation of words like *via* ("way" or "route") and *expeditio* ("expedition" or "campaign"), as well as their emphasis on Jerusalem as the pilgrims' goal.[58] Medieval scribes also copied narratives of the First Crusade alongside Holy Land itineraries, as well as devotional texts set in, or focused upon, the holy places of the East.[59]

Early medieval pilgrimage literature is characterized by what Ora Limor calls "a deep religious aura, a lack of interest in the present, and casualness about space and time (unless it is sacred space and sacred time)."[60] Likewise, in early crusading narratives time and space have an elastic quality; distances expand and contract in a way befitting a journey that was as much spiritual as physical, while time is as likely to unfold typologically as in linear fashion. As in contemporary guides to the Holy Land, in crusade chronicles the Jerusalemites move through a landscape where time has slowed almost to a standstill. So deeply have the events of the biblical age impressed the topography of the Levant that history cannot seem to move on; instead, the crusaders, like early generations of Holy Land

---

[56] Niskansen, "The Origins of the *Gesta Francorum*," 298.

[57] Keskiaho, "On the Transmission of Peter Tudebode's *De Hierosolymitano Itinere*," 74–75.

[58] The anonymous Monte Cassino chronicle is titled *Hystoria de via et recuperatione Antiochiae atque Ierusolymarum*; the first lines of Albert of Aachen's narrative present his work as "De via et expeditione Ierusalem" (AA, 2); the works of Fulcher of Chartres, Robert of Reims, and Baldric of Bourgueil circulated under the title *Historia Iherosolimitana*; the composite text by Gilo of Paris and the Charleville Poet is known as the *Historia de vie Hierosolimitane*. The twelfth-century crusade compilation in Bibliothèque de l'Arsenal, ms. latin 1102 also identifies this last work as a "liber super Jherosolimitana expeditione factus" (fol. 1r).

[59] In addition to the Maillezais collection described above at n. 3, examples include three mss. of Robert of Reims' *Historia* which were copied with two topographical works written in the wake of the First Crusade, the anonymous *De situ urbis Ierusalem* and Rorgo Fretellus's *Descriptio locorum* (see Kempf and Bull's Introduction to RR, xliii); the sole ms. of the Monte Cassino Anonymous, which also contains the *Evangelium Nicodemi* and *Gesta Pilati* (see D'Angelo's editorial comments at MC, xiv); and a ms. of Baldric of Bourgueil's *Historia*, Paris, Bibliothèque nationale ms. latin 5134, which contains the late antique *Cena Cypriani*, an anonymous allegorical retelling of the wedding at Cana. See, too, the comments by Rubenstein, *Nebuchadnezzar's Dream*, 53, and examples at 233, nn. 14–15.

[60] Ora Limor, "Early Pilgrimage Itineraries (333–1099)," in *The Encyclopedia of Medieval Pilgrimage*, ed. Larissa J. Taylor et al. (Leiden, 2010), 170.

pilgrims, are themselves drawn into the biblical narratives. At the same time, the Jerusalemites' victories led to profound changes in the sacred geographies of the East, as evidenced by new building programs in conquered cities and a proliferation of new itineraries aimed at Latin pilgrims.[61] Such initiatives reflected Christian rulers' conviction that God had collectively entrusted adherents of the Latin Church, as he had once entrusted the Israelite conquerors of Canaan, with a vast store of sacred treasure that demanded to be exalted and defended.[62]

Pilgrimage literature offered models for how to orient the first crusaders within the sacred space of the East. Early medieval guidebooks to the Holy Land were organized spatially, allowing pilgrims to follow established routes, and entries combined topographical descriptions with historical background and information on local shrines. The following entry, a description of the biblical site of Jericho from Bede's enormously popular *De locis sanctis*, is typical:

> Jericho lies to the east of Aelia [Jerusalem] at a distance of eighteen miles. It was three times razed to the ground and only the House of Rahab (Josh. 2:1–6) remains as a sign of faith: the walls of her house are still there, but it has no roof. The site of the city is planted with wheat and vines. Between this and the Jordan, a distance of five or six miles, there are large palm-groves separated by small fields. The inhabitants are Canaanites. The twelve stones which Joshua commanded to be taken from the Jordan lie beside the walls on each side of the church erected at Gilgal (Josh. 4:20). ... Beside Jericho is a spring of plentiful drinking water which provides a good supply for irrigation. Once this had been fatal to growth and unhealthy for drinking, until the prophet Elisha purified it by putting in a bowl of salt (4 Kgs. 2:21).[63]

---

[61] Morris, *The Sepulchre of Christ*, 183–97.

[62] For insights into the spiritual climate of the twelfth-century Levant, see Brett E. Whalen, "The Discovery of the Holy Patriarchs: Relics, Ecclesiastical Politics, and Sacred History in Twelfth-Century Crusader Palestine," *Historical Reflections / Réflections Historiques* 27 (2001): 139–76 (esp. 154–56).

[63] Bede, *De locis sanctis*, 9.1–2, ed. J. Fraipont, in *Itineraria et alia geographica*, ed. Ezio Franceschini and Robert Weber, CCSL 175 (Turnhout, 1965), 267: "Hiericho ab Aelia orientem versus novemdecim mille passibus abest, qua tertio ad solum destructa, sola domus Raab ob signum fidei remanet: ejus enim adhuc parietes sine culmine durant. Locus urbis segetes et vineas recipit. Inter hanc et Jordanem, quinque vel sex ab ea millibus separatum, grandia sunt palmeta campulis interpositis et inhabitatoribus Chananaeis. Duodecim lapides, quos Josue de Jordane tolli praeceperat, in ecclesia Galgalis facta altrinsecus juxta parietes ejusdem jacent ... Est juxta Hiericho fons uber ad potum, pinguis ad irrigandum; qui quondam sterilis ad geuerandum, parum salubris ad potandum, per Elisaeum prophetam dum vas salis in eum mitteret, sanatus est." Trans. John Wilkinson, *Jerusalem Pilgrims Before the Crusades* (Warminster, 2002), 224.

Compare the following description of Caesarea from Robert of Reims's crusade chronicle:

> Caesarea is a famous city of Palestine, reputed to be the home of the apostle Philip: the house is still shown today, as is the bedroom of his daughters, who had the gift of prophecy (Acts 21:9). The city is on the coast and used to be called Pyrgos, or 'the Tower of Strato.' It was made more magnificent and beautiful by King Herod, who improved the sea defences; and it was named Caesarea in honor of Augustus Caesar. Herod constructed a temple to him in white marble: it was here that his nephew Herod was struck by the angel (Acts 12:23), Cornelius the centurion was baptized (Acts 10), and Agabus the prophet was tied by Paul's belt (Acts 21:11).[64]

The similarities here are striking. Not only do both authors convey the same sort of information – information chosen to appeal to a very specific group, pilgrims – but they display a similar attitude toward time. Bede, who was keenly interested in scriptural history, represents the actions of Joshua and Elisha to the reader as though they had just happened;[65] likewise, Robert's presentation minimizes the distance between the biblical then and the twelfth-century now. The crusaders walk in the footsteps of the earliest Christians and, indeed, it seems that their biblical predecessors have never left the scene. Further, such a narrative strategy has the effect of eliding the post-biblical history of the Levantine holy places, effectively erasing centuries of rule by Muslims (rendered as Canaanites by Bede, who anticipates a connection made by crusade chroniclers).

A pilgrimage guide-like sensibility pervades the lengthy descriptions of Antioch found in early crusading narratives. Unlike Jerusalem, Antioch was, for early medieval pilgrims, a waystation that generated little spiritual excitement, despite its biblical associations and prominence in the early church.[66] As

---

[64] RR, 94: "Est autem Cesarea insignis civitas Palestine, in qua Philippus apostolus dicitur domum habuisse, que usque hodie monstratur, nec non et cubiculum filiarum eius virginum prophetantium. Est autem in litore maris sita, olim Birgos, id est Turris Stratonis, appellata. Sed ab Herode rege nobilius et pulchrius contra vim maris utilius extructa, in honorem Cesaris Augusti Cesarea est cognominata; cui etiam in ea templum albo marmare construxit, in quo nepos eius Herodes est ab angelo percussus, Cornelio centurio baptizatus, et Agabus propheta zona Pauli est ligatus." Trans. 194. Cf. the descriptions of Ramlah by BB, 102; and WM, 1:640. Here Robert evidently confuses the coastal city of Caesarea Maritima with the inland city of Banias, also known as Caesarea Philippi (which the first crusaders did not visit); the latter was also believed to be the site of an important miracle, Christ's healing of the bleeding woman (Mat. 9:20–22; Mk. 5:25–34; Lk. 8:43–48); on Banias, see Wilkinson, *Jerusalem Pilgrims*, 336–37.

[65] Ray, "Bede, the Exegete," 125–26.

[66] E.g., Theodosius, *The Topography of the Holy Land*, c.32b; and the itinary of the Piacenza Pilgrim, c.46, in *Jerusalem Pilgrims*, ed. Wilkinson, 116, 150.

the crucible of the First Crusade, however, it became worthy of extensive topographical and historical descriptions, as well as gazetteers of the city's holy sites.[67] Had they consulted early medieval Latin itineraries of the East, the chroniclers would have found little useful information on Antioch, though a description of the city's dramatic topography and defenses, along with snippets of its history, could be found in the popular Pseudo-Ambrosian treatise *De excidio urbis Hierosolymitanae*.[68] The crusade's apologists looked instead to the Scriptures and eyewitness accounts to situate Antioch on the spiritual map. Peter Tudebode boasted of Antioch's 1,200 churches and 360 monasteries, while Fulcher of Chartres singled out for praise the church dedicated to Saint Peter, with the apostle's throne-relic, and the rotunda of the Virgin Mary.[69] "Although these had long been under the Turks," Fulcher added, "God, knowing all things beforehand, saved them intact for us so that they might be properly venerated in our time."[70] The crusaders' discovery of the controversial relic of the Holy Lance in the basilica of Saint Peter further cemented Antioch's place in the sacred geography of the Levant.[71] While acknowledging the Turkish occupation, such stories diminish its importance by denying the Turks power over Antioch's shrines,[72] and emphasize the direct link between the apostolic age – via its perfectly preserved churches and relics – and the Jerusalemites. A similar strategy was employed by the Charleville Poet, whose

---

[67] Crusader-era descriptions of Antioch are reviewed by Krijnie Ciggaar, "Antioche: Les sources croisées et le plan de la ville," in *Les sources de l'histoire du paysage urbain d'Antioche sur l'Oronte: Actes des journées d'études des 20 et 21 septembre 2010 à l'Université de Paris-8* (Paris, 2010), 223–34.

[68] The descriptions of Antioch by Raymond of Aguilers (RA, 47–48) and the *Gesta Francorum* Anonymous (GF, 76–77) may have been informed by the *De excidio* (3.5, PL 15: 2175), as suggested by John and Laurita Hill in their translation of Peter Tudebode, *Historia*, 96 n. 24. The treatise, however, omits any description of the city's buildings or cultic geography. Cf. the description by RC, 47–48.

[69] Peter Tudebode's account (PT, 119–20) is an elaboration of GF, 76–77; cf. MC, 38–39. (Guibert of Nogent rephrased the *Gesta* to indicate Antioch had a mere 360 churches; GN, 249.) FC, 217–18.

[70] FC, 218: "Quae quamvis sub potestate Turcorum diu exstiterant, Deus tamen cuncta praesciens nobis eas integras reservavit, ut quandoque a nobis in eis honorificaretur." William of Malmesbury, who used Fulcher's *Historia* as his main source on the crusade, went a step further, suggesting that the church of the Virgin "exercised its beauty such a sway over the eyes of the beholder that, strange to relate, the Turks revered the shrine of her whose faith they persecuted." WM, 1:633.

[71] On this famous incident, see Thomas Asbridge, "The Holy Lance of Antioch: Power, Devotion and Memory on the First Crusade," *Reading Medieval Studies* 33 (2007): 3–36.

[72] There is a tension here between the wish to emphasize God's power to restrain Muslims and the anxiety about threatened harm to Christian sanctuaries and bodies which permeates many crusade narratives; e.g., EP, no. 16, p. 177.

work, in the manner of an *itinerarium*, traces Antioch's history from Moses' time to the present, collapsing the centuries between Saint Peter's tenure and the crusaders' arrival:

> [Antioch] ranked third among the great cities until the Byzantine empire took its strength. It was also among the first to take up the marks of Christ, since the use of the name 'Christian' first began here. Here too the apostolic seat flourished under Saint Peter, before ... [being assumed? ms. damaged] by Rome. And so the armies of Christ, grieving that it was so wickedly profaned (*profanatam male*), came in great numbers to recapture it for Christ.[73]

Like the examples above, this description affects a timeslip, so that the crusaders seem to arrive at Antioch on the heels of Saint Peter, while the poet avoids any direct reference to the Turkish rulers, focusing instead on the city's suffering. Such an elision, paired with the suggestion that the Byzantines bore responsibility for Antioch's decline, bolsters the Charleville Poet's presentation of the crusaders as the city's saviors and rightful heirs.

The endpoint of the crusaders' journey, Jerusalem, was the focus of numerous early medieval guidebooks, whose authors had confronted the same challenge now facing narrators of the crusade: how to do justice to the innumerable holy sites crammed inside the city's walls? While some writers, like Raymond of Aguilers, interspersed hurried sketches of the holy sites with descriptions of strategy and siege-works,[74] others included fuller pilgrimage itineraries within their accounts of the 1099 conquest. Both Ralph of Caen, who wrote while living in Jerusalem in the second decade of the twelfth century,[75] and Fulcher of Chartres, who gained an intimate knowledge of Jerusalem in later life,[76] created detailed visual maps of the city's holy sites. The *Descriptio sanctorum locorum Hierusalem*, which medieval readers encountered as an appendix to the *Gesta Francorum* and Peter Tudebode's history, offered an even more comprehensive guide to the holy city and its environs. Unsurprisingly, given that it is modeled

---

[73] CP, 96–97: "Tercia maiores inter fuit hec prius urbes / Quam res acciperet Byzantica [tollere] uires. / Haec etiam Christi in primis insignia sumpsit / Christocolum nomen quando hic primordia coepit. / Hic et apostolica Petro residente cathedra / Floruit ante foret quam ... . pre ... a Roma. / Ergo profanatam male Christi turma dolentes / Ad recoaptandam Christo uenere frequentes." The poet indicates that his information on the city derives from the works of "many notable historians" (*nobilium complures hystoricorum*); CP, 94.

[74] RA, 138–39.

[75] Bachrach and Bachrach, Introduction to *The Gesta Tancredi*, 4.

[76] Fulcher may have been a canon of the Holy Sepulcher; see Marcus Bull, "Fulcher of Chartres," in *Christian–Muslim Relations: A Bibliographical History, Vol. 3: 1050–1200*, ed. David Thomas and Alex Mallett (Leiden, 2009), 402–3.

on a fourth-century Holy Land itinerary,[77] the *Descriptio* bears the hallmarks of a guidebook: a spatial ordering of landmarks, precisely measured distances between shrines, observations on the present-day uses of each site, and employment of the second-person 'you' as a means of drawing readers into the cultic landscape. Similar concerns inform Fulcher and Ralph's narratives. Ralph invites readers to undertake a circuit (*ambitus*) of Jerusalem's ancient walls, pausing to notice their irregularities and take in various vistas: Galilee to the north, the Tower of David adjoining the western wall, the Mount of Olives east of the city. Concerned to "follow things in order" (*ut rem ordine prosequar*), Ralph describes the holy sites of the Mount of Olives together, as he does the cluster of structures on the Temple Mount.[78] In his virtual tour of Jerusalem, Fulcher specifies distances between holy sites, as measured in bowshots (*quantum iactus est arcus*), a unit used nowhere else in Fulcher's *Historia* but employed by early medieval pilgrimage guides.[79] Fulcher's descriptions of the architecture, biblical pedigrees, and treasures of the *Templum Domini* (the Dome of the Rock) and Temple of Solomon (the al-Aqsa mosque) are also reminiscent of earlier Holy Land itineraries.[80] Given this, it is easy to imagine why the twelfth-century scribes at the abbey of Saint-Bertin were inspired to create a detailed map of Jerusalem's holy sites to accompany this section of Fulcher's *Historia Iherosolymitana*. Here, again, in Jay Rubenstein's words, "Crusade and travel narrative blended together into a single project aimed at uncovering mysteries and bringing the activity of man more into concert with the designs of God."[81]

The deep concern with sacred geography and history visible throughout these narratives reflects the authors' desire to underscore the crusaders' status as pilgrims, while also asserting the justness of their military conquests and the legitimacy of the new polities founded in the East, and eliding or condemning Muslim rule. Adding a new typological layer to the Holy Land's thick historical strata, the chroniclers suggested that the crusaders' sufferings and triumphs had enhanced the sanctity of the East, in the process creating a new *iter* with its own sacred landmarks for future pilgrims to follow. For clerical writers who approached the crusade as a text to be glossed, the narrative mapping of the expedition onto the

---

[77] For commentary on this text and its connection to the account of the Bordeaux Pilgrim, see Keskiaho, "The Transmission of Peter Tudebode's *De Hierosolymitano itinere*," 73–74.

[78] RC, 95 (on the Temple Mount) and 97.

[79] FC, 282–83. Cf., for example, the sixth-century Piacenza Pilgrim's use of this measurement; *Pseudo Antonini Placentini Itinerarium*, c.25, ed. Paul Geyer in *Itineraria et alia geographica*, ed. Franceschini et al., 142. For a somewhat different reading of Fulcher, see Cole, "Theme of Religious Pollution," 90.

[80] FC, 285–91. For a fuller discussion of the crusaders' responses to these sites, see Chapter 4.

[81] Rubenstein, *Nebuchadnezzar's Dream*, 50–55 (quoting 53).

scriptural landscape entailed a virtual pilgrimage that they performed themselves and invited readers to undertake. As Ralph of Caen explained, "Since it is not possible to nourish (*pascere*) the [reader's] eyes because of the distance, the [material] transmitted by hand and absorbed by the ears at least may nourish the soul."[82] Virtual pilgrimages had a long history in the Latin West, where a variety of devotional aids – including replicas of the Holy Sepulcher, detailed *mappae mundi*, geographical treatises, and devotional texts – were available to those unable to travel to the Holy Land in the flesh.[83] Indeed, as Daniel Connolly has shown, foundational works of monastic spirituality encouraged this sort of "translocative thinking," whereby cloistered men and women undertook virtual pilgrimages without compromising their vows of stability.[84] The First Crusade's chroniclers participated in this tradition, offering readers on the home front not only detailed accounts of the Jerusalem journey but a means of vicarious participation. But whereas such virtual crusading entailed crossing vast distances in the spirit, those who actually answered the pope's call to arms were seen to have undertaken an equally impressive virtual journey, one that took them back through the centuries to a time when the ancient Israelites fought idolatrous tribes for control of the Promised Land.

Crusaders as New Israelites

As the First Crusade's armies starved outside Antioch through the winter of 1097–98, harrassed by the city's Turkish garrison, jolted by an earthquake, and reduced by desertions, clerics tried to bolster morale by maintaining the familiar rhythm of the liturgical calendar and preaching uplifting sermons.[85] While we

---

[82] RC, 97: "ut quorum pascere non ualet oculos propter remotionem, saltem animos iuuet transmissa ad manus et infusa per aurem." Trans. 132. This suggests Ralph assumed that his work would be read aloud.

[83] Recent studies of virtual pilgrimage include: Bianca Kühnel, "Virtual Pilgrimages to Real Places: The Holy Landscapes," in *Imagining Jerusalem in the Medieval West*, ed. Lucy Donkin and Hanna Vorholt (Oxford, 2012), 243–64; Kathryn M. Rudy, *Virtual Pilgrimages in the Convent: Imagining Jerusalem in the Late Middle Ages* (Turnhout, 2011); and Daniel K. Connolly, *The Maps of Matthew Paris: Medieval Journeys through Space, Time, and Liturgy* (Woodbridge, 2009).

[84] Connolly, *The Maps of Matthew Paris*, 30–31. Classic studies of the tension between pilgrimage and the monastic ideal are Jean Leclercq, "Monachisme et pérégrination du IXe au XII siècle," *Studia Monastica* 3 (1961): 33–52; and Giles Constable, "Monachisme et pèlerinage au moyen âge," *Revue historique* 258 (1977): 3–27. William Purkis has shown that many professed religious participated in the First Crusade, ignoring the directives of their superiors and the pope; see *Crusading Spirituality*, 14–15.

[85] Gaposchkin, *Invisible Weapons*, 97–99.

cannot know the preachers' exact words, this is how they were imagined in the crusade's immediate aftermath, in a letter attributed to the crusade's leaders:

> [O]ur spiritual Mother Church cries out, "Come, my most beloved sons, come to me, take away the crown from the sons of idolatry (*idolatriae filii*) who are rising up against me. This crown has been destined for you since the beginning of the world (cf. Mat. 25:34)." ... Come, then: hurry to be paid the double reward, that is, the *land of the living* (Ps. 26:13, Is. 38:11, Jer. 11:19, Ez. 26:20, etc.) and *the land that floweth with milk and honey* (Ex. 3:8, 17, Num. 13:28) and abounding in all things.[86]

This passage neatly encapsulates the typological logic used by the crusade's narrators to justify the Jerusalemites' enterprise: heirs of both Moses and Christ, the crusaders are pitted against Muslim enemies burdened with their own exegetical inheritance derived from biblical paganism. Adopting the close connection between covenant and land – between the 'double reward' of salvation and the terrestrial Promised Land – which they discerned in the Old Testament, Latin chroniclers glossed the crusade as a reprisal of the wanderings and wars which had led the ancient Hebrews to Israel. While this interpretation followed the time-honored Christian practice of reading the Old Testament allegorically, in Latin narratives of the holy war the eerily close resemblance between the accomplishments of the crusaders and those of the ancient Israelites blurred the traditional exegetical boundaries between the *sensus spiritualis* and *sensus literalis*.

While numerous scholars have noted Latin chroniclers' presentation of the crusaders as new Israelites,[87] more work remains to be done to contextualize these descriptions and parse their relationship to earlier traditions of exegesis and

---

[86] EP, no. 9, p. 148: "materque nostra spiritualis ecclesia clamat: uenite, filii mei dilectissimi, uenite ad me, suscipite coronam ab insurgentibus in me idolatriae filiis, ab initio mundi uobis praedestinationam. ... Uenite ergo, festinate duplici praemio remunderandi, uidelicet terra uiuentium terraque melle et lacte manante omnique uictuali abundante." Trans. (slightly revised) 21–22. Cf. Robert of Reims's account of Clermont; RR, 6. The promise of the "double reward" (*duplex praemium*), echoed in Fulcher of Chartres's version of the Clermont sermon (FC, 136, which speaks of an "*honor duplex*"), is a hagiographical commonplace; see, for instance the tenth-century *Passio sancti Pelagii* by the Iberian priest Raguel, ed. Rodriguez Fernández, *La pasión de S. Pelayo: edición crítica con traducción y comentarios* (Santiago de Compostela, 1991), 52. The "land of the living" (*terra viventium*), too, was a common allegorical convention for heaven; see Gaposchkin, *Invisible Weapons*, 86.

[87] Alphandéry, "Les citations bibliques," 153–54; idem, *La chrétienté et l'idée de croisade*, ed. Auguste Dupront (Paris, 1954), 1:9–54; Rousset, "L'idée de croisade," 547–63; Green, *The Millstätter Exodus*, ch. 8; Whalen, *Dominion of God*, ch. 2; Rubenstein, *Armies of Heaven*, 132–33, 320–22; Lapina, *Warfare and the Miraculous*, ch. 5; eadem, "Maccabees and the Battle of Antioch"; Morton, *Encountering Islam*, ch. 3; idem, "The Defense of the Holy Land"; and Miriam Rita Tessera, "The Use of

propaganda. By 1095, there was a long tradition in the Latin West of invoking ancient Israel as a model for Christian rulership, ecclesiastical governance, and warfare. Behind such positive valuations lay the conviction that the "Old Israel" (*vetus Israel*) was a prototype of the "new Israel" (*novus Israel*) which far surpassed its antecedent in virtue, just as the Hebrew patriarchs anticipated but could never equal Christ.[88] Patristic commentators on the Pentateuch, who focused on Genesis and Exodus' narratives of human sinfulness and redemption, tended towards allegorical readings, identifying numerous passages that seemed to them to foretell Christ's life; to cite just a few, the falling of manna in the wilderness foreshadowed the multiplication of the loaves and fishes, while the sacrifice of Isaac presaged the Passion.[89] Encouraged by the allegorical use of the Psalter throughout the New Testament, Christian commentators similarly read the Psalms through a messianic lens, as prophecy; thus, even as they expressed admiration for the Israelites' faith and forbearance, exegetes interpreted the Psalms christologically, as texts which foreshadowed the Church's history.[90] As we saw in Chapter 2, these biblical books feature prominently in crusading narratives, whose authors drew upon venerable typologies to present Christian holy warriors as new Israelites.

If patristic writers pioneered the Christian appropriation of an Israelite identity, Carolingian exegetes elevated it to an art form. In law, liturgy, art, and court ceremonial, Frankish rulers became reincarnations of the Old Testament kings David, Solomon, and Josiah, ruling over a new chosen people, aided by bishops whose spiritual leadership recalled that of Moses.[91] Nor were biblical models mere window-dressing for the Carolingian imperial revival; as Wilfried Hartmann has argued, Old Testament history and law were seen as the basis for

---

the Bible in Twelfth-Century Papal Letters to Outremer," in *The Uses of the Bible*, ed. Lapina and Morton, 179–205 (esp. 181–82).

[88] For a case study of one patristic exegete's approach to the patriarchs, see Marcia L. Colish, *Ambrose's Patriarchs: Ethics for the Common Man* (Notre Dame, IN, 2005).

[89] David L. Balás and D. Jeffrey Bingham, "Patristic Exegesis of the Books of the Bible," in *Handbook of Patristic Exegesis: The Bible in Ancient Christianity*, 2 vols., ed. Charles Kannengiesser (Leiden, 2004), 1:278–83.

[90] Balás and Bingham, "Patristic Exegesis," 1:297–301. Patristic writers' use of the Maccabees as spiritual exemplars akin to Christian martyrs follows a similar pattern, as shown by Daniel Joslyn-Siemiatkoski, *Christian Memories of the Maccabean Martyrs* (New York, 2009), ch. 2.

[91] Johan Chydenius, *Medieval Institutions and the Old Testament* (Helsinki, 1965), 46–70; Rosamund McKitterick, *The Frankish Church and the Carolingian Reforms* (London, 1977), 1–2, 5; Thomas F. X. Noble, "The Bible in the Codex Carolinus," in *Biblical Studies in the Early Middle Ages: Proceedings of the Conference on Biblical Studies in the Early Middle Ages*, ed. Claudio Leonardi and Giovanni Orlandi (Florence, 2005), 61–74; Ildar H. Garipzanov, *The Symbolic Language of Royal Authority in the Carolingian World (c. 751–877)* (Leiden, 2008), 274.

a *renovatio* of society that would assure the Franks of God's continued favor.⁹² By the late eighth century Frankish courtiers and reformers had thoroughly internalized this new self-definition as the *beata gens*, the blessed nation *"whose God is the Lord, the people whom he hath chosen for his inheritance"* (Ps. 32:12).⁹³ Ninth-century rulers and the exegetes who served them perpetuated the Frankish identification with the 'New Israel,' even as Charlemagne's empire collapsed around them; indeed, recent scholarship has emphasized the close relationship between conflict, disorder, and typology in the Carolingian world. As Mary Garrison has shown, confrontations with foreign peoples encouraged Franks to see themselves in Old Testament terms as an elect group, distinct from and superior to Lombards, Avars, and Greeks. Within this framework, typological thinking encouraged the Carolingians (and their allies at the papal court) to compare their victories to the God-given triumphs of the Hebrew patriarchs and kings of Israel, and to attribute their enemies' defeats to the loss of divine favor.⁹⁴ In the precarious political climate of the ninth century, Mayke De Jong has found, typology remained vitally important, helping Carolingian exegetes and rulers to make sense of an empire beset by invaders and religious dissidents.⁹⁵ Samantha Zacher's work suggests that the rewriting of Hebrew heroism as vernacular epic may have served a similar purpose in tenth-century England.⁹⁶

---

⁹² Wilfried Hartmann, "Die karolingische Reform und die Bibel," *Annuarium Historiae Conciliorum* 18 (1986): 57–74.
⁹³ For a careful reconstruction of the Carolingians' gradual adoption of an Israelite identity, see Mary Garrison, "The Franks as the New Israel? Education for an Identity from Pippin to Charlemagne," in *Uses of the Past in the Early Middle Ages*, ed. Yitzhak Hen and Matthew Innes (Cambridge, 2000), 114–61 (reference to Ps. 32:12 at p. 160). Uses of Old Testament models in earlier medieval contexts are discussed by Rob Meens, "The Uses of the Old Testament in Early Medieval Canon Law," in *The Uses of the Past*, ed. Hen and Innes, 67–77; and Yitzhak Hen, "The Uses of the Bible and the Perception of Kingship in Merovingian Gaul," *Early Medieval Europe* 7 (1998): 277–90.
⁹⁴ Garrison, "Franks as the New Israel?" 120, 150–53. For the longer-term trajectory of the Franks-as-chosen-people idea, see Gabriele, *Empire of Memory*.
⁹⁵ Mayke De Jong, "The Empire as *Ecclesia*: Hrabanus Maurus and Biblical *Historia* for Rulers," in *The Uses of the Past*, ed. Hen and Innes, 191–226 (esp. 222–23); and Abigail Firey, "The Letter of the Law: Carolingian Exegetes and the Old Testament," in *With Reverence for the Word: Medieval Scriptural Exegesis in Judaism, Christianity, and Islam*, ed. Jane Dammen McAuliffe, Barry D. Walfish, and Joseph W. Goering (Oxford, 2003), 204–24. Such typological connections were also underscored in the developing liturgies of war from the ninth century on, as discussed by Gaposchkin, *Invisible Weapons*, 46–47; and Michael McCormick, "Liturgie et guerre des Carolingiens à la première croisade," in *'Militia Christi' e Crociata nei secoli XI–XIII: Atti della undecima Settimana internazionale di studio, Mendola, 28 agosto – 1 settembre 1989* (Milan, 1989), 209–38 (at 226–27).
⁹⁶ Samantha Zacher, *Rewriting the Old Testament in Anglo-Saxon Verse: Becoming the*

In the eleventh century, developers of competing reform agendas found ideological ammunition in the histories, laws, and prophecies of 'Old Israel.' While some polemicists condemned such use of the Hebrew scriptures as anachronistic, or even "judaising,"[97] a perusal of the *Libelli de lite* reveals that papal and imperial partisans alike supported their claims through extensive use of the Pentateuch, Books of Kings, and prophets (as well as patristic and Carolingian exegesis of these).[98] In their wrangling over the proper relationship between *regnum* and *sacerdotium*, pro-imperial clerics exalted the model of the priest-king Melchizedek, and pointed to Solomon's deposition of the priest Abiathar as anticipating Henry IV's righteous struggle against Pope Gregory VII, while papal supporters celebrated the prophets Nathan, Elijah, and Elisha, whose principled resistance to royal authority seemed to foreshadow their own.[99] Nor was such allegorical thinking confined to the realm of polemic; as I. S. Robinson demonstrated, in these turbulent decades exegetes like Bruno of Segni also turned to the Old Testament with a new urgency.[100] Such rhetoric pervades eleventh-century monastic chronicles and letters as well. Thus, we find Abbot Hugh of Flavigny (d. aft. 1114) expressing sympathy for Gregory VII by likening the pope's position to that of the Israelites beset by the Amorites, while Hugh's mentor Abbot Jarento of Saint-Bénigne (d. 1113) offered refuge to monastic "Israelites" who supported Pope Urban II against the latter-day "pharaoh" Bishop Otbert of Liège.[101] Such examples show that in the decades immediately preceding the First Crusade, typology continued to be an essential hermeneutical tool for articulating difference and justifying opposition.

Like exegetical traditions and propaganda, liturgy offered crusade chroniclers models of how to 'think with' the Israelites. As Cecilia Gaposchkin notes, the historical books of the Old Testament's "cycles of sin, military loss, repentance, and forgiveness" were embedded in the liturgical year, and reinforced particular connections – between spiritual purity and victory, moral turpitude and defeat, 'pagans' and the devil – that served as a bedrock upon which to build scripturally

---

Chosen People (London, 2013).

[97] As discussed by Robinson, "The Bible in the Investiture Contest," 79–83.
[98] Leclercq, "Usage et abus," 99.
[99] Leclercq, "Usage et abus," 102–3; Chydenius, *Medieval Institutions*, 71–75; Beryl Smalley, *The Becket Conflict and the Schools: A Study of Intellectuals in Politics* (London, 1973), 32–33.
[100] Robinson, "Political Allegory," 81, 86–9; and, for eleventh-century exegetes' amendment of patristic glosses in the service of reform, idem, *Authority and Resistance*, 24–25 and 139–40. For the role of the Maccabees as exemplars in this context, see Münsch, "Hate Preachers and Religious Warriors," 161–76.
[101] Cited by Patrick Healy, *The Chronicle of Hugh of Flavigny: Reform and the Investiture Contest in the Late Eleventh Century* (Aldershot, 2006), 1, 61. Urban II also deployed such language, as noted by Gabriele, "Last Carolingian Exegete," 797–98.

inflected readings of the holy war.[102] Further, for centuries liturgies of war had invoked the divinely sanctioned conflicts of the Israelites, beseeching similar protection for Christian armbearers. The following prayer from the late eleventh-century Le Puy Sacramentary, which may well have been performed by Bishop Adhemar and the canon Raymond of Aguilers prior to their contingent's departure on crusade, identifies the Israelites as both paradigmatic holy warriors and types of Christ:

> Lord, look kindly upon the work of our army, and allow them to advance with your help under clear skies, just as [you] gave your protection to Israel hastening out of Egypt, so send your angel, the author of light, to guide your people as they go forth into battle and defend them from every danger by day and night. Let him be with them, so that their journey may be unimpeded, they may foresee what is to come and their weakness may be tempered, they may be free of care, and strong without fear, they may have an abundance of goods and the right intent for doing battle, and emerge victorious under the leadership of your angel; and may he bestow it not by his strength, but may your grace return to them the victory of Christ, your son, who, by the humility of his passion defeated the death of death and triumphed upon the cross.[103]

Finally, pre-1095 liturgical rites for the blessing of pilgrims situated *peregrini* within a spiritual genealogy that included the Hebrew patriarchs, even as they emphasized the christomimetic nature of pilgrimage.[104] A rite from the Romano-Germanic Pontifical, for instance, beseeches God to protect the pilgrim as he had Abraham, "so that he might go forth from the land of his birth and come into the land of promise (*terra repromissionis*), which you promised to give to him, as well as the Israelite people whom you taught, by means of many wonders, to worship you in the desert."[105] Taken together, this evidence raises a tanta-

---

[102] Gaposchkin, *Invisible Weapons*, 41–42, 53, 112–13 (quoting 42).

[103] Le Puy Sacramentary (privately owned), fol. 80v: "Prebe domine misericordie tue opere exercitui nostro, et sub aeris claritate presta eis optatum proficendi auxilium et sicut israhel properante ex egypto securratis tribuisti munimen, ita populo tuo in prelium pergenti lucis auctorem dirige angelum, qui eos die noctuque ab omni adversitate defendat, sit eis iterandi sine labore profectus, ubique providus eventus moderata fragilitas, sine metu, fortitudo sine terrore, copia rerum et preliandi recta voluntas et cum tuo angelo duce victor extiterit; non suis tribuat viribus, sed ipsi victori christo filio tuo gratias referat de triumpho qui humilitate sue passionis de morte mortisque principe, in cruce triumphavit." For discussion, see Gaposchkin, *Invisible Weapons*, 47. I am most grateful to Cecilia Gaposchkin for suggesting this connection, sharing her transcription, and helping with the translation.

[104] Gaposchkin, *Invisible Weapons*, 37, 58; Green, *Millstätter Exodus*, 242–43.

[105] *Le Pontificale Romano-Germanique du dixième siècle*, c. 212, ed. Cyrille Vogel and R. Elze, Studi e Testi 226–227, 266 (Rome, 1963–72), 2:362. Cf. *El Sacramentario de Vich*, c. 1430, ed. Alejandro Olivar (Barcelona, 1953), 215.

lizing possibility that liturgical experiences encouraged crusaders to adopt a 'new Israelite' identity even before heading east.[106] What is certain is that, in the coming years, Latin chroniclers actively promoted this view of the holy war.

A review of citation patterns in early crusading narratives reveals that the presentation of crusaders as new Israelites largely depends upon shared readings of a handful of biblical books: Exodus, Numbers, Deuteronomy, 1 and 2 Maccabees, and, especially, Psalms. At the same time, individual authors made use of Old Testament imagery in distinctive ways; in fact, a mere six verses from these books appear in the works of four or more authors,[107] reminding us that, as we saw in Chapter 2, Latin writers brought considerable originality and creativity to their glosses of the crusade 'text.' Through a closer look at how these and related verses function in early crusade narratives, we can better understand how twelfth-century Christians used the Scriptures to define the terms of God's covenant with the Jerusalemites and associate their Muslim enemies with biblical 'paganism.'

Latin chroniclers could not doubt that the God of Israel, having transferred his favor to a new chosen people, watched over the crusade from beginning to end, and they expressed this divine guardianship in language from the Psalter.[108] Reversing a longstanding exegetical tradition that interpreted the Psalms' martial imagery in terms of spiritual struggle against evil,[109] chroniclers, like contemporary liturgists, instead saw these texts as prefiguring and justifying the crusaders' physical combats.[110] In Baldric of Bourgueil's account

---

[106] In this way, the rites for pilgrims may have served a didactic function, a point made about medieval laity's experience of the liturgy by Evelyn Birge Vitz, "Liturgy as Education in the Middle Ages," in *Medieval Education*, ed. Ronald B. Begley and Joseph W. Koterski (New York, 2005), 20–34. Derek A. Rivard comments on the ways in which liturgies for pilgrims may have encouraged particular kinds of self-fashioning; see *Blessing the World: Liturgy and Lay Piety in Medieval Religion* (Washington, D. C., 2009), 134–42.

[107] These are: Deut. 11:24–25, Deut. 32:30, Ps. 9:10, Ps. 32:12, Ps. 62:3, and Ps. 78:6. For references to these verses in individual sources, see Appendix 2.

[108] When the crusaders called upon God for aid in battle, chroniclers put the language of the Psalms into their mouths, emphasizing that, just as the crusaders fought in God's cause, so too did God fight for them; for example, see RA, 60. Cf. *Gesta Adhemari episcopi podiensis, hierosolymitana*, RHC Oc. 5:354–55, at 355 (on Ps. 19:8) and Robert of Reims's extensive use of Exodus 15:6–13 (RR, 27–28) for a similar interpretive effect.

[109] As discussed by Katherine Allen Smith, *War and the Making of Medieval Monastic Culture* (Woodbridge, 2011), 24–28. This tradition can be traced back to the highly influential glosses on the Psalms by Augustine and Cassiodorus, but was still very much alive in the eleventh and twelfth centuries; for later examples of spiritual interpretations of the Psalms' military imagery, see Pseudo-Bruno of Chartreuse, *Expositio in Psalmos*, c. 44 (Ps. 44:4), PL 152:827; and Hildebert of Lavardin, *De diversis*, c. 27, PL 171:867–71.

[110] Gaposchkin, *Invisible Weapons*, 52–53.

of Clermont, for example, Urban II invokes Psalm 44:4 ("*Gird thy sword upon thy thigh, O thou most mighty*") to explain what he is calling upon Christian warriors to do: "Gird yourselves, every one of you, I say, and be valiant sons; for it is better for you to die in battle than to behold the sorrows of your race and of your holy places."[111] This was the pugnacious God of the Psalms, the "*God of revenge*" (Ps. 93:1),[112] "*strong and mighty in battle* (Ps. 23:8), who shielded his children"[113] against their enemies "like *a tower of strength*" (Ps. 60:4)[114] as long as they showed themselves worthy. Several writers supported this claim by reference to Psalm 9:10 ("And the Lord is become a refuge for the poor, a helper in due time in tribulation"). In the *Gesta Francorum* and Peter Tudebode's *Historia* the verse is a promise of divine aid, spoken by Christ to the priest Stephen at Antioch; for Raymond of Aguilers, the psalmist's words described how God fought for the crusaders during the siege of that city; and Guibert of Nogent invoked the passage to illustrate God's special relationship with Jerusalem's inhabitants, as members of the "house of David."[115] The verb tenses Guibert used to describe this elect group – "to whom omnipotent God has given and still gives (*donavit et donat*) many victories" – emphasize the durable typological bond between Jerusalem's old and new masters.[116]

Latin writers constructed the crusaders as a new *beata gens* through judicious citations of Psalm 32:12 ("*Blessed is the nation whose God is the Lord: the people whom he hath chosen for his inheritance*"), a liturgically prominent verse with a rich exegetical history.[117] The Michelsberg Continuator

---

[111] BB, 9: "*Accingere, o homo unusquisque, gladio tuo super femur tuum, potentissime*. Accingimini, inquam, et estote filii potentes: quoniam melius est uobis mori in bello, quam uidere mala gentis uestre et sanctorum." Trans. McGinty, in *The First Crusade*, ed. Peters, 32. As Cecilia Gaposchkin points out, this verse was used in earlier liturgies of war in connection with the girding on of a warrior's sword; see *Invisible Weapons*, 68–69.

[112] AA, 59.

[113] RA, 57, 73; trans. 40. Compare the depiction of "deus omnipotens et bellipotens" in GF, 54.

[114] RR, 72.

[115] GF, 58; PT, 99; RA, 60; GN, 307.

[116] GN, 307: "Ipsos 'habitores Iherusalem' dixerim 'domum David,' quos Omnipotens etsi frequentibus victoriis donavit et donat ... ." Trans. (slightly revised) 144. As Matthew Gabriele has shown, medieval writers employed verb tenses with great care when situating the crusaders' accomplishments within sacred history; see "From Prophecy to Apocalypse."

[117] As a responsory, the verse was used at various times in the medieval liturgical calendar, including during the seasons of Pentecost and Lent, from the tenth century onward; e.g. Debra Lacoste and Jan Koláček, *Cantus: A Database for Latin Ecclesiastical Chant*, accessed January 28, 2018, at www.cantusindex.org.

voices this claim through the priest Arnulf of Chocques, who glosses the verse in a sermon to the crusaders gathered outside Jaffa in 1102:

> *Blessed is the nation whose God is the Lord, the people whom he hath chosen* (Ps. 32:12). You, O most beloved brothers, are that blessed people, that holy people; are that people of *Christ's inheritance* (cf. Rom. 8:17), the *purchased people* (1 Pet. 2:9), who have *left all things* (Lk. 5:11) – homeland, parents, and possessions (cf. Mat. 19:29) – to bear the cross daily after Christ (cf. Mat. 16:24, Mk. 8:34, Lk. 9:23). You have handed over your bodies unto suffering for Christ. You seemed to fight, but Christ of his own will has deemed it worthy to cleanse the place of his sanctification with your blood and with the costly deaths of your brothers and comrades.[118]

The chronicler builds upon an allegorical tradition in which the *beata gens* referred to the Israelites, and, more importantly, to Christ's followers, whose spiritual obligations Arnulf details in an impressive string of biblical references. Early medieval exegesis of Psalm 32:12 built upon a patristic foundation exemplified by Cassiodorus, for whom the *beata gens* consisted of virtuous Christians dwelling, as it were, in the heavenly Jerusalem and enjoying God's special favor.[119] While later exegetes such as Remigius of Auxerre (d. 908) and the Pseudo-Bruno of Chartreuse (fl. c. 1100) generally accepted this spiritualized reading,[120] Alcuin of York (d. 804) broke with tradition by identifying the *beata gens* with the Franks.[121] The First Crusade's narrators followed suit, employing Psalm 32:12, like Psalm 9:10, in a variety of contexts but with a common hermeneutic goal: the identification of the Jerusalemites – or more specifically, as in Robert of Reims's *Historia*, Frankish crusaders – as God's

---

[118] FE, 174: "Beata gens, cuius est dominus Deus eius, populus quem elegit. Vos, o fratres karissimi, gens estis illa beata, illa gens sancta, vox estis populus ille Christi hereditatis, populus acquisitionis, qui relictis omnibus patria, parentibus et rebus crucem cotidianam post Christum tulistis, vos corpora vestra pro Christo ad supplicia tradidistis. Vos pugnasse videmini, sed Christus vestro voluntarie sibi sacrificato sanguine vestrorum fratrum et commilitonum preciosa morte locum sanctificationis sue dignatus est mundare ... ." Trans. 168.

[119] Cassiodorus, *Expositio psalmorum I–LXX*, c. 32, ed. M. Adriaen, CCSL 97 (Turnhout, 1958), 289; and cf. the *Glossa Ordinaria*'s adoption of Cassiodorus's reading, PL 113: 889. As Theresa Gross-Diaz notes, Cassiodorus's *Expositio Psalmorum* remained a schoolroom staple through the twelfth century; *The Psalms Commentary of Gilbert of Poitiers: From Lectio Divina to the Lecture Room* (Leiden, 1996), 97.

[120] Remigius of Auxerre, *Enarrationes in Psalmos*, c.32, PL 131: 309; Pseudo-Bruno of Chartreuse, *Expositio in Psalmos*, PL 152: 766. Cf. Pseudo-Haimo of Auxerre, *Explanatio in Psalmos*, c. 32, PL 116: 304.

[121] Alcuin, *Epistolae*, no. 229, ed. Ernst Dümmler, MGH Epp. 4: Epistolae Karolini aevi, 373; cited by Garrison, "Franks as the New Israel?" 159–60.

new "blessed nation."[122] Raymond of Aguilers used the verse to describe the Latins' confidence as they faced down Kerbogha at Antioch, and later put the psalmist's words into the mouth of the Muslim ruler of Shaizar, who explains that he cannot resist the crusaders "because God has chosen this people" (*Deus hanc gentem elegit*).[123] Raymond's fellow crusader Fulcher of Chartres described how the crusaders "blessed and glorified God" in the words of Psalm 32:12 after their victory at Ascalon,[124] while Gilo of Paris used the verse to gloss the pilgrims' military successes in Syria:

> While that blessed people (*gens ... beata*) rejoiced over the bountiful produce of that fine land, plundering the cornfields of Syria, three emirs (for that is what the kings and leaders of Jerusalem, Aleppo, and Damascus are called) attacked them, but then they too handed over their possessions to our men; in truth they retreated in defeat, and many died. Heartened by this victory, they joyfully returned to their tents.[125]

Such usage is a far cry from most earlier exegesis, which represented "blessedness" as a spiritual state and promised the *beata gens* the incomparable, but decidedly intangible, reward of salvation. As proof of their status as God's "blessed nation," however, the crusaders, like the pious warriors of ancient Israel, reaped not only spiritual but material rewards in the form of wealth and sacred land.

Led as they were by "He who led the sons of Israel from Egypt dry-shod across the Red Sea,"[126] the pilgrims' route was glossed as a symbolic reenactment

---

[122] As in the prologue to Robert of Reims's *Historia;* RR, 209: "huic tanto gentem istam deum reservasse negotio [i.e., the crusade]." Descriptions of the French as the "blessed nation" became increasingly common over the course of the twelfth and thirteenth centuries, as described by Claire Weeda, "Violence, Control, Prophecy and Power in Twelfth-Century France and Germany," in *Reading the Bible in the Middle Ages*, ed. Jinty Nelson and Damien Kempf (London, 2015), 147–66 (at 157); and Colette Beaune, *The Birth of an Ideology*, trans. Fredric L. Cheyette (Berkeley, CA, 1991), 173.

[123] RA, 79 and 103. Cf. RA, 154 for the description of the crusaders as a people "quod Deus ... elegit."

[124] FC, 318; trans. 95. Cf. the use of the verse in this context in the anonymous *Narratio profectionis Godefridi ducis ad Jerusalem*, a reworking of Fulcher's *Historia;* 3.4, RHC Oc. 5: 193.

[125] GP, 104–5: "Telluris grate dum gaudet fertilitate / Diripiendo sata Syrie gens illa beata, / Tres ammirati (sic reges quippe uocati / Iherusalem, Scalapi ductores atque Damasci) / Ipsos inuadunt, sed et hi nostris sua tradunt. / Quippe recesserunt uicti, plures perierunt. / Hac palma freti repetunt tentoria leti."

[126] RR, 19: "quis ad hec peregrina loca vos adduxit [says Bohemond], nisi ille qui filios Israel ex Egypto per mare Rubrum sicco vestigio transduxit?" Cf. CJ, 647 (ref. to Ps. 119:1).

of the Exodus narrative.[127] Albert of Aachen wrote that God guided the army to Jerusalem, as he had led their Old Testament predecessors, *"with a strong hand"* (Ex. 13:3),[128] while Ralph of Caen identified the miracle of living water flowing from the rock (Num. 20:11) with God's healing of the Norman crusader Tancred of Hauteville (d. 1112).[129] Like the Israelites whose journey to Canaan prefigured their own, the crusaders were led to the land of promise by God's representatives, who were models of military prowess and piety. For Albert of Aachen, Godfrey of Bouillon was "a spiritual leader of Israel (*dux spiritualis Israhel*), preordained by God and appointed prince of the people," who embodied "the spirit and gentleness of Moses," while Baldric of Bourgueil likened Count Raymond IV of Toulouse (d. 1105) to Moses' brother Aaron.[130] Other writers invoked the conquests of Joshua as antecedents of the Latins' victories.[131] Bishop Adhemar of Le Puy (d. 1098) was also regarded as a second Moses in his piety, his mission, even the manner of his death.[132] "Nurturing our army with his deeds and divinely inspired sermon," wrote Raymond of Aguilers, Adhemar "was another Moses" (*Moyses alter*).[133] Reflecting on Adhemar's untimely death at Antioch, Ralph of Caen offered this epitaph:

> Here lies buried the most brilliant follower (*imitator*) of Moses in doctrine, zeal, habit, and office. Moses was the leader of his people and this one was the leader of his people. Both were leaders of Christ (*duces Christi*), and both were born in heaven. Both pursued justice and doctrine. Both were the voice of God and his mediator with his people. It is recalled that the land of Canaan was the reason for Moses' journey. So, too, was the land of Canaan the reason for his journey. Moses was granted the ability to see but not to reach this land. This one also was not allowed to reach it, and was almost given to see it. Long fasts reconciled Moses to God. God consecrated this one through long hunger

---

[127] At least one early twelfth-century vernacular work similarly reinterpreted the Exodus story in light of the First Crusade; see Green, *Millstätter Exodus*.

[128] AA, 2.

[129] RC, 100.

[130] AA, 448–49; BB, 11. Baldric's sentiment is repeated verbatim by OV, 5:18.

[131] E.g., CJ, 649; GN, 276.

[132] Jonathan Riley-Smith noted that such comparisons emphasize qualities in keeping with contemporary reformers' vision of an ideal episcopate; see "The First Crusade and Saint Peter," in *Outremer: Studies in the History of the Crusader Kingdom of Jerusalem Presented to Joshua Prawer*, ed. Benjamin Z. Kedar, H. E. Meyer, and R. C. Smail (Jerusalem, 1982), 44.

[133] RA, 152; RR, 8. Significantly, in Albert of Aachen's *Historia* (AA, 192), Adhemar is made to speak the words of Moses from Ex. 14:14, and he is described in the anonymous *Gesta Adhemari* (RHC Oc. 5:355) using the language of Deuteronomy 32, the "Canticle of Moses."

Into the Promised Land

as well. God himself chose Moses, and Pope Urban chose this one, but he was following God's command, and thus God sent both of them.[134]

Such descriptions of Moses as a *dux spiritualis* or *dux Christi* are in keeping with a long exegetical tradition which understood him as a *figura* of Christ, and thus rendered him an acceptable model of spiritual leadership for Christians.[135]

In their presentation of the crusade as a spiritual as well as a physical journey, in which the crusaders were led from a state of sin, via purgative suffering, to a state of grace, the chroniclers again emphasized Old Testament precedents.[136] The Jerusalemites' trials could be read as a sign of God's concern for his new chosen people,[137] or of divine wrath, which might be assuaged by the avoidance of vice and the smoothing out of discord, as well as fasting and penitential processions.[138] No less than five Latin writers used the language of Psalm 62:3 to compare the

---

[134] RC, 82–83: Conditus est Moysis clarissimus hic imitator doctrina, studio, moribus, officio. Dux populi Moyses, et dux populi fuit iste. Ambo duces Christi, coelitus ambo sati, ambo justitiae, doctrinae ambo studiosi. Ambo fuere Dei vox media et populi. Causa viae Moysis tellus Chanaan memoratur, huic quoque causa viae terra fuit Chanaan. Cernere, non uti Moysi conceditur illa, huic quoque non uti, cernere ferme datum est. Longa Deo Moysen jejunia conciliarunt, hunc quoque longa Deo consecrat esuries. Ipse Deus Moysen, hunc papa Urbanus, et ipse praeco Dei sequitur, misit utrumque Deus." Trans. 114.

[135] For late antique and medieval Christian interpretations of Moses, see Jean Daniélou, *From Shadows to Reality: Studies in the Biblical Typology of the Fathers*, trans. Wulstan Hibberd (London, 1960), 202–16; Ruth Mellinkoff, *The Horned Moses in Medieval Life and Thought* (Berkeley, CA, 1970); and Averil Cameron, "Eusebius' *Vita Constantini* and the Construction of Constantine," in *Portraits: Biographical Representation in the Greek and Latin Literature of the Roman Empire*, ed. M. J. Edwards and Simon Swain (Oxford, 1997), 145–74. The idea that Moses could be read as a *figura* of Adhemar is also reflected in contemporary church art; at the cathedral of Le Puy a series of frescoes depicting the life of Moses was created around the time of Adhemar's death, according to Anne Derbes, to express the typological connection between the two leaders. See "A Crusading Fresco Cycle at the Cathedral of Le Puy," *Art Bulletin* 73 (1991): 561–76.

[136] The army's suffering was glossed with reference to biblical passages suggestive of how such privations were an expression of God's love. For example, Guibert of Nogent offered Heb. 12:6 as a lens through which to read the army's trials at Antioch; GN, 233. More generally, Orderic Vitalis likened the trials of the participants in the 1101 expedition, many of whom "were led away captive by the barbarians into unknown lands" where, "as they piously fulfilled their duty to the supreme Deity they experienced his grace, and were miraculously helped in many ways, as were the Israelites among the Assyrians and Chaldeans"; OV, 5: 338–39.

[137] E.g., RR, 39; trans. 126.

[138] GF, 34; AA, 228 and 412; OV, 5:154. Earlier exegetes glossed this verse as a reference to a state of spiritual degradation caused by a lack of the "water" of God's life-sustaining word; see Cassiodorus, *Expositio psalmorum* I–LXX, c. 62, ed. M. Adriaen, 550–51; Remigius of Auxerre, *Enarrationes in Psalmos*, 62, PL 131: 455–56 (and

crusaders' suffering to the privations endured by the Israelites in the desert of Edom,[139] while Deuteronomy 11:24–25 functions in several chronicles as a reminder that God would reward the new Israelites as he had their predecessors.[140] Purified by suffering, the pilgrims became worthy of divine mercy. As the Michelsberg Continuator reminded readers, "God, looking upon his people (cf. Ex. 33:13), whom he had scourged for so long (cf. Ps. 72:14), benevolently comforted them" with signs of favor, the greatest of which was the gift of the Holy Sepulcher, which the chronicler likened to the "fountain of living water" brought forth from the rock by Moses' staff (Num. 20:6).[141] Discovering plentiful food and water after a period of dearth was another clear sign of divine approval; Guibert of Nogent wrote that after the first battle of Antioch, "such great abundance seemed everywhere to pour in a sudden eruption from the earth, and God seemed to have opened the *cataracts of heaven*" (Mal. 3:10).[142] The crusaders also rejoiced when God granted them the spoils of war, materially rewarding their spiritual fortitude as he had once done for the Israelites. For Robert of Reims, it was a clear fulfillment of Proverbs 13:22 ("the wealth of the sinner is kept for the just") that the crusaders were able to replenish their foodstuffs from the stores of Turks who fled at their approach,[143] while a similar incident following Kerbogha's defeat reminded Raymond of Aguilers of how the Israelites had pillaged the camps of their enemies at Samaria (4 Kgs. 7:15f.).[144]

Such spiritual testing established the crusaders' worthiness to possess what early medieval Christians called the "land of promise" (*terra repromissionis*).[145]

---

cf. the Cassidorean gloss in *Glossa ordinaria*, PL 113:934); and Pseudo-Bruno of Chartreuse, *Expositio in Psalmos*, PL 152:927.

[139] GF, 23; PT, 57; MC, 34; RA, 36; and AA, 148. Some earlier exegetes had applied this verse to discussions of terrestrial conquests, while others had read it as an allegory of passing from earthly existence to the "promised land" of eternal life; e.g., compare the canons of the Synod of Pistres (862), c. 1, ed. Georg Pertz, MGH Leges 1: *Capitularia regum Francorum* (Hannover, 1835), 477; with the commentary on this verse by Hrabanus Maurus, *Enarratio super Deuteronomium libri quattuor*, 2.2 PL 108:876–78.

[140] GF, 54; PT, 94; MC, 73; RR, 63; and *Historia Nicaena vel Antiochena*, c. 43, RHC Oc. 5:165.

[141] FE, 150: "Respiciens autem Domini populum, quem tam diu flagellaverat, benigne consolatur ... ." The glossing of the Holy Sepulcher with reference to Num. 20: 6 is at FE, 154.

[142] GN, 242–43: "ut subita emersione passim exoriri videretur omnis plenitudo rei et aperuisse putaretur dominus *cataractas caeli*." Trans. 112.

[143] RR, 37 and 90.

[144] RA, 83.

[145] See Erdmann, *Origin of the Idea*, 300; and Robert L. Wilken, *The Land Called Holy: Palestine in Christian History and Thought* (New Haven, 1992), 52–53. This

As we have seen, this land could be understood historically and literally as a physical landscape marked by biblical miracles, or symbolically as a state of purity, or both. It is important to remember that early medieval exegetes interpreted God's promise to Abraham in Genesis 13:15 ("All the land which thou seeest I will give to thee, and to thy seed forever") literally, as a pledge that Christians – Abraham's spiritual "seed" – would rule the land of Canaan.[146] Thus, in learned Latins' eyes, the crusade offered not only a means of attaining salvation but a chance to redeem God's pledge. What purports to be a letter written by the army's ecclesiastical leaders in 1098 invites fellow Latin Christians to join the pilgrims in reaping "a double reward, that is, the land of the living and *the land that floweth with milk and honey*" (Ex. 3:8, 17, Num. 13:28).[147] Like Robert of Reims's version of Urban II's Clermont speech,[148] the letter emphasizes the fecundity of the land as an adjunct to the spiritual rewards associated with the expedition. In so doing, these writers followed traditional glosses of Exodus 3:8, which held that the "land of milk and honey" had been given to the Israelites (as it was now entrusted to the crusaders) "so that they might be called to a better way of life" and avoid damnation.[149] The chroniclers had no doubt that the land first promised to Abraham, and later granted to Moses' followers, was now the legitimate patrimony of Latin warriors who had, like the Hebrew patriarchs, left their homes and reformed their lives at God's command.[150] In his version of Urban II's speech, Guibert of Nogent further developed the themes of inheritance and predestination by linking the crusaders to Abraham as well as Christ:

> If what was said by the Lord remains true, namely that *salvation is of the Jews* (Jn. 4:22), and it remains true that the Lord of the Sabbath has left his seed for us, lest we become like those of Sodom and Gomorrah (cf. Is. 19, Rom. 9:29),

---

terminology, which appears in Hebr. 11:9, is used in early crusade texts; e.g., EP, no. 23, p. 180.

[146] Lozovsky, *"The Earth is Our Book,"* 41–42. Particularly influential in this regard were Jerome's *Hebraicae quaestiones in libro Geneseos*, c. 13, ed. de Lagarde, 17; and Augustine, *De Genesi ad litteram*, 12.6, ed. J. Zycha, Corpus Scriptorum Ecclesiasticorum 28/1 (Vienna, 1894), 387. Intriguingly, the verse is invoked to this effect in the Encyclical of Sergius IV; for the text, see Hans Martin Schaller, "Zur Zreuzzugsenzyklika Papst Sergius' IV," c. 3, in *Papsttum, Kirche und Recht im Mittelalter: Feschschrift für Horst Fuhrmann zum 65. Geburtstag*, ed. Hubert Mordek (Tübingen, 1991), 135–53 (at 151).

[147] EP, no. 9, p. 148 (with Latin text at n. 86 above); trans. 22. Cf. William of Malmesbury's version of Urban's speech for a similar dual promise of a "lost fatherland" (*amissa patria*) and "the kingdom of God" (*regnum Dei*); WM, 1:602.

[148] RR, 6; and cf. RR, 90.

[149] E.g., Gregory the Great, *Liber pastoralis*, 3.26, ed. F. Rommel, SC 382 (Paris, 1992), 442.

[150] As suggested by the Michelsberg Continuator's use of Heb. 11:9; FE, 134.

and that Christ is our seed (*semen nostrum Christus est*; cf. Gal. 3:29), in whom lies salvation and blessing for all people (cf. Ps. 3:9, Gal. 3:14), then the earth and the city in which he lived and suffered is called holy by the testimony of Scripture (i.e., in Joel 3:17). ... [T]his land is the inheritance of God, and his holy temple, even before the Lord walked and suffered there, as the sacred and prophetic pages tell us ....[151]

Guibert's reading rests on a chain of associations familiar to medieval exegetes: God's promises to Abraham and his descendants in Genesis 12–15, and Paul's typological gloss in Galatians 3, which insists that Christ and, through him, the Christian community, became "the seed of Abraham, heirs according to the promise" (Gal. 3:29).[152] As Guibert would have known, earlier commentators had used Galatians 3 as a lens through which to reread the Psalter in a christological mode, and proposed that God had in mind future Christians when he spoke of Abraham's descendants.[153] Thus crusade chroniclers amended earlier interpretations of Scripture, so that to inhabit the "land of milk and honey" or be the "seed of Abraham" now entailed not merely spiritual kinship but physical possession of the Israelites' patrimony.[154] In the eyes of contempo-

---

[151] GN, 111–12: "Si enim verum constat quod a domino dicitur, quia videlicet *salus ex Iudeis est*, et dominum sabaoth semen nobis reliquisse constat ne sicut Sodoma sicut Gomorrae similes fiamus, et *semen nostrum Christus est*, in quo salus et omnium gentium benedictio est, ipsa terra et civitas, in qua habitavit et passus est, Scripturarum testimonio sancta vocatur. Si enim et terra dei hereditas et templum sanctum antequam ibi obambularet ac pateretur dominus in sacris et propheticis paginis legitur ... ." Trans. 42. Orderic Vitalis also refers to the "men of all nations predestined (*predestinatos*) by God to join the army of the almighty Messiah" on crusade (OV, 5:30); and Fulcher of Chartres uses similar language to describe how God foreordained the death of so many Turks at Antioch (FC, 227).

[152] For a thorough study of Paul's interpretation and its significance within its original cultural context, see Bradley Trick, *Abrahamic Descent, Testamentary Adoption, and the Law in Galatians* (Leiden, 2016).

[153] E.g., Bede, *Libri quatuor*, 4.15.5, ed. Jones, 195; Augustine, *Enarrationes in Psalmos*, 82.5, 88.5, ed. Dekkers and Fraipont, 2: 1142, 1222. For a survey of patristic commentary on this verse, see Martin Meiser, *Galater*, Novum Testamentum Patristicum 9 (Göttingen, 2007), 175–77. It is noteworthy that in the eighth and ninth centuries, the Franks and their Carolingian rulers were keen to don the mantle of Abraham's heirs, as befitting their model of sacral kingship and territorial ambitions, while the Capetian kings, in turn, were linked to Abraham through their liturgies of war; see Constance Brittain Bouchard, "The Carolingian Creation of a Model of Patrilineage," in *Paradigms and Methods in Early Medieval Studies*, ed. Celia Chazelle and Felice Lifshitz (New York, 2007), 135–52 (at 140); and Renie S. Choy, *Intercessory Prayer and the Monastic Ideal in the Time of the Carolingian Reforms* (Oxford, 2016), 158; and Peter Rietbergen, *Europe: A Cultural History*, 3rd edn (London, 2015), 112–13.

[154] Sylvia Schein made a similar point with regard to the altered status of Jerusalem in the Latin Christian world post-1099; see *Gateway to the Heavenly City*, ch. 2. The

raries, the new geopolitical realities of the Levant post-1099 seemed to be proof that God's promises to Abraham had been fulfilled, yet again, with Latin settlement in the Levant.

In addition to modeling the terms of divine covenant, the Old Testament contained numerous examples of God's just punishment of unbelievers. Several chroniclers invoked Deuteronomy 32:30 ("How should one pursue after a thousand, and two chase ten thousand? Was it not because their God had sold them, and the Lord had shut them up?") to explain the crusaders' defeat of larger Muslim armies. Soon after the fall of Jerusalem, Pope Pascal II (r. 1099–1118) cited the verse as proof that "without doubt God has renewed the ancient miracles," fulfilling his promise in Leviticus 26:12 to "walk among you."[155] Guibert of Nogent used the verse to describe the Battle of Dorylaeum, while Robert of Reims, Gilo of Paris, and the authors of the *Historia Nicaena vel Antiochena* and the *Gesta Adhemari* applied it to the Franks' victory at Antioch.[156] Deuteronomy 32:30 lacked a rich exegetical history, perhaps because it did not readily lend itself to allegory; as Hrabanus Maurus wrote, it appeared to be a straightforward threat of destruction aimed at those who failed to respect God's might.[157] The verse's biblical context, in particular its proximity to Moses' first sight of the Promised Land, may have recommended it to chroniclers eager to link the crusaders' triumphs to the Israelites' victories over the idolatrous Canaanites, whose dispossession paved the way for the founding of Israel.[158] Such logic clearly appealed to writers like Raymond of Aguilers, who wrote that the guardians of the Holy Sepulcher delivered the True Cross to the crusaders because "clearly God has chosen you (*vos elegit*), has delivered you from all of your trials, and given you this and many other cities, not by virtue of your great strength but because in his wrath he has blinded the blasphemers."[159] Here, as so often

---

pilgrim-crusader's status as the heir of Abraham's promise is echoed in later formulae for the blessing of the crusader's cross, as in a late twelfth-century example from Ely cited and analyzed by Gaposchkin, *Invisible Weapons*, 85–86.

[155] EP, no. 22, p. 178.

[156] GN, 158; RR, 45 and 62; GP, 160; *Historia Nicaena vel Antiochena*, c. 42, RHC Oc. 5:164; *Gesta Adhemari*, RHC Oc. 5:355. Cf. FC, 364; and the anonymous twelfth-century *Secunda pars historiae Hierosolimitanae*, c. 5, RHC 3:554.

[157] Hrabanus Maurus, *Enarratio super Deuteronomium*, 4.2, PL 108:980. This reading is echoed by Bruno of Würzburg (d. 1045), *Commentarius in Cantica*, PL 142:551.

[158] My analysis is indebted to Green, *The Millstätter Exodus*, 243–44. This passage continued to be associated with crusading in later decades; see Tessera, "The Bible in Twelfth-Century Papal Letters," 203–4; Giles Constable, "A Report of a Lost Sermon by St Bernard on the Failure of the Second Crusade," in *Studies in Medieval Cistercian History*, ed. Joseph F. O'Callaghan (Shannon, Ireland, 1971), 49.

[159] Here is another echo of the crusaders as a *beata gens*. RA, 154: "Manifestum est quod Deus vos elegit, et ex omnibus tribulationibus vos eripuit, et hanc civitatem et alias

in early crusading narratives, a competing faith group (in this case, Greek Christians) is made to use biblical logic to demonstrate the Latins' divine mandate.

Finally, Latin writers summoned divine wrath upon the crusaders' enemies in the words of Psalm 78:6 ("Pour out thy wrath upon the nations that have not known thee, and upon the kingdoms that have not called upon thy name"), a verse which was to have a distinguished place in crusading liturgies of the twelfth and thirteenth centuries.[160] Attributed to Kerbogha's mother in the *Gesta Francorum*, Monte Cassino chronicle, and Guibert of Nogent's *Dei gesta per Francos*, and to crusading clerics at Ma'arra by Robert of Reims,[161] the verse allowed the chroniclers to cast Latin victories as just punishments of those who, in Augustine's gloss of Psalm 78:6, "call upon idols, demons, or even beasts, rather than upon the Creator."[162] Such unbelievers, who were, in the words of the Pseudo-Bruno of Chartreuse, already "blinded in their souls," deserved to be "sent bodily and soul into the fires of Gehenna."[163] There, Latin exegetes imagined, space was set aside for all of the enemies of the chosen people, past, present, and future. For just as the crusaders were accorded a privileged place in a genealogy of chosen people stretching back to the first covenant described in Genesis, equal care was taken to situate their Muslim opponents within the history of unbelief. Here, too, the Scriptures and their exegetical traditions provided crucial inspiration.

Muslims as Biblical Polytheists

The chroniclers further emphasized the crusaders' status as God's elect by linking contemporary Turks, Syrians, and Egyptians to the biblical opponents of Israel. The typological association of Levantine Muslims with Amalekites, Edomites,

---

multas vobis tribuit, non in virtutis vestre robore sed in furore suo execans impios, et civitates munitissimas vobis aperuit et bella formidolosa vobis ductor et dominus vester pro vobis ipse peregit." Raymond might have had in mind any one of the numerous biblical examples of blinding as a divine punishment, e.g., Deut. 28:28, 4 Kgs. 6:18, Is. 44:18, Jn. 12:40.

[160] For examples, see Gaposchkin, *Invisible Weapons*, Table 1 and 218, 316, and 318–19; see also Thomas W. Smith, "The Use of the Bible in the *Arengae* of Pope Gregory IX's Crusade Calls," in *The Uses of the Bible*, ed. Lapina and Morton, 206–35 (at 235); and Debra Higgs Strickland, "Looking Back: The Westminster Psalter, the Added Drawings, and the Idea of 'Retrospective Crusade,'" in *The Crusades and Visual Culture*, ed. Lapina et al., 157–84 (at 171).

[161] GF, 54; MC, 72; GN, 214; and RR, 86.

[162] Augustine, *Enarrationes in psalmos*, c.78.9, ed. Dekkers and Fraipont, 2:1104: "Invocant enim pro eo vel simulacra, vel daemonia, vel quamlibet creaturam ... ."

[163] Pseudo-Bruno of Chartreuse, *Expositio in Psalmos*, c.78, PL 152:1060.

Jebusites, and other ancient *gentes* (i.e., "peoples" or "races"[164]) was inspired by the Scriptures, where these groups serve as anti-models to set off the chosen people's piety and obstacles to the fulfillment of God's promise to Abraham, and was informed by earlier medieval exegesis. Nonetheless, the nature of this influence has not been fully explored, even as studies by John V. Tolan, Nicholas Morton, Jean Flori, and Kristin Skottki have greatly enhanced our understanding of how the first crusaders and their chroniclers viewed Islam through the related lenses of ethnography, history, and prophecy.[165] The following analysis adds to this work, demonstrating how glosses of Muslims as Old Testament 'pagans' drew upon earlier exegetical traditions, even as they reflected concerns about religious 'others' that took hold in Christendom post-1099.

The anxieties about paganism which inform depictions of Muslims in crusading contexts were hardly new. While the Vulgate does not explicitly denounce *pagani* – a word whose connotations changed dramatically with the ascendance of the Roman Church[166] – the Old Testament includes numerous descriptions of forbidden beliefs and practices, including polytheism, idol worship, sorcery, and violations of ritual purity, which were retroactively labelled 'pagan.' The earliest Christians, coming of age in a hostile, largely polytheistic Roman world, had denounced non-believers as unfeeling, barbaric, even inhuman, framing paganism and its attendant vices as inherently antithetical to

---

[164] On the associations of the medieval Latin term *gens* with descent, race and ethnicity, and religion, see Geraldine Heng, *The Invention of Race in the European Middle Ages* (Cambridge, 2018), 118f.; and Robert Bartlett, "Medieval and Modern Conceptions of Race and Ethnicity," *Journal of Medieval and Early Modern Studies* 31, no. 1 (2001): 39–56 (esp. 42–44).

[165] See Morton, *Encountering Islam, passim*; John V. Tolan, "Muslims as Pagan Idolaters in Chronicles of the First Crusade," in *Western Views of Islam in Medieval and Early Modern Europe: Perception of Other*, ed. Michael Frassetto and David R. Blanks (New York, 1999), 97–117; idem, *Saracens: Islam in the Medieval European Imagination* (New York, 2002), ch. 5–6; Jean Flori, *L'Islam et la fin des temps: l'interprétation prophétiques des invasions musulmanes dans la chrétienté médiévale* (Paris, 2007), ch. 13–14; idem, "La caricature de l'Islam dans l'Occident médiéval: origine et signification de quelques stéréotypes concernant l'Islam," *Aevum* 2 (1992): 245–56; Kristin Skottki, *Christen, Muslime und der Erste Kreuzzug: Die Macht der Beschreibung in der mittelalterlichen und modernen Historiographie* (Münster, 2015), ch. 4; and the ground-breaking work of Svetlana Loutchitskaja: "*Barbarae Nationes*: Les peuples musulmans dans les chroniques de la Première Croisade," in *Autour de la Première Croisade, Actes du Colloque de la Society for the Study of the Crusades and the Latin East (Clermont-Ferrand, 22–25 juin 1995)*, ed. Michel Balard (Paris, 1996), 99–107; and eadem, "L'Image des musulmans dans les chroniques des croisades," *Le Moyen Age* 105 (1999): 717–35.

[166] Peter Brown, "Pagan," in *Late Antiquity: A Guide to the Postclassical World*, ed. G. W. Bowersock, Peter Brown, and Oleg Grabar (Cambridge, MA, 1999), 625.

Christianity.¹⁶⁷ While early medieval exegetes who inherited these stereotypes of *pagani* tended to gloss Old Testament polytheism allegorically, some writers harnessed anti-pagan discourses to disparage living enemies; Bede, for instance, compared the bellicose Britons to the Philistines.¹⁶⁸ In Carolingian Francia, the apostasy of the Saxons, as well as debates over the proper role of images in Christian worship, prompted a reexamination of Old Testament prohibitions of idols.¹⁶⁹ Ninth-century exegetes identified Old Testament polytheists as "pagans" and "heretics," and suggested that the devil had worked through these peoples to oppose Israel, just as latter-day unbelievers sought to undermine the Frankish church.¹⁷⁰ Anxieties about paganism became more pronounced still in the tenth century, as monastic missionary efforts that targeted Christendom's frontiers heightened Latins' awareness of polytheism as an existential threat.¹⁷¹ The ancient *gentes* of the Old Testament remained touchstones in the evolving discourse on paganism; eleventh-century reformers likened biblical 'pagans' to other agents of social and ritual pollution, like simoniacal and unchaste clerics, as well as

---

[167] See Sara Lipton, "Christianity and Its Others: Jews, Muslims, and Pagans," in *The Oxford Handbook of Medieval Christianity*, ed. John H. Arnold (Oxford, 2014), 413–35 (at 424–25); and Daniel Baraz, *Medieval Cruelty: Changing Perceptions, Late Antiquity to the Early Modern Period* (Ithaca, NY, 2003), 29–46.

[168] Ian Wood, "Who are the Philistines? Bede's Readings of Old Testament Peoples," in *The Resources of the Past in Early Medieval Europe*, ed. Clemens Gantner, Rosamund McKitterick, and Sven Meeder (Cambridge, 2015), 172–87 (at 179). John Tolan has shown that some eighth-century Iberian writers called their Muslim overlords "Chaldeans," a moniker implying cruelty, tyranny, and allegiance to Antichrist; see *Saracens*, 88–100. Some Eastern Christians made similar connections, which may have inspired some of the First Crusade's chroniclers; see Morton, *Encountering Islam*, 200–3.

[169] Robert Flierman, "Religious Saxons: Paganism, Infidelity and Biblical Punishment in the *Capitulatio de partibus Saxoniae*," in *Religious Franks: Religion and Power in the Frankish Kingdoms in Honour of Mayke de Jong*, ed. Rob Meens et al. (Manchester, 2016), 172–92 (esp. 181–84); and Thomas F. X. Noble, *Images, Iconoclasm, and the Carolingians* (Philadelphia, 2009), 187–91.

[170] A nice example is Hrabanus Maurus' allegorical reading of the Syrian king Ben-Hadad and the siege of Samaria (4 Kgs. 6 and 8); see *Commentaria in libros Regum*, 3.20, 4.8, PL 109:213–14 and 236. See, too, Scott G. Bruce's discussion of tenth-century Cluniacs' association of Muslims with the biblical figure Belial; *Cluny and the Muslims of La Garde-Freinet: Hagiography and the Problem of Islam in Medieval Europe* (Ithaca, 2015), 36–37.

[171] John Marenbon has emphasized the relative paucity of writings about paganism in the centuries separating Boethius and Abelard; see *Pagans and Philosophers: The Problem of Paganism from Augustine to Leibnitz* (Princeton, NJ, 2015), 57–72. For the revival of missionizing in the century preceding the First Crusade, see Phyllis G. Jestice, *Wayward Monks and the Religious Revolution of the Eleventh Century* (Leiden, 1997), 44–89.

heretics and Jews.[172] In the words of Humbert of Silva Candida (d. 1061), pagans "hold in their hearts, and spew from their mouths, the faithlessness of idolatry (*perfidiam ydolatriae*)," and are "like beasts in their savagery" (*in sua saevitia similes sunt bestiis*).[173]

As much as the Scriptures and their commentary traditions shaped medieval Christian views of paganism, prior to the advent of crusading much of what educated Latins knew, or thought they knew, about Muslims came from these same sources. Christian exegetes traditionally identified Muslims as descendants of Ishmael, Abraham's son by Hagar, the handmaiden of his wife Sarah. This interpretation, developed by Jerome and expanded upon by Cassiodorus and Bede, had huge implications for later views of 'Saracens': as blood descendants of earlier 'Ishmaelite' peoples, including the Midianites (Gen. 37, Num. 10, 25, 31), they were believed to be tainted by the curse laid upon their common biblical ancestor (Gen. 16:11–12), though, early medieval exegetes claimed, 'Saracens' denied their lineage, falsely claiming to be descendants of Sarah.[174] Such a reading eroded the temporal distance between Old Testament events and the present, as it was a short step from identifying 'Saracens' as the descendants of ancient Levantine tribes to identifying them as *living* members of these tribes. To paraphrase one anonymous monastic exegete, 'Saracen' was just a pejorative name for Midianites, Ishmaelites, and Hagarenes.[175] Nor did exposure to actual 'Saracens' necessarily undermine such views. As Nicholas Morton has shown, well-informed Christians in the Levant continued to describe the ancient Chaldeans and Medes as living peoples even in the thirteenth century.[176] Certainly this sense of sojourning among biblical *gentes* is present in narratives of the First Crusade; consider, for instance, Fulcher of Chartres's casual mention of passing

---

[172] The letters of Peter Damian, whose rhetoric strongly influenced later reformers, provide many such examples; e.g., Letters 141 and 174, in *Die Briefe des Petrus Damiani*, 4 vols., ed. Kurt Reindel, MGH Briefe der deutschen Kaiserzeit 4.1–4 (Munich, 1983–93), 3: 499–501 and 4: 272–74.

[173] Humbert of Silva Candida, *Libri tres adversus simoniacos*, 2.11, ed. Friedrich Thaner (Berlin, 1877), MGH Lib. de lite 1:151. For context, see Lipton, "Christianity and Its Others," 425–28. It is also noteworthy that Jews were sometimes associated with savagery or wild animals in early medieval Christian exegesis and homilies; see Michael Berger, "St. Peter Damian: His Attitude toward the Jews and the Old Testament," *Yavneh Review* 4 (1965): 80–112, repr. in David Berger, *Persecution, Polemic and Dialogue: Essays in Jewish-Christian Relations* (Boston, 2010), 261–88 (at 266–67).

[174] On the development of these ideas, see Katharine Scarfe Beckett, *Anglo-Saxon Perceptions of the Islamic World* (Cambridge, 2003), 90–98, 125–58; and Ekkehart Rotter, *Abendland und Sarazenen: Das okzidentale Araberbild und seine Entstehunt im Frühmittelalter* (Berlin, 1986), 231–64.

[175] Cited by Beckett, *Anglo-Saxon Perceptions*, 118.

[176] Morton, *Encountering Islam*, 208.

through "Philistine" territory en route to Jerusalem in 1099.[177] This background helps us to appreciate that when Latin narrators declared the holy war to be a revival of the campaigns of ancient Israel they meant this in both a spiritual and a literal sense.

In their presentation of Muslims as Old Testament polytheists, crusading narratives recycle venerable stereotypes of pagans as cruel, wrathful, idolaters and emphasize God's use of the 'Saracens' to test his new chosen people.[178] Describing the nadir of the army's fortunes at Antioch, Orderic Vitalis compared the crusaders to "the children of Israel" (*filios Israel*) who "were often afflicted and conquered in war by the Philistines, Edomites, Midianites, and other neighboring peoples, so that they might be compelled to turn again to God."[179] This view of battle as a mass trial by ordeal could equally be applied to single combats; thus, Robert of Reims staged Godfrey of Bouillon's confrontation with a particularly tall and fearsome Turk as a rematch between David and Goliath.[180] Similar logic is evident in the presentation of Turks as "Egyptians," an association which emphasizes the crusade's status as a second Exodus. Consider Gilo of Paris's foretelling of Kerbogha's defeat at Antioch:

> God will send his legion of angels to help (cf. Mat. 26:53), he will overwhelm this people as he overwhelmed Pharaoh (*uelut oppressit Pharaonem*). Oh, how great is the frenzy (*furor*) with which this senseless race (*gens insensata*) is seized! In their madness (*malesana*), they are buying hell with their own blood, they earn pain with pain, their flesh is twice crucified, and through this death they merit death without end (cf. 1 Cor. 10:13).[181]

The Muslims-as-Egyptians motif allowed chroniclers to present Christian victories in the East as divine rewards for unwavering faith. This is clear in Ralph of Caen's use of Psalm 135:13–14 to liken Jerusalem's fall to the parting of the Red Sea, another great miracle by which God punished "the blasphemies of the perfidious" and "consoled his desolate people."[182]

---

[177] FC, 274.
[178] Morton, *Encountering Islam*, 152.
[179] OV, 5:132–33: "Sic nimirum filios Israel in sacris codicibus frequenter afflictos legimus, et in bellos uictos a Philastiim et Edom atque Madian aliisque uicinis gentibus ut cogerentur ad Deum semper recurrere, et in obseruatione mandatorum eius perseuerare."
[180] RR, 44. Similarly, Ralph of Caen has Ademar of Le Puy encourage the crusaders to emulate David's courage when facing Goliath; RC, 61.
[181] GP, 184–86; and for commentary, Green, *Millstätter Exodus*, 261. The Danishmend Malik Ghazi, who imprisoned Bohemond of Antioch from 1100–1103, was cast as a new Pharaoh in Orderic Vitalis' *History*; see OV, 5:358, 376.
[182] RC, 104; trans. 141.

The casting of Muslims as biblical polytheists also bolstered the crusaders' claim to the terrestrial Promised Land. A twelfth-century hymn from the abbey of Saint-Martial commemorated the conquest of July 15. 1099 as "the day on which Dagon [a Philistine deity] was destroyed, and Amalek conquered; the one born of Hagar banished, and Jerusalem rescued and returned to the Christians."[183] The casualness of these references, it should be noted, presupposed a fair amount of biblical knowledge on the part of readers and listeners. When Baldric of Bourgueil had Urban II describe the Turks as "more execrable than the Jebusites," and command his audience to "brandish the sword against Amalek,"[184] or Guibert of Nogent styled Baldwin I of Jerusalem (r. 1100–18), as "that tireless lion, whose roars silenced the Philistines and Egyptians, and terrified the Arabs, Amalekites, and Edomites,"[185] they counted on their audiences to know that these ancient peoples had been disinherited or destroyed by divine command; God ordered King Saul to annihilate Amalek (1 Kgs. 15:2–3), while Saul's successor David subjected the Jebusites and Edomites (2 Kgs. 5:6–8, 8:14). For the crusade's narrators, who knew these stories well,[186] the advent of Latin armies in the Levant marked the beginning of a new cycle of conquests which brought a new chosen people to power. Robert of Reims explicitly framed the crusaders' conquests this way, while the Ripoll account of the capture of Jerusalem typologically links the 1099 victory to the Israelites' defeat of Amalek on the plain of Raphidim (Ex. 17).[187] Bartolf of Nangis (fl. c. 1108) went even further, suggesting that the first crusaders consciously modeled their treatment of Muslim adversaries on Old Testament precedent. Reflecting on the motivations behind the massacre of Jerusalem's inhabitants, Bartolf suggested that the Latins "were mindful, I believe (*credo*), of how King Saul spared Agag, thereby incurring God's wrath, and perished."[188] In the passage in question, Saul orders all the Amalekites

---

[183] Cited and discussed by Gaposchkin, *Invisible Weapons*, 188–89.

[184] BB, 9, 10: "et Turcos qui in ea [i.e., Jerusalem] sunt, nefandiores quam Iebuseos ... ." And again: "uos exerite et uibrate intrepidi preliatores in Amalech gladium." Trans. Krey in *The First Crusade*, ed. Peters, 32.

[185] Guibert of Nogent, *Petite chronique du règne de Baudouin Ier*, ed. Huygens in *Dei gesta per Francos*, 361 (Appendix 2): "impiger ille leo, rugitu cuius eo regnante siluit Philistim et Egypts, tremuit Arabs, Amalech et Ydumeus ... ."

[186] This is evident from the capsule histories of Jerusalem included in many of the crusade chronicles, which show the authors were aware that the city had a long history prior to its conquest by the Israelites; e.g., RR, 109; WM, 1:640. The role of Levantine landmarks in the Israelite conquests was also of interest to the chroniclers; e.g., Fulcher of Chartres's reference to Joshua's victory at Gibeon (Josh. 10:13) in FC, 280–81.

[187] RR, 62; CJ, 647, 649. This battle also seems to be referenced by BB, 10.

[188] Bartolf of Nangis, *Gesta francorum*, c. 25, RHC, Oc. 3:515: "nullusque ex eis [i.e., Jerusalem's non-Christian inhabitants] vitae est reservatus: sed neque feminis, neque parvulis pepercerunt: vitae memores, credo, Saul regis, qui Agag perpercit, iramque Dei incurrit et periit." While this appears to be an addition by Bartolf to his main

killed, but spares their king, Agag, in contravention of God's command to "*smite Amalek, and utterly destroy all that he hath*," down to the last man, woman, child, and animal (1 Kgs. 15:3–8). Strikingly, though Bartolf stopped short of insisting that the massacre of 1099 had followed a biblical script, he certainly thought it *could* have, and that God's command to Saul might have resonated with these new Israelites even more than it had with their spiritual forebears. Following a line of thinking familiar to medieval exegetes, Bartolf might even have seen God's command in 1 Kings 15 as being intended for the first crusaders.

The use of 'pagan' (*paganus* or *gentilis*) as a synonym for 'Muslim' in early crusade chronicles[189] is part of a larger narrative strategy that frames the holy war in terms of spiritual opposition. While one function of the Muslim-as-pagan label may be to associate the enemy with the early Church's Roman persecutors, attributing to them similar qualities – cruelty, lust, inconstancy – while bolstering fallen crusaders' claims to martyrdom,[190] in the larger exegetical context of the chronicles the charge of paganism also strengthens the typological bond between Muslims and the idolatrous enemies of ancient Israel, and thus between crusaders and Israelites. Robert of Reims makes this connection, describing how, during the siege of Antioch, the clerics among the crusading army (whom he refers to as "priests and Levites") called upon God for aid, using the language of the Israelites denouncing their gentile enemies: "*Pour out thy wrath upon the nations that have not known thee, and upon the kingdoms that have not called upon thy name*" (Ps. 78:6).[191] Likewise, Albert of Aachen's claim that the sultan of Baghdad "summoned the *magicians, prophets, and soothsayers* (Dan. 2:27) of their gods and asked about future victory" in the war with the Christians is voiced in the words of the prophet Daniel's denunciation of Babylonian religion, again aligning the Muslim enemy with biblical polytheism.[192] The equation of the ancient Egyptians, Philistines, and Amalekites with Levantine Muslims reflects the widespread ignorance of and hostility toward Islam on the part of Latin

---

source, Fulcher of Chartres's *Historia*, following the recent reassessment of Bartolf's work, this passage may have come from an earlier redaction of Fulcher's history; see Susan B. Edgington, "The *Gesta Francorum Iherusalem expugnantium* of 'Bartolf of Nangis,'" *Crusades* 13 (2014): 21–35. For discussion of this and other passages related to Amalek in crusading narratives, see Christian Hofreiter, *Making Sense of Old Testament Genocide: Christian Interpretations of Herem* (Oxford, 2018), 171–82.

[189] For representative references, see GF, 82; PT, 103; RR, 37; GN, 112; RC, 7; OV, 5:114; and FE, 132.

[190] As argued by Tolan, "Muslims as Pagan Idolaters," 97–117; and idem, *Saracens*, 117–20.

[191] RR, 86; and cf. RR, 62, for a speech by Kerbogha's mother that presents a similar message.

[192] AA, 258.

Christians, who were reluctant to acknowledge Islam as a monotheistic faith.[193] But this exegetical strategy also justified the holy war by presenting it not as an act of conquest but as a renewal of the ancient Israelites' aggression against unbelieving tribes, and thus as a war unquestionably in keeping with the will of God. The Old Testament justified the Israelites' wars as divine punishment for their neighbors' idolatry, and the crusaders proved their right to the Promised Land in a similar fashion.[194] Latin writers' insistence that Muslims worshiped idols fit neatly into this typological model, even as it drew upon a longstanding exegetical tradition that identified Ishmaelites, Hagarenes, and other biblical opponents of the chosen people with idolatry and the adjunct vices of greed and lust.[195]

But we must not forget that when early twelfth-century writers linked the First Crusade allegorically to Old Testament migrations and conflicts they asserted the superiority of the crusaders to the Israelites, of 'new Israel' to old, of the type to the archetype. Granted the chance to reenact the Exodus and conquer Jerusalem anew, the crusaders, God's new elect, avoided the spiritual pitfalls that entrapped the first Israelites. Baldric of Bourgeuil made this point via a comparison of the crusaders' encampment at Nicaea to the Israelites' preparations for battle with the Midianites:

> I confess, truly I confess, that if [the prophet] Balaam had been worthy of being present at such a lovely sight, he would have admired those tents even more than the *tents of the Israelites* (Num. 24:5), since in the Christian camps [the priest] Phineas would not have discovered the Midianite [harlot] whom he stabbed with a dagger (cf. Num. 25:16), nor would an evil serpent have been sent to burn the people [as punishment] for evil-doing (Num. 21:6).[196]

---

[193] For the development of "polemical images" of Islam in Europe pre-1200, including that of the pagan Saracen, see Tolan, *Saracens*, chaps. 4–6; on the association of Islam with idolatry and unreason from the First Crusade on, see Suzanne Conklin Akbari, *Idols in the East: European Representations of Islam and the Orient, c. 1100–1450* (Ithaca, 2009). Despite the widespread dissemination of such negative views, there existed a range of European attitudes towards Islam, as argued by Jo Ann Hoeppner Moran Cruz, "Popular Attitudes Toward Islam in Medieval Europe," in *Western Views of Islam*, ed. Frassetto and Blanks, 55–81.

[194] For the themes of idol-worship and pollution, see Jean Flori, "La caricature de l'Islam," 245–56; and Cole, "Theme of Religious Pollution," 85–88; as well as the discussion in Chapter 4.

[195] Beckett, *Anglo-Saxon Perceptions*, 104–09, 212–13.

[196] BB, 25: "Fateor, et uerum fateor, quoniam, si Balaam huic tam formose speculationi adesse meruisset tentoria ista tentoriis Israeliticis preposuisset. In castris siquidem Christianis, nec Finees Madianitem, quam pugione confocere debuisset, inueniret; nec serpens malignus, quem pro malignitate sua torreret, haberet."

The Bible and Crusade Narrative in the Twelfth Century

In Baldric's view, whereas the new chosen people retained the moral purity that was a condition of their victories, it is clear that the ancient Israelites had been rewarded by God *despite* their spiritual shortcomings. In the collective logic of the chronicles, the crusaders proved their obedience to the divine will not only by embracing suffering but by meting out terrible punishments to their defeated adversaries, who were themselves condemned to repeat the blasphemies of their biblical predecessors. But while Levantine Muslims were, in Latin eyes, as irredeemable as the Midianites or Amalekites, the crusaders, strengthened by their faith, so far surpassed their archetypes as to reduce the original Israelites to the status of mere predictors of the Jerusalemites' triumphs. Indeed, as we shall see in the next section, the crusaders' status as new Israelites depended on the denigration not only of Muslims-as-pagans but of living Jews, as well as on the christological interpretation of Old Testament prophecy in the light of the holy war.

Crusade History as Polemic

Crusade apologists turned to the Old Testament for inspiration at a moment when the status of Jewish communities was deteriorating in the West and theologians were becoming increasingly preoccupied with the 'problem' of Judaism. While various explanations have been adduced to explain the declining position of Jews, and scholars disagree about the first crusaders' role in this story, it is clear that the late eleventh and early twelfth centuries saw a proliferation of anti-Jewish polemic, in the form of traditional *Adversus Judaeos* treatises as well as biblical commentaries, religious poetry, and liturgical drama.[197] Such works participated in a larger effort to reform and strengthen the Christian community by clarifying key doctrinal points challenged by Jews. Scholars of the First Crusade have long been concerned with its short- and long-term impact on European Jewry, and numerous studies have interrogated the anti-Jewish sentiment in crusade chronicles. This work has understandably concentrated on explicit references to living Jews, especially in the context of the Rhineland massacres of 1096.[198] Focusing instead

---

[197] For the variety of anti-Jewish genres, see Gilbert Dahan, *The Christian Polemic against the Jews in the Middle Ages*, trans. Jody Gladding (Notre Dame, IN, 1988), 41–79. It is important to note that the late eleventh and early twelfth centuries saw not only an increase in polemical output but the articulation of new ways of thinking about conversion, as well as heightened frustration on the part of Christians about the failure of missionary efforts directed at Jews; see Ryan Szpiech, *Conversion and Narrative: Reading and Religious Authority in Medieval Polemic* (Philadelphia, 2012), 7f; and David Berger, Introduction to *The Jewish-Christian Debate in the High Middle Ages: A Critical Edition of the* Nizzahon Vetus (Philadelphia, 1979), 8–11.

[198] Among the large body of scholarship on the Rhineland massacres and their aftermath,

on the chronicles' substantial biblical content offers another, virtually untapped, means of addressing this important issue. As we shall see, this strategy makes visible the indebtedness of early crusade narratives to anti-Jewish polemic, whose christological approach to Old Testament prophecy and combative exegesis of key verses inspired Latin writers' approach to new theological challenges related to Islam. While Christians accorded Jews and Muslims different roles in salvation history, early crusading narratives bear out Jeremy Cohen's assertion that the 'hermeneutical Jew' of medieval polemic served as a model for the creation of a 'hermeneutical Muslim' in the early twelfth century.[199]

An analysis of the influence of anti-Jewish polemic on the First Crusade's chronicles must begin with the chroniclers themselves, at least some of whom were personally invested in ongoing debates about Jews' place in Christendom. It is well known that Guibert of Nogent, whose *Dei gesta per Francos* features strident anti-Jewish rhetoric, subsequently authored a polemical work on the Incarnation, the *Contra iudaizantem et Iudeos* (c. 1111).[200] Orderic Vitalis was familiar with similar works, having supervised the copying of Gilbert Crispin's popular *Disputatio Iudei et Christiani* (c. 1092) for the library at Saint-Evroul,[201] and William of Malmesbury avidly collected scurrilous stories about Jews.[202]

---

key works are Jeremy Cohen, *Sanctifying the Name of God: Jewish Martyrs and Jewish Memories of the First Crusade* (Philadelphia, 2004); and Robert Chazan, *In the Year 1096: The First Crusade and the Jews* (Philadelphia, 1996).

[199] Here I follow Jeremy Cohen, though he is not explicitly concerned with the First Crusade chronicles; see "The Muslim Connection, or On the Changing Role of the Jew in High Medieval Theology," in *From Witness to Witchcraft: Jews and Judaism in Medieval Christian Thought*, ed. Cohen, Wolfenbütteler Mittelalter-Studien 11 (Wiesbaden, 1996), 141–62; and idem, *Living Letters of the Law: Ideas of the Jew in Medieval Christianity* (Berkeley, CA, 1999), 158f.

[200] See *Contra iudaizantem et Iudeos*, ed. R. B. C. Huygens in *Serta mediaevalia: textus varii saeculorum X–XIII in unum collecti*, CCSL 171 (Turnhout, 2000), 310–73. Elizabeth Lapina has examined the use of Jewish models in the *Dei gesta* within the context of Gilbert's other works; see "Anti-Jewish Rhetoric," esp. 242–43, 252. For the place of the *Contra iudaizantem* within Gilbert's oeuvre and worldview, see Rubenstein, *Guibert of Nogent*, ch. 5.

[201] Saint-Evroul's copy of Gilbert Crispin's work is preserved in Rouen, Bibliothèque municipale, ms. 1174, fols. 106r–115v; for discussion, see Chibnall, *The World of Orderic Vitalis: Norman Monks and Norman Knights* (Woodbridge, 1984), 157 and n. 39.

[202] Kati Ihnat, "Getting the Punchline: Deciphering Anti-Jewish Humor in Anglo-Norman England," *Journal of Medieval History* 38, no. 4 (2012): 408–23 (esp. 412–21); P. N. Carter, "The Historical Content of William of Malmesbury's Miracles of the Virgin," in *The Writing of History in the Middle Ages: Essays Presented to Richard William Southern*, ed. R. H. C. Davis and J. M. Wallace-Hadrill (Oxford, 1981), 146–54; Adrienne Williams Boyarin, *Miracles of the Virgin in Medieval England: Law and Jewishness in Marian Legends* (Cambridge, 2010), 69–73.

Polemical works circulated widely in France and the Anglo-Norman world in the decades around 1100, and it is likely that many, if not most, of the crusade's narrators knew such texts. Even those who did not would have encountered the ideological building-blocks of anti-Judaism in the patristic and Carolingian homiletic and exegetical works that were the foundation of monastic and cathedral libraries.[203] Interactions with living Jews in a still relatively unsegregated society may have heightened some chroniclers' interest in a theological confrontation between Christianity and Judaism that was entering a higher-stakes phase.[204] Finally, it is suggestive that some later copyists viewed crusading historiography and anti-Jewish polemic as related genres, as is apparent from the tradition of copying Baldric of Bourgueil's *Historia* alongside the Jewish convert Peter Alfonsi's *Dialogus contra Judaeos* (c. 1100).[205]

The crusade's narrators signaled their engagement with the Jewish–Christian debate in various ways. First, for all that Christian writers embraced the Israelites as prototypical crusaders, they took pains to show that these latter-day chosen people were superior to their predecessors in intention and deed. According to Ralph of Caen, Adhemar of Le Puy preached a sermon at Antioch in which he recounted David's exploits against the Philistines (1 Kgs. 18) not only to inspire his listeners with "examples from antiquity" (*de antiquis exempla*) but to contrast the biblical hero's motivation with the purer motives of the Christian warriors; David was roused to fight "by the promise of the king's daughter and the liberty of his father's house," in other words, by worldly rewards, but Adhemar ordered the crusaders to "act, so that it is not the ambition of rule which moves you but rather the completion of this journey we have undertaken."[206] In a similar interpretive move, Guibert of Nogent qualified his comparison of the crusaders'

---

[203] For example, from an inventory taken in c. 1000 we know that in the library of Le Puy Raymond of Aguilers could have read commentaries by Augustine and Gregory the Great, whose interpretations helped define the Church's position on the Jews; see Léopold Delisle, "Recherches sur l'ancienne bibliothèque du Puy," *Annales de la Société Académique du Puy* 28 (1866–67), 1–21 (at 7–8).

[204] Aachen, for instance, had a Jewish community which dated to the Carolingian period; see Bernard S. Bachrach, *Early Medieval Jewish Policy in Western Europe* (Minneapolis, 1977), 166 n. 22.

[205] The works appear together in three manuscripts: Chartres, Bibliothèque municipale, mss. 127 (now lost) and 130 (both 12th century); British Library, Harley 3707 (13th century, probably French). For descriptions of these, see Biddlecombe, Introduction to the *Historia*, lxxiv, lxxxv, xcviii; and Omont et al., *Catalogue générale des manuscrits des bibliothèques publiques de France* (Paris, 1890), 9:68–69.

[206] RC, 61: "Non fuit in Hebraeis, qui contra Goliath surgeret, donec regis filia et libertas patria domui promissa David suscitarunt. ... Quare agite, non moveat uos ambitus regnandi, sed potius viae coeptae consummatio ... ." Trans. 90. Cf. Raymond of Aguilers's report that the clerics in the crusader army objected to the election of a king in Jerusalem out of fear that he might "become a David, degenerate in faith and

accomplishments with those of the ancient Israelites, writing: "Let us rejoice then in the battles [the crusaders] won, undertaken purely out of spiritual desire (*spirituali desiderio*), granted by divine power, which had never before appeared, but was made manifest in modern times; and let us not admire the fleshly wars (*carnalia bella*) of Israel, which were waged merely to fill the belly."[207] Such declarations rest on a substrate of dichotomies – carnal/spiritual, literal/allegorical, worldly/celestial – often used by medieval writers to compare Judaism unfavorably with Christianity.

Chroniclers also staged their co-religionists' encounters with Muslims in a manner reminiscent of the disputations between Christians and Jews that were a common feature of the intellectual landscape in twelfth-century Europe. For instance, the accounts of Peter the Hermit's embassy to the Turkish magnate Kerbogha on the eve of the Battle of Antioch have an unmistakably *disputatio*-like flavor. According to the *Gesta Francorum*, Peter hopefully asked Kerbogha if "perhaps you have come here with the full intent of being christened?" whereupon the great man thundered, "We neither want nor like your God and your Christendom, and we spit upon you and them."[208] While Peter's attempt at conversion was a spectacular failure, this aspect of the embassy clearly interested later writers, who added details that smacked of the aggressive give and take of contemporary interreligious debate. Albert of Aachen played up Peter's proselytizing, having him ask the Turkish leader to "consent to believe in the Lord Christ, who is the true God and son of God, and renounce the filthy ways of the gentiles" (*gentilium spurcitiis*).[209] In Gilo of Paris's narrative, Peter demands that Kerbogha "discard the law of error" (*erroris lege*), while his interlocutor, in turn, derides "the people ... eager to pay homage to some Christ, whoever he may be."[210] Ralph of Caen writes that after his retainers mocked Peter for his humble mien, Kerbogha followed suit, laughing at Christ and at Saint Peter,

---

goodness, [and then] the Lord, no doubt, [would] overthrow him and be angry with the place and people." RA, 143; trans. 121.

[207] GN, 267: "De his itaque spirituali solum desiderio ceptis patratisque preliis, divina, quae a seculo numquam acciderit, tempora moderna insigniri virtute letemur nec Israhelis carnalia pro ventrium plenitudine bella miremur." Trans. 124.

[208] GF, 66–67: Peter's question is: "Putamus forsitan et credimus, quia ideo huc uenistis, quoniam per omnia uultis effici Christiani?" To which Kerbogha replies, "Deum uestrum et uestram christianitatem nec optamus nec uolumus, uosque cum illis omnino respuimus." Cf. PT, 108–09 and the bare-bones account in RA, 79. In Robert of Reims's account, Kerbogha demands that Christians "renounce their God and his Christianity or be destroyed"; see RR, 71–72.

[209] AA, 318–19 (trans. slightly modified): "Christo Domino qui uerus est Deus et Dei filius credere concesseris, et gentilium spurcitiis abreuntiaueris ... ."

[210] GP, 182–85: Kerbogha derides the Christians (at 184) as "Gens que nescio cui studet obsequium dare Christo." Here there is an echo of the longstanding critique of Jews as enslaved to the law, in contrast to Christian adherence to the *spirit* of the law.

Antioch's saintly guardian.[211] The two sides accuse one another of "madness" (*dementia*) and "ignorance" (*inscitia*) in the version by Guibert of Nogent, who describes the encounter using the dialectical language of proofs.[212] According to Baldric of Bourgueil, Kerbogha angrily rejected Peter's offer of baptism in a speech that echoes the Jews' mocking of the crucified Christ in the Gospel of Mark (15:30–31):

> We totally reject and spit upon (*respuimus*) your Christianity, which is a form of idolatry and an abomination (*idolatria et abominatio*). You pretend you will rescue from our hands your crucified one (*crucifixus vester*), who could not even save himself from the insult of the cross (cf. Mk. 15:30–31)? We wonder by what madness you presume to call yours the land which we have long held, which our ancestors possessed long before that superstitious Peter of yours; but he drew them away from the worship of their God with his lies, and seduced the deceived ones into that most ridiculous sect (*nugacissimam sectam*) of yours.[213]

Narratively speaking, these scenes support Christian exegesis of the Battle of Antioch as a divine punishment of disbelief, a victory marked by "wonders" (*mira*) so great that some Muslims were said to have accepted baptism in its aftermath.[214] But these exchanges also touch upon key issues that preoccupied early twelfth-century Christian (and Jewish) polemicists; Jews living in the West openly denied Christ's divinity, decried baptism, and equated Christian worship with idolatry, while authors of *Adversus Judeaos* literature went to great lengths to refute Jewish critiques.[215] The framing of recalcitrant converts as mad is

---

[211] RC, 72–73.

[212] GN, 234–36.

[213] BB, 78: "Christianitatem enim uestram, que idolatria et abominatio est, omnino respuimus et habominamur. Crucifixus uester, quem pretenditis, qui se crucis improperio non potuit eripere, uos nostris eripiet manibus? Miramur quo hiatu terram, quam diu possedimus, uestram uocare presumitis, quam ante Petrum illum, superstitiosum uestrum, progenitores nostri possederunt; sed illos fallaciis suis a Deitatis sue cultura auertit, eosque in nugacissimam sectam uestram deceptos seduxit." Kerbogha's framing of Christianity as a "sect" whose members "seduced" believers away from the true God aligns with medieval Jewish characterizations of Christianity. Cf. OV, 5:108, for a similar story, and OV, 5:166, for Muslim women's mocking of Christian belief at the siege of Jerusalem.

[214] Several writers describe the subsequent conversion of the leader of Antioch's garrison (and, in some accounts, other Muslims); see GF, 71; BB, 84; and OV, 5: 116. Gilo of Paris connects the conversions at Antioch to the wonders (*mira*) observed at the battle for the city; GP, 192.

[215] Robert Chazan, *Fashioning Jewish Identity in Medieval Western Christendom* (Cambridge, 2004), ch. 11–12, 14; Anna Sapir Abulafia, *Christians and Jews*, 70–71, 86, 118–19; and Bernhard Blumenkranz, *Juifs et chrétiens dans le monde occidental, 430–1096* (Paris, 1960), 279–89.

another commonplace in contemporary polemic, in which clerical writers cast the Jews' rejection of Christ as irrational, and, ultimately, a mark of their diminished humanity.[216]

Crusade apologists also shared with polemicists a keen interest in Christ's crucifixion. It is well known that the first crusaders were regarded as imitators of Christ, who had, by taking the cross, literally fulfilled the Gospel commandment to this effect (Mat. 16:24, Mk. 8:34, Lk. 9:23).[217] As Susanna Throop has shown, early crusading narratives framed the holy war – and, in particular, the assault on Jerusalem in 1099 – as a means of avenging the crucifixion,[218] and, in their active defense of Christ's honor against 'Saracens,' crusade chroniclers echoed early twelfth-century polemicists and exegetes, who claimed – in a sharp departure from earlier Christian tradition – that the Jews had persecuted Christ in full knowledge that he was the messiah.[219] Raymond of Aguilers recounted how the crucified Christ appeared to the priest Peter Bartholomew at Antioch to castigate faithful crusaders, who, he said, "are like my crucifiers who said, 'He deserves death (cf. Mk. 14:64, Lk. 23:21); to the cross with him because he claims to be a king, the son of God.'" The Jerusalemites must remain steadfast in their faith, Christ continued, or, as unbelievers (*increduli*), they "will be with the Jews, and I shall choose other people for whom to fulfill my promises."[220] Visions of the crucifixion also drove the crusaders to attack the Muslim enemy,[221] whom they likened to the Jews who had betrayed Christ. In Baldric of Bourgueil's *Historia*

---

[216] Abulafia, *Christians and Jews in the Twelfth-Century Renaissance*, ch. 6. See also eadem, "Christians Disputing Disbelief: St Anselm, Gilbert Crispin and Pseudo-Anselm," *Religionsgespräche im Mittelalter*, ed. Bernard Lewis and Friedrich Niewöhner (Wiesbaden, 1992), 131–48; repr. in *Christians and Jews in Dispute: Disputational Literature and the Rise of Anti-Judaism in the West (c. 1000–1150)* (Aldershot, 1998), 131–48.

[217] This verse was widely cited by the chroniclers in support of the Jerusalem journey: GF, 1; PT, 31; MC, 12; GN, 178. William J. Purkis has demonstrated the importance of such imitation in motivating crusaders, who might mark their bodies in token of their deep commitment to following Christ's example; see Purkis, "'Zealous imitation': The Materiality of the Crusader's Marked Body," *Material Religion* 14, no. 4 (2018): 438–53.

[218] Throop, *Crusading as an Act of Vengeance*, 59–61. Philippe Buc suggests educated Christians would have viewed the Rhineland Massacres in terms of the *vindicta Domini* legend; see "La vengeance de Dieu," 452–53.

[219] Jeremy Cohen, "The Jews as Killers of Christ in the Latin Tradition, from Augustine to the Friars," *Traditio* 39 (1983): 1–27 (at 13–16).

[220] RA, 114–15: "Hi tales similes illis sunt, qui dixerunt: 'reus est mortis, crucifigatur, quia se regem fecit, et Dei filium se dixit.' ... Alioquin vobis remanentibus cum Iudeis alios populos assumam, et per ipsos compleo, quod vobis promiseram." Trans. (slightly revised) 93–94.

[221] GN, 240; and OV, 5:168 (both cited by Throop, *Crusading as an Act of Vengeance*, 59).

a priest primes the crusaders for their assault on Fatimid-held Jerusalem with this comparison:

> Let us rouse ourselves, kinsmen of Christ (*familia Christi*); let us rouse ourselves, knights and footsoldiers, to seize this city, which indeed belongs to us. Attend to Christ, who has until today (*adhuc hodie*) been persecuted and crucified within its walls, and, with Joseph [of Arimathea] take him down from the cross, lay that most dear, most desired one's body down in the sepulcher of your heart, and manfully take hold of those unbelievers (*impiis*) who crucified him. For just as the Jews, accomplices of Herod and Pilate, crucify (*crucifigunt*) Christ, so do those evildoers (*mali*) mock and abuse your brethren. Just as they torment and kill them [i.e., Jerusalem's Christians], so, with Longinus, do they wound Christ in his side with a lance. They do all of this, and, what is worse, they deride and insult our law and Christ, provoking us with their reckless mouths.[222]

This rhetoric elides the distinction between Jerusalem's past and present, the body of Christ and the bodies of Christians, while reinforcing believers' corporate membership in Christ's family. Equally importantly, the distinction between Jew and Muslim dissolves, reminding us that, following Suzanne Conklin Akbari, medieval Christians' constructions of the 'Saracen' drew heavily upon earlier ideas about Jews.[223] Muslims become, in Baldric's presentation, dialectical opponents of Christianity who oppose the crusaders in word as much as deed; in the logic of the passage, it seems as important for the crusaders to stop their opponents from mocking and insulting the faith as to conquer the holy city. This same urgency is a familiar feature of contemporary anti-Jewish treatises, in which Jews are reproached for jeering at Christian belief and practice. In an eleventh-century polemical exchange reported by Alpert of Metz (d. 1024), for example, the Christian chastises his Jewish interlocutor for "vomiting forth calumny from [his] unbelieving mouth" and "murmuring with infamous arrogance in an attempt

---

[222] BB, 108: "Expergiscimini igitur, familia Christi; expergiscimini, milites et pedites expediti; et ciuitatem hanc, rem quidem publicam nostram, constanter capessite; et Christum, qui adhuc hodie in ciuitate ista proscribitur et crucifigitur, adtendite; et de cruce, cum Ioseph, uobis illum deponite; et in sepulcro cordis uestri thesaurum incomparabilem, thesaurum illum concupiscibilem, collocate; et istis impiis crucifixoribus illum uiriliter eripite. Quociens enim isti mali Iudices, Herodis et Pilati complices, fratribus uestris illudunt uel angariant, tociens Christum crucifigunt. Quociens eos tormentant et occidunt, tociens lateri Christi cum Longino lanceam infligunt. Hec quidem omnia faciunt; et quod peius est ipsi Christo legique nostre subsannant et improperant, et ore temerario nos exacerbant." For commentary, see Throop, *Crusading as an Act of Vengeance*, 60–61 and Biddlecombe, "Baldric of Bourgueil and the *Familia Christi*," 18, 21–22.

[223] Akbari, *Idols in the East*, 112–54.

to refute the Christian religion."[224] Equally importantly, within this web of connections Muslims are made complicit in the crucifixion and the crusade is rendered as a means of inflicting upon them the same punishment – disinheritance and disgrace – that the Jews had long suffered.

These connections are reinforced through chroniclers' claims that Muslims mocked and abused Christian symbols. Peter Tudebode relates that at the siege of Jerusalem, as the pilgrims processed barefoot around the city, on the walls above, the city's Muslim defenders "performed all kinds of acts of mockery" (*omne genus derisionis*). Worst of all, Peter continues,

> To add insult to injury they made from wood a cross similar to the one on which the merciful Christ redeemed mankind, pouring forth his blood. Afterward, in order to inflict great sorrow on the Christians, in the sight of all they beat upon the cross with sticks and shattered it against the walls, shouting loudly, 'Frango agip salip,' which means, 'Franks, is this a good cross?'[225]

In Raymond of Aguilers's version, the Muslims "placed many crosses on the walls on gibbets, and tormented them with blows and insults."[226] As Albert of Aachen tells it, "to arouse the Christians' anger, they affixed on the walls crosses in mockery and abuse (*in derisam etiam et obprobrium*), upon which they spat (*spuebant*), nor they did shrink from urinating on them in full view of everyone."[227] Albert attributes similar behavior to Christian apostates at the siege of Haifa in 1100, suggesting that he saw such blasphemy as intrinsic to Islamic praxis. The offenders' odious actions were cut short, Albert writes, when God made their tower collapse, fulfilling Christ's prophecy that the Jerusalem Temple would be destroyed, so that *"there shall not be left here a stone upon a stone"*

---

[224] Anna Sapir Abulafia, "An Eleventh-Century Exchange of Letters between a Christian and a Jew," *Journal of Medieval History* 7 (1981): 153–74 (at 165–66). As Abulafia shows elsewhere, mockery of Christianity was indeed omnipresent in Jewish life and speech in this period; see *Christians and Jews in the Twelfth-Century Renaissance*, 70.

[225] PT, 137: "Insuper sanctissimam crucem qua fundendo sanguinem suum misericors Christus humanum genus redemit, videntibus omnibus Christianis, cum quodam ligno verberabant. Et postea, ut maiorem Christianis inferrent dolorem, ad murum eam frangebant, dicentes alta voce: 'Frangi agip salip,' quod nos sonat: 'Franci, est bona crux?'" Trans. (slightly revised) 115. This story does not appear in the *Gesta Francorum*.

[226] RA, 145: "Saraceni et Turci infra civitatem girabant, multimode nos deridentes, multas cruces super muros ponebant in patibulis, afficientes eas cum verberibus atque contumeliis." Trans. (slightly revised) 123.

[227] AA, 414–15: "Hoc etiam in loco ad suscitandam iram Christianorum in derisum etiam et obprobrium cruces fixerunt, super quas aut spuebant, aut in oculis omnium mingere non abhorrebant."

(Mat. 24:2, Mk. 13:2, Lk. 21:6).[228] Here it is worth noting that Albert repurposed a verse which medieval Christians read as foretelling the Jews' punishment for rejecting Christ, making it into a prophecy of the crusaders' triumphs.[229] The Ripoll account of the sack of Jerusalem drew a similar conclusion, insisting that the events of July 1099 "fulfilled God's very just sentence of [the city's] destruction," something Christ himself could have accomplished during his time on earth, had he not wished to reserve this honor for "his chosen ones" (*electi sui*), the crusaders.[230] Such glosses – in which Jerusalem's conquest becomes a double act of vengeance, against the Jews for Christ's death and against Muslims for their pollution of Christian symbols and spaces[231] – are a reminder that Jews and Muslims often occupy a common ideological space in crusading narratives.[232] It is noteworthy that the acts of desecration attributed to Muslims in the East recall charges commonly levelled in the West against Jews, whom Christians accused of breaking crosses or defiling them with bodily fluids.[233] Such accusations circulated in the aftermath of the First Crusade in connection with stories of Christians forcibly baptizing Jews in the Rhineland.[234] As we

---

[228] AA, 762. It is notable that the apostates of this story are said to be enraged by the presence at the siege of the relic of the true cross, which eastern Christians had hidden from Jerusalem's Muslim rulers out of fear they would desecrate or destroy it.

[229] Cohen, "The Jews as Killers of Christ," 10, 21. Albert knew this exegetical tradition well, and even references it to explain Titus's conquest of Jerusalem in 70 CE; see AA, 432. Cf. GN, 283.

[230] CJ, 644: "Completa quippe fuerat de eius excidio sententia Dei iustissima, complenda restabat de eius consolatione misericordissima uisitatio eius, ut appareret quid fecisset prius longe, si uoluisset potentiam suam demonstrare, sicut uolebat dissimulare ut electorum suorum mala tot perferentium … ." Cf. GN, 283.

[231] This connection is suggested by GP, 244–45; RC, 94; and WM, 1:648.

[232] This is driven home throughout the chronicles; e.g., Orderic Vitalis's characterization of the Muslim forces at Ascalon as "the synagogue of Satan" (*sinagogam Sathanae*), OV, 5: 176; and Gilo of Paris's categorization of "Jews, Turks, and Arabs" as *gentiles*, GP, 236. While this connection predates the First Crusade, being visible in early medieval exegesis (on which see Becket, *Anglo-Saxon Perceptions*, 134), it is only fully developed post-1099.

[233] Merrall Llewelyn Price, "Medieval Antisemitism and Excremental Libel," in *Jews in Medieval Christendom: Slay Them Not*, ed. Kristine T. Utterback and Merrall L. Price (Leiden, 2013), 177–88 (esp. 178–81); Christoph Cluse, "Stories of Breaking and Taking the Cross: A Possible Context for the Oxford Incident of 1268," *Revue d'histoire ecclésiastique* 90 (1995): 396–442 (at 405–8). An example of such a story in circulation at the time of the First Crusade comes from Ademar of Chabannes (d. 1034), who claims the Jews of Rome were punished with a deadly earthquake after they mocked a crucifix; *Chronicon*, 3.52, ed. Richard A. Landes and Georges Pon, CCCM 129 (Turnhout, 1999), 171. Such *exempla* continued to be told in crusading contexts, as noted by Throop, *Crusading as an Act of Vengeance*, 106–7.

[234] Robert Chazan notes that the cross and Holy Sepulcher became "objects of scorn and hatred" among Latin Jewry post-1096; *In the Year 1096*, 92. In the early twelfth

shall see in Chapter 4, the first crusaders' triumph over Muslim 'Babylon' was likewise presented as the punishment of a blasphemous enemy who proudly refused to embrace Christianity.

The most pervasive – but to modern readers, least visible – form of dialogue between early crusading narratives and anti-Jewish polemic was carried on through the medium of biblical exegesis, in particular the glossing of Old Testament verses to demonstrate the truth of Christian revelation more generally and the crusade's divine inspiration more specifically. The belief that the Old Testament was spiritually fulfilled in the New was, of course, foundational to medieval hermeneutics, and the crusade's narrators leaned heavily on this idea, lacing their accounts of the Jerusalem journey with the language of fulfillment, as signaled by the verbs *complere*, *explere*, and *adimplere*.[235] Trained as most of them were in a monastic exegetical tradition which sought, in Elisabeth Mégier's words, "to include in the Christian fulfillments of Old Testament prophecy not only the spiritual achievements of the Church but also the historical, corporal reality of Christian life," such a strategy came as second nature to our writers.[236] Through the liberal citation of Old Testament prophecy, the crusade's narrators embedded the Jerusalem journey in the deep history of God's relationship with humanity, claiming that the crusaders, not the Jews, were the chosen people whose victories the Hebrew prophets had foreseen. While, as Cecilia Gaposchkin, Matthew Gabriele, Elizabeth Lapina, and Sylvia Schein have shown, Christians saw the Book of Isaiah as a blueprint for the crusader conquest,[237] the chroniclers' christological readings of prophecy from elsewhere in the Old Testament have gone largely unnoticed. Crucially, the crusade's narrators repurposed common pericopes from medieval *Adversus Judaeos* literature as crusading proof-texts. Debates over the right interpretation of Scripture had played a central role in anti-Jewish polemic from the genre's beginnings and, as a result, by 1095 key biblical *testimonia* in Psalms, Isaiah and Daniel (among other books) had

---

century Jews told stories of co-religionists urinating on crosses during the pogroms of 1096; Elliott S. Horowitz, *Reckless Rites: Purim and the Legacy of Jewish Violence* (Princeton, NJ, 2006), 165–66.

[235] As observed by Green, using examples from the *Secunda pars historiae Hierosolimitanae*, a redaction of Fulcher of Chartres's chronicle; *Millstätter Exodus*, 256–57. *Complere*: GN, 115; RR, 7; and BB, 8. *Explere*: GN, 106; FC, 306. *Adimplere*: AA, 448; RR, 109; FC, 162.

[236] Elisabeth Mégier, "Christian Historical Fulfilments of Old Testament Prophecies in Latin Commentaries on the Book of Isaiah (ca. 400 to ca. 1150)," *Journal of Medieval Latin* 17 (2007): 87–100 (quoting 97).

[237] See Gaposchkin, *Invisible Weapons*, 141–51; Gabriele, "From Prophecy to Apocalypse," 304–16; Lapina, *Warfare and the Miraculous*, 135–37; and Schein, *Gateway to the Heavenly City*, 21–33.

acquired a rich christological patina reflecting their polemical associations.[238] The chroniclers' awareness of these associations is suggested by a comparison of their work with anti-Jewish polemics circulating in the early twelfth-century West. Such a comparison reveals that the crusade's narrators shared polemicists' concerns about incarnational theology, the fate of the Jewish people, and the future of Jerusalem. Further, it allows us to see that anti-Jewish exegesis offered chroniclers a model upon which to construct an image of Muslims as a people deserving of divine censure and disinheritance.

In support of the crusaders' territorial claims, the chroniclers enlisted Old Testament pericopes which Christian polemicists had long associated with the advent of Jesus as messiah. Twice in his *Dei gesta per Francos*, for instance, Guibert of Nogent cites Isaiah 2:3, a verse Christians read as heralding the coming of Christ, "the word made flesh" (Jn. 1:14). In the *Dei gesta per Francos*, Urban II admonishes would-be crusaders, "Surely this fact alone should be enough to drive you to come to the aid of the land and the city: that *the law shall came forth from Zion, and the word of the Lord from Jerusalem*" (Is. 2:3), before offering a christological reading of this verse as meaning that "all Christian preaching flows from the fountain of Jerusalem" and "into the hearts of the Catholic multitude."[239] Guibert circles back to Isaiah 2:3 near the end of his narrative, embedding it within his complex gloss of the siege of Jerusalem to underscore the city's value for all Christians, and its worthiness of the sacrifices the crusaders made for its liberation.[240] As Guibert would have known, this verse had an established place among the arsenal of texts that exegetes used to contend that Israel's prophets foresaw the Incarnation.[241] In his *Tractatus adversus Iudaeos*, for example, Augustine wrote that Isaiah 2:3 predicted Christ's preaching in Jerusalem, as well as the subsequent miracle of Pentecost, when a new law, a "law of faith" (*lex fidei*) was "written by the Holy Spirit on the tablets of the holy Evangelists'

---

[238] For the close relationship between biblical exegesis and polemic in the early twelfth century, see Timmer, "Biblical Exegesis and the Jewish-Christian Controversy," 309–21; Abulafia, *Christians and Jews in the Twelfth-Century Renaissance*, ch. 7; Chazan, *Fashioning Jewish Identity*, ch. 6–11; Rosemary Radford Ruether, "The *Adversus Judaeos* Tradition in the Church Fathers: The Exegesis of Christian Anti-Judaism," in *Essential Papers on Judaism and Christianity in Conflict: From Late Antiquity to the Reformation*, ed. Jeremy Cohen (New York, 1991), 174–89; and Signer, "*Peshat, Sensus Litteralis*, and Sequential Narrative," 203–11.

[239] GN, 113: "Certe, si haec deessent omnia, solum illud ad subveniendum terrae et civitati vos excitare debuerat quia *de Symon exierit lex et verbum domini de Iherusalem*." Trans. 43.

[240] GN, 301–02 (Is. 2:3 quoted at 301).

[241] Heinz Schreckenberg, *Die christlichen Adversus-Judaeos-Texte und ihr literarisches und historisches Umfeld (1.–11. Jh.)* (Frankfurt, 1999), 51–52, 236; Gilbert Dahan, *Les intellectuels chrétiens et les juifs au moyen âge* (Paris, 1990), 393.

hearts, rather than on the tablets of stone" used to record Moses' law.²⁴² Isidore of Seville's polemical *De fide catholica* insisted on the fulfillment of Isaiah's prophecy, proclaiming that "the law went forth from Zion" – substituting the past tense *"exiit"* for the Vulgate's future tense *"exhibit"* – in the person of Christ, though "the Jews were left behind on account of their unbelief."²⁴³

A similar christological agenda underlies Raymond of Aguilers's gloss of Godfrey of Bouillon's election as advocate of the Holy Sepulcher by means of Daniel 9:24 (*"Seventy weeks are shortened upon thy people and upon thy holy city, that transgression may be finished, and sin have an end, and iniquity may be abolished, and everlasting justice may be brought, and vision and prophecy may be fulfilled, and the saint of saints may be anointed"*). This verse appears within a stretch of Daniel 9 which Christian exegetes read as the Old Testament's clearest prophecy of Jesus's mission and which, by c. 1100, had become a flashpoint in the Christian–Jewish debate.²⁴⁴ In Raymond's account, clerics in the crusading army objected to crowning an earthly king to rule over the city of Christ's Passion on the following grounds:

> Suppose that in the elected one's heart he said, "I sit upon the throne of David, and I possess his dominion." Suppose he became a David, denying faith and virtue, the Lord would undoubtedly overthrow him and be angry with the place and its people. Moreover, the prophet cries out, *"When the holy of holies (sanctus sanctorum) shall have come, unction will cease"* (Dan. 9:24), because it was made clear to all people that he had come.²⁴⁵

---

²⁴² Augustine, *Tractatus adversus Iudaeos*, c. 7, PL 42:57: "ita Lex ista, quae processit de Sion et Jerusalem, non in tabulis lapideis, sed in tabulis cordis sanctorum Evangelistarum scripta est per Spiritum sanctum ... ."

²⁴³ Isidore of Seville, *De fide catholica ex Veteri et Novo Testamento contra Judaeos*, 2.1.13, PL 83:502: "Lex autem de Sion exiit, et verbum Domini de Jerusalem, sive ut veniret in gentes, relictis ob incredulitatem Judaeis ... ." The influence of Augustine and Isidore's texts is discernible in Peter Damian's polemic use of the verse; see Ep. 1 (*Antilogus contra Iudaeos*, c. 1040), c.2, in *Die Briefe des Petrus Damiani*, ed. Reindel, 1: 71–72.

²⁴⁴ For early Christian readings of this verse, see William Adler, "The Apocalyptic Survey of History Adapted by Christians: Daniel's Prophecy of 70 Weeks," in *The Jewish Apocalyptic Heritage in Early Christianity*, ed. James C. VanderKam and William Adler (Minneapolis, 1996), 201–38; and for its role in polemic, see Dahan, *Les intellectuels chrétiens*, 377–78; Robert Chazan, "Daniel 9:23–27: Exegesis and Polemics," in *Adversus Iudaeos: Ancient and Medieval Polemics between Christians and Jews*, ed. Ora Limor (Tübingen, 1996), 143–60; and idem, *Fashioning Jewish Identity*, 148–61.

²⁴⁵ RA, 143: "Quod si in corde suo diceret, sedeo super solium David et regnum eius obtineo, deneger a fide et virtute David. Fortassis disperdet eum Dominus et loco et genti irasceretur. Propterea clamabat propheta: *Cum venerit sanctus sanctorum, cessabit unctio*, qui advenisse cunctis gentibus manifestum erat." Trans. (slightly revised) 121.

Raymond aligns Jerusalem's Latin conquerors with Christ (identified by Christian exegetes with the *sanctus sanctorum* anticipated by Daniel), whose incarnation changed the rules of salvation, while the city's Jewish past is evoked by King David. As a denier of the faith and object of God's righteous anger, David – who was in other contexts embraced as a model by the crusader kings of Jerusalem – is aligned with contemporary Jews. The Jews' present state as a people without a temple, king, or priests, waiting in vain for a messiah who had already (so Christians believed) arrived, was, eleventh-century polemicists wrote, clearly foretold in Daniel 9:24.[246] Guibert of Nogent went further in his *Contra iudaizantem et Iudeos*, linking the prophecy to the fate of Jerusalem in what seems an oblique reference to the decade-old crusader conquest: "that city, already sanctified by Christ's blood, will exchange old age for new honors, thereby diminishing the guilt of that sinner Adam and forsaking the sins of idolatry (*idolatria*) and infidelity (*infidelitas*)."[247] By linking the eschatological fates of two previous peoples who ruled Jerusalem – ancient Jews (who were often accused of infidelity) and medieval Muslims (who were regularly denounced as idolaters) – Guibert demonstrates how earlier traditions of polemical exegesis could be pressed into the service of the crusade.

The chroniclers' use of Psalm 58:12 ("*God shall let me see over my enemies; slay them not, lest at any time my people forget. Scatter them by thy power, and cast them down, O Lord, my protector*") offers an even more provocative example of how the crusade encouraged a rethinking of traditional anti-Jewish exegesis. Evidence of this verse's association with the crusade from an early date comes from the *Gesta Francorum*, which tells how Christ appeared to desperate crusaders at Antioch and instructed them to perform a liturgy featuring Psalm 58:12.[248] Baldric of Bourgueil elaborated upon the *Gesta* account, clarifying that Christ desired the army's members to ceaselessly sing (*indesinenter psallent*) a series of verses from the Psalter, culminating in the last words of Psalm 58:12: "*Disperge illos in virtute tua et depone eos protector meus, Domine.*"[249] Robert of Reims repurposed this same part of the verse to gloss the crusaders' final assault on Ma'arra in December 1098, when the Latins scaling the walls were urged on by priests who sang the words of Psalm 58:12.[250] No cleric could fail to know that this

---

[246] E.g., Peter Damian, Epistle 1.2, in *Die Briefe des Petrus Damiani*, ed. Reindel, 1: 72–73; and Fulbert of Chartres, *Tractatus contra Judaeos*, PL 141:310–11.

[247] Guibert of Nogent, *Contra iudaizantem et Iudeos*, c. 3, PL 156:510.

[248] GF, 58 (and cf. PT, 100); for this insight, see Gaposchkin, *Invisible Weapons*, 112–13.

[249] BB, 69.

[250] RR, 86. Minor discrepancies in wording between Robert and Baldric's citation (with Robert's corresponding to the *Biblia Sacra Vulgata* version and Baldric's to the redaction of Ps. 58:12 in the Dumbarton Oaks Medieval Library edition (*The Vulgate Bible, Vol. 3: The Poetical Books*, ed. Swift Edgar with Angela M. Kinney [Cambridge,

verse was a cornerstone of the Church's longstanding position towards the Jews, and the proof-text of the concept of "Jewish witness" first articulated by Augustine, who famously wrote:

> [W]hen [the Jews] do not believe in our Scriptures, their own Scriptures are fulfilled in them, while they read them with darkened eyes. ... To us, however, those prophecies which are produced from the books of our adversaries [i.e., the Jews] themselves are enough; for we recognize that it is for the sake of such testimony, with which, even against their will, they furnish us by having and preserving those books, that they themselves are scattered through all the nations, wherever the Christian church spreads. Indeed, a prophecy concerning this scattering was given long ago in the Book of Psalms, which they also read, where it is written: '*My God, his mercy shall prevent me. God shall show me concerning my enemies; slay them not, lest they should at last forget your law; scatter them by thy power*' (Ps. 58:11–12).[251]

This passage demonstrates how Augustine's insistence that Jews be tolerated as living witnesses to the fulfillment of the prophecies they deny relies on the first part of Psalm 58:12 – "*Slay them not, lest at any time my people forget*" – and allows us to see how fundamentally Baldric's and Robert's omission of those words alters the verse's meaning. Prefacing as they do their accounts of the crusaders' massacre of Ma'arra's inhabitants and defeat of Kerbogha's army, the chroniclers' curated quotation of Psalm 58:12 present these events as prophetic fulfillments; indeed, this point is underscored by the chroniclers' inclusion of the verse's final words – "and cast them down" – which Augustine had just as deliberately omitted. The use of Psalm 58:12 in crusading narratives reinforces our impression that anti-Jewish rhetoric gave Christian writers a deep ideological well from which to draw, but also suggests these writers' concern to distinguish

---

MA, 2011], 302) are a salutary reminder of the lack of a single authoritative Vulgate text in this period.

[251] Augustine, *De civitate Dei*, 18.46, CCSL 48, ed. B. Dombart and A. Kalb (Turnhout, 1955), 2:329: "Proinde cum Scripturis nostris non credunt, complentur in eis suae, quas caeci legunt ... . Nobis quidem illae sufficiunt, quae de nostrorum inimicorum codicibus proferuntur, quos agnoscimus propter eosdem codices habendo atque servando, per omnes gentes etiam ipsos esse dispersos, quaquaversum Christi Ecclesia dilatatur. Nam prophetia in Psalmis, quos etiam legunt, de hac re praemissa est, ubi scriptum est: *Deus meus, misericordia eius praeveniet me. Deus meus demonstrauit mihi in inimicis meis, ne occideris eos, ne quando obliviscantur legem tuam: disperge eos in uirtute tua.*" Trans. R. W. Dyson, *The City of God against the Pagans* (Cambridge, 1998), 892. Cf. Augustine, *Tractatus adversus Iudaeos*, c. 7, PL 42:57. For Augustine's formulation of this position, see Paula Frederiksen, *Augustine and the Jews* (New Haven, 2008), 290–352; and on this reading's immense influence – visible, in later exegetical works such as the *Glossa Ordinaria* (PL 113:929–30), see Dahan, *Les intellectuels chrétiens*, 405, 544; and Cohen, *Living Letters*.

Jews from Muslims as peoples assigned to play different roles in God's plan. While Jews were to be tolerated in Christian society as witnesses to the truth of the majority faith, Muslims were not eligible for such protected status; like the polytheistic tribes of the Old Testament, their role in salvation history was simply to be defeated and displaced, thereby cementing the crusaders' elect status.

If the holy war prompted sustained consideration of Muslims' place in salvation history, it is clear that the crusaders' achievements also led Latin writers to reevaluate God's plan for the Jews. In the first place, the crusade reinforced the longstanding Christian conviction that Old Testament prophecy was deeply concerned with the future of the Church. Fulcher of Chartres, for instance, began to tally the many biblical verses which seemed to presage the Jerusalem journey, but soon gave up, noting, "We have read much about this in the prophets which it is tedious to repeat."[252] The conquest of Jerusalem in particular supported the centuries-old belief that the Jews' reprobate status was well deserved and permanent.[253] One anonymous chronicler of the fall of Jerusalem addressed himself to the "miserable Jews" of his own day, mocking their expectation that Jerusalem would be returned to them upon the advent of their long-awaited messiah; instead, the author invoked the parable of the cornerstone (Mat. 21:42, Mk. 12:10, Lk. 20:17; cf. Ps. 117:22) and Daniel's prophecy to King Nebuchadnezzar (Dan. 2:45) to remind the Jews of their rejection of Christ and assert that the crusaders' conquest of the city heralded not the fulfillment of their hopes but the advent of a new kingdom, established by God's will, that would last forever.[254] The author's christological agenda is reflected in the juxtaposition of the Gospel story with Daniel 2:45, whose "stone cut out of the mountain without hands" Christians understood to herald the virgin-born Christ; but he goes a step further, scolding Jews not only for rejecting "the cornerstone" (i.e., Christ) but also for not recognizing that Daniel's prophecy was capacious enough to foretell another event, one nearly as momentous as the Incarnation: the crusaders' liberation of the Holy Sepulcher.[255]

This analysis of the interplay between early crusade historiography and anti-Jewish polemic points to a larger conclusion: Latin writers regarded the First Crusade as an unprecedented proof of the truth of their own faith. The chroniclers made this clear in various ways; they marshaled accounts of miraculous victories (and punishments) that punctuated the Jerusalem journey, linked

---

[252] FC, 162: "de hoc itinere plurima etiam in prophetiis legimus, quae revolvendi taedium est." Trans. 58.
[253] Ruether, "The *Adversus Judaeos* Tradition," 182–83.
[254] CJ, 652.
[255] CJ, 652–53. For christological readings of Dan. 2:44, see Chazan, *Fashioning Jewish Identity*, 234; and Schreckenberg, *Die christlichen Adversus-Judaeos-Texte*, 71–72; and for an eleventh-century example, Peter Damian, Epistle 1.2, in *Die Briefe des Petrus Damiani*, ed. Reindel, 1: 77.

the crusaders' accomplishments to biblical prophecies, and harnessed the vitriol of polemic. For clerical authors familiar with the conventions of *disputatio* and accustomed to viewing one familiar non-Christian group, the Jews, as rhetorical and textual adversaries – that is, as competing readers of sacred texts and debaters of doctrinal issues – it was a short step to transferring some of these expectations to Muslims. And indeed, the 'hermeneutical Muslims' of early crusading narratives exhibit many of the characteristics of contemporary 'hermeneutical Jews': scornful, blasphemous, and spiritually blind, they testify to the truth of Christianity by advertising the obvious falsity of their own unbelief.[256] Thus, the First Crusade's chroniclers added a new chapter to a centuries-old polemical tradition, even as they helped to define the future ideological rules of engagement between Latin Christendom and the Islamic world.

Conclusion

In 1147, just as the Second Crusade was getting underway, the Cluniac abbot Peter the Venerable reflected on the First Crusade's legacy in a sermon that took his clerical listeners on a virtual pilgrimage to Jerusalem and the Church of the Holy Sepulcher.[257] Peter invited his audience to reflect on the achievements of the first crusaders as the holy sites' "purifiers," chosen by God to help carry history forward in whatever short time remained before Christ's return. The Scriptures, Peter believed, were the master key that could unlock the holy war's larger significance within this divine plan, and select verses demanded to be reread in light of the events of 1095–99. To this end, he glossed Genesis 49:10 (*"The scepter shall not be taken away from Judah nor a ruler from his thigh, till he come that is to be sent, and he shall be the expectation of nations"*), a verse which had long been used to explain the degraded status of Jews in Christendom.[258] For Peter, this pericope proved that the crusade represented

---

[256] Here one might note that the Muslims of early crusading narratives absorb the traditional associations of *infidelis* and *perfidus* with blindness, heresy, and Judaism; for these etymologies, see H. Schmeck, "*Infidelis*: Ein Beitrag zur Wortgeschichte," *Vigiliae Christianae* 5 (1951): 129–47; and Bernard Blumenkranz, "*Perfidia*," *Bulletin du Cange* 22 (1952): 157–70.

[257] Peter the Venerable, "Sermo de laude Domini sepulchri," ed. Giles Constable, "Petri Venerabilis Sermones Tres," *Revue Bénédictine* 64 (1954): 224–72 (at 232–65). For analysis of this text, see Cohen, *Living Letters*, 249–52; Purkis, *Crusading Spirituality*, 81–82; and Cole, "Theme of Religious Pollution," 103.

[258] For the use of Gen. 49:10 in anti-Jewish polemic from early Christianity up to the eleventh century, see Schreckenberg, *Die christlichen Adversus-Judaeos-Texte*, 189, 231, 279, 306, 336, 440, 469, 486, 511, 520, 533, and 552. This verse provides the basis for the initial discussion in Fulbert of Chartres' *Tractatus contra Judaeos* (PL

a divine judgment not only on the Jews, who had rejected the one "that is to be sent," namely Christ, but also upon unbelieving Muslims in the East.[259] The conquest of Jerusalem was a sign that, in Peter's words, God "rejects the Jews as he did the enemy Cain, and rejects the pagans (*gentiles*) as he did the worshippers of Baal," even as he "chooses the Christian people," making known their elect status through miraculous signs.[260] This identification of the Jerusalemites as a new chosen people, and of their enemies with biblical idolatry, echoes earlier crusade chronicles, as does the association of Jews with Muslims as common enemies of Christendom. For Peter, as for earlier crusade apologists and later commentators like the monks of Maillezais with whom this chapter began, interpreting the First Crusade entailed an impressive marshalling of intellectual resources and a willingness to borrow methodologies and interpretations from pilgrimage literature, religious polemic, and biblical exegesis. A contextualized reading of early crusading narratives reveals the boundaries between these medieval genres to have been more fluid than modern scholars generally acknowledge.

Peter's sermon is also a reminder of the durability of the exegetical connections forged in the heat of the years immediately following 1099, when Latin writers waged a rhetorical war aimed at justifying co-religionists' rule in the Levant. These connections between crusaders and Israelites, Muslims, and Canaanites informed later twelfth-century writers' commemoration of the crusade as a new chapter in biblical history, a literal fulfillment of God's will that complicated allegorical readings of Old Testament prophecy. The association of Muslims and Jews, too, endured in later theology, historiography, literature, and art.[261] While this association certainly predated 1095, the First Crusade's early narrators played a crucial role in its propagation through their creative deployment of the building-blocks of anti-Jewish polemic in service of the holy war. A fundamental assumption of this interpretive work was that 'Israelite,' 'Hebrew,' and 'Jew' were not interchangeable categories.[262] Crusade chroniclers correlated Jewishness to carnality, blindness, and stubborn antipathy to Christ, even as they affirmed 'Israelite' as a positive

---

141: 308f.) and also features in Peter Damian's *Antilogus contra Judaeos*; Ep. 1.2, in *Die Briefe des Petrus Damiani*, ed. Reindel, 1: 73.

[259] Peter the Venerable, "Sermo de laude Domini sepulchri," 247.

[260] Peter the Venerable, "Sermo de laude Domini sepulchri," 252: "Reprobas Iudaeos sicut inuidium Cain; reprobas gentiles sicut cultores Baal, nec super sacrificia eorum inflammas; eligis Christiani populi hostias, sicut munera Abel ...."

[261] Studies of the related representations of Jews and Muslims in later medieval Europe include: Akbari, *Idols in the East*, ch. 3; Sofia Rose Arjana, *Muslims in the Western Imagination* (Oxford, 2015), ch. 2; and Debra Higgs Strickland, *Saracens, Demons & Jews: Making Monsters in Medieval Art* (Princeton, NJ, 2003), ch. 3–4.

[262] As observed by Green, *Millstätter Exodus*, 200–1.

spiritual identity implying the enjoyment of divine favor and entitlement to Abraham's patrimony. This positive evaluation of 'Israelite' identity, it must be remembered, served the typological project of situating a long succession of Christian heroes within salvation history. Writing in the 1130s, the Frankish canon Rorgo Fretellus remembered the first crusaders as a "second Israel" (*secundus Israel*), who had won the Promised Land (*terra promissionis*) by virtue of their victories over the Philistines and Amalekites and continued to guard the true homeland (*patria*) of Christ "like new Maccabees keeping watch over the bed of the true Solomon" (cf. Song of Sol. 3:7–8).[263] Underlying Rorgo's description are specific exegetical methodologies and associative networks that resonate throughout the corpus of early crusading narratives and, indeed, came so naturally to medieval clerical writers as to constitute a language all its own, one requiring no explanation to initiates. As we shall see in the following chapter, Latin chroniclers made use of these same interpretive skills to situate the crusaders within the two poles of the Christendom's spiritual geography: Jerusalem and Babylon.

---

[263] Rorgo Fretellus, *Descriptio de locis sanctis terre Jerusalem*, c. 1, ed. P. C. Boeren (Amsterdam, 1980), 53. Cf. the similar description of the Templars by Bernard of Clairvaux, *De laude novae militiae*, c. 4, in *Sancti Bernardi Opera*, 8 vols., ed. Jean Leclercq, C. H. Talbot and Henri Rochais (Rome, 1957–77), 3: 221. More generally, 'guarding Solomon's bed' (Song 3:7) was a popular metaphor for monastic life as spiritual warfare; see Smith, *War and the Making*, 127.

Chapter 4

Babylon and Jerusalem

> But ours, with minds uplifted
> Unto the heights of God,
> With our whole heart's desiring,
> To take the homeward road,
> And the long exile over,
> Captive in Babylon,
> Again unto Jerusalem,
> To win at last return.
>
> — Peter Abelard, "Sabato ad Vesperas"[1]

While many contemporaries were struck by the novelty of the crusading enterprise, it could also be read as the latest chapter in a very old story, one that encompassed the entirety of sacred history and deeply informed the medieval Christian worldview. This was a tale of two cities, created, in the famous words of Saint Augustine, by two kinds of love: "the love of self (*amor sui*), extending even to the contempt of God" and "the love of God (*amor Dei*), extending to the contempt of self." In the first, earthly city (*civitas terrena*) where the devil held sway as sovereign (*princeps*), pride and ambition drove men to compete and oppress their fellows while, by contrast, the inhabitants of the city of God (*civitas Dei*) sought only to glorify God and live in a state of harmony.[2] Inspired by Scripture, Augustine identified the two cities allegorically with Babylon, which he defined as "confusion," and Jerusalem, which he labeled "the vision of peace."[3] In subsequent centuries, Augustine's vision of the two cities, transmitted via the *City of*

---

[1] Peter Abelard, "Sabbato ad Vesperas," in *Mediaeval Latin Lyrics*, ed. and trans. Helen Waddell (New York, 1929), 164–65: "Nostrum est interim / mentem erigere / et totis patriam / votis appetere, / et ad Jerusalem / a Babylonia / post longa regredi / tandem exsilia."

[2] Augustine, *De civitate Dei*, 14.28, ed. Dombart and Kalb, 2: 56–57: "Fecerunt itaque ciuitates duas amores duo, terrenam scilicet amor sui usque ad contemptum Dei, caelestem uero amor Dei usque ad contemptum sui. Denique illa in se ipsa, haec in Domino gloriatur." Trans. Dyson, 632.

[3] Augustine, *De civitate Dei*, 16.4 and 19.11, ed. Dombart and Kalb, 2: 130, 371. For commentary, see Johannes Van Oort, *Jerusalem and Babylon: A Study into Augustine's City of God and the Sources of His Doctrine of the Two Cities* (Leiden, 1991), 118–21. Augustine inherited the gloss of Jerusalem as *visio pacis* from Ez. 13:16, via Jerome's *In Hieremiam libri VI*, 1.59.2, CCSL 74, ed. S. Reiter (Turnhout, 1960), 37. This association was widely known at the time of the First Crusade; see, for example, RR, 109.

God and his extremely popular *Enarrationes in Psalmos*, remained a touchstone of medieval theology, history, and political theory.[4] But, whereas Augustine had resisted a literal equation of the two cities to worldly counterparts – viewing, as he did, the idea of a Christian polity as a contradiction in terms – later writers explicitly identified the two cities with various worldly powers and institutions, including the Holy Roman Empire and the Church. Thus, by the ninth century Hincmar of Reims (d. 882) could write that "as Augustine showed in the book of *The City of God*, the two cities are intermingled (that is, Jerusalem, which is the Church, and Babylon, which is worldly power)."[5] The early chroniclers of the First Crusade participated in this tradition, building upon the work of eleventh-century reformers and polemicists who compared the two cities to the papal and imperial factions of their own day. But the crusade actualized the conflict between the two cities in a new way when a Christian army challenged a new Babylon for control of Jerusalem.[6] Such a venture begged to be read allegorically, as a typological echo of the ancient wars between Israel and Babylon, as well as morally, as an exemplary narrative of how Christians might escape the earthly city *en masse* and become worthy residents of the heavenly Jerusalem.

While scholars have debated how much Urban II's message of holy war owed to Augustine's just war theory, the related question of how Augustinian theology more broadly, and the scheme of the 'two cities' more particularly, influenced the early crusading movement has been comparatively overlooked. In approaching this issue, it is useful to remember that eleventh- and early twelfth-century understandings of salvation history were fundamentally Augustinian,[7] and that

---

[4] Sylvia Schein, "Babylon and Jerusalem: The Fall of Acre, 1291–1996," in *From Clermont to Jerusalem. The Crusades and Crusader Societies 1095–1500*, ed. Alan V. Murray (Turnhout, 1998), 141–50; Jacques Le Goff, *The Medieval Imagination*, trans. Arthur Goldhammer (Chicago, 1988), 170–71. One of the best-documented early crusade chroniclers, William of Malmesbury, certainly knew both the *De civitate dei* and the *Enarrationes*; see Thomson, *William of Malmesbury*, 41, 51, 190, 204–5.

[5] Hincmar of Reims, *Ad episcopos et procere provinciae Rhemensis*, c. 41, PL 125:984: "sicut sanctus Augustinus in libro de Civitate Dei ostendit (i.e., *De civ. Dei*, 19.26–27), 'Quamdiu, inquiens, permistae sunt ambae civitates (scilicet Hierusalem, hoc est Ecclesia, et Babylon, quae est mundana potestas) ... .'" Quoted in J. N. Hillgarth, "L'Influence de la *Cité de Dieu* de saint Augustin au Haut Moyen Age," *Sacris Erudiri* 28 (1985): 5–34 (at 9).

[6] At least one Latin chronicler, Hugh of Flavigny, summarized the crusade in precisely these terms; see *Chronicon Hugonis Monachi Virdunensis et Divionensis*, lib. 2, MGH Scriptores 8, ed. G. H. Pertz, 481.

[7] As M.-D. Chenu observes, "The Latin civilization of the Middle Ages ... was born out of Augustine." *Toward Understanding St. Thomas*, trans. A.-M. Landry (Chicago, 1964), 58. For a thorough overview of Augustine's influence on medieval intellectual life, see Willemien Otten, "The Reception of Augustine in the Early Middle Ages (c. 700–c. 1200)," in *The Oxford Guide to the Historical Reception of Augustine, Vol. 1*, ed. Karla Pollman and Willemien Otten (Oxford, 2013), 22–39.

the decades around 1100 witnessed the beginning of a veritable "Augustinian Renaissance" in the Latin West.[8] We know, too, that the First Crusade's chroniclers had access to those works in which Augustine most clearly articulated his concept of the 'two cities'; the *Enarrationes in Psalmos* was a staple of ecclesiastical libraries,[9] while the *City of God* circulated widely, via both *florilegia*[10] and stand-alone copies. Indeed, Michael Gorman has turned up an impressive twenty-nine manuscripts, and numerous excerpts, of *The City of God* produced in the eleventh and early twelfth centuries, including several associated with the schools where our chroniclers studied.[11] Further, the scheme of the 'two cities' was disseminated at second hand through the works of influential authors like Cassiodorus, Orosius, Gregory the Great, Bede, and Hrabanus Maurus, whose writings were well known to the crusade's narrators.[12] In the eleventh century, with the advent of competing theories about how to order the world and balance

---

[8] Eric L. Saak, "Augustine in the Western Middle Ages to the Reformation," in *A Companion to Augustine*, ed. Mark Vessey (London, 2009), 465–68 (quoting 467); also see Chenu, *Nature, Man, and Society*, 60–64; and Bernard McGinn, "From Admirable Tabernacle to House of God: Some Theological Reflections on Medieval Architectural Integration," in *Artistic Integration in Gothic Buildings*, ed. Virginia Chieffo Raguin, Kathryn Brush, and Peter Draper (Toronto, 1995), 41–56 (esp. 47–48).

[9] On the enduring popularity of the *Enarrationes* see Joseph Dyer, "The Psalms in Monastic Prayer," in *The Place of Psalms*, ed. Van Deusen, 69–70; and Matter, "The Church Fathers and the *Glossa Ordinaria*," 92–93.

[10] See Alain J. Stoclet, "Le 'De civitate Dei' de saint Augustin: Sa diffusion avant 900 d'après les caractères externes des manuscrits antérieur à cette date et les catalogues contemporains," *Recherches Augustiniennes et Patristiques* 19 (1984): 185–209; Joseph T. Lienhard, "Florilegia," in *Augustine through the Ages: An Encyclopedia*, ed. Allan D. Fitzgerald and John C. Cavadini (Grand Rapids, MI, 1999), 370–71; and Julie Kerr, *Monastic Hospitality: The Benedictines in England, c. 1070–c. 1250* (Woodbridge, 2007), 24n. As J. N. Hillgarth shows ("L'Influence de la Cité de Dieu," 11–34), most *florilegia* focused on the second half of the *City of God* (ch. 11–22), where Augustine develops the idea of the 'two cities.'

[11] For mss. from Paris, Reims, and Monte Cassino, see Michael M. Gorman, "A Survey of the Oldest Manuscripts of St. Augustine's *De Civitate Dei*," *Journal of Theological Studies* n.s. 33, pt. 2 (1982): 398–410 (at 405–07); and for mss. from Chartres, see Lucien Merlet, "Catalogue des livres de l'abbaye de Saint-Père de Chartres, au XIe siècle," *Bibliothèque de l'Ecole des Chartes* 3rd ser., vol. 5 (1854), 263–70 (at 270).

[12] On Cassiodorus, see *Expositio psalmorum*, e.g., 108.15, 136.1–2, 147.14, ed. Adriaen, 2: 998, 1230–32, 1311; on Orosius, see Andrew Scheil, *Babylon under Western Eyes: A Study of Allusion and Myth* (Toronto, 2016), 55–66; on Gregory the Great, see, e.g., *Registrum Epistularum*, 8.33, ed. Paul Ewald and Ludwig M. Hartmann, MGH Epistolae 2 (Berlin, 1898), 35–36; on Bede, see Conor O'Brien, *Bede's Temple: An Image and Its Interpretation* (Oxford, 2015), 132–44, and Benedicta Ward, *The Venerable Bede* (Kalamazoo, MI, 1990), 74; and for Hrabanus Maurus, see Choy, *Intercessory Prayer*, 144–46. For the chroniclers' knowledge of these authors' works, see Chapter 2, nn. 5–6.

different kinds of power, Christian thinkers returned to Augustine with a new urgency, and the symbolic language of the 'two cities' came to figure prominently in both pro- and anti-Gregorian polemic.[13] At the same time, in the decades around 1100 monastic thinkers like Rupert of Deutz and Hugh of Fleury (d. aft. 1118) incorporated the 'two cities' model into new frameworks for understanding salvation theology and human history.[14] Augustine's dualist scheme also naturally appealed to the thinkers who crafted a new 'discourse of opposites' in Capetian schools during the decades in which the crusading movement and its early historiography took shape.[15] It is fair to say that the First Crusade's chroniclers came of age intellectually in a milieu steeped in Augustinian ideas about sin and salvation, time and history. Our authors need not have read specific works by Augustine to have been familiar with his model of the 'two cities'; it was simply part of the air one breathed in the monastic and cathedral schools where these men were trained.[16]

This chapter considers how, at a remove of seven centuries, Augustine's theology of the 'two cities,' in combination with the Scriptures, created a lens through which medieval narrators understand the crusading project. As we shall see, Augustine bequeathed to the twelfth century a terminology that could be used to define both the crusaders and their enemies in terms of mankind's age-old struggle for grace in a fallen world.[17] By associating the Jerusalemites

---

[13] Marcia L. Colish, *Medieval Foundations of the Western Intellectual Tradition, 400–1400* (New Haven, 1997), 337–38; Bede Lackner, *The Eleventh-Century Background of Cîteaux* (Washington, D.C., 1972), 153. The most thorough study of this usage remains C. Mirbt, *Die Stellung Augustins in der Publicistik des gregorianischen Kirchenstreits* (Leipzig, 1888). Margaret Gibson's work on Lanfranc of Bec also reflects the use of *De civitate Dei* as a teaching text in the eleventh century; see "Lanfranc's Notes on Patristic Texts," *The Journal of Theological Studies*, new ser. 22 (1971): 435–50, esp. 436–41.

[14] For Rupert of Deutz, see *De sancta Trinitate, In Deuteronomium*, 1.20, ed. Haake, 2: 1041–42; and for commentary, Van Engen, *Rupert of Deutz*, 90–91. For Hugh of Fleury, see *Historia Ecclesiastica*, book 2, prol., PL 163:830; and for commentary, Matthew Kempshall, *Rhetoric and the Writing of History, 400–1500* (Oxford, 2011), 87.

[15] Constance Brittain Bouchard, *"Every Valley Shall Be Exalted": The Discourse of Opposites in Twelfth-Century Thought* (Ithaca, NY, 2003), 16–18. Bouchard stresses, however, the fundamental differences between Augustine's methodology and that of twelfth-century thinkers influenced by him.

[16] Jay Diehl's discussion of "subterranean" lines of influence connecting medieval writers across generations seems to me useful for understanding the transmission of Augustinian ideas; see "Harmony between Word and World: Anselm of Canterbury, Aelred of Rievaulx, and Approaches to Language in Twelfth-Century Monasticism," in *Saint Anselm of Canterbury and His Legacy*, ed. Giles E. M. Gasper and Ian Logan (Toronto, 2012), 95–113 (at 97).

[17] In his study of the polemical literature of the Investiture Contest, the nineteenth-century

with *caritas* (selfless love), *concordia* (concord), and *humilitas* (humility) and emphasizing their status as exiles and pilgrims (*peregrini*), the crusade's chroniclers identified them as worthy denizens of the city of God, sojourning in the city of the world *en route* to the heavenly Jerusalem. Conversely, the crusaders' non-Christian enemies (and, in some cases, wicked crusaders) were identified with the earthly city, beset as they were by pride (*suberbia*), confusion (*confusio*), and the misdirected love that led to greed (*avaritia* or *cupiditas*). This oppositional discourse of virtue and sin had long been central to monastic spirituality, whose values – themselves strongly Augustinian – strongly influenced the crusade idea.[18] Augustine had, indeed, envisioned the monastery as the closest approximation of the city of God on earth,[19] and the chroniclers who portrayed the Jerusalemites as (in Jonathan Riley-Smith's memorable phrase) "a military monastery on the move," drew upon this tradition.[20] In this very monastic way of thinking, crusaders defended Christ and his patrimony not only through worldly combat but through a Psychomachia, a bloody spiritual face-off between the virtues and vices.

Augustine's vision of an archetypal clash between 'two cities', a confrontation understood as simultaneously historical and mystical, also powerfully influenced the narrative structure of early crusade chronicles. Thus, the crusaders defied a new 'Babylon' – the Fatimid caliphate – that was both a military and political rival and an embodiment of the worldly city of sin and unbelief. The crusaders' goal of Jerusalem, too, had a well-established multivalence for medieval Christians: as a city set within a landscape of competing worldly powers, it could be subjected to all the horrors of medieval warfare; as a likeness (*instar*) of the heavenly city on earth and a symbol of mankind's redemption, its *virtus* could dissolve the worst sins. In these two cities, one profoundly sacred and the other deeply profane, the crusaders acted out an Augustinian salvific drama every bit as momentous as the events which had originally prompted the *City of God*'s composition. As

---

historian Carl Mirbt found that Augustine's teachings, often mediated by *florilegia* or other theologians' works, strongly influenced Gregorian and especially anti-Gregorian clerics, but that this influence was manifest not so much in direct quotations as in the appropriation of a distinctly Augustinian vocabulary to describe key concepts and institutions. Likewise, Augustine's stamp is visible on crusading narratives less through direct quotations from his works than through the use of a vocabulary of crusading spirituality that owes much to Augustine's writings on sin and salvation. Mirbt, *Die Stellung Augustins*.

[18] Purkis, *Crusading Spirituality*, 30–58. For the long Christian tradition of the 'conflict of virtues and vices,' from Late Antiquity forward, see Morton W. Bloomfield, *The Seven Deadly Sins: An Introduction to the History of a Religious Concept, with Special Reference to Medieval English Literature* (East Lansing, 1952).

[19] R. A. Markus, *The End of Ancient Christianity* (Cambridge, 1990), 78–82.

[20] Riley-Smith, *The Idea of Crusading*, 2.

they played out their divinely appointed roles in this contest, the crusaders fully realized their potential as new apostles, and their holy war took on the status of a new apostolic mission. For the crusade's Augustinian trajectory was inextricably linked to the glossing of the crusaders as living embodiments of the apostolic life (*vita apostolica*), an ideal very much on the minds of the holy war's chroniclers.

This chapter focuses on the twin themes of Babylon's defeat and Jerusalem's capture in the early narratives of the First Crusade, aiming to uncover the multiple levels of meaning that twelfth-century observers ascribed to this chain of events. It emphasizes medieval narrators' use of two overlapping interpretive frameworks: an Augustinian lens, in which the oppositional nature of the 'two cities' and their residents loomed large, and a typological lens borrowed from biblical exegesis, which emphasized the crusaders' apostolicity and linked key turning-points in the holy war to New Testament precedents.[21] An initial examination of the language of salvation and sin in early crusading narratives demonstrates how crusade chroniclers used highly charged terminology to create for the Jerusalemites a venerable spiritual pedigree, one that combined an Augustinian conceptual framework with the ideals of the *vita apostolica*. From there, I situate the first crusaders within a spiritual landscape defined by the symbolic-turned-literal opposition of Jerusalem and Babylon, reconstructing the prolonged encounter between the crusaders, the earthly representatives of the heavenly city, and their 'Babylonian' enemies. Finally, the chapter follows the salvific trajectory of the crusade to Jerusalem, where, for some observers, the heavenly city seemed to have come to earth in 1099.

Crusading, the City of God, and the Apostolic Ideal

In his *Historia Ierosolimitana*, the Benedictine Baldric of Bourgueil described how, in the year 1096, the primitive church was refounded by a group of Christians who agreed to share all of their possessions and hold every believer to an equally strict standard of moral conduct. Baldric described this praiseworthy way of life with language borrowed from the famous description of the apostolic church in the fourth chapter of the Acts of the Apostles:

---

[21] Such a blending of biblical comparisons and Augustinian theology would have been encouraged by educational practice in this period, since students were urged to deepen their understanding of the Scriptures through engagement with Augustine; indeed, one anonymous twelfth-century cleric recommended reading the *City of God* as a prelude to advanced study of the allegorical and moral senses of the Bible. See Philippe Delahaye, "L'Organization scholaire au XIIe siècle," *Traditio* 5 (1947): 211–68 (at 232–33).

Hereafter theirs was a community of all goods to such an extent that hardly any man could call anything his own; as in the early church (*primitiua ecclesia*), nearly *all things were common to them* (Acts 4:32). They had entirely driven out brothels and prostitution from their camps, and, above all, judged matters of morality with great virtue. Men still lived alongside women, but only within the bonds of marriage or lawful service. If anyone was convicted of immorality, he was publicly punished in order to inspire in the rest a dread of misconduct. Indeed, bishops preached daily sermons on the virtue of continence, and all harlotry and wastefulness were abhorred.[22]

Given the spiritual climate of northern France, Baldric's home at the time he wrote, this could be a description of one of the many new religious movements that had sprung up there in recent decades with the aim of replicating the singleness of heart of the early church.[23] As Baldric would have known, many of these reformers justified their way of life using Acts 4.[24] That Baldric was in fact describing the armies of the First Crusade on the march tells us a great deal about how he and his contemporaries understood the apostolic life as a living tradition, and how they conceived of crusading spirituality in terms of the fulfillment of the injunctions of Christ and the missions of his disciples as described in the New Testament.

If, as we saw in the previous chapter, one way of interpreting the holy war was as a typological reenactment of the wars of ancient Israel against its idolatrous neighbors, chroniclers were equally eager to claim apostolic status for the first crusaders. They saw nothing contradictory in these two interpretations: the glossing of crusaders as Israelites played a crucial role in justifying Latin claims to mastery over the Promised Land, while the crusaders-as-apostles reading did the equally important ideological work of promoting the crusade as an extension of the ideals of *imitatio Christi*, as well as a revival of the primitive church. Thanks to the work of Jonathan Riley-Smith, H. E. J. Cowdrey, and William

---

[22] BB, 26: "Preterea ibi erat tanta rerum omnium communitas ut uix aliquis aliquid sibi diceret proprium; sed, sicut in primitiua ecclesia, ferme *illis erant omnia communia*. Lupanar et prostibulum omnino a castris suis procul eliminauerant, et potissimum de morum honestate disceptabant. Ibi tamen cum hominibus mulieres cohibitabant, sed uel in coniugio uel in legali ministerio. Si quis enim alicuius conuincebatur inhonestatis, uel in faciem, uet ceteris metus incuteretur, castigandus increpabatur, uel grauiter de eo uindicabatur. Cotidie siquidem de continentia sermocinabantur episcopi, et omne scortum et abusum de medio castrorum abominabantur." Cf. OV, 5:54.

[23] It is instructive to compare Baldric's account of the early history of Fontevrauld in his *Vita beati Roberti de Arbrisello*, c.17–19, PL 162:1052–53; this too was a community that included men and women, laypeople and clerics, dedicated to poverty, and "joined together in fraternal love" with "one common will."

[24] Emmanuel Bain, *Église, richesse et pauvreté dans l'Occident médiéval: L'Exégèse des Évangiles aux XIIe–XIIIe siècles* (Turnhout, 2014), 33–34.

Purkis, the indebtedness of crusading spirituality to christo-mimetic practice and the eleventh-century apostolic revival has been well established.[25] The following discussion extends this work, highlighting the ways in which Augustinian ideas undergirded representations of the crusade as an apostolic activity, and of the crusaders as heirs of the city of God, and exploring how exegesis of Matthew 19:29 – the most frequently cited biblical verse in early crusading narratives – supported the presentation of the crusaders as new apostles.

The later eleventh and early twelfth centuries witnessed a great revival of interest in the *vita apostolica*. In debates that often intersected with the drive for ecclesiastical reform, clerical writers pondered how Christians might best imitate Christ's life and suffering, and how a return to the ideals of the apostolic age might revitalize the embattled church. These deliberations intersected with scriptural exegesis at every turn. Some would-be reformers were judged heretics for their insistence that the Gospels' injunctions must be obeyed literally, and their rejection of post-scriptural *auctoritates*, while less radical thinkers used exegesis to carve out a place for the new evangelism within the existing ecclesiastical hierarchy.[26] Whereas early medieval Christians believed the primitive church had survived in the monastic ideal, eleventh- and early twelfth-century writers developed allegorical and moral readings of key New Testament passages which identified other groups – including regular canons, hermits, wandering preachers, and pious laypeople – as the apostles' true heirs.[27] It is no coincidence that many of the scriptural pericopes that featured in these debates about the 'true church' also appear in the First Crusade's historical corpus; after all, the crusade enjoyed the backing of the reformed papacy, counted among its leaders lay and ecclesiastical supporters of reform,

---

[25] Riley-Smith, *The Idea of Crusading*, 24–25; idem, "Death on the First Crusade," in *The End of Strife*, ed. David Loades (Edinburgh, 1984), 14–31; H. E. J. Cowdrey, "Pope Urban II and the Idea of Crusade," *Studi Medievali* 36 (1995): 721–42; and Purkis, *Crusading Spirituality*, 30–58.

[26] Lobrichon, "The Early Schools," 546, 553.

[27] Numerous studies have traced this shift in meaning in the context of reform; see Kathleen Cushing, *Reform and the Papacy in the Eleventh Century* (Manchester, 2005), 139–57; Giovanni Miccoli, *Chiesa Gregoriana: Ricerche sulla riforma del secolo XI*, 2nd edn. (Rome, 1999), 368–73; Andrew Garrett Traver, "The Identification of the '*vita apostolica*' with a Life of Itinerant Preaching and Mendicancy: Its Origins, Adherents, and Critics ca. 1050–1266," unpublished PhD diss. (University of Toronto, 1996), 18–28; Glenn W. Olsen, "The Idea of the *Ecclesia Primitiva* in the Writings of the Twelfth-Century Canonists," *Traditio* 25 (1969), 61–86; M.-D. Chenu, "Monks, Canons, and Laymen in Search of the Apostolic Life," in his *Nature, Man, and Society in the Twelfth Century*, 202–38; Ernest W. McDonnell, The *Vita apostolica*: Diversity or Dissent," *Church History* 24 (1955): 15–31; and Charles Dereine, "Le problème de la vie commune chez les canonistes: d'Anselme de Lucques à Gratian," *Studi Gregoriani per la storia di Gregorio VII e della riforma gregoriana* 3 (1948): 287–98.

and exhibited many characteristics that could be linked to various definitions of the apostolic life then current in the Latin West. As with the primitive church, the crusade lacked a single leader; it included large numbers of the poor; and its adherents professed a willingness to suffer and die for Christ. The crusade itself could be seen as a new interpretation, a divinely inspired gloss, of the Gospels, a point which clerical writers drove home by interweaving the words and deeds of Christ and the first disciples with their accounts of the crusaders' progress. The chroniclers' emphasis on the Jerusalemites' fraternal love, unity, and humility situated them within the allied traditions of the apostolic life and monastic spirituality which shared a common vocabulary of virtue. Earlier scholars have noted that the meritorious practices traditionally associated with the practice of the *vita apostolica* by pilgrims and monks – such as voluntary exile, flight from the world, and ascetic self-denial – are celebrated in early crusading narratives,[28] and that crusade apologists selectively appropriated New Testament concepts as a means of 'monasticizing' lay pilgrims.[29] But this conceptual framework is also strongly indebted to Augustine, and it is possible to reconstruct chroniclers' use of a specifically Augustinian scheme of virtue and vice to justify their fellow Christians and disparage Muslim enemies.

The centrality of the Christian ideal of *caritas*, love for God and neighbor, within crusading rhetoric is well known, thanks to a seminal article by Jonathan Riley-Smith.[30] While Riley-Smith carefully traced the influence of Augustine's thought on medieval just war theory,[31] we might go even further in mapping out the Augustinian pedigree of *caritas* as the opposite of *cupiditas*, the carnal appetite for wealth or sex that the New Testament condemned as "the root of all evil" (1 Tim. 6:10) and contrasted with *caritas* as the greatest virtue (1 Cor. 13:13).[32] As he asserted in *De doctrina christiana*, Augustine believed that "Scripture enjoins nothing but love (*caritas*), and censures nothing but greed" (*cupiditas*), and indeed he viewed the opposition of these two impulses as a – if not *the* – major theme of human history.[33] The *City of God* equates *cupiditas*

---

[28] Giovanni Miccoli, "Dal pellegrinaggio alla conquista: povertà e ricchezza nelle Prime Crociate," in *Povertà e ricchezza nella spiritualità dei seccli XI e XII* (Todi, 1969), 49–52; A. Dupront, "La spiritualité des croisés et des pélerins d'après les sources de la première croisade," in *Pellegrinaggi e culto dei santi*, 451–83.

[29] Purkis, *Crusading Spirituality*, 47–58.

[30] Riley-Smith, "Crusading as an Act of Love," *passim*.

[31] Riley-Smith, "Crusading as an Act of Love," 42–46.

[32] William S. Babcock, "*Caritas* and *Cupiditas*: The Early Augustine on Love and Human Fulfillment," in *Augustine Today*, ed. Richard Neuhaus (Grand Rapids, MI, 1993), 1–34 (esp. 13–34).

[33] Augustine, *De doctrina christiana*, 3.35–38, ed. Green, 148: "Non autem praecipit scriptura nisi caritatem, nec culpat nisi cupiditatem, et eo modo informat mores hominum." Note that while Green translates *cupiditatem* as "lust," I have rendered it

to carnal desire (*concupiscentia*), and unfavorably compares the "culpable desire" (*culpabilis cupiditas*) of the residents of the earthly city with the "praiseworthy love" (*laudabilis caritas*) of the city of God's inhabitants.[34] The opposition of these loves was a matter of great interest to early twelfth-century monastic writers and schoolmen, whose theorizing on the subject owed much to Augustine's influence.[35] For medieval observers, the crusade could be understood to exemplify the conflict between different kinds of love – that is, love for God and neighbor (*caritas*) and lust for wealth and power (*cupiditas*) – in two related ways. In the first place, the expedition's promoters demanded that the Jerusalemites abandon their misguided attachment to worldly possessions and honors to embrace the selfless love of God and fellow Christians; in the second place, the journey east pitted the crusaders, as embodiments of *caritas*, against enemies whose *cupiditas* was advertised by their greed, cruelty, and pride.[36]

The crusaders' devotion to *caritas*, and to the virtues of the city of God more generally, was reflected in the language used to describe their endeavor. Those who took the cross did not, of course, call themselves 'crusaders,' nor refer to their endeavor as a 'crusade;' they were *peregrini*, pilgrims of a new sort, on a pilgrimage (*peregrinatio*) to the Holy Land.[37] This terminology, modern scholars generally agree, reflected the crusaders' adoption of the traditional rituals and ethos of pilgrimage, to which they added a new church-sanctioned privilege: arms-bearing.[38] Latin chroniclers' consistent identification of the first

---

as "greed," in keeping with how twelfth-century readers would have understood it, and indeed Augustine often treated *cupiditas* as a synonym of *avaritia*. For explanations of how these oppositional concepts inform Augustine's work more generally, see D. Dideberg, "*Caritas*," in *Augustinus-Lexikon*, ed. Cornelius Petrus Mayer et al. (Basel, 1986), 1: 730–43; and G. Bonner, "*Cupiditas*," ibid., 2: 166–72 (esp. 168–69).

[34] Augustine, *De civitate Dei*, 14.7, 14.9, ed. Dombart and Kalb, 2:15, 23.

[35] Barbara Newman, *God and the Goddesses: Vision, Poetry, and Belief in the Middle Ages* (Philadelphia, 2005), 141–46.

[36] For instance, in William of Malmesbury's account of Clermont, Urban II explicitly warns against *cupiditas*; see *Gesta regum*, 4.347, 1:604–05. The crusaders' shortcomings were also described in terms of a lack of *caritas*; e.g., OV, 5:187.

[37] For a thorough survey of how chroniclers used this language, see Léan Ní Chléirigh, "*Nova Peregrinatio*: The First Crusade as a Pilgrimage in Contemporary Latin Narratives," in *Writing the Early Crusades*, ed. Bull and Kempf, 63–74. See also Giles Constable, Appendix A: "The Terminology of Crusading," in *Crusaders and Crusading in the Twelfth Century* (Burlington, VT, 2008), 349–52. Note that chroniclers also sometimes referred to the crusade as a "mission" (*legatio*), a term associated in the Vulgate (e.g., 2 Cor. 5:2, Eph. 6:20) with the apostles' travels; for example, see AA, 6.

[38] Important studies include: Marcus Bull, "The Pilgrimage Origins of the First Crusade," *History Today* 47, no. 3 (1997): 10–15; Christopher Tyerman, "Were There Any Crusades in the Twelfth Century?" *English Historical Review* 110, no. 437 (1995): 553–77 (at 567–70); Purkis, *Crusading Spirituality*, 12–22; and Cowdrey, "New

crusaders as pilgrims, however, cannot be easily separated from their interpretation of the Jerusalemites as heirs to the city of God and new apostles; indeed, these three identities overlapped with and mutually reinforced one another.

For Augustine, the city of God was a "pilgrim city" (*civitas peregrina*), and its residents were *peregrini*, a term which for Augustine meant 'strangers' or 'aliens' but which connoted 'pilgrims' for his medieval readers.[39] A "pilgrim city which dwells in this wicked world" (*ciuitatem in hoc saeculo maligno tamquam in ... peregrinantem*) under God's protection, the city of God endures in the midst of the earthly city.[40] Unified by virtue and sustained by prayer, the inhabitants of the city of God were fated to remain, like the ancient Israelites and first apostles, "strangers (*peregrinos*) even in their own dwelling-places" until they reached the goal of their pilgrimage, the heavenly city which was their true homeland.[41] The worldly sojourn of the city of God – which was for Augustine the true church and its members – would remain the natural state of the elect in the fallen world during the time remaining before Christ's return and the heavenly city's descent to earth.[42] Rather than identifying the elect with a particular group, Augustine stressed that the city of God brought together "citizens of all nations and every tongue" (*ex omnibus gentibus ciues atque in omnibus linguis*), thus creating a "society of pilgrims" (*peregrina societas*) who, despite lacking a common language and customs, nonetheless lived together in perfect concord and abstinence, free from pride and greed.[43]

This vision of the city of God resonates throughout the First Crusade's narratives, which describe a pilgrim army comprising Christians from many nations. These *peregrini*, we are told, willingly left their old lives behind to become strangers in a hostile land, living lives of apostolic simplicity under the

---

Dimensions of Reform," 11–24. For a contrary view, see Janus Møller Jensen, "*Peregrinatio sive expeditio*: Why the First Crusade Was Not a Pilgrimage," *Al-Masaq: Journal of the Medieval Mediterranean* 15 (2003): 119–37.

[39] For a comprehensive analysis of *peregrinari*, *peregrinus*, and *peregrinatio* in Augustine's work, see Van Oort, *Jerusalem and Babylon*, 131–42; and M. A. Claussen, "*Peregrinatio* and *Peregrini* in Augustine's City of God" *Traditio* 46 (1991): 33–76 (at 42ff).

[40] Augustine, *De civitate Dei*, 15.26 (quote) and 18.51, ed. Dombart and Kalb, 2: 115 and 336.

[41] Augustine, *De civitate Dei*, 1.35, 5.18, 19.17 (quote), 19.27, ed. Dombart and Kalb, 1: 51, 227–28, 2: 384–86, and 402. Note the resonance with Rev. 9:7's description of the elect gathered in the presence of the Lamb: "turbam magnam quam dinumerare nemo poterat ex omnibus gentibus et tribubus et populis et linguis stantes ante thronum et in conspectu agni amicti stolas albas et palmae in manibus eorum."

[42] Augustine, *Enarrationes in Psalmos*, 147.5, ed. Dekkers, 3: 2142–43; Augustine, *De civitate Dei*, 18.32, ed. Dombart and Kalb, 2: 300–1.

[43] Augustine, *De civitate Dei*, 14.9 and 19.17 (quote), ed. Dombart and Kalb, 2: 21–22, 385–86.

leadership of Christ, the king of Augustine's celestial city. Echoing a common theme in the chronicles, Fulcher of Chartres described how the "innumerable people coming together from everywhere" to join the crusade "were diverse in languages, but nevertheless seemed to be brothers in the love of God and very close to being of one mind."[44] Like the inhabitants of the city of God, the crusaders created their own society amidst the fallen world, a "sacred society of God's faithful" (*sacra fidelium Dei societas*), in the words of Robert of Reims.[45] Theirs was a pilgrim society, or, as Raymond of Aguilers put it, a "pilgrim church" (*peregrina ecclesia*), under the unerring leadership of Christ.[46] The linkage between the concepts of *peregrinatio* and *caritas* helped to define the crusade, since to take up this new pilgrimage was to commit to a love that eschewed worldly entanglements as manifestations of *cupiditas*. As Urban II wrote to Bolognese crusaders in 1096,

> We strongly encourage your love (*caritas*), so that if you love God you may show that devotion to His vicar. For as He says about this, *who that heareth you, heareth me* (Lk. 10:16). We hear that some of you have conceived a desire to undertake the journey to Jerusalem, and wish you to know that this pleases us greatly. Let it be known to all, however, that they must not undertake to go there out of greed for earthly goods (*terreni commodi cupiditate*) but solely for the health of their souls and the liberation of the Church ....[47]

The chroniclers assured their readers that the crusaders had indeed followed Urban's instructions. Orderic Vitalis reconstructed a conversation in which the expedition's leaders insisted to the Byzantine emperor Alexius I (r. 1081–1118), "We have abandoned our worldly wealth and set out on a pilgrimage by our own choice, in order to throw back the pagans and free the Christians for the love of Christ" (*pro amore Christi*).[48] Their *caritas* bound the Jerusalemites to

---

[44] FC, 161: "de innumera gente concrevit exercitus exercituum undique convenientium, ut de linguis quamplurimis et regionibus multis ... " and 203: "sed qui linguis diversi eramus, tamquam fratres sub dilectione Dei et proximi unanimes esse videbamur." Trans. McGinty in Peters, ed., *The First Crusade*, 58 and 68. Cf. FE, 136; and GN, 86.
[45] RR, 40.
[46] RA, 83.
[47] EP, no. 3. p. 137: "caritati uestrae attentius commendamus, ut si Deum diligitis, in eius uicario ostendatis. Ipse enim de huiusmodi dixit: *qui uos audit, me audit*. Nonnullos uestros in Hierusalem eundi desiderium concepisse audiuimus, quod nobis plurimum complacere noueritis. Sciatis autem eis omnibus, qui illuc non terreni commodi cupiditate sed pro sola animae suae salute et ecclesiae liberatione profecti fuerint ... ."
[48] OV, 5:48–49: "Nos diuitias nostras dereliquimus, et peregrinationem sponte aggressi sumus ut pro amore Christi paganos confundamus, et Christianos liberemus." Cf. OV, 5:142–43, where Raymond of Toulouse is praised because "[p]reposuit enim causam Dei suae uoluntati uel utilitati."

live at peace with – and willingly die for – fellow Christians.[49] At the same time, as we shall see, the projection of the sin of *cupiditas* onto the Muslim enemy became an essential ideological prop of the holy war in the East.

The ultimate sign of the Jerusalemites' *caritas* and apostolic virtuosity was their self-imposed exile. The scriptural proof-text for this claim was Christ's dramatic injunction in Matthew 19:29: "*Every one that hath left houses or brethren or sisters or father or mother or wife or children or lands for my name's sake shall receive a hundredfold (*centuplum*), and inherit eternal life.*"[50] The verse's message – that bonds of kinship, marital affection, and property were mere distractions from the quest for salvation – was echoed elsewhere in the Scriptures in descriptions of the Israelites as strangers or sojourners (*peregrini* or *advenae*; e.g., Gen. 23:4, 1 Chron. 29:15), an identity which early Christians appropriated to signal their detachment from the world (e.g., Mat. 25:35, 1 Pet. 2:11, Heb. 11:13). While Matthew 19:29's association with the First Crusade was noted decades ago,[51] however, the verse's close relationship to the early crusading idea has never been fully explored. This connection warrants further scrutiny, given that Matthew 19:29 is quoted or paraphrased a total of twenty-four times across fourteen narratives, making it by far the most frequently cited biblical verse in the narrative corpus of the First Crusade.[52] A closer look at how contemporaries used Matthew 19:29 to gloss the crusade reveals the extent to which early crusading spirituality was defined in terms of the *vita apostolica*, as well as how the crusade idea intersected with exegetical tradition to forge a new vision of the apostolic life, one which exhorted lay Christians to become exiles in a pilgrim collective.

By the late eleventh century, Matthew 19:29 – which medieval writers often shorthanded as "the *centuplum*" – had a long and colorful exegetical history. Early Christians believed it foreshadowed the sacrifices of the martyrs.[53] More controversially, Late Antique chiliasts found in the text a coded description of Christ's imminent one thousand-year reign on earth, while their opponents – most influentially, Jerome – insisted that the text simply exalted spiritual over material

---

[49] E.g., BB, 9.
[50] Cf. Mk. 10:29–30 and Lk. 18:29–30.
[51] Riley-Smith, "Death on the First Crusade," 25.
[52] MC, 10; BB, 3; RR, 6; FE, 132; HH, 422; GN, 87–88; FC; SF, 162; CJ, 647; AA, 2, 107, 236, 480; CP, 12; OV, 5:16, 34; WM, 1:609; and *Beati Gaufridi castaliensis prioris, dictamen de primordiis ecclesiae castaliensis*, c. 3, RHC Oc. 5:349. In addition, Mat. 19:29 is cited in the Encyclical of Sergius IV; see Schaller, "Zur Zreuzzugsenzyklika," 152.
[53] For example, see Augustine, Sermon 326 (On the Birthday of the Twenty Martyrs), c. 2, ed. John E. Rotelle and trans. Edmund Hill in *Sermons 3/9 (306–340A): On the Saints, The Works of Saint Augustine: A Translation for the 21st Century* (Hyde Park, NY, 1994), 171.

rewards.⁵⁴ In the early Middle Ages this verse was regarded as an exhortation to pilgrimage, both the short-term journey to a saint's shrine and the perpetual exile of ascetics who forsook their homelands for Christ's sake.⁵⁵ Above all, monks were believed to embody Matthew 19:29, as they renounced blood ties, marriage, and private property to devote themselves to things of the spirit.⁵⁶ Monastic treatises and cartularies cited the Gospel verse as proof that monks literally fulfilled Christ's command, and, on this premise, clerical reformers promised lay patrons that they too could share in the hundredfold reward of eternal life.⁵⁷ While such a sacrifice had traditionally been synonymous with monastic profession, in the eleventh century it came to be associated with other dramatic gestures of devotion, such as giving one's life to defend the Church. By the time of the First Crusade, then, the time was ripe for an exegetical revision of Matthew 19:29, and the crusade's early chroniclers were well placed to carry this out.

Across the chronicles, Matthew 19:29 serves to justify the expedition to Jerusalem as a perfect, literal realization of Christ's command to his disciples. Although only two writers, Robert of Reims and William of Malmesbury, attributed it to Urban II at Clermont,⁵⁸ most authors referenced the Gospel verse near the beginnings of their narratives as a means of framing the crusade idea as

---

[54] See the introductory comments by Thomas P. Scheck in his translation of Jerome's *Commentary on Matthew*, FC 117 (Washington, D. C., 2008), 41–42; and Jerome's gloss in *Commentariorum in Matheum libri IV*, 19.29, CCSL 77, ed. D. Hurst and M. Adriaen (Turnhout, 1969), 173. Jerome's commentary continued to be widely read throughout the Middle Ages. Hrabanus Maurus, for example, reproduced Jerome's remarks on Mat. 19:29 verbatim in his *Expositio in Matthaeum*, lib. 6, ed. Bengt Löfstedt, CCCM 174–174A (Turnhout, 2000), 2: 521–22, and it supplied much of the material for the *Glossa Ordinaria* on Matthew. On the long-term influence of Jerome's commentary, see Kevin Madigan, *Olivi and the Interpretation of Matthew in the High Middle Ages* (Notre Dame, IN, 2003), 15–19.

[55] As in Bede's commentary on Mat. 19:27–29 in *Homiliarum evangelii libri II*, 1.13, ed. D. Hurst, CCSL 122 (Turnhout, 1955), 88–94 (esp. 92–93).

[56] This is beautifully illustrated by early commentaries on the *Rule of Benedict*: Hildemar of Corbie, *Expositio regulae*, c.58, ed. Rupert Mittermüller (Ratisbon, 1880), 542; Smaragdus of Saint-Mihiel, *Expositio in Regulam S. Benedicti*, 3.49, ed. Alfred Spannagel and Pius Engelbert, Corpus Consuetudinum Monasticarum 8 (Siegburg, 1974), 276. For a similar reading from the early twelfth century, see the *Tractatus de professione monachorum*, ed. Giles Constable and trans. Bernard S. Smith in *Three Treatises from the Abbey of Bec on the Nature of Monastic Life* (Toronto, 2008), 56. For commentary on medieval readings of Mat. 19 as a guide to monastic life, see Bain, *Église, richesse et pauvreté*, 22–37.

[57] Miccoli, *Chiesa Gregoriana*, 71 and n. 18; Placidus of Nonantola, *Liber de honore ecclesiae*, c.72, ed. L. de Heinemann and E. Sackur, MGH Libelli de lite 2:599.

[58] RR, 6; William of Malmesbury has Urban II refer to the "hundredfold reward" (*centuplicatum ... pretium*) awaiting those who heed the call to crusade; WM, 1:606.

an apostolic, exilic enterprise.[59] Several writers circled back again and again to the sacrifices demanded in Matthew 19:29 in homiletic fashion, meditating on the meaning of the scriptural passage and its application to the Jerusalem journey.[60] It was, as Guibert of Nogent wrote, a wondrous thing that entire "nations, inspired by God, shut the doors of their hearts towards all kinds of needs and feelings," while the most powerful laymen suddenly found that "the most splendid honors, the castles and towns over which they held power, meant nothing to them," and, "abandoning their possessions, spurning their wives and fleeing from their children, they took up arms."[61] Countless men and women abruptly left behind everything, claimed the Monte Cassino Anonymous, because they had heard the voice of Christ speaking the words of Matthew 19:29 and rushed to obey, confident that they would thereby earn the hundredfold reward.[62] If the first apostles had fulfilled Matthew 19:29, the leaders of this new apostolic age answered the Gospel's call with equal alacrity, and on a far greater scale.

The chroniclers' reading of Matthew 19:29 as a command to go into voluntary exile in a foreign, hostile land[63] calls to mind Augustine's presentation of the city of God encamped among its worldly enemies. This was an exegetical innovation, insofar as earlier glosses of the Gospel text did not emphasize the concept of exile.[64] The chroniclers may have been influenced by other Scriptural passages which allegorized God's elect as strangers, as well as by two strands of contemporary clerical rhetoric: in the first, hagiographers celebrated the willingness of holy men and women to leave their own countries to preach the Gospel;[65] in the second, reformers urged monks to follow the footsteps of the apostles into exile from a sinful world.[66] But if the concept of exile was being woven into the *vita apostolica* by the time our chroniclers wrote, their glosses of Matthew 19:29 took this

---

[59] GN, 87–88; AA, 2; CP, 12; OV, 5:16; and WM, 1:609.
[60] The Charleville Poet references Mat. 19:29 three times (CP, 12, 14, 16); Albert of Aachen four times (AA, 2, 107, 236, 480); and Guibert of Nogent five times (as in n. 61 below).
[61] GN, 87–88: "Deo ergo incentore motas vidimus nationes et, ad omnia necessitudinum affectionumque genera precordiales aditus predurantes .... Honores amplissimi, castellorum et urbium dominia spernebantur, uxores pulcherrimae quasi quiddam tabidum vilescebant ... ." and 266: "abrenuntiationes possessionum, uxorum aspernatio, filiorum fuga ... ." Trans. 28–29, 124. Cf. GN, 132, 148, 156; and CJ, 647.
[62] MC, 10. Cf. FC, 162–63 and the verbatim description in SF, 162.
[63] Modern historians have discussed imagery of exile in texts related to the crusade, though without linking it to specific exegetical traditions; e.g., Riley-Smith, "Death on the First Crusade," 25; Purkis, *Crusading Spirituality*, 40–41.
[64] Note, too, that the word *exilium* is uncommon in Vulgate, where strangers or exiles are usually called *peregrini* or *hospites*.
[65] For example, Geoffrey of Vendôme, Sermon 64, PL 157:273–74.
[66] For example, Peter Damian, Letter 110, ed. Reindel, *Die Briefe*, 3:225.

development a step further. Consider William of Malmesbury's account of Clermont, in which Urban II's exhortation to would-be crusaders takes the form of a discursus on the Gospel verse:

> clear the impious out of God's sanctuary, drive out the robbers (cf. Mat. 21:12–14, Mk. 11:15–18, Lk. 19:45–47, Jn. 2:13–16) and install the godfearing. Let no devotion to the ties of kinship restrain you, for man's first devotion must be to God. Let no man be diverted by love (*caritas*) of his native soil, because from different points of view a Christian must find the whole world exile (*exilium*) and the whole world home, so that exile is home and home is exile. Let no man be held back by the greatness of his patrimony, for what is promised us is greater still ... The things I speak of are sweet but transitory, and such as for those who despise them bring a hundredfold reward (*centuplicatum ... pretium*; cf. Mat. 19:29).[67]

Albert of Aachen echoed this sentiment, celebrating those who had willingly left behind "their homeland, kinsmen, wives, sons and daughters, castles, cities, lands, estates, and all the sweetness of this world, left settled things for unsettled, and sought exile in the name of Jesus" among "distant and barbarous nations ... for the sake of the Redeemer."[68] Repeatedly, the chroniclers insist that the crusaders not only endured exile, but did so joyfully, out of love for Christ and in confident expectation of the reward promised to the original apostles.[69] Crusading exile, however, did not entail passive suffering at the hands of persecutors, nor did it emphasize spreading the Gospel among unbelievers; unlike the original apostles – or the inhabitants of Augustine's *civitas Dei* – the first crusaders left their homes to fight for possession of a specific holy site. Further, this model of exile was incompatible with traditional monastic interpretations of the apostolic life, which emphasized peaceful contemplation and physical stability.[70] In this respect, as in so many others, the crusade necessitated a rereading of allegory

---

[67] WM, 1:605–7: "uacuate ab impiis Dei sacrarium, extrudite latrones, inducite pios. Nulla uos necessitudinis pietas contineat, quia prima hominis pietas in Deum. Nullum natalis soli caritas tricet, quia diuersis respectibus Christiano totus est mundus exilium et totus mundus patria; ita exilium patria, et patria exilium. Nullum patrimoniorum amplitudo remoretur, quia ampliora sunt quae promittuntur ... . Et haec quidem sunt dultia, sed caduca et quae centuplicatum contemptoribus suis pretium importent."

[68] Quoting AA, 1–2: "quomodo reliquerint patriam, cognatos, uxores, filios filiasque, castella, urbes, agros, regna et omnem huius mundi dulcedinem, certa pro incertis, et in nomine Iesu exilia quesierint ... ." and 480–81: "in tam longinquas et barbaras nationes facere non dubitastis ... pro redemptoris nostri gratia sustinuistis." Cf. AA, 474.

[69] FE, 132; GN, 87–88, 132; OV, 5:34 and 70.

[70] A point stressed by church leaders who wished to prevent monks from taking the cross. See Elizabeth Siberry, *Criticism of Crusading, 1095–1274* (New York, 1985), 38–43; and Purkis, *Crusading Spirituality*, 12–14.

as simple truth. The crusaders' literal fulfillment of the Gospel command to sacrifice home, family, and wealth – sacrifices traditionally only demanded of the holiest members of Christian society – had, it seemed, made it possible for them to accomplish anything, and had set into motion a new apostolic age, an age of hitherto unimaginable miracles.

A New Babylon in the East

Even as the first crusaders made their way towards Jerusalem, some among them cast their eyes towards Babylon. Associated with moral degeneracy, spiritual confusion, and tyranny, the biblical Babylon was the historical site of the captivity and testing of the chosen people, a theme that animates many of the historical and prophetic books of the Old Testament. As an apocalyptic symbol, Babylon was also the "great harlot," "full of the abomination and filthiness of her fornication" (Rev. 17:1, 4) whose annihilation was foretold in Revelation 18. As we have seen, Augustine built upon these traditions in his identification of Babylon with the earthly city, and early medieval exegetes followed his lead, assigning Babylon a negative but essential role in the span of salvation history, past and future: looking backwards, Babylon's conquest of Judah marked the beginning of the fifth age of the world,[71] while looking ahead, the city was identified as the fated birthplace of Antichrist.[72] Further, Babylon played a key role in the *translatio imperii*, a theme of great interest to some crusade apologists.[73] As the symbolic 'father' of the Roman Empire, Babylon set an example of corrupt *imperium* – characterized by pagan idolatry and persecution of the Jews – which Rome had followed in its oppression of the first Christians.[74] But, whereas Rome had been redeemed through the triumph of the true church, Babylon remained beyond redemption; it was, in the words of Bede, "the devil's city," peopled by "the instigators of heresies" who assaulted "the acknowledged faith of the truth with wicked deeds and words."[75]

---

[71] Guenée, *Histoire et culture historique*, 150–52. Especially influential was the timeline included by Isidore of Seville in his *Etymologies*, 5.39, ed. Lindsay, 1: n.p.; trans. Stephen A. Barney, W. J. Lewis, J. A. Beach, and Oliver Berghof (Cambridge, 2010), 131–32.

[72] Richard Kenneth Emmerson, *Antichrist in the Middle Ages: A Study of Medieval Apocalypticism, Art, and Literature* (Seattle, 1981), 80, 93.

[73] Rubenstein, *Nebuchadnezzar's Dream*, esp. ch. 3 and 9; and Scheil, *Babylon*, 60–63.

[74] The key figure here is Orosius (d. 420); see Scheil, *Babylon under Western Eyes*, 60–63; and Rubenstein, *Nebuchadnezzar's Dream*, 26–29.

[75] Bede, *Libri quatuor in principium Genesis*, 3.11, ed. Jones, 157: "Quia uero iuxta spiritalem sensum Babylon est diaboli ciuitas, hoc est reproba hominum multitudo uniuersa, structores Babyloniae qui sunt nisi magistri errorum, qui contarium ueritati

Its very corruption made Babylon the perfect foil for the purity of Jerusalem; as a vice-ridden place of spiritual confusion, it contrasted with Jerusalem, the city of charity, peace, and eternal truth.[76]

While the biblical Babylon had long since disappeared from the landscape of worldly power, its memory was very much alive in the Latin West at the time of the First Crusade. Christians were reminded of the Babylonian Captivity through the liturgy, especially during Septuagesima and Lent, when seasonal prayers and sermons encouraged worshippers to meditate on the sufferings of the enslaved Jews, as well as to rejoice at their liberation from bondage.[77] In the later eleventh century, the discourse of ecclesiastical reform also accorded an important place to Babylon and its rulers, in particular within discussions of the proper relationship between the Church and secular authorities. During the Investiture Contest, the papal party's champions proclaimed that the Church had been enslaved by a new Babylon, and exhorted her faithful sons to remain defiant in their captivity, following the model of the prophet Daniel and his companions at the court of Nebuchadnezzar (viz. Emperor Henry IV).[78] The German emperor's partisans were quick to remind their opponents that many scriptural passages enjoined submission to worldly authorities, and some writers even speculated that Babylon had been reborn in Rome itself.[79] As Sigebert of Gembloux (d. 1112) wrote: "There was formerly great confusion in Babylon, just as there is today in the Church. In Babylon there was a confusion of the tongues of the people; so now in the Church both the tongues and minds of the believers are divided."[80] Augustine's explication of the earthly and heavenly cities, and his identification of these with Babylon and Jerusalem, loomed large in these debates. For instance,

---

cultum diuinitatis introducunt uel agnitam fidem ueritatis malis actibus siue uerbis impugnant?" Trans. Calvin B. Kendall as *Bede, On Genesis* (Liverpool, 2008), 233.

[76] These associations reflected, in part, medieval etymologies of the two cities' names, as exemplified by Isidore of Seville, *The Etymologies*, 15.1, ed. Lindsay, 2: n.p.; trans. Barney et al., 301.

[77] The twelfth-century liturgist Jean Beleth explains why the Babylonian Captivity was an appropriate subject to reference at these moments in his *Summa de ecclesiasticis officiis,* c. 77 and 87, ed. Heribert Douteil, CCCM 41A (Turnhout, 1976), 141–42, 157. My thanks to Jessalynn Bird for this observation.

[78] See, for example, Bernard of Hildesheim, *Liber canonum contra Heinricum quartum*, c. 21, ed. F. Thaner, MGH Lib. de lite 1:491; Bonizo of Sutri, *Liber ad amicum*, ed. E. Dümmler, MGH Lib. de lite 1:571–72; and Bernold of Constance, *De damnatione scismaticorum*, ed. Thaner, 46, 101.

[79] This reading followed scriptural and patristic precedent, as shown by Schein, *Gateway to the Heavenly City*, 58–59.

[80] Sigebert of Gembloux, *Leodicensium epistola adversus Paschalem Papam*, ed. E. Sackur, MGH Lib. de lite 2:451: "Quae enim maior olim confusio fuit in Babilonia, quam hodie est in aecclesia? In Babylone confusae sunt linguam gentium; in aecclesia dividuntur lingae et mentes credentium."

the anonymous monastic author of the *Liber de unitate ecclesiae conservanda*, building on Book 18 of the *City of God*, condemned "those who belong to Babylon, that is to say the earthly city," as "adversaries and enemies of Jerusalem, which is interpreted as the vision of peace, and whose adversary and enemy is the king of Babylon, namely he who guards the secrets of the devil."[81] If the city of God – Jerusalem – was a place of peace and concord, Babylon embodied tyranny, confusion, and heresy.[82]

Babylon continued to be regarded as a real polity as well as a potent symbol. By the ninth century, Latin Christian writers had relocated Babylon to Egypt,[83] specifically to Cairo, capital of the Shia Fatimid caliphate from 973 to 1171.[84] While Latin Christians identified this new Babylon as a reincarnation of the biblical city of unbelief, by the eleventh century they also recognized its significance within the contemporary Islamic world, a context Latins widely associated with paganism and heresy. We see this tradition in the early *chansons de geste*, for instance in the figure of Baligant, the idolatrous "emir of Babylon" of the *Chanson de Roland*.[85] Concerns about the actual "king of Babylon" were revived in the Latin West when, in 1009, the Fatimid caliph al-Ḥākim (r. 996–1021) ordered the Holy Sepulcher's destruction. Latin writers believed that the "king of Babylon" was motivated by a desire to halt the annual miracle of the New Fire, which drew ever-larger flocks of Christian pilgrims to Jerusalem after the millennium; further, Jews were accused of encouraging al-Ḥākim's assault.[86] For Ademar of Chabannes (d. 1034), al-Ḥākim was an Antichrist-like figure, "the Nebuchadnezzar of Babylon" who "had in his pride (*superbia*) rebelled against God,"[87] while his fellow Benedictine Ralph Glaber had no doubt that the caliph

---

[81] *Liber de unitate ecclesiae conservanda*, ed. W. Schwenkenbecker, MGH Lib. de lite 2:273: "Haec sunt verba eorum, qui pertinent ad Babylonem, ad terrenam scilicet civitatem, qui sunt adversarii et hostes Hierusalem, quae interpretatur visio pacis, cuius adversarius est quoque atque hostis rex Babylonis, qui utpote gerens mysterium diaboli ... ." For commentary, see Robinson, *Authority and Resistance*, 140.

[82] For example, see Bruno of Segni, *Expositio in Psalmos*, Ps. 136, PL 164:1195.

[83] For example, we find this usage in Bernard the Monk's ninth-century itinerary; *Bernardi Itinerarium*, c. 7, PL 121:570.

[84] Scheil, *Babylon under Western Eyes*, 258–59. As Anne Wolff has shown, Europeans still employed this terminology as late as the sixteenth century; *How Many Miles to Babylon? Travels and Adventures to Egypt and Beyond, 1300 to 1640* (Liverpool, 2003), 138.

[85] Gerard J. Brault, *The Song of Roland: An Analytical Edition*, 2 vols. (University Park and London, 1978), 1:61 (commentary) and 2:158, line 2614 (text). For a discussion of Babylon and the 'Sultan of Babylon' as themes in later medieval romance, see Akbari, *Idols in the East*, 52–65, 226–27.

[86] For an overview of this event and its reception, see Morris, *The Sepulchre of Christ*, 134–39.

[87] Ademar of Chabannes, *Chronicon*, 3.47, ed. Bourgain, 166–67; and for discussion,

was a tool of the devil.[88] Though there are frustratingly few extant western commentaries on this event, it is clear that for some clerical observers this was, as Matthew Gabriele has argued, "an event unprecedented in sacred history," which smacked of cosmic conflict and continued to shape what we might in hindsight identify as proto-crusading rhetoric.[89]

The First Crusade's chroniclers thus inherited a tradition of reading Babylon as a site of historical, allegorical, and mystical meaning, and each level of signification is visible in their narratives. In historical-political terms, Latin writers followed contemporary usage in identifying Babylon with Cairo, and sometimes with Egypt more generally; likewise, they commonly referred to the Fatimid caliph as the "emperor" (*imperator*), "emir" (*admirabilis* or *ammirarius*), or, most commonly, "king" (*rex*) of Babylon, a title recalling his status as ruler of the *civitas terrena* and stand-in for the devil.[90] While modern editors and translators have consistently noted this terminology, they have generally treated it as a point of geographical confusion requiring clarification; indeed, the conceptual role of 'Babylon' within the early ideology of crusading has received only a small fraction of the scholarly attention paid to its counterpoint, Jerusalem.[91] This usage surely merits further exploration, given that, in John Tolan's words, it represents "a deliberate choice to use a very charged image" on the part of crusade narrators.[92] Such a choice is particularly interesting, given that it entailed a rejection of the rich typological potential of Egypt, the center of Fatimid power and a location of immense historical and symbolic importance in the Scriptures. As the following reading shows, the chroniclers' persistent and purposeful identification of the Fatimid caliphate with Babylon supported their larger interpretive strategy of situating the holy war within the ongoing conflict between the earthly and heavenly cities.

As we saw in Chapter 3, twelfth-century authors were eager to orient the crusaders within scriptural geography, and while the location of 'Babylon' within the crusading landscape might at first seem like part of the same strategy, this

---

Daniel F. Callahan, *Jerusalem and the Cross in the Life and Writings of Ademar of Chabannes* (Leiden, 2016), 154–55.
[88] Radulfus Glaber, *Historiarum libri quinque*, 3.7.24, ed. Neithard Bulst and trans. John France and Paul Reynolds (Oxford, 1989), 132–34.
[89] Gabriele, *An Empire of Memory*, 141–42.
[90] The following are representative of the numerous references throughout the chronicles: GF, 93; RA, 58; FC, 312; BB, 101; RR, 46; GN, 268; AA, 864; CP, 97; OV, 5:186; WM, 1:658.
[91] The most substantive discussion to date, by Andrew Scheil, focuses mostly on later medieval vernacular literature; see *Babylon*, 258–62.
[92] John V. Tolan, *Sons of Ishmael: Muslims through European Eyes in the Middle Ages* (Gainesville, FL, 2008), 165–66, n. 22. The rendering of "Babylon" as "Cairo" or "Egypt" in most modern translations of crusading chronicles, while helpful as a geographical clarification, obscures this choice.

remapping of sacred geography actually put medieval narrators at odds with biblical history. Anticipating confusion on the part of their readers, a few writers took pains to distinguish the biblical Babylon from its Egyptian namesake. "Lower Egypt is now called Babylon," Guibert of Nogent explained, while William of Malmesbury noted that while the original Babylon was "thought now to be deserted ... the other Babylon in Egypt, built by Cyrus's son Cambyses on the site of the former [city of] Taphnis," was now called by the same name.[93] But the majority of writers made no such efforts. Baldric of Bourgueil, for example, alternated descriptions of the biblical Babylon's role in Jerusalem's history with explanations of the Fatimid 'Babylonians'' involvement in the crusade.[94] That the erudite Baldric, who certainly knew his history and geography, followed the majority of chroniclers in strategically blurring the lines between the biblical Babylon and Babylon-in-Egypt suggests a typological view of the two cities' relationship.[95] Many centuries after the conquest of the Jewish capital of Jerusalem by the Babylonians, another power had arisen in the East to oppress the new chosen people, the Christians, in the holy city. Among the "prophetic signs" (*signa propheta*) that preceded the First Crusade, the Michelsberg Continuator noted, was that "Jerusalem was made a slave to Babylon, whose seat is now in the kingdom of Egypt."[96] This wording presents the Fatimid Caliphate (which ruled Jerusalem from 969 until the Seljuks' arrival in 1073) not simply as the namesake of the ancient Babylonian Empire but as its continuation. As we shall see, Christian writers further elided the differences between the two cities by associating Babylon-in-Egypt with the vices of the biblical Babylon, especially perfidy, cruelty, and greed, as well as with the characteristics of Augustine's Babylon-as-earthly-city, namely, spiritual confusion and rebellion against God. In so doing, they constructed Fatimid "Babylon" as both spiritual successor of the biblical Babylon and allegory of the *civitas terrena*. Against the forces of this new Babylon Latin narrators arrayed the crusaders in the guise of an apostolic army, a veritable city of God on the march.

Underpinning these glosses was a series of diplomatic and military encounters between the crusaders and Fatimids spanning the period from the siege of Nicaea (May to June 1097) to the battle of Ascalon (August 1099).[97] In the summer of

---

[93] GN, 83; WM, 1:650–52. Cf. CP, 148.
[94] BB, 112 (for the biblical Babylon), and 47–48, 52, 101 (for Babylon-in-Egypt).
[95] As noted by Scheil, who provides additional examples; see *Babylon*, 258–59.
[96] FE, 132: "Iam Hierosolima Sarracenis civibus possessa Babylonie, que nunc sedes est regni Egyptie."
[97] Michael Köhler has made the most in-depth study of Fatimid-crusader diplomacy: see his "Al-Afdal und Jerusalem – was versprach sich Äegypten von ersten Kreuzzug?" *Saeculum: Jahrbuch für Universalgeschichte* 37 (1986): 228–39; and Allianzen und Verträge *zwischen fränkischen und islamischen Herrschern im Vorderen Orient* (Berlin, 1991), 55–69. Also see Morton, *Encountering Islam*, 145–47.

1097, apparently at the suggestion of Emperor Alexius I, the crusade's leaders named three men, Hugh of Bellefaire, Bertrand of Scabrica, and Bertrand's chaplain Peter of Picca, as ambassadors (*legatos*) to the emir of Babylon (*in Babyloniam ... Ammirario*), probably the vizier al-Afḍal Shāhanshāh.[98] According to the Monte Cassino Anonymous, they were instructed to give the following message to the Fatimid ruler:

> Make known to him that all of the princes of the Franks have embarked together on a journey to Jerusalem, in order to liberate the city from the hands of the impious pagans (*impiorum manibus paganorum*) and to drive them out of the Christians' lands. Thus, it seems to us that he should wish to become a Christian (*vult ... Christianitatem recipere*) and become one with us as a brother and friend; or, if he prefers the friendship of the pagans, he must prepare to do battle with us.[99]

While the crusaders clearly hoped to enlist Fatimid aid against their mutual enemy, the Sunni Seljuk Turks, what is most striking is the proposal that their would-be ally should embrace Christianity.[100] While there is no record of how this proposal was received, Hugh, Bertrand, and Peter apparently spent over a year at the Fatimid court, and the Fatimids dispatched their own ambassadors to the Latin camp outside Antioch in 1098. A second Egyptian embassy, probably accompanied by the returning Christian envoys, joined the crusaders at the siege of Arqa in the spring of 1099.[101] Although negotiations went on for nearly two years, the Fatimid reconquest of Jerusalem from the Seljuks in February 1098 doomed any possible alliance. Even after the crusaders' defeat of a Fatimid army at Ascalon in August 1099, scant weeks after the Christian capture of Jerusalem, Egypt remained a formidable adversary of the Latin Kingdom, and in later decades the First Crusade's heroes continued to be memorialized as opponents of Babylon.[102]

---

[98] The only account of this embassy is in MC, 28. For discussion, see Köhler, "Al-Afdal und Jerusalem," 230. A second crusader embassy was dispatched to Egypt from the siege of Antioch, according to AA, 230–32 and CP, 152–54.

[99] MC, 18: "Sciat ille quod omnes Francorum principes Jerosolymorum insimul veniunt itinera et viam ab impiorum liberare manibus paganorum, illosque prudentissime ejicere de Christianorum terra. Videat ergo nos agere vult, aut Christianitatem recipere, et esse una nobiscum ut frater atque amicus, aut si paganorum vult amicitiam habere, et obviam nobis ad bellum exire."

[100] If such a suggestion were really made, it may have been prompted by memories of the Fatimids' traditional protection of Christian pilgrims to Jerusalem, which was common knowledge to the chroniclers; see Morton, *Encountering Islam*, 148.

[101] Köhler, "Al-Afdal und Jerusalem," 230–31 and n. 13 for a complete list of references to the Latin chroniclers' accounts of these embassies.

[102] See, for example, the epitaph of Count Eustace of Boulogne, of whom it was remembered that "Babylon timuit qua timor orbis erat"; Heather J. Tanner, *Families,*

Latin chroniclers transferred the biblical Babylon's associations with cruelty, idolatry, and persecution to these new Muslim adversaries, thereby identifying Babylon-in-Egypt as a *figura*, or type, of both biblical Babylon and the *civitas terrena* – a place, as Albert of Aachen termed it, of "pride" (*superbia*) and "opulence" (*opulentia*).[103] Christian writers further claimed that Babylon-in-Egypt was ruled by an immoral tyrant who was, as the Charleville Poet wrote, "treacherous" (*perfidus*) and "false" (*fictus*), and, the Michelsberg Continuator insisted, willing to use "trickery" (*dolus*) to reconquer Jerusalem.[104] In the chroniclers' characterization the Fatimid ruler recalls his biblical predecessor, the Babylonian King Nebuchadnezzar: both are despots punished for their overweening pride; pagan idolaters overawed by displays of God's power; and captors whose testing of the righteous reveals their own faithlessness.[105] The arrogance and inconstancy of this new "king of Babylon" and his subjects serves as a foil for the Jerusalemites' humility and obedience to the divine will, thereby allowing for a presentation of the crusade as a virtuoso moral performance.

In the narrative lead-up to Jerusalem's fall, chroniclers emphasize the craven treachery and faithlessness of the new 'Babylonians' in order to set off the crusaders' bravery and constancy and illustrate their worthiness to possess the holy city. While the Fatimid ruler repeatedly dangled the prospect of his conversion to Christianity before the crusade's leaders, he is said to have acted in bad faith all along; indeed, the chroniclers signal this to their readers in stage-whispers, assuring us that the king was "treacherous" (*perfidus*) and "deceitful" (*dolus*) and that his promise to become Christian was made "falsely" (*falso*).[106] According to the Charleville Poet, when the crusaders joined the Fatimids in a treaty of alliance and dispatched envoys to Cairo in good faith, the caliph had them seized and imprisoned while he considered how he might "slaughter them in covert treachery" (*mactare ... sub operta proditione*).[107] Fortunately, the ruler's advisors dissuaded him, but his foreboding that "if such a race were to capture Jerusalem and then invade [Fatimid] territory, there would be nothing that could withstand their courage" proved well founded.[108] In defeat, the Fatimids' collective spiritual

---

Friends and Allies: Boulogne and Politics in Northern France and England, c. 879–1160 (Leiden, 2004), 343 (Appendix 4). My thanks to Heather Tanner for this reference.

[103] AA, 862.
[104] CP, 152, 156; FE, 154.
[105] David Wells, "The Medieval Nebuchadnezzar: The Exegetical Tradition of Daniel IV and Its Significance for the *Ywain* Romances and for German Vernacular Literature," *Frühmittelalterliche Studien* 16 (2010): 398–405; David J. Bernstein, *The Mystery of the Bayeux Tapestry* (Chicago, 1987), 181–84.
[106] GN, 189; FE, 152; CP, 152.
[107] CP, 154–56.
[108] CP, 156: "si gens talis Francigenarum / Hierusalem capta fines peruadat eorum, / Nil

confusion – a defining feature of the *civitas terrena*[109] – was made manifest; thus an anonymous account of the conquest of Jerusalem described how the city's Egyptian defenders fled from the crusaders to the Tower of David, as to a second Tower of Babel (*turris Babel*), a typological reading which powerfully reasserted the centuries-old linkages between Babylon, spiritual confusion, and rebellion against God.[110]

Latin accounts of the battle of Ascalon make much of the Fatimids' concern with the trappings of the earthly city: worldly power and its adjunct vices, pride and greed. Even as the crusaders were giving thanks to God for delivering Jerusalem into their hands, the Fatimid ruler arrogantly boasted that he would easily retake the holy city and enslave the Christians, and even stock-piled chains and shackles for the purpose.[111] This detail sets up a reading of the subsequent crusader victory at Ascalon as a just punishment of the 'Babylonians' who failed to discern God's hand in Jerusalem's conquest. In this engagement the crusader army routed a significantly larger Egyptian force, leading contemporaries to view the outcome as miraculous, even apocalyptic.[112] Twelfth-century descriptions of Ascalon, a city allied with unbelief and threatened with divine wrath in the Scriptures (Jer. 47:7), strongly associate the Fatimids with the trappings of the earthly city. Latin writers described how the Egyptian army arrived at the battlefield laden with "a treasury of gold and silver," as well as "gold plate" and "rare gems," in a conspicuous display of worldly consumption.[113] By contrast, the Frankish force had been worn so thin by years of campaigning that they gave the appearance of "a mendicant people (*gens mendica*), unarmed and poverty-stricken," ever mindful of the dangers of greed (*cupiditas*) – in short, a truly apostolic army, adorned only with the relics of the True Cross and Holy Lance.[114] Unmindful that "men's power is fleeting," Robert of Reims wrote, the Fatimid

---

fore uirtuti quod eorum obsistere possit … ."

[109] As the name "Babylon" was said to mean "confusion," per Augustine, *De civitate Dei*, 16.4, ed. Dombart and Kalb, 2: 129–31.

[110] CJ, 649. The Babylon–Babel connection was undergirded by medieval Christians' identification of Nimrod, the king of Babylon descended from Ham (Gen. 10:8–12), as the builder of the Tower of Babel; see Kathleen Glenister Roberts, *Alterity and Narrative: Stories and the Negotiation of Western Identities* (Albany, NY, 2007), 78–79.

[111] PT, 143: "amirauissus Babylonie … deferens cathenas et alia ferrea vincula cum quibus iuvenes Christianorum ligasset, qui amplius in servitute haberentur." Trans. 121. This detail is not present in the *Gesta Francorum*. Cf. RA, 155 and EP, no. 18, p. 171.

[112] See the discussion in Rubenstein, *Armies of Heaven*, 305–11; and cf. idem, "Lambert of Saint-Omer," 85.

[113] GN, 300; and WM, 1:652.

[114] Quoting GF, 96; for the clergy's warning against greed, see GN, 296. Cf. RA, 133; BB, 118; and RR, 107.

ruler placed his trust in his own strength and numbers, and in defeat lamented that "the glory of the kingdom of Babylon (*gloria regni Babilonie*) has been foully disgraced."[115] That this was no ordinary defeat but, rather, a triumph of the city of God over the worldly city, was underscored by Fulcher of Chartres, whose description of the crusaders' battle-spoils references the gem-studded walls of the heavenly Jerusalem described in Revelation 21:19–21.[116] Fulcher's reference suggests that when the crusader–Fatimid confrontation was mapped onto the conflict between the 'two cities,' Christian observers perceived the very future of the heavenly city, symbolized by Jerusalem, to be at stake.

Building on traditional associations of the biblical Babylon and the Augustinian earthly city, twelfth-century writers linked Fatimid "Babylon" with captivity and spiritual testing. Early crusading narratives routinely describe pre-crusader Jerusalem as a captive mother (*mater*) or handmaiden (*ancilla*), typologically bonding the city's ancient term of Babylonian captivity with later periods of Muslim rule.[117] Some Latin writers would have known, too, of Augustine's insistence that part of Jerusalem – that is, a portion of the population of the *civitas Dei* – remained hostage in Babylon, awaiting deliverance by Christ.[118] Consider that Baldric of Bourgueil used strikingly Augustinian language in his description of Jerusalem's period of Fatimid rule as a term of captivity:

> Since in the days of that Christianity the city obeyed its Christ less than was fitting, she was once more brought under the yoke of an earthly king (*terrenus rex*), because she scorned to serve the heavenly prince (*celestis imperator*). Therefore, Christ decreed that she be made subject for a long time to the emir of Babylon, so that she might be cured of her proud obstinacy. On this account the city's inhabitants served the impious lords in order to escape death or captivity ....[119]

Baldric's reading reminds us that medieval Christians understood Jerusalem as simultaneously a terrestrial, historical city and a heavenly city, one which could keep faith with its eternal master even as it endured physical captivity under a series of unbelieving kings.[120] The crusade pitted Christ, the ruler of the spiritual

---

[115] RR, 102 and 107.

[116] As noted by Rubenstein, *Armies of Heaven*, 310; see FC, 317.

[117] Morris, "The Servile Mother," 174–94.

[118] Augustine, *Enarrationes in Psalmos*, 136.1, ed. Dekkers, 3: 1964.

[119] BB, 5: "Que ciuitas, quoniam in ipsius sue Christianitatis temporibus Christo suo quam oportuit minus obtemperauit, terreno regi subiugata rursum seruiuit, quia celesti imperatori militare pedetentim contempsit. Facta est igitur Babilonico admirabili tempore diutino tributaria, que superba ceruicositate a Christo suo deuiauerat. Quamobrem seruierunt dominis prophanis si qui mortem euaserunt uel captiuitatem, eiusdem urbis coloni ... ."

[120] Cf. the ruminations on the historical and anagogical meanings of the city in FE, 328–30.

city and the crusade's invisible general, against the ruler of the worldly city, the devil, in the persons of their respective representatives, the crusaders and the Fatimid 'Babylonians.' Here again the identification of Egypt as a new Babylon enabled chroniclers to elevate the holy war to a cosmic level. Robert of Reims's symbolically charged commentary on the Battle of Ascalon is a perfect case in point:

> It was the Friday on which the Redeemer of the human race defeated utterly with the victorious symbol of the cross the Devil of the human race, the King of Babylon; now in the same way the Lord overcame the Emir of the Devil's Babylon through his followers.[121]

Robert's degradation of the Fatimid ruler to the status of devil's stand-in recalls Augustine's *Enarrationes in Psalmos*, a foundational work of monastic exegesis that Robert could have encountered in various contexts, which offers a similar characterization:

> There is one city, and over against it another city, one people and another one people, a king and a king. What am I talking about – one city and another one city? Babylon is one, and Jerusalem is one. ... One has the devil for its king, but Christ is king of the other.[122]

With these words in mind, we can see that Robert's presentation of Ascalon as a conflict between two kings, the *rex Hierosolimitani* – Godfrey of Bouillon, earthly stand-in for Christ the King – and the *rex Babilonis*, heightens the conflict's Augustinian feel.[123]

Babylon-in-Egypt also served as an arena for the performance of the crusaders' apostolicity and figurative martyrdom, where they were given numerous

---

[121] RR, 103: "Erat autem feria VI, in qua Salvator generis humani diabolum, regem Babilonie, tropheo crucis prostravit; et nunc iterum ammiravisum sue Babilonie per satellites suos Dominus superavit." Trans. 206.

[122] Augustine, *Enarrationes in Psalmos*, 61.6, ed. Dekkers, CCSL 39, 2:776: "Quia una civitas et una civitas, unus populus et unus populus, rex et rex. Quid est: una civitas et una civitas? Babylonia una; Jerusalem una. Quibuslibet aliis etiam mysticis nominibus appelletur, una tamen civitas et una civitas: illa rege diabolo; ista rege Christo." Trans. Maria Boulding, *Expositions of the Psalms, 51–72* (Hyde Park, NY, 1990), 207.

[123] RR, 103–5. On the issue of Godfrey's title, see John France, "The Election of and Title of Godrey of Bouillon," *Canadian Journal of History* 18, no. 3 (1983): 321–29, and more recently Jay Rubenstein, "Godfrey of Bouillon versus Raymond of Saint-Gilles: How Carolingian Kingship Trumped Millenarianism at the End of the First Crusade," in *The Legend of Charlemagne in the Middle Ages: Power, Faith, and Crusade*, ed. Matthew Gabriele and Jace Stuckey (New York, 2008), 59–75.

opportunities to demonstrate their obedience to God's will and, in the process, reveal their captors' spiritual confusion. As mentioned earlier, the Charleville Poet maintained that the crusaders' delegates had been held hostage in Cairo, and similar stories seem to have been making the rounds in Latin clerical circles after 1099. The most detailed version comes from the Monte Cassino chronicle, an underappreciated compendium that contains a good deal of unique material. Framed as "the story of what the envoys saw with their own eyes in Babylon (*in Babylone ... oculis suis conspexerunt*) ... and which they faithfully recounted,"[124] this remarkable narrative is suggestive of the richness of Babylon as a locus for continued exegesis of the First Crusade well into the second quarter of the twelfth century.[125]

The Monte Cassino narrative opens with the delegates' arrival in Babylon, "where they discovered many captive Christians held in chains," among them the bishops of Taranto, Beauvais, and Reims, various unnamed prelates, and a holy hermit named William.[126] The engineer of these captives' torments was another Latin churchman, "a certain Ursus, formerly bishop of Bari, who had been captured while on pilgrimage and *led to Babylon* (2 Chron. 36:20), where, compelled by torture, he abjured the Christian faith" and became a confidant of the king (*rex*), "who loved him so much that he did nothing without his counsel."[127] Together, the pair hatched a plan to humiliate and kill both the captives and the newly arrived envoys: they would insist upon the Christians proving the literal truth of Christ's promise in the Gospel of Matthew that "*If you have faith as a grain of mustard seed, you shall say to this mountain, 'Remove from hence to yonder place,' and it shall remove*" (Mat. 17:19). If the captives failed, they would be executed. The Christians sought a three-day respite to fast and pray, during which time the hermit William exhorted them to stand fast, reminding them of the Jerusalemites' sworn duty to die for Christ:

> My brethren and my lords, do not mistrust any word of Christ, but let us ask him with our whole hearts that he may prove the truth of the words he spoke, not to us who believe, but to the unbelievers (*infidelibus*), whether

---

[124] MC, 105.

[125] On the value of this source, see Edoardo D'Angelo's introduction to MC, xl–xliii; John France, "The Use of the Anonymous *Gesta Francorum* in the Early Twelfth-Century Sources for the First Crusade," in *From Clermont to Jerusalem*, ed. Murray, 37; and Rubenstein, "What is the *Gesta Francorum*?" 181.

[126] MC, 105.

[127] MC, 105: "Porro in aula rega erat vir quidam, Ursus nomine, qui olim Barensium episcopus fuerat, sed captus post in peregrinationis itinere *Babylonem ductus est*; sicque dein, poenis constrictus, fidem Christianam negaverat. Rex enim valde eum diligebat, in tantum ut fere nihil sine ipsius consiliis ageret."

to bring about their conversion (*conversionem*) or to the glory of his name. If, however, it does not please him to do this, nevertheless we must not deny those words to be true; let us freely yield ourselves to death in the faith for the sake of those words, so that we might receive the eternal reward![128]

Three days later, the king and "all the people of Babylon" accompanied the Christians outside the city's walls, where the king mockingly pointed out a nearby mountain upon which the captives might test the words of Matthew 17:19. While his companions tearfully beseeched God, William commanded the mountain to rise up in the name of Christ, "indicating with his finger the place to which he would have it move," and, with a deafening thunderclap, the mountain obligingly "rose up from the earth and advanced through the air to the indicated spot." Thereupon the apostate Bishop Ursus "was driven mad, and fell to the ground as if dead," while the terror-struck king promised to free the captives and load them with rich gifts.[129] But the Christians' trials were not over; the Fatimid ruler insisted on conveying the Frankish captives to his newly recaptured city of Jerusalem, where he subjected their faith to yet another impossible test. This being Lent, the king's thoughts turned to the miracle of the New Fire, believed to occur each Easter at the Holy Sepulcher, when one of the lamps of the Anastasis was lit by a divine spark.[130] Summoning the Christians, he cast doubt on the miracle: "I cannot believe," he declared, "the reports that at the Easter vigil the fire kindles itself in the lamps of the Lord's Sepulcher."[131] In a further display of "infidelity" (*infidelitas*), the king insisted upon being allowed to prepare the lamps – equipped with lead wicks, no less – himself to eliminate any possibility of trickery. While the skeptical king stood by, the hermit William once again led the Christians in prayer, until "at the ninth hour, suddenly the heavenly fire began to burn very brightly in all the lamps" of the sanctuary.

---

[128] MC, 106: "Nolite, fratres et domini mei, de uerbo Christi quicquam diffidere, sed eum toto corde rogemus, quatenus uerbum suum, quod locutus est, uerum esse patefaciat non nobis, qui credimus sed infidelibus, uel ad ipsorum conuersionem uel ad gloriam nominis suis. Si autem ei istud non agere placuerit, nos tamen uerbum illud uerum esse non negantes, pro ipsius fide morti succumbamus libenter mercede eterna donandi." While I have rendered *verbum* as plural for clarity in translation, the repeated use of the singular noun in the Latin suggests a play on Christ as the Word (Jn. 1:1, 14).

[129] MC, 107–8.

[130] See Jay Rubenstein, "Holy Fire and Sacral Kingship in Post-Conquest Jerusalem," *Journal of Medieval History* 43 (2017): 470–84 (esp. 477–78); McGinn, "*Iter Sancti Sepulchri*," 33–37; and Benedicta Ward, *Miracles and the Medieval Mind: Theory, Record, and Event, 1000–1215*, 2nd edn. (Philadelphia, 1987), 120–22.

[131] MC, 108: "Non possum credere, quod sabbato uigiliarum Paschae ignis ille, ut fertur, apud Sepulchrum Dominicum per semetipsum in lampadibus accendatur."

"Greatly amazed and seized with wonder (*ingenti stupore atque ammiratione excipitur*) at such a great miracle," nevertheless the king returned to Babylon unconvinced of the truth of Christianity.[132]

This remarkable tale has attracted virtually no attention from scholars, likely because it reads more like an *exemplum* than historical reportage,[133] but it was evidently popular in the Latin West, with versions of it being retold for centuries. Early thirteenth-century iterations appeared in the chronicle of Santa Maria of Ferraria,[134] a Cistercian monastery about thirty miles southeast of Monte Cassino, and in the sermons of the Franciscan Luca of Bitonto (fl. 1230s);[135] by the late thirteenth century it had made its way into Marco Polo's *Devisement du Monde*,[136] and by the mid-fourteenth century into the Second Crusade Cycle.[137] While the number of later accounts is suggestive of the story's wide circulation in the two centuries after the First Crusade, the narrative likely had its genesis in the crusade's immediate aftermath, and there are hints that it was inspired by actual events, albeit ones distorted in the retelling. First, as we have seen, a diplomatic relationship between the crusaders and Fatimids did exist, although later chroniclers downplayed its extent.[138] Moreover, there was indeed an apostate bishop of Bari, Andreas, who converted to Judaism (rather than Islam) in the late eleventh century and subsequently travelled to Constantinople before taking refuge in Egypt.[139] A certain Obadiah, a Norman priest from southern Italy, followed a similar trajectory around this time, ending his days as a Jewish convert in Egypt.[140] These

---

[132] MC, 108–09.

[133] See the dismissive comments by the text's original editors on its many "embellissements et … additions merveilleuses," RHC Oc. 3: xv.

[134] *Chronica Santa Maria of Ferraria*, ed. Umberto Caperna (Cassino, 2008), 48–50.

[135] Luke of Bitonto's unedited sermon appears in Paris, Bibliothèque nationale, ms. latin 16481, fol. 293rv. See also D. L. D'Avray, *The Preaching of the Friars: Sermons Diffused from Paris before 1300* (Oxford, 1985), 156 and n. 4.

[136] Marco Polo, *The Description of the World*, 2 vols., ed. A. C. Moule and Paul Pelliot (London, 1938), 2: viii–x.

[137] *Li romans de Baudouin de Sebourc, IIIe roy de Jhérusalem, poëme du XIVe siècle*, 2 vols, ed. M. L. Boca (Valenciennes, 1841); 1: 345, ll. 573–75; and for commentary, see Vander Elst, *The Knight, the Cross, and the Song*, 164–65.

[138] Rubenstein (*Armies of Heaven*, 113) has pointed to "the ambivalence, or embarassment, that the strategy [of allying with the Fatimids] inspired among the army in general" as a possible explanation for the chroniclers' strategy. Interestingly, Yaacov Lev offers a similar explanation for the silence of the Arabic sources concerning the proposed alliance, in light of the crusade's success; *State and Society in Fatimid Egypt* (Leiden, 1991), 53–54.

[139] Blumenkranz, *Juifs et chrétiens*, 161 and n. 6, 169.

[140] A. Scheiber, "A Fragment from the Chronicle of Obadiah, the Norman Proselyte: From the Kaufmann Geniza," *Acta orientalia academiae scientiarum Hungari* 4 (1954): 271–96.

scandalous stories, either or both of which may have contributed something to the "moving mountain" *exemplum*, were still within living memory when the Monte Cassino Anonymous wrote. We also know of at least ten bishops who accompanied the First Crusade,[141] and while there is no independent record of participation by the bishops of Reims or Taranto, there is a tradition that Bishop Roger II of Beauvais took the cross and was subsequently imprisoned in Egypt.[142] The travails of several high-profile captives in Cairo following the second battle of Ramleh (1102) were also celebrated in the West, and could have inspired the Monte Cassino chronicler – as they did the original author of the Old French romance *Les Chétifs*, who wrote around the same time.[143] Finally, the miracle of the New Fire was widely known in the West, and the Monte Cassino account may have been inspired by a tale that had circulated among eastern Christians since the tenth century, and was perhaps carried west by returning crusaders. In this story, a visiting "emir from Baghdad" accused the Holy Sepulcher's guardians of faking the miracle, and attempted to cancel the Easter liturgy, whereupon all of the lamps in the sanctuary spontaneously caught fire, humiliating the Muslim dignitary.[144] An avid story collector, the Monte Cassino chronicler could have interwoven these fragments from history and hagiography with oral traditions from the first crusaders to create

---

[141] Riley-Smith, *The Idea of Crusading*, 79.

[142] Denis Simon, *Supplément à l'histoire du Beauvaisis* (Paris, 1704), 90. Given that the Monte Cassino chronicle of the crusade exists in a single manuscript (Monte Cassino, Archivio capitolare, MS 300), and that Simon's book predates the first published edition of the chronicle (by J. Mabillon as *Historia belli sacri*, Museum Italicum, i/2 [Paris, 1724]), it seems unlikely that the chronicle was the source of this tradition.

[143] For the captivity of leaders of the Crusade of 1101, including Duke William IX of Aquitaine and Odo Arpin, the viscount of Bourges, and the influence of this historical event on *Les Chétifs*, see Giles Constable, "The Three Lives of Odo Arpinus: Viscount of Bourges, Crusader, Monk of Cluny," in *Religion, Text, and Society in Medieval Spain and Northern Europe: Essays in Honor of J. N. Hillgarth*, ed. Thomas E. Burman, Mark D. Meyerson, and Leah Shopkow (Toronto, 2002), 190–92; and Linda M. Paterson, "Occitan Literature and the Holy Land," in *The World of Eleanor of Aquitaine: Literature and Society in Southern France between the Eleventh and Thirteenth Centuries*, ed. Marcus Bull and Catherine Léglu (Woodbridge, 2005), 88–89.

[144] Andrew Jotischky, "The Christians of Jerusalem, the Holy Sepulchre and the Origins of the First Crusade," *Crusades* 7 (2008): 43–44. It is worth remembering that, as Jotischky notes (ibid., 55), Monte Cassino's ties to the Christian clergy of Jerusalem predated the crusade by nearly a century; the abbey also had friendly ties with Emperor Alexius I (on which, see H. E. J. Cowdrey, *The Age of Abbot Desiderius* [Oxford, 1983], 218). Ralph Glaber tells another story about a Muslim who suffered divine punishment for attempting to halt the holy fire ceremony in the year 1033; *Historiarum libri quinque*, 4.6.19, ed. Bulst and trans. France and Reynolds, 202.

a memorable new narrative.¹⁴⁵ Alternately, the chronicler could have adopted the story wholesale from among the sermons or *exempla* about the crusade circulating in Norman Italy after 1099.¹⁴⁶

If the tale of the crusaders' Babylonian captivity has historical underpinnings, it is also set against a complex background of biblical associations and exegesis that could hardly have been lost on the Monte Cassino Anonymous or his intended audience. While there are echoes here of the Babylonian captivity and the prophet Daniel's experiences at the court of Nebuchadnezzar, the narrative's centerpiece is an extended gloss on Matthew 17:19, a verse which is quoted in full no fewer than three times, and whose meaning both the Christian and Muslim characters are made to ponder. The context for the original Gospel account is Jesus's exorcism of an epileptic boy (called a *lunaticus* in the Vulgate) whose father had initially brought him, without success, to the apostles (Mat. 17:14–17). After driving an evil spirit (*daemonium*) out of the child, Jesus admonished his disciples for their unbelief (*incredulitas*), which prevented them from working the miracle, and went on to make his famous pronouncement about the mustard-seed, concluding that "nothing will be impossible" to those who have faith (Mat. 17:19). It is important to note that early Christian commentators agreed Christ's words should be taken figuratively rather than literally. Jerome's highly influential *Commentary on Matthew* is representative of this view:

> Some think that faith that is compared to a mustard-seed is called small in order that the kingdom of heaven may be compared with a mustard-seed. For the apostle says, "*And if I have all faith so that I may move mountains*" (1 Cor. 13:2). Faith is large, then, which is equated with a mustard seed. The movement of the mountain signifies the removal not of the mountain that we see with the fleshly eyes, but of that one which had been removed by the Lord from the lunatic. For what does he say? "*You will say to this mountain: 'Move from here,' and it will move.*" From this it is possible to refute the follies of those who claim that, since none of the apostles and no believers have ever removed mountains, they did not possess even a little faith. For no great advantage comes from the removal of a mountain from one place to another, only the vain display that is sought in signs. But when that mountain is removed that is said by the prophet to corrupt the whole earth (cf. Jer. 51:25), this brings very great advantage for everyone involved.¹⁴⁷

---

¹⁴⁵ For the chronicler's working methods, see Luigi Russo, "The Monte Cassino Tradition of the First Crusade: From the *Chronica Monasterii Casinensis* to the *Hystoria de via et recuperatione Antiochae atque Ierusolymarum*," in *Writing the Early Crusades*, ed. Bull and Kempf, 59–61.

¹⁴⁶ This seems the more likely scenario, given that the story continued to circulate in later decades, and that later versions were unlikely to have been directly inspired by the Monte Cassino chronicle, which survives in a single twelfth-century manuscript.

¹⁴⁷ Jerome, *Commentariorum in Matheum libri IV*, 17.19, ed. Hurst and Adriaen, 153:

Bede added another layer of commentary to Jerome's words; Christ, he suggested, was referring to the need to purge one's heart of vice, making room therein for the heavenly gift of faith, through which believers became worthy of God's favor.[148] The resulting two-part gloss of Matthew 17:19 was repeated, often verbatim, by later authors such as the ninth-century commentator Hrabanus Maurus.[149] The moving mountain itself continued to be associated with evil and the demonic: in the words of Hrabanus's contemporary Haimo of Halberstadt (d. 853), it stood for "the serpent, that is, infidelity (*infidelitas*), or the venomous thoughts which try to destroy the soul."[150] By the time of the First Crusade, the mountain had become the devil himself, as is clear from the exegesis of Bruno of Segni, whose status as both crusade apologist and abbot of Monte Cassino (r. 1107–11) makes him of particular interest here:

> What is the mountain [Bruno asks], if not the evil [spirit] which the apostles failed to remove from the said man? It is, however, equally valid to identify the mountain as the devil (*diabolus*), on account of the height of his pride (*superbiae altitudo*) and because he oppresses miserable mankind with great heaviness, so that he cannot be moved by such men. *This kind is only cast out by prayer and fasting* [as Christ goes on to say in Mat. 17:20]. Both this mountain and this kind of demon may only be moved and driven out by faith, and so it is necessary to oppose them with prayers and fasts. This, then, is the great and special defense for the rest of the faithful .... And so let us emphasize this point, and commit it well to memory, and always bear in mind this conclusion in the face of all temptation.[151]

"Putant aliqui fidem grano sinapis comparatam paruam dici, quo regnum caelorum grano sinapis conferatur, cum apostolous dicat: *Et si totam fidem habuero ita ut montes transferam,* ergo magna est fides quae grano sinapis coaequatur. Montis translatio non eius significatur quem oculis carnis aspicimus sed illius qui a Domino translatus fuerat ex lunatico. Quid enim ait? *Dicetis monti huic: Transi hinc, et transibit.* Ex quo stultitiae coarguendi qui contendunt apostolos omnesque credentes ne paruam quidem habuisse fidem quia nullus eorum montes transtulerit. Neque enim tantum prodest montis de alio in alium locum translatio et uana signorum quaerenda ostentatio quantum in utilitatem omnium iste mons transferendus est qui per prophetam corrumpere dicitur omnem terram." Trans. Scheck, *Commentary on Matthew,* 203–4. Cf. Ambrose's commentary in *Explanatio psalmorum XII,* 45.9, ed. Michael Petschenig and Michaela Zelzer (Vienna, 1999), 335–36.

[148] Bede, *In Lucam Evangelium Expositio,* 5.17.6, ed. D. Hurst, CCSL 120 (Turnhout, 1960), 309–10.

[149] Rabanus Maurus, *Expositio in Matthaeum,* lib. 5, ed. Löfstedt, 1:485–86.

[150] Haimo of Halberstadt, *Homiliae de tempore,* c. 92, PL 118:533: "est serpens, videlicet infidelitas, sive venenosae cogitationes, quae animam interimere conantur."

[151] Bruno of Segni, *Commentaria in Matthaeum,* 3.72, PL 165:222–23: "Quid est monti huic, nisi illi iniquo, quem apostoli de supradicto homine nec ejicere nec movere poterunt? Quamvis enim propter superbiae, altitudinem mons diabolus dici possit, hoc

Bruno's emphasis is on the devil's power in the world, and on the ascetic struggle of evil. But we should also note that the gloss remains very much in the realm of allegory; the mountain is a *figura* of an evil spirit, the devil, and temptation – anything except an actual mountain. While, as the French scholastic Godfrey of Babion (fl. 1110) acknowledged, Christ's promise in Matthew 17:19 "can be understood in real terms (*realiter potest intelligi*), just as we read that the blessed Benedict [of Nursia] transported a stone from the middle of his garden with a single word,"[152] medieval exegetes generally agreed that this pericope was best understood as an allegory about the power of faith.

With this background in mind, it is easier to appreciate how the Monte Cassino chronicle's account of the envoys' captivity responds to, and indeed dramatically challenges, earlier exegesis of Matthew 17:19. Up to a point, the chronicler follows earlier glosses of the Gospel verse: the narrative centers on a test of faith, in which a faithful people (*populus fidelis*) confronts the forces of unbelief, personified by the king of Babylon, his apostate councilor, and the city's faithless populace (*populus infidelis*); the king, who has already forced one Christian to renounce his faith through torture and aims to sow doubt in the minds of the captives, reads like a *figura* of the devil; and finally, the Christians follow time-tested monastic advice by defending themselves with the spiritual weapons of fasting and prayer. But from this point the narrative dramatically departs from the exegetical script, unequivocally rejecting a symbolic fulfillment of Christ's words for a literal fulfillment. What had hitherto seemed *spiritually* true had been *historically* proven, in a dramatic display of the Gospel's veracity that reversed the traditional ordering of the exegetical 'senses' of scripture.[153] But the narrative also demands to be read typologically, in conjunction with the story of Christ's

---

tamen in loco propter ponderis gravitatem qua hunc miserum hominem opprimebat, et a talibus tantisque viris moveri non poterat, satis congrue mons vocatur. *Hoc autem genus non ejicitur, nisi per orationem et jejunium.* Quamvis, inquit, hic mons et hoc genus daemonum per fidem moveatur et ejiciatur, ad hoc tamen agendum et orationes et jejunia necessaria sunt. Est igitur hoc magnum et singulare praesidium cunctis fidelibus, ut in magnis tentationibus ad orationem et jejunia confugiant .... Hoc itaque valdo notemus, hoc valde memoriae commendemus, hujusque clausulae semper in omnibus tentationibus memores sunt." Cf. ibid., 3.69, cols. 215–16, where, as Matt Phillips kindly pointed out to me, Bruno makes a series of similar points about resisting the devil by bearing the cross of Christ.

[152] Godfrey of Babion (as pseudo-Anselm of Laon), *Enarrationes in Matthaeum*, PL 162:1404. Godrey is referring to Gregory the Great, *Dialogues*, 2.9, in which several monks of Benedict's abbey were unable to move a large rock because the devil was sitting upon it, whereupon Benedict blessed the rock and made it light enough to be lifted easily. See *The Life of St. Benedict*, ed. and trans. Terrence Kardong (Collegeville, MN, 2009), 50.

[153] For analysis of a similar instance in which a chronicler reversed the order of the historical and spiritual senses of a biblical text (Is 60:10–11), see Gabriele, "From

healing of the epileptic. In this reading, the captive crusaders, reprising the role of apostles, are given a test of faith that pits them against evil forces (here, embodied by the Babylonian king, who stands in for the demon of the Gospel account). But whereas the first disciples' incredulity prevented them from working the sought-after miracle, and indeed earned them a reprimand from Christ, there is no question either of the crusaders' perfect faith or of their possession of divine favor. If the original disciples belonged to "an unbelieving and perverse generation" (Mat. 17:16), the first crusaders, in their flawless embrace of the *vita apostolica*, were a new generation of apostles for whom nothing was impossible.

Even in the midst of Babylon, the crusaders held fast to the faith that marked them as citizens of the city of God, in the sense of the heavenly Jerusalem that the First Crusade seemed to have brought to earth in 1099. The triumph of Jerusalem over Babylon, of the *civitas Dei* over the *civitas terrena*, was manifested in the miracle of the moving mountain and the victory at Ascalon, but this cosmic confrontation informed the Jerusalemites' entire undertaking from the moment they took the cross in obedience to the injunction of Matthew 19:29. In an inversion of the biblical narrative, in 1099 Babylon was made to serve Jerusalem, a new hierarchy underscored by the Latins' installation of the standard of the "king of Babylon" in the Holy Sepulcher following his defeat at Ascalon.[154] Overshadowed by the *virtus* emanating from Christ's empty tomb, this relic recalled not only the crusaders' military triumph over a formidable foe but the victory of faith and humility over doubt and pride. It was a reminder, too, that the story of Jerusalem – of the city of God – could not be separated from that of Babylon; indeed, as we have seen, the crusaders' apostolic character, and their mission's cosmic significance, came into sharper focus when set against the backdrop of a 'new Babylon' in the East.

The Conquest of Jerusalem and Christ's Cleansing of the Temple

When the first crusaders breached Jerusalem's northern wall on July 15, 1099, following a desperate five-week siege, they gained possession of the physical embodiment of the heavenly city.[155] This was a homecoming for the city of

---

Prophecy to Apocalypse," 313–14. See also Schein, *Gateway to the Heavenly City*, 24–26.

[154] This detail is included in several chronicles: PT, 148; AA, 468; GN, 299–300; BB, 119; OV, 5:188. The capture of the Egyptian standard became a well-known story in the twelfth-century west; see Paul, *To Follow in Their Footsteps*, 231; and Elizabeth A. R. Brown and Michael W. Cothren, "The Twelfth-Century Crusading Window at the Abbey of Saint-Denis: *Praeteritorum Enim Recordatio Futurum est Exhibitio*," *Journal of the Warburg and Courtauld Institutes* 49 (1986): 1–40 (at 16–17).

[155] For recent overviews of the conquest and its medieval reception, see Benjamin Kedar,

Babylon and Jerusalem

God's residents and a defeat for the earthly city's forces. As Albert of Aachen proclaimed, "Jerusalem, city of God on high (*ciuitas Dei excelsi*), has been recovered ... and restored to her own sons and delivered from the hands of the king of Babylon."[156] The crusader conquest of 1099 effectively closed the typological gap that separated the first and second apostolic ages. Surely it could be no coincidence, Latin writers protested, that the conquest occurred on the feast of the *divisio apostolorum*, which commemorated the apostles' dispersal from Jerusalem and the beginning of their missionary work.[157] Raymond of Aguilers believed that the conquest had completed the cycle of history begun with the *divisio* of Christ's first disciples:

> It is also noteworthy that on this day the apostles were thrown out of Jerusalem and dispersed throughout the world. On this day the children of the apostles (*filii apostolorum*) freed the city for God and the Fathers. This day ... shall be commemorated to the praise and glory of the name of God, who in response to the prayers of his church returned in faith and blessing to his children Jerusalem as well as its lands which he had pledged to the Fathers.[158]

Several years later Ralph of Caen attributed similar sentiments to his former teacher Arnulf of Chocques, the first Latin patriarch of Jerusalem:

> O blessed Ides, glorious above all others. It was in you that those who had been ordered to spread the articles of the faith through the world were separated out. They were the beginning of the seed. Behold, the renewed seed now gathers its harvest in this time. It was in the Ides *during the morning that the Father sent out his household servants into the vineyard* (cf. Mat. 20:1). Behold, it is in the evening that vines fill the cellar.[159]

"The Jerusalem Massacre of July 1099 in the Western Historiography of the Crusades," *Crusades* 3 (2004): 15–75; and Alan V. Murray, "The Siege and Capture of Jerusalem in Western Narrative Sources of the First Crusade," in *Jerusalem the Golden*, ed. Edgington and Ramos, 191–215.

[156] AA, 440 (trans. slightly revised): "Ierusalem ciuitas Dei excelsi, ut uniuersi nostis ... et liberata de manu regis Babilonie ... ."

[157] Other writers also commented on the significance of the date: EP, no. 18, p. 171; AA, 438; RA, 151; RC, 111; FE, 152.

[158] RA, 151: "In hac eadem die apostolorum filii, Deo et patribus urbem et patriam vendicaverunt. Hec celebrabitur dies, idus iulii, ad laudem et gloriam Dei, qui dedit precibus ecclesie sue urbem et patriam quam iurauit patribus et reddidit in fide et benedictione filiis." Trans. 128. On the significance of the *divisio* as a liturgical celebration before and after 1099, see Gaposchkin, *Invisible Weapons*, 172.

[159] RC, 111: "O beatus idus ac prae ceteris gloriosas! In his siquidem diuisi sunt, qui in orbem terrarum fidei rudimenta spargere iussi sunt; ab his cepit exordium seminis: ecce in iisdem seges rediuiua horreum cumulat. In his pater ille familias operarios mane in

Viewed this way, the crusade marked the completion of the apostolic mission by a new generation of disciples.[160] This reading highlighted the centrality of Jerusalem – as terrestrial and heavenly city – within the early crusading idea, as well as the crusade's significance within the holy city's divinely planned history.[161]

As long as the first crusaders had waited to gain admission to the holy city, Jerusalem had waited longer for them. The holy city was not just another stronghold to be won; it was a symbol whose meanings had been multiplied by generations of Jewish and Christian exegetes until the holy city staggered under their weight.[162] As with Babylon, the Scriptures assigned Jerusalem historical, moral, and mystical significance, forming the basis for a rich exegetical tradition that looked simultaneously backward and forward in sacred time.[163] Historically, Jerusalem was the city of God's first chosen people, the Jews, and subsequently hallowed by Christ's preaching and Passion; allegorically, it was the Church, monastery, or soul; and mystically, it represented what the Apostle Paul termed "the Jerusalem above," the heavenly city that remained free even as its earthly double suffered in bondage (Gal. 4:26–27). For Augustine, this Jerusalem was the *civitas Dei*, a gathering of the good angels and deceased believers, as well as the living elect who opposed the earthly city, Babylon,

---

uineam misit: ecce in his uesperi uinea penum replet: o igitur merito has iduum idus sua gloria has meruit indici!" Trans. 149.

[160] For other explicit comparisons between the crusaders and the apostles, see RA, 92–93, 113; and CJ, 645.

[161] Jean Flori has identified three goals of the First Crusade that illustrate the multivalent nature of Jerusalem in early crusading narratives: "reconquérir la Jérusalem terrestre, gagner la Jérusalem céleste, bâtir la Jérusalem spirituelle." See "Jérusalem terrestre, céleste, et spirituelle: Trois facteurs de sacralisation de la première croisade," in *Jerusalem the Golden*, ed. Edgington and Ramos, 25–50 (quoting 26).

[162] Thomas Renna identifies no fewer than ten meanings attributed to Jerusalem by patristic exegetes; see "Zion and Jerusalem in the Psalms," in *Augustine: Biblical Exegete*, ed. Frederick Van Fleteren and Joseph C. Schnaubelt (New York, 2001), 279–98 (at 282).

[163] The following discussion builds upon Schein, *Gateway to the Heavenly City*, 1–5; Joshua Prawer, "Christian Attitudes Towards Jerusalem in the Early Middle Ages," in *The History of Jerusalem: The Early Muslim Period*, ed. Joshua Prawer and Haggai Ben-Shammai (New York, 1996), 311–48; Adriaan H. Bredero, "Jerusalem in the West," in *Christendom and Christianity in the Middle Ages: The Relations between Religion, the Church, and Society*, trans. Reinder Bruisma (Grand Rapids, MI, 1994), 79–104; Sibylle Mähl, "Jerusalem in mittelalterlicher Sicht," *Die Welt als Geschichte* 22 (1962): 11–26; Van Oort, *Jerusalem and Babylon*, 118–23; Ann R. Meyer, *Medieval Allegory and the Building of the New Jerusalem* (Cambridge, 2003), 47–65; Gaposchkin, *Invisible Weapons*, 31–35; and Thomas J. Renna, "The Idea of Jerusalem: Monastic to Scholastic," in *From Cloister to Classroom: Monastic and Scholastic Approaches to Truth*, ed. E. Rozanne Elder (Kalamazoo, MI, 1986), 96–109.

through their self-effacing love of God and rejection of the world. The Scriptures, their commentary traditions, and the widely read Josephan historical corpus conditioned Christian views of Jerusalem as a place of prophecy fulfilled and prophecy-to-be-fufilled, its earthly history bound up in a cycle of revelation, disbelief, and violent retribution that would be broken only at the end of time.[164] Learned Latin observers believed that the first crusaders' arrival outside Jerusalem's walls marked a new phase in this cycle.

As in their descriptions of the crusaders' confrontation with Babylon, the First Crusade's narrators read the events of 1099 through a biblical lens, ransacking the exegete's toolkit in their efforts to locate the conquest as precisely as possible on the arc of sacred history. Several scholars have noted that medieval narrators of the conquest creatively redeployed and combined scriptural passages as a way of endowing this momentous event with meaning, while later chroniclers continued this hermeneutical endeavor, mining the crusader capture of Jerusalem as they would a sacred text to uncover historical, typological, moral, and eschatological lines.[165] While historians have become more attuned to eschatological thinking in narratives of 1099,[166] less effort has been made to understand Latin writers' typological glosses. On the typological level, the conquest seemed to have been predicted by numerous types (*figurae*) in both the Old and New Testaments; for instance, chroniclers associated the crusaders' victory with the parting of the Red Sea, Saul's defeat of Amalek, and the dispersal of Christ's followers from Jerusalem, analogies which reflected widespread views of the crusaders as new Israelites or new apostles.[167]

---

[164] For the influence of Josephus on early crusading narratives, see Throop, *Crusading as an Act of Vengeance*, 205–6; and on the medieval reception of Josephus and pseudo-Josephan texts more generally, see Karen M. Kletter, "Christian Reception of Josephus in Late Antiquity and the Middle Ages," in *A Companion to Josephus*, ed. Honora Howell Chapman and Zuleika Rodgers (Malden, MA, 2016), 368–81.

[165] See Jay Rubenstein, "Miracles and the Crusading Mind: Monastic Meditations on Jerusalem's Conquest," in *Prayer and Thought in Monastic Tradition: Essays in Honour of Benedicta Ward SLG* (London, 2014), 197–210 (esp. 203–10); Luigi Russo, "The Sack of Jerusalem in 1099 and Crusader Violence Viewed by Contemporary Chroniclers," in *The Uses of the Bible*, ed. Lapina and Morton, 63–73; Kaspar Elm, "Die Eroberung Jerusalems im Jahre 1099. Ihre Darstellung, Beurteilung und Deutung in den Quellen zur Geschichte des Ersten Kreuzzugs," in *Jerusalem im Hoch- und Spätmittelalter: Konflikte und Konfliktbewältigung: Vorstellungen und Vergegenwärtigungen*, ed. Dieter Bauer, Klaus Herbers, and Nikolas Jaspert (Frankfurt, 2001), 31–54; and Philippe Buc, *Holy War, Martyrdom, and Terror*, 275–78.

[166] Buc, *Holy War, Martyrdom, and Terror*, 264–74; Rubenstein, *Nebuchadnezzar's Dream*, 35–48.

[167] For the Red Sea analogy, see RC, 104 (citing Ps. 135:13–14); for the comparison with Saul's victory, see Bartolf of Nangis, *Gesta francorum*, c. 25, RHC, Oc. 3:515; and for the conquest and the dispersal of the apostles, see EP, no.18, p. 171; AA, 438; RA, 151; RC, 111; FE, 152.

The Bible and Crusade Narrative in the Twelfth Century

The most insistent typological interpretation, adopted by no fewer than six twelfth-century writers, linked the 1099 conquest with the so-called "cleansing of the Temple," when Christ drove the merchants and moneychangers from the Temple in Jerusalem and afterwards worked thaumaturgical miracles in the Temple precincts.[168] The number of accounts, as well as the fact that, while some of these sources are closely related[169] others have no apparent linkage, suggests that the 1099 conquest was widely understood as a second cleansing of the Temple, a typological drama in which crusaders collectively played the role of Christ and Muslims stood in for the merchants and moneychangers of the Gospel accounts. Spanning a period from c. 1105 (when Baldric of Bourgueil began his *Historia*) to the 1170s (when William of Tyre [d. 1186] composed the relevant portion of his chronicle), these accounts attest to the early appearance and longevity of this exegetical reading, which has, however, escaped the notice of most modern scholars.[170] Its enduring popularity is especially striking, given that, as we saw in Chapter 2, relatively few scriptural passages appear in multiple crusading narratives, suggesting the significance of instances in which multiple authors invoked common biblical passages to explain the Jerusalemites' actions. These typological and moral glosses of the 1099 conquest offer an excellent vantage point from which to consider the complex interplay between scriptural exegesis, theology, and early crusade historiography. As will become clear, when twelfth-century writers likened the sack of Jerusalem to the cleansing of the Temple, they entered into dialogue not only with the Scriptures but with earler exegetes, and especially with eleventh-century reformers who had revisited the Gospel narrative within the context of the revival of the apostolic life. Further, in their accounts of the crusaders' contest with Fatimid "Babylon," in glossing the 1099 conquest Latin writers once again married typology to Augustinian dualist imagery, emphasizing the greed, cruelty, and idolatry of Jerusalem's Muslim overlords as evidence of their affiliation with the earthly city.

The cleansing of the Temple, and particularly the account in John 2:13–16 in which Christ wields a whip of knotted cords (*flagellum de funiculis*), is Christ's

---

[168] These are: BB, 5; CJ, 648; RC, 112; CP, 2; WM, 1: 604; and William of Tyre, *Chronicon*, 1.15, ed. R. B.C. Huygens, 2 vols., CCCM 63(A) (Turnhout, 1986), 1: 132. For the biblical narratives, see Mat. 21:12–14; Mk. 11:15–18; Lk. 19:45–47; Jn. 2:13–16.

[169] For example, William of Tyre knew of Baldric's account, as discussed by Peter W. Edbury and John Gordon Rowe, *William of Tyre: Historian of the Latin East* (Cambridge, 1988), 46–47.

[170] The only studies I have found which discuss this particular interpretation are Bain, "Les marchands chassés du Temple," §31–32; and idem, *Église, richesse et pauvreté*, 277–93. Also see my "The Crusader Conquest of Jerusalem and Christ's Cleansing of the Temple," in *The Uses of the Bible in Crusader Sources*, ed. Lapina and Morton, 19–41.

only act of violence in the Gospels, and has accordingly played a central role in Christian debates over the just use of force from Late Antiquity to the present.[171] The biblical texts themselves demand to be read on multiple levels beyond the literal. The account in the Gospel of John offers the first symbolic interpretation of the Temple as Christ's body, soon to be sacrificed and resurrected. Here Christ challenges the Jews: "'Destroy this Temple, and in three days I will raise it up.' The Jews reply, 'Six and forty years was this temple in building, and wilt thou raise it up in three days?' But He spoke of the Temple of his body" (Jn. 2:19–21). Rejecting the literal interpretation of Christ's words proposed by the Jews, the evangelist offers an allegorical interpretation that was taken up by Paul, who described each believer as a "temple of God" (*templum dei*).[172] These readings threatened to render obsolete the physical Temple, like the rituals traditionally performed therein, and indeed in Late Antiquity and the early Middle Ages Christians cared little for the Temple's physical ruins.[173] But, as text and symbol, the Temple continued to occupy a prominent place in the landscape of Christian theology.[174]

Early Christian exegetes often downplayed the violence of the cleansing story by insisting that the passages be read as allegories for the expulsion of sin from the soul.[175] In the West, one of the most influential such readings was offered by Jerome in his *Commentary on Matthew*, where he decreed the cleansing to be Christ's greatest miracle.[176] Jerome presented what he termed (following Origen) a "mystical understanding" of the cleansing as the constant struggle to preserve the "house of the heart" as a pristine dwelling for God. The chief lesson to be drawn concerned the dangers of avarice, which had of old afflicted the Jewish priesthood and continued to degrade believers and erode the dignity of the clergy.[177] So, Jerome warned,

> May there not be business in the house of our heart. May there not be the commerce of selling and buying. May there not be greed (*cupiditas*) for

---

[171] For a survey of interpretive trends, see Andy Alexis-Baker, "Violence, Nonviolence and the Temple Incident in John 2:13–15," *Biblical Interpretation* 20 (2012): 73–96.

[172] 1 Cor. 3:16–17 and 2 Cor. 6:16.

[173] Schein, *Gateway to the Heavenly City*, 92–93.

[174] For an overview of the Temple's place in medieval thought, see Thomas Renna, "Bernard of Clairvaux and the Temple of Solomon," in *Law, Custom, and the Social Fabric in Medieval Europe: Essays in Honor of Bryce Lyon*, ed. Bernard S. Bachrach and David Nicholas (Kalamazoo, MI, 1990), 73–88.

[175] Jennifer A. Harris, "The Body as Temple in the High Middle Ages," in *Sacrifice in Religious Experience*, ed. Albert I. Baumgarten (Leiden, 2002), 233–56.

[176] For a close reading of Jerome's commentary and its later influence, see Hubert Silvestre, "Le 'plus grand miracle' de Jésus," *Analecta Bollandiana* 100 (1982): 1–15.

[177] Jerome, *Commentariorum in Matheum*, 21.13, ed. Hurst and Adriaen, 187–88; trans. Scheck, *Commentary on Matthew*, 236–37.

donations, lest an angry and stern Jesus enter and cleanse (*mundet*) his own [house] with a whip that he wields in order to make a house of prayer out of a den of thieves and a house of business.[178]

While Jerome had restricted the cleansing's violence to the confines of believers' souls, a parallel commentary tradition forged by Augustine unleashed Christ's anger on a wider world of sinners. In his *Homilies on John*, Augustine justified Christ's scourging of the temple-merchants as a form of prophetic vengeance against the Jews who, with "carnal mind and stony heart" (*carnalitate et corde lapideo*), would later turn him over to be whipped and executed. In Augustine's eyes, the heretics of his own day, who seemed to scourge Christ anew with their blasphemies, were the Jews' heirs.[179] Elsewhere, Augustine explicitly invoked Christ's actions in the Temple to justify the violent ejection of heretics from the Church, and recommended that righteous Christians imitate Christ, who "bodily persecuted those whom he expelled from the Temple."[180]

Early medieval exegetes thus inherited from Late Antiquity a complex chain of associations surrounding the cleansing of the Temple. The biblical pericope could serve as an anti-Jewish or anti-heretical proof-text, as a warning against avarice, or a condemnation of worldly clergy. Building on Jerome's gloss of John 2:13–16, Gregory the Great took his precedessor's anxiety about the sale of the gifts of the Holy Spirit further, declaring that the dove-sellers of the Gospel narratives were guilty of the "heresy of simony" (*simoniacam haeresim*).[181] Gregory's unprecedented equation of simony with heresy, and his insistence that Christ had denounced this specific form of heresy by his actions in the Temple, paved the way for the eleventh-century war on simoniacal clergy.[182] In Bede's homilies on the Gospels, the cleansing became a focal point for concerns about the purity of

---

[178] Jerome, *Commentariorum in Matheum*, 21.13, ed. Hurst and Adriaen, 188: "Non sit in domo pectoris negotio, non uendentium ementiumque commercia, non donorum cupiditas, ne ingrediatur Iesus iratus et adhibito, ut de spelunca latronum et domo negotiationis domum faciat orationis." Trans. based on Scheck, 237. Though ostensibly commenting on the version of the story in Mat. 21:12–13, by importing the element of the whip from the Gospel of John and attributing Christ's actions to righteous anger, Jerome enhances the biblical story's violent flavor and subtly undermines a purely spiritual reading.

[179] Augustine, *In Iohannis Evangelium tractatus CXXIV*, 10.4, ed. Radbod Willems, CCCM 36 (Turnhout, 1954), 102.

[180] Quoted in Alexis-Baker, 80 and n. 14. When it suited his purposes, Augustine could also read the cleansing narrative literally, as an injunction against exchanging money or sacrificing animals on sacred ground; see *Sancti Aurelii Augustini Epistolae I–LV*, 29.3, ed. Daur, 99.

[181] Gregory the Great, *Homiliarum in Evangelia*, ed. R. Étaix, C. Morel, and B. Judic, SC 485 (Paris, 2005), 1:385.

[182] Bain, "Les marchands chassés du Temple," §11–14.

Christian bodies and cult-spaces. For Bede, as for the Carolingian commentators who expanded on his exegesis, the Gospel's chief lesson was that sacred spaces must be safeguarded against polluting agents, be they criminals, sinners, or impious activities.[183]

Several developments led to a revival of interest in the cleansing of the Temple after c. 1050. In the first place, the allegorical association between Christ's body and the Temple clearly suggested in the biblical texts, gained new significance as the nature of Christ's embodiment in the Eucharist received unprecedented theological scrutiny. By the time of the First Crusade, the Temple had come to symbolize not only Christ's body but the entire body of Christians, the *corpus Christianorum*, who collectively participated in the mystery of the Eucharist and bore responsibility for safeguarding the Temple's purity.[184] Ranged against this sacred body were the new temple-merchants and moneylenders: heretics, as well as profit-makers of all kinds, but especially usurers.[185] In the decades following 1099, as the First Crusade's historiography took shape, growing Christian anxieties about the monetary economy were being displaced onto Jews, as part of a process whereby Jewish moneylending was linked to avarice, idolatry, carnality, and pollution.[186] The cleansing of the Temple was a natural exegetical locus for these anxieties, and indeed we know that by this period Latin writers had begun to depict usurers not only as avaricious but as thieves (*latrones*), like those Christ had expelled from the Temple.[187]

Finally, the cleansing became part of the textual arsenal of reformers eager to purge the Church of various pollutants. Lay armsbearers who occupied monastic enclosures might be said to have turned these "temples of God" into "dens of thieves."[188] Earlier exegetes' concerns about avarice and impurity also seemed uncannily familiar – and their glosses very *à propos* – to eleventh-century clerics embroiled in what was framed as a new "Donatist" controversy over the sacramental authority of married and simoniacal priests.[189] Eleventh-century reformers

---

[183] Bain, "Les marchands chassés du Temple," §15–18.

[184] Harris, "The Body as Temple."

[185] Diana Wood, *Medieval Economic Thought* (Cambridge, 2002), 112–13.

[186] Anna Sapir Abulafia, *Christian–Jewish Relations, 1000–1300: Jews in the Service of Medieval Christendom* (Harlow, 2011), 213–16; Rist, *Popes and Jews*, 140–47.

[187] J. T. Noonan, *The Scholastic Analysis of Usury* (Cambridge, MA, 1957), 17–18. Noonan dates this shift to works composed in the 1060s–1090s that immediately preceded the crusade.

[188] Marjorie Chibnall, "Orderic Vitalis on Castles," in *Studies in Medieval History Presented to R. Allen Brown*, ed. Christoper Harper-Bill et al. (Woodbridge, 1989), 43–56 (at 53).

[189] Louis I. Hamilton, "Sexual Purity, 'the Faithful,' and Religious Reform in Eleventh-Century Italy: Donatism Revisited," in *Augustine and Politics*, ed. John Doody, Kevin L. Hughes, and Kim Paffenroth (Lanham, MD, 2005), 237–60.

like Peter Damian and Anselm of Lucca (d. 1086) seized on the cleansing as proof of the sinfulness of simony. Christians who wished to imitate Christ were advised, as the crusade preacher Bruno of Segni wrote in his *Commentary on Luke*, to "violently expel simoniacs from the Church."[190] In the hands of reforming exegetes, the moneychangers also became heretics and idolaters, who adored false images just as simoniacs worshipped the false god of money.[191] As the twelfth century progressed, reformers went further, associating the moneychangers of the Gospel with Jews, heretics, schismatics, and other agents of Antichrist, and encouraging the righteous to imitate Christ's anger against any who polluted the "Temple," that is, Christendom.[192]

The crusade's narrators were well aware of reformist exegesis of the cleansing of the Temple. In his memoirs, Guibert of Nogent connected the Gospel story to his own brush with simony, when well-connected relatives had sought to buy him a prebend, causing Guibert to protest, "I have always been reluctant to buy or, worse, sell, doves" in God's Temple.[193] Fulcher of Chartres claimed to have heard Pope Urban II make a similar connection at Clermont, warning the clerics present that if they wished to be "friends of God" and of the reformed papacy, they must remain on guard, so that "no simoniac heresy will take root among you ... lest the vendors and moneychangers, flayed by the scourges of the Lord, be miserably driven out into the narrow streets of destruction."[194] A manuscript containing Urban II's decrees against simoniacs, including what may be excerpts from a sermon

---

[190] Bruno of Segni, *Commentaria in Lucam*, 46, PL 165:440: "Si igitur eum [i.e., Christ] in hoc quoque imitari velimus ... violenter simoniacos ab Ecclesia pellere debemus." See also Robert H. Rough, *The Reformist Illuminations in the Gospels of Matilda, Countess of Tuscany* (The Hague, 1973), 17–36; Joseph H. Lynch, *Simoniacal Entry into the Religious Life from 1000 to 1260* (Columbus, OH, 1976), 66–67; and Fiona J. Griffiths, "The Trouble with Churchmen: Warning against Avarice in the 'Garden of Delights,'" in *Frauen – Kloster – Kunst: Neue Forschungen zur Kulturgeschichte des Mittelalters*, ed. Jeffrey Hamburger et al. (Turnhout, 2007), 147–54.

[191] Humbert of Silva Candida, *Libri tres adversus simoniacos*, ed. Thaner, 1:174; and for commentary, see Buc, "La vengeance de Dieu," 479.

[192] See, for example, Gerhoh of Reichersberg, *De investigatione Antichristi*, ed. E. Sackur, MGH Lib. de lite, 3:314–15 (and cf. Orderic Vitalis's characterization of the Muslim forces at Ascalon as *sinagogam Sathanae*, OV, 5: 176); and Thomas of Chobham, *Summa Confessorum*, ed. F. Broomfield, Analecta mediaevalia Namurcensia 25 (Louvain, 1968), 414; trans. Throop, *Crusading as an Act of Vengeance*, 158–59.

[193] Guibert of Nogent, *De vita sua*, ed. Labande, 160: "Etsi enim multotiens nefarie alias labi potuerim, emptor tamen, imo proditor columbarum semper esse timuerim." Trans. Paul J. Archambault, *A Monk's Confession: The Memoirs of Guibert of Nogent* (University Park, PA, 1996), 71 and n. 115.

[194] FC, 126–27: "res ecclesiasticas praecipue in suo iure constare facite, ut et simoniaca haeresis nullatenus apud uos radicet; carete ne uendentes ac ementes flagris flagellati dominicis per angiportus in exterminium confusionis miserabiliter propellantur."

delivered at Clermont, supports Fulcher's claim that the pope referenced the cleansing of the Temple as an anti-simony proof-text at Clermont,[195] and gives special significance to those chronicles which claim that Urban employed the cleansing as a rhetorical device in his call to arms. By the time the first crusaders headed east, then, a monumental body of interpretation had grown up around the cleansing of the Temple, and the words of the fathers and reformers clung so tightly to the original biblical narrative that they could not easily be disengaged. The First Crusade's historians inherited a rich store of commentaries that identified the cleansing as a moment of rupture between Judaism and Christianity, a parable for the struggle of righteousness against sin, and a battle cry in the war against simony. After 1099, chroniclers reassessed the meaning of the Gospel narrative yet again, in the light of the crusaders' astonishing capture of Jerusalem.

After the crusading army breached Jerusalem's walls on July 15, 1099, the Christians carried out one of the most infamous massacres in the annals of medieval warfare. Seeking to understand these events, several studies have emphasized the importance of biblical models, both to the crusaders themselves and to their clerical chroniclers.[196] Certainly it is significant that some of the bloodiest scenes took place at sites with recognized biblical pedigrees; thousands of Muslims were killed inside the al-Aqsa mosque upon the Temple Mount, which Latin Christians identified as the Temple of Solomon, and outside the Dome of the Rock, which Latin Christians called the Temple of the Lord.[197] Remembering that the conquest was also perceived as part of an ongoing conflict between the 'two cities,' Jerusalem and Babylon – whose representatives, the Fatimids, had reconquered the holy city just months earlier – can also help to contextualize Latin reactions. As we shall see, the opposition of the *civitas Dei* and *civitas terrena*, which was traditionally described in terms of a battle between virtue and vice, informed the interpretative framework for the chroniclers' presentation of the 1099 massacre as a cleansing process.

Trans. 51. William of Malmesbury also emphasizes the place of simony on the agenda at Clermont; WM, 1:594.

[195] *The Councils of Urban II, Vol. 1: Decreta Claromontensia*, ed. Robert Somerville (Amsterdam, 1972), 33–34. Greed (usually termed *avaritia*) is a persistent theme of the council's canons; see ibid., 34 (c. 15) and 117 (c. 36).

[196] See especially Kaspar Elm, "Die Eroberung Jerusalems im Jahre 1099. Ihre Darstellung und Deutung in den Quellen zur Geschichte des Ersten Kreuzzugs," in *Jerusalem im Hoch- und Spätmittelalter. Konflikte und Konfliktbewältigung – Vorstellungen und Vergegenwärtigungen*, ed. Deiter Bauer, Klaus Herbers, and Nikolas Jaspert (Frankfurt, 2001), 31–54; Buc, *Holy War,* 135–36 and 265–72; and Rubenstein, *Armies of Heaven,* 273–92.

[197] The various contemporary versions of these events are discussed by Kedar, "The Jerusalem Massacre of July 1099," 16–25.

Immediately after the Temple Mount was washed in the blood of their enemies, the triumphant army laid claim to nearby sacred sites, solemnly processing to the Holy Sepulcher and thence to the Temple of the Lord to offer prayers of thanksgiving.[198] In the decades to come, the Temple of the Lord took second place only to the Holy Sepulcher in the crusader capital's spiritual geography; Jerusalem's rulers, clergy, and people regularly gathered here to do penance, pray for divine intercession before battles, and celebrate the anniversary of the city's conquest. Under the auspices of a community of Augustinian canons, the mosque was transformed into a church in the early twelfth century.[199] Although most educated Christians knew this structure was not actually the Second Temple, it was believed to stand on its exact site, and to encompass locations where key events from the life of Christ, including the cleansing, had occurred.[200] The events of 1099 served to heighten the physical Temple's cultic importance within Christendom. Earlier medieval writers had emphasized that such holy sites were, as Samuel Collins writes, "tied by unbreakable chains of meaning to the sacred architecture of the Old Testament past and the coming eschatological future,"[201] and the crusaders' actions powerfully reaffirmed these associative bonds, confirming the value of the Temple as symbol – of the resurrection, of the defeat of the old law, and of avarice. At the same time, Latin writers expressed a concern with the Temple as a physical holy site hallowed by two typologically linked acts of purgation.

The Temple's transformation was of great interest to Latin chroniclers, who described the site's pollution under Muslim rule and its capture by the crusaders in terms reminiscent of earlier exegesis of the cleansing of the Temple. It is noteworthy that the verb *mundare*, used throughout the Latin narratives to describe the crusaders' actions as a spiritual as well as physical purification of the city, had been used by earlier exegetes to describe Christ's violence against the moneychangers.[202] Some twelfth-century writers went so far as to identify

---

[198] PT, 142; FC, 305; *Historia Nicaena vel Antiochena*, RHC Occ. 5:176; and for commentary Amnon Linder, "The Liturgy of the Liberation of Jerusalem," *Mediaeval Studies* 52 (1990): 110–31 (128).

[199] Sylvia Schein, "Between Mount Moriah and the Holy Sepulchre: The Changing Traditions of the Temple Mount in the Middle Ages," *Traditio* 40 (1984): 175–95; Denys Pringle, *The Churches of the Crusader Kingdom of Jerusalem, a Corpus, Vol. 3: The City of Jerusalem* (Cambridge, 2010), 401–2.

[200] Pringle, *Churches of the Crusader Kingdom*, 3: 401. Some twelfth-century Christians apparently believed the Dome of the Rock to be an exact replica of the Second Temple; see Schein, *Gateway to the Heavenly City*, 106. This seems to have been Ralph of Caen's view; RC, 112–13.

[201] Samuel W. Collins, *The Carolingian Debate over Sacred Space* (New York, 2012), 4.

[202] J. F. Niermeyer, *Mediae Latinitatis lexicon minus* (Leiden, 1976), 708. For examples, see GP, 248; FC, 304; AA, 460n. (manuscript C variant); RR, 100; HH, 442. As Nicholas Morton shows, earlier medieval authors used similar language to describe Christian defeats of non-Christians; see *Encountering Islam*, 36. E.g., Jerome,

the liberation of the Temple, alongside that of the Holy Sepulcher, as the original motivation for the First Crusade.[203] Several justified the crusaders' slaughter of their enemies by charging that under Muslim rule the Temple site had been profaned by sacrilegious practices. Raymond of Aguilers spoke for many of his contemporaries when he claimed, "It was undoubtedly a just judgement [of God] that their blood was spilled in that same place where they had blasphemed God for so long."[204] In this reading, the crusaders became agents of divine vengeance, their hatred of the enemy glossed as righteous anger on God's behalf. As Baldric of Bourgueil explained, the Christians "pursued them [i.e., the Muslims] with such hatred because they had appropriated the Temple of the Lord and the Holy Sepulcher and the Temple of Solomon as well as other churches, and polluted them with such shameful practices."[205] These "shameful practices," Latin chroniclers agreed, were motivated by avarice and idolatry, sins commonly linked in the earlier moral exegesis of the cleansing narrative, as well as in Augustine's characterization of the earthly city.

As we have seen, crusading spirituality emphasized *caritas*,[206] the selfless and self-effacing love for fellow Christians, but avarice – the evil opposite of *caritas* – also had an important role to play in the ideology of holy war. Medieval writers blamed the first crusaders' earlier defeats on their avarice, which was regarded by many as the vilest of the seven deadly sins.[207] In the crusading context, avarice, like *caritas*, was defined in terms of biblical models; for instance, the chronicler Ralph of Caen reported that Arnulf of Chocques had cited the cleansing of the Temple when he rebuked the Norman leader Tancred for stripping the silver from the Dome of the Rock's walls. (Tancred, for his part, defended his actions as an attack on idolatry.[208]) Moreover, representations of the Muslim enemy in the Latin chronicles connect avarice with heresy, idolatry, and pollution of the sacred, using language recalling the biblical cleansing narrative as well as contemporary diatribes against simony. In making these connections,

---

Commentariorum in Matheum, 21.13, ed. Hurst and Adriaen, 188 (as cited at n. 178 above).

[203] For references, see Schein, *Gateway to the Heavenly City*, 100–1 n.

[204] RA, 150–51: "Iusto nimirum iudicio, ut locus idem eorum sanguinem exciperet, quorum blasphemias in Deum tam longo tempore pertulerat."

[205] BB, 110: "Tanto siquidem odio persequebantur eos, quia templum domini et Sancti Sepulchri ecclesiam et Templum Solomonis et alias ecclesias suis usibus illicitis peculiauerant ac indecenter contaminauerunt." Cf. OV, 5:172.

[206] See Riley-Smith, "Crusading as an Act of Love"; and Purkis, *Crusading Spirituality*, 30–58.

[207] See Siberry, *Criticism of Crusading*, 101; and Lester K. Little, "Pride Goes Before Avarice: Social Change and the Vices in Latin Christendom," *American Historical Review* 76 (1971): 16–49.

[208] RC, 112.

the chroniclers drew from a hermeneutical well whose depths reached to the patristic age, and here again, we can discern Augustine's influence. As we have seen, the Augustinian conflict between the city of God and the earthly city was defined in terms of the opposition of *caritas* (selfless love) and *cupiditas* (greed or lust).[209] Further, Augustine identified idolatry as an incitement to the self-love that ruled the earthly city, where the sin of avarice, defined as the worship of temporal goods rather than God, was a form of idolatry. The historical examples of ancient Israel and pagan Rome, Augustine concluded, demonstrated that those guilty of idolatry in its various manifestations could not escape God's wrath.[210] The language and logic of Latin accounts of the fall of Jerusalem owe much to this way of thinking.[211]

Latin chroniclers dwelt upon the avarice of Jerusalem's Muslim rulers, who were said to have amassed wealth by charging Christian pilgrims for entrance to the city's sacred places – a practice that, in medieval Christian eyes, amounted to the sale of the gifts of the Holy Spirit, and so could be seen as a form of simony.[212] Such was their greed, claimed Guibert of Nogent, that guardians of shrines routinely cut open pilgrims' very bodies in the hopes of finding coins they had swallowed.[213] Other writers accused the Muslims themselves of ingesting gold coins in an attempt to conceal their filthy lucre, thereby aligning the crusaders' enemies with the hellbound usurers of Romanesque art and hagiography.[214] The chroniclers further charged that, like contemporary moneylenders and simoniacs, the Muslims' adoration of gold and silver found expression in idolatry.[215] In

---

[209] Edward Morgan, *The Incarnation of the Word: The Theology of Language of Augustine of Hippo* (London, 2010), 73–75. See Augustine, *De doctrina christiana*, 3.35–38, ed. Green, 148; and idem, *Enarrationes in Psalmos*, 118.11.6, ed. Dekker, 3: 1698–99.

[210] Augustine, *De civitate Dei*, 2.19–20, 2.22–25, ed. Dombart and Kalb, 1: 76–79, 85–91; cf. idem, *De libero arbitrio*, 1.15.33–1.16.34, ed. William M. Green, CCSL 29 (Turnhout:, 1970), 234–35. For a concise summary of Augustine's position, see Matthew A. Shadle, *The Origins of War: A Catholic Perspective* (Washington, D.C., 2011), 16–18.

[211] This oppositional thinking, of course, also played an important role in the spirituality of contemporary monastic groups such as the Cistercians, as shown by Martha G. Newman, *The Boundaries of Charity: Cistercian Culture and Ecclesiastical Reform, 1098–1180* (Stanford, CA, 1996).

[212] For example, AA, 2–4; CP, 4; WM, 1:600; OV, 5:172.

[213] GN, 116. Ironically, the crusaders are said to have engaged in similar practices to extract money from the corpses of their dead enemies; e.g., FC, 301–2.

[214] For example, Bartolf of Nangis, *Gesta Francorum*, RHC Oc, 3:516; WM, 1:678. For the visual depiction of usury, see Charles Reginald Dodwell, *The Pictorial Arts of the West, 800–1200* (New Haven, CT, 1993), 326; for hagiographical conventions, see James Davis, *Medieval Market Morality: Life, Law and Ethics in the English Marketplace, 1200–1500* (Cambridge, 2012), 126–27; and an early example of the motif in *The Memoirs of Guibert of Nogent*, trans. Archambault, 205–6.

[215] These descriptions are discussed in detail in Tolan, *Saracens*, 109–20; and Cole, "The

Robert of Reims's history, the "Babylonian" emir Clemens laments his failure to defend Jerusalem in terms that link Muslim idolatry to luxury and greed: "O Mahommed, Mahommed," he cries, "who has ever invested more in the magnificence of your worship with shrines ornate with gold and silver, decorated with beautiful images of you …?"[216] Significantly, the center of idol-worship in Muslim Jerusalem was identified as the Temple of the Lord, said to house an "idol of Mahomet" (*simulacrum* or *idolon Mahumet*).[217] In the climax of Ralph of Caen's narrative of the conquest of Jerusalem, Tancred orders this image removed from the sacred precincts, torn limb from limb, and melted down.[218] Suzanne Conklin Akbari has shown that such depictions of Muslim idolatry formed part of a larger nexus of accusations that associated Islam (like Judaism) with the flesh rather than the spirit.[219] They also speak to the contemporary glosses of Islam as Old Testament paganism that, as we saw in Chapter 3, were a stock feature of early crusading narrative.

Accusations of avarice and idolatry against the Turks and Fatimids provide a cultural context for the identification of the crusaders' capture of Jerusalem with the cleansing of the Temple. Given the preexisting associations of the cleansing narrative and the Temple site, such charges could do various kinds of interpretive work. In the first place, these moral readings linked Muslims with other groups – simoniacs, heretics, usurers, and Jews – who were reckoned enemies of the true Church, and thereby enabled extreme acts of violence, like the 1099 massacre, to be read as necessary acts of purification. The four twelfth-century writers who referenced the cleansing of the Temple in their accounts of Urban II's Clermont speech clearly understood the Gospel narrative as part of the justificatory framework not only for the sack of Jerusalem but for the entire crusade.[220] For instance, William of Malmesbury had the pope liken Muslims to the "thieves" (*latrones*) who did business in the Temple until Christ drove them out, and proclaim that it is now the crusaders' duty to emulate Christ and "clear the impious out of God's sanctuary … and install the godfearing."[221] This sentiment is echoed by the Charleville Poet, who had Urban chastise Christians for their tolerance of the deplorable state of Jerusalem, now become once again "a hideout and den of thieves" (*speluncam latronum*), as it had been

---

Theme of Religious Pollution," 87–101.
[216] RR, 107: "O Mathome, Mathome! Quis unquam venustiori te cultu colitur in delubris auro argentoque insignitis, pulchrisque de te imaginibus decorates … ?" Trans. 210.
[217] FC, 290; WM, 1:642–43.
[218] RC, 107.
[219] Akbari, *Idols in the East*, 235–42.
[220] I.e., Baldric of Bourgueil, the Charleville Poet, William of Malmesbury, and William of Tyre.
[221] WM, 1:604–05: "vacuate ab impiis Dei sacrarium, extrudite latrones, inducite pios."

before the cleansing of the Temple.[222] Baldric of Bourgeuil explicitly compared the crusaders' enemies to the moneychangers of the Gospel, charging that under Muslim rule,

> The holy Temple of God has undoubtedly been polluted (*pollutum est*), and God's courtyard irreverently made into a gathering-place for vagabonds; *the house of prayer has been turned into a den of thieves* (cf. Mat. 21:13), and Mother Church made a foreign-born stepmother to her sons. They [i.e., the Muslims] allow the church of the Holy Sepulcher to be looked after a little, not out of regard for the Christian religion, but so that they may thereby satisfy their desire for profit and their greed (*cupiditas*).[223]

Drawing on interpretative traditions that likened the pollution of money with that of idolatry, one anonymous witness to the conquest of Jerusalem directed his words not to an imagined audience of crusaders but to Christ himself:

> Your people, Lord, have been cast down and your inheritance laid waste. They [i.e., the Muslims] desecrate (*polluuerunt*) your Temple and holy house, of which you said, "*My house shall be called the house of prayer.*" Now, however, it is made not into a *den of thieves* but rather a temple of demonic idols (*demoniorum idolium*) (Mat. 21:13).[224]

Writing in the 1170s, William of Tyre broadcast a similar message in his version of Urban II's speech: "The Temple of the Lord, from which the Lord, full of zeal (*zelans*), cast out the buyers and sellers lest his father's house become a *den of thieves*, is now the residence of demons" (*sedes daemoniorum*).[225] This last turn of phrase, significantly, invokes the fall of Babylon as described in

---

[222] CP, 8: "Nunc fore speluncam protectricemque latronum, / Perque eius caueam lacerari membra piorum / Et blasphemari nomen super omnia sanctum / Calcarique Dei templum spernique sepulchrum."

[223] BB, 5: "Pollutum est nimirum sanctum Dei templum; et facta est aula Dei gentium conuenarum irreuerenter conuenticulum. Domus orationis spelunca latronum facta est, et filiis suis mater Ecclesia in nouercam alienata est. Sane Sancti Sepulchri ecclesiam Paulo seruari sinebant honorificentius: non quia multum de religione Christiana curabant, sed quoniam taliter utilitatibus et cupiditatibus suis satisfaciebant." Cf. FE, 134, which emphasizes the Muslim preservation of the Holy Sepulcher solely for profit (*quaestus*).

[224] CJ, 648: "Populum tuum humiliauerunt et hereditatem tuam uexauerunt. Polluuerunt Templum Sanctum tuum et domum sanctum de qua dixeras: '*Domus mea domus orationis uocabitur*' nunc autem non spelanca [sic] latronum, sed demoniorum idolium efficitur."

[225] William of Tyre, *Chronicon*, c. 1.15, ed. Huygens, 1:132: "Templum domini, de quo zelans dominus vendentes eiecit et ementes ne domus patris eius fieret spelunca latronum, facta est sedes demoniorum." William could plausibly have borrowed the

Revelation 18:2, a verse which William may have seen as foretelling the events of 1099.[226] For these writers, the profanation of Jerusalem's holy sites by the new 'Babylonians' was even worse than the actions of the original temple-merchants who prefigured them; the thieves of the Gospel narrative had been replaced by idolaters and demons, necessitating a second, far more violent, cleansing of the Temple by God's new agents of purification.

Readings of the 1099 conquest as a second cleansing of the Temple also typologically linked the crusaders to Christ and other biblical heroes and gave their undertaking christo-mimetic status. As lovers of justice and zealous defenders of the Church's purity, the crusaders declared themselves the heirs (*heredes*) of Christ, who had modeled these qualities in the original cleansing.[227] Baldric of Bourgeuil's account of the siege of Antioch makes this connection in the tale of a vision in which Christ gave renewed support to the crusade after being reminded of how "for so many years that pagan race have held and defiled with their filth that house which was *a house of prayer*" (Mat. 21:13), after the expulsion of the original moneychangers and merchants.[228] In their cleansing of Jerusalem, the crusaders were said to have imitated not only Christ but also the Jewish priest Mattathias, who, because he had refused to sacrifice to the Greek gods in the Temple and killed a fellow-Jew who carried out the act in his stead,[229] could be seen as a *figura* of Christ. As William of Tyre wrote,

> It was this [i.e., the profanation of the Temple] that roused the laudable zeal (*zelem commendabilem*) of that great priest Mattathias, founder of the line of Maccabees, as he himself bears witness, saying "*The Temple of the Lord is like a man without honor*," and "*the vessels of her glory are carried away captive*" (1 Macc. 2:8–9).[230]

In these typological readings, the crusaders, Christ, and the Maccabees are united by zeal (*zelus*), a term associated in the Vulgate with the terrifying, unappeasable wrath of God.[231] This righteous anger could be channeled into acts

---

basic comparison from Baldric's history, which he knew, but he has clearly made it his own (see n. 230 below).

[226] The Vulgate reads: "cecidit Babylon magna et facta est habitatio daemoniorum."

[227] CJ, 648.

[228] BB, 68: "tot annis gens pagana domum istam, que domus erat orationis, obtinuit; suisque spurcitis, proh pudor, eam delegauit ...."

[229] 1 Mac. 2:15–24. For the uses of the Maccabees in crusader sources, see Lapina, *Warfare and the Miraculous*, ch. 5; and Morton, "The Defense of the Holy Land."

[230] William of Tyre, *Chronicon*, c. 1.15, ed. Huygens, 1: 132: "Idipsum enim et Matathiam sacerdotem magnum, sanctorum progenitorem Machabeorum, ad zelum accendit commendabilem, sicut ipse testatur, dicens: *templum domini quasi vir ignobilis, vasa glorie eius abducta sunt captiva.*"

[231] For example, Wis. 5:18, Is. 9:7, and Ez. 16:42.

of violence – whipping the moneychangers, overturning the merchants' tables, executing an idolater, or murdering many thousands of 'pagans' – which Latin writers deemed legitimate, even praiseworthy, because they preserved the honor of God and his holy spaces.

As the sacred geography of the Temple Mount was reconfigured under the Latin rulers of Jerusalem, the biblical cleansing narrative and its allegorical repetition by the crusaders continued to serve as an interpretive touchstone. The early masters of the Temple, who were keenly interested in the renovation of holy sites, explicitly reminded would-be patrons of the cleansing's status as a key moment in the history of the holy city and, by extension, the pre-history of their own order.[232] The cleansing also occupied a privileged place within the renovated visual fabric of the crusader capital. As part of the transformation of the Dome of the Rock into a church,[233] the building's interior was painted with scenes from its (or rather, its architectural predecessors') history, including a large image of Christ – the triumphant, militant Christ who had just expelled the buyers and sellers – repeating his words from Matthew 21:13: "My house shall be called a house of prayer" (*Haec domus mea domus orationis vocabitur*).[234] Half a mile away, an early twelfth-century lintel on the western façade of the Holy Sepulcher greeted pilgrims with another depiction of the cleansing story.[235] The fabric of Jerusalem's holy sites, glossed by the crusaders' addition of new images and texts, thus served as a powerful reminder of the events of 1099 and their biblical precedents. Regular liturgical observances at these sites, in particular those surrounding the feast of the capture of Jerusalem celebrated

---

[232] See Achard of Arrouaise, "Poème sur le Templum Domini," in *Archives de l'Orient Latin, I*, ed. Paul Riant (Paris, 1884), 575; and Rudolf Hiestand, "Gaufridus abbas Templi Domini: An Underestimated Figure in the Early History of the Kingdom of Jerusalem," in *The Experience of Crusading, Vol. 2: Defining the Crusader Kingdom*, eds. Peter Edbury and Jonathan Phillips (Cambridge, 2003), 48–59 (at 58). I am grateful to Eyal Poleg for these references.

[233] It is important to note that some Christians believed the present building had originally been built as a Byzantine church, and ignored its original status as a Muslim place of worship; see Benjamin Z. Kedar and Denys Pringle, "1099–1187: The Lord's Temple (*Templum Domini*) and Solomon's Palace (*Palatium Salomonis*)," in *Where Heaven and Earth Meet*, ed. Oleg Grabar and Benjamin Z. Kedar (Jerusalem, 2009), 132–49.

[234] Schein, "Between Mount Moriah," 183. The image and inscription are described by the pilgrim John of Würzburg, in *Peregrinationes tres*, ed. R. B. C. Huygens, CCCM 139 (Turnhout, 1994), 90. The narrative of the English pilgrim Saewulf suggests that guardians at the Temple of the Lord also reminded their visitors of the cleansing story; see *Peregrinationes tres*, ed. Huygens, 68.

[235] Nurith Kenaan-Kedar, "The Figurative Western Lintel of the Church of the Holy Sepulcher in Jerusalem," in *The Meeting of Two Worlds*, ed. Vladimir P. Goss (Kalamazoo, MI, 1986), 123–31.

every 15 July between 1099 and 1187,[236] amplified these iconographical commentaries. As attested by a sacramentary in use in Jerusalem in c. 1130, the crusader conquest was explicitly identified with the cleansing of the Temple in the liturgy for the feast of "the liberation of Jerusalem," which featured a Gospel reading from Matthew 21:10–17.[237]

The transformation of the al-Aqsa mosque, or Temple of Solomon, into the headquarters of the Templars after 1119 further encouraged Latin Christians to reflect on the relationship between the cleansing and the ongoing crusading movement. In his *De laude novae militiae*, Bernard of Clairvaux, who never visited Jerusalem, asserted that the Templars had consciously imitated Christ's actions in the cleansing when they rededicated the Temple to the knight-service of Christ.[238] As he wrote,

> Moved therefore by their King's example, his devoted soldiery, considering it far more unfitting and infinitely more intolerable for a holy place to be polluted by unbelievers (*pollui ab infidelibus*; cf. Lev. 19:8) than to be crowded with merchants, have installed themselves in this holy house .... Having expunged it and the other holy places of every infidel stain (*infidelitas spurca*) and the tyrannical horde, they occupy themselves day and night with work as distinguished as it is practical. They honor the Temple of God earnestly with fervent and sincere worship, in their devotion offering up, not the flesh of animals according to the ancient rites (cf. 1 Kgs. 8:63), but true peace offerings, brotherly love, devoted obedience, and voluntary poverty.[239]

In the wake of its second cleansing by the crusaders, the Temple was reborn in a twofold sense: allegorically, it signified the new apostolic church centered on

---

[236] On the feast's development, see Amnon Linder, "The Liturgy of the Liberation," *passim*.

[237] Bibliothèque nationale de France, ms. latin 12056, fols. 31v–32r. My thanks to Cecilia Gaposchkin for this reference. For a detailed discussion of the manuscript's provenance and contents, see Cristina Dondi, *The Liturgy of the Canons Regular of the Holy Sepulchre: A Study and a Catalogue of the Manuscript Sources* (Turnhout, 2004), 253–66.

[238] For a fuller analysis of Bernard's exegesis of the temple as symbol and holy site, see Renna, "Bernard of Clairvaux and the Temple," 80–85.

[239] *De laude novae militiae*, ed. Leclercq, Talbot and Rochais, 3:222: "Talis proinde sui Regis permotus exemplo devotus exercitus, multo sane indignius longeque intolerabilius arbitrans sancta pollui ab infidelibus quam a mercatoribus infestari, in domo sancta ... commoratur, tamque ab ipsa quam a ceteris sacris omni infidelitatis spurca et tyrannica rabie propulsata, ipsi in ea die noctuque tam honestis quam utilibus officiis occupantur. Honorant certatim Dei templum sedulis et sinceris obsequiis, iugi in eo devotione immolantes, non quidem veterum ritu pecudum carnes, sed vere hostias pacificas, fraternam dilectionem, devotam subiectionem, voluntarium paupertam." Trans. M. Conrad Greenia, *In Praise of the New Knighthood* (Kalamazoo, MI, 2000), 50.

the traditional monastic virtues of *caritas* and *povertas* which loomed so large in the spirituality of Bernard and his fellow Cistercians; historically, it had become the home of a new model Christian, the monk-knight, born from the crusading project. For Bernard, the cleansing of the Temple was the inspiration for the Templars' particular form of *imitatio Christi*:

> By all these signs the knights clearly show that they are animated by the same zeal (*zelo*) for the house of God which of old vehemently inflamed the leader of knighthood himself, who, having his most sacred hands armed, not with a weapon but with a whip which he had fashioned from lengths of cord, entered the Temple, ousted the merchants, scattered the coins of the moneychangers, and overturned the chairs of the dove-sellers, considering it totally unfitting that this house of prayer be polluted (*incestari*) by such traffic (Mat. 21:12–13, Jn. 2:14–16).[240]

Though he makes no explicit mention of the 1099 massacre, Bernard's characterization of the Templars as followers of the apostolic life and defenders of Jerusalem's sacred places is very much in the exegetical tradition of earlier crusade narratives, and suggests how the conquest of 1099 was remembered in the Latin West three decades later: as an act of purification justified by righteous zeal which reenacted the biblical cleansing of the Temple. It is also clear that the memories of the First Crusade inherited by Bernard's generation included (imagined) memories of Muslim defilement of the Temple by idolatry, memories which could be rhetorically deployed to justify the perpetuation of the holy war.

It has often been noted that Christian accounts of the 1099 conquest of Jerusalem describe the slaughter of the city's Muslim inhabitants as an act of purification. But we have overlooked the ways in which medieval constructions of Muslims as agents of contamination depended on centuries of exegesis of scriptural texts such as the cleansing of the Temple, as well as on the links between avarice, idolatry, and simony established by eleventh-century reformers. If the 'purification' of Jerusalem could be clearly linked to biblical precedents, it could be justified, and the crusaders' actions understood as part of an ongoing, universal project of purging the Church of polluting practices and bodies. Within this project, as in the chroniclers' glosses of the 1099 massacres, Muslims were closely linked to Jews – the objects of the first cleansing of the Temple – through the discourses of avarice and idolatry. These same discourses associated

---

[240] *De laude novae militiae*, 3:222: "Plane his omnibus liquido demonstrantibus eodem pro domo Dei fervere milites zelo, quo ipse quondam militum Dux, vehementissime inflammatus, armata illa sanctissima manu, non tamen ferro, sed flagello, quod fecerat de resticulis, introivit in templum, negotiantes expulit, nummulariorum effudit aes et cathedras vendentium columbas evertit, indignissimum iudicans orationis domum huiuscemodi forensibus incestari." Trans. 49.

non-Christians with bad Christians, especially those tainted by profiteering and simony. Twelfth-century readings of the conquest of Jerusalem thus participated in the creation of what Jeremy Cohen has termed "a genus of hermeneutically constructed *infideles* who undermined the unity of Christian faith."[241]

As they glossed the capture of Jerusalem, the First Crusade's chroniclers not only carved out a place for the events of 1099 within salvation history but, by transforming the usurers and simoniacs of exegetical tradition into avaricious, idolatrous Muslims, added an original chapter to the corpus of Gospel commentary that stretched back to Late Antiquity. This is exactly the sort of intellectual work these men were trained to do, steeped as they were in the rhetoric of ecclesiastical reform and in the modes of reading and thinking associated with the monastic and cathedral schools. As a second, and then a third, generation of historians tackled the events of 1099, the connection between the cleansing of the Temple and the capture of Jerusalem remained a durable one, and became an accepted part of the 'culture of remembrance' that grew up around the First Crusade in both the Latin West and Outremer.[242] Within this culture, biblical texts and the crusade-text exercised a mutual influence on one another; that is, the Scriptures and their commentary traditions provided an indispensable lens through which to read the crusade, even as the crusade prompted twelfth-century Christians to reassess the meaning of familiar scriptural narratives.

Conclusion

In the early narratives of their expedition, the first crusaders move through a sacred landscape that feels at once profoundly foreign and deeply familiar; on the one hand, the inhabitants, topography, fauna, and food of the East seem utterly strange to the Latins, but, on the other hand, they have no doubt that they belong in this land, just as it belongs – indeed, has always belonged – to them. According to the typological logic which was second nature to clerical writers, the Jerusalemites had been there and done these things before; they were pilgrims and warriors, yes, but also reenactors of sacred scripts composed long before they were born. The Scriptures made this point clearly, provided one knew how to read them. Of the various scripts which the sacred texts proffered, the story of a new apostolic mission was one of the most appealing to medieval Christians narrators steeped in the discourse of reform and convinced of the perfection of

---

[241] Cohen, "The Muslim Connection," 162.
[242] On the 'culture of remembrance' of the crusading movement, see Megan Cassidy-Welch and Anne E. Lester, "Memory and Interpretation: New Approaches to the Study of the Crusades," *Journal of Medieval History* 40, no. 3 (2014): 1–12; and the essays in *Remembering the Crusades and Crusading*, ed. Cassidy-Welch.

the primitive church. The confrontation of Jerusalem and Babylon, too, derived from biblical precedent by way of Augustine, supplied an equally compelling, complementary hermeneutical script, one that presented the holy war as equal parts pilgrimage and cosmic battle. In the decades to come, as new expeditions marched east, Latin writers continued to identify Augustine's model of the 'two cities' as a particularly apt one for the holy war. We might see the Cistercians Otto of Freising (d. 1158) and Henry of Marcy (d. 1189), both of whom adopted explicitly Augustinian schemes to explain recent events in Outremer, as following a hermeneutic path forged by earlier generations of crusade chroniclers.[243] The First Crusade had, in Philippe Buc's words, "rematerialized the Holy City in the Holy Land," thereby lending a new and unprecedented immediacy to the struggle between Jerusalem and Babylon that would inform Latin Christian thought over the next two centuries.[244]

For the clerical narrators who parsed this struggle, scriptural motifs were more than convenient metaphors; they were accurate descriptors of the Jerusalemites' experiences in the East, experiences that some chroniclers had shared in the flesh, others vicariously, through conversations with veterans, reading or hearing firsthand accounts, and, finally, their own acts of interpretation and composition. For these witnesses, the sacred texts offered narrative models and, on a fundamental level, helped to constitute reality. Here it seems apt to borrow an insight from Thomas Head's analysis of the meaning of hagiographical topoi to medieval Christians. As Head memorably wrote, for twelfth-century Christians "being a 'bride of Christ' was not *like* marriage to Christ, it *was* marriage to Christ."[245] Similarly, early crusading narratives make clear that for medieval Christians taking the cross was not *like* being an apostle; it *was* being an apostle, an inhabitant of a scriptural world in which, as in the days of the primitive church, wonders were commonplace. The war between the earthly and heavenly cities was equally real, a spiritual–temporal contest involving the highest possible stakes. Early crusading narratives suggest that medieval Christians believed the years 1095–99 had seen numerous literal reenactments of biblical events, fulfillments of biblical prophecy, and a renewal, in the East, of the age-old confrontation between Jerusalem and Babylon. What had been described figuratively in Scripture and by the Fathers had now been rendered literally true; if Christ had promised that faith *could* move mountains, in the twelfth century it was widely reported that

---

[243] Otto of Freising, *Chronica sive Historia de duabus civitatibus*, ed. A. Hofmeister and Walther Larnmers, MGH SSRG 45 (Hannover, 1912); and for commentary, Rubenstein, *Nebuchadnezzar's Dream*, 126–31. Henry of Marcy, *Tractatus de peregrinante civitate Dei*, PL 204:251–402.

[244] Buc, *Holy War*, 291.

[245] Thomas Head, "The Marriages of Christina of Marykate," in *Christina of Markyate: A Twelfth-Century Holy Woman*, ed. Samuel Fanous and Henrietta Leyser (London, 2005), 116–37 (at 116).

captive crusaders actually *had* moved a mountain through the power of prayer. As its historiography took shape, these stories of the First Crusade intensified Latin Christians' relationship with the Scriptures and deepened their sense of living in a world animated by spiritual struggle, in which the power of virtue and the threat of sin were equally real.

Conclusion

That the early crusading movement was widely understood in terms of scriptural precedent and described in scriptural language might seem like a truism hardly in need of explication. And yet, as the previous chapters have shown, to accept this and to *understand* it are two quite different things. Serious engagement with the biblical context of the First Crusade leads us into the deep waters of medieval notions of sacred space and time, narrative practice and genre, authority and originality, election and damnation. Indeed, this sort of engagement opens up many more questions than can be answered by any single book, and it is to be hoped that future researchers will continue to explore the interplay between history, exegesis, and theology in crusading narratives. More generally, though focused on a single, remarkable group of texts, this study has suggested the importance of taking seriously the scriptural framing and citational practices of *all* medieval narrative sources. Such an approach can help to clarify the linkages between closely related texts, as well as demonstrate the powerful impact of medieval educational practices and spiritual training on contemporary writers, whatever their chosen genres. Perhaps most meaningfully for scholars who work on the distant past, it brings us closer to understanding what our authors were thinking, that is, what words and chains of association were in their minds, as they wrote. By extension, an attentiveness to citation, and allegory helps us to approximate the experience of medieval readers, who were primed to appreciate and ruminate over much of what modern readers overlook in privileging facticity and chronological story lines. The multitude of biblical references found in the First Crusade's early chronicles, and in many other medieval narratives, can function as so many breadcrumbs along a trail, leading historians back into the writers' cultural world. While some of these references were no doubt unconscious, testimony to the thoroughness with which scriptural language and diction permeated Latin writers' minds, others are juicy morsels indeed. They reveal the indebtedness of early crusading narratives to a variety of genres, ranging from biblical exegesis and theology to pilgrimage guidebooks and polemic. Further, they suggest the similarities between the rhetoric of holy war and that of the ecclesiastical reform movement, and show how the habits of mind inculcated by the cloisters and schools of the Latin West conditioned initiates to see the world, and gave them the tools needed to respond when the dramatic events of the 1090s threatened to shatter this worldview.

The Latin narratives of the First Crusade are not only sources of historical data, then, but products of a particular intellectual context, one which produced no professional crusade historians but numerous highly trained exegetes, liturgists, and theologians who brought their whole selves to bear on the project of understanding the holy war. The education these men received in monastic and cathedral schools imparted a reverence for the authority of the Scriptures and earlier exegetical traditions, as well as a confidence that the dramatic events of their lifetimes – what Augustine termed "the book of the world" – could, and indeed must, be explicated in the manner of a sacred text. The astonishing victories of the first crusaders in the East offered Latin clerics an ideal opportunity to put their training to use, but also posed interpretive problems of a far greater magnitude than other significant events in living memory, such as the Norman Conquest. Clerical authors embraced this challenge, in the process pioneering new kinds of historical writing that leaned heavily on the traditional tools of biblical exegesis and self-consciously adopted biblical language and symbolism as the most appropriate available discourse for the narration of events. Yet, even as they agreed on the central interpretive importance of the Scriptures to the holy war, individual writers privileged different biblical books and themes, showcasing their deeply personal relationships with the sacred texts. Considered from this perspective, the First Crusade's chronicle tradition seems to be characterized not so much by progressive "theological refinement," as Jonathan Riley-Smith famously suggested,[1] as by a consistently high level of theological engagement and creativity.

Despite their multiplicity of approaches to glossing the holy war, Latin clerical writers shared broader conclusions about the First Crusade's biblical underpinnings. They agreed upon the suitability of particular scriptural forebears, above all the ancient Israelites and the first apostles, as models for the first crusaders, even as they shared the conviction that the Jerusalemites had surpassed their antecedents in virtue. Likewise, chroniclers concurred in their typological association of Muslim opponents with Old Testament paganism. A handful of biblical pericopes, too, were widely used to gloss the crusade as a fulfillment of scriptural injunctions, such as Christ's demand that believers renounce their homes and families (Mat. 19:29), or as a literal reenactment of scriptural events, such as the expulsion of the moneychangers from the Temple (Mat. 21:12–14, Mk. 11:15–18, Lk. 19:45–47, Jn. 2:13–16). Underlying these shared exegeses were common concerns with models of spiritual authority and inheritance, election and supercession, and the place of unbelievers in an expanding Christendom. These were old apprehensions, grounded in ancient texts, but given new life by victories in the East which demanded a reexamination of scriptural promises of

---

[1] Riley-Smith, *Idea of Crusading*, 135–52.

sacred land, divine favor, and retribution. Looking into the future as our medieval writers could not, we can appreciate the long afterlives of the problems raised by the First Crusade's early historiography; the later twelfth- and thirteenth-century thinkers who continued to debate the mutual obligations of Christian community, the spiritual autonomy of laypeople, and the relative exegetical value of history and allegory stood on the shoulders of the crusade's early narrators, who had in turn drawn inspiration from patristic and early medieval writers.

Privileging the scriptural material and exegetical methods in early crusading narratives, finally, allows us to see that we know more about these texts and their authors than we have hitherto realized. Even as crusades historians have developed exciting new methods of textual excavation, using focused, side-by-side analyses to reconstruct the complex relationships between individual works,[2] we have often focused on how much we do not know, and probably cannot know, about our sources. To be sure, the authorship of many narratives remains in doubt, and the surviving textual corpus of the First Crusade, while impressive by medieval standards, is clearly incomplete. The extant texts have a good deal more to tell modern scholars than we have recognized, however: not so much about the chronological events of 1095–99 as about the ways in which these events were recounted, debated, preached, and mythologized. We may not know the precise affiliations or even the names of many of the crusade's early narrators, but we are on much firmer ground when it comes to the ideas, institutions, and events that shaped their outlook. Their own words betray their intellectual training, spiritual formation, and moral convictions, and tell us much about what they read, as well as what they admired or sought to improve upon in other authors' work. Collectively, they give the impression of men engrossed in a spirited, lifelong conversation with the Scriptures, mediated by earlier generations of commentators and liturgists. Seeking meaning in the crusade, they discovered a natural means of extending this conversation with the past and its texts.

---

[2] Two fine examples are Bull, "Robert the Monk and His Source(s)," and Rubenstein, "What is the *Gesta Francorum*?"

Appendix 1: Tables and Charts of Biblical References

Table 1. Distribution of 739 Old Testament references

	Pentateuch[1]	Historical books[2]	Wisdom books[3]	Prophets[4]
Total number	133	163	255	188
Percentage of total	18%	22%	35%	25%

[1] Genesis, Exodus, Leviticus, Numbers, Deuteronomy.
[2] Joshua, Judges, Ruth, 1–4 Kings, 1–2 Chronicles, Ezra, Nehemiah, Tobit, Judith, Esther, 1–2 Maccabees.
[3] Job, Psalms, Proverbs, Ecclesiastes, Song of Songs, Wisdom, Sirach (Ecclesiasticus), Lamentations.
[4] Isaiah, Jeremiah, Ezekiel, Daniel, Hosea, Joel, Jonah, Micah, Habakkuk, Zechariah, Malachi (not cited: Baruch, Amos, Obadiah, Nahum, Zephaniah, Haggai).

Table 2. Distribution of 630 New Testament references

	Gospels[1]	Acts	Epistles[2]	Revelation
Total number	326	54	216	34
Percentage of total	52%	9%	34%	5%

[1] Matthew, Mark, Luke, and John.
[2] Romans, 1–2 Corinthians, Galatians, Ephesians, Phillippians, Colossians, 1–2 Thessalonians, 1–2 Timothy, Philemon, Hebrews, James, 1–2 Peter, 1 and 3 John, Jude (not cited: Titus, 2 John).

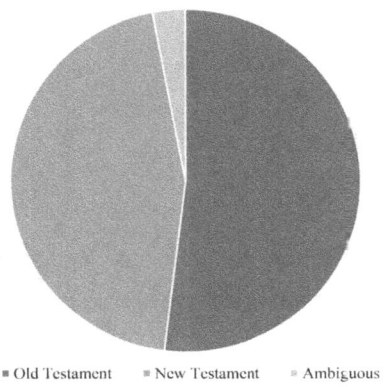

Chart 1. Total citations to Old and New Testaments

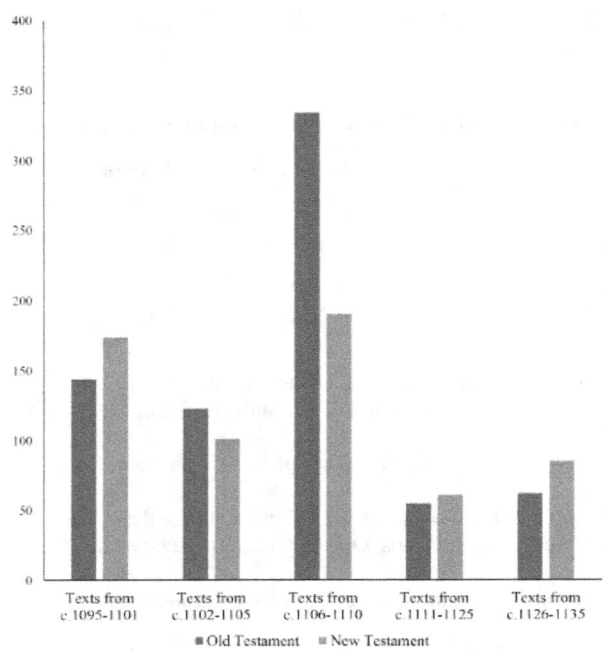

Chart 2. Old and New Testament references over time

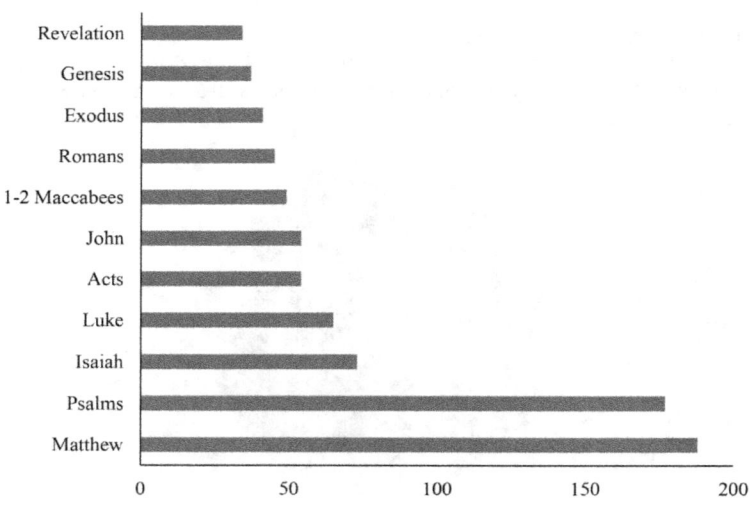

Chart 3. Most frequently cited biblical books

Table 3. Biblical references in major chronicles of the First Crusade, c. 1099–c. 1135

Author	Date	Length[1]	Total references	Old Testament	New Testament	Ambiguous references[2]	Most-cited books
Guibert of Nogent, *Dei gesta per Francos*	c. 1107–8	146 pp.	309	190	113	6	Psalms, Isaiah
Robert of Reims, *Historia Iherosolimitana*	c. 1109–10	161 pp.	128	92	34	2	Psalms, Isaiah
Albert of Aachen, *Historia Ierosolimitana* (books 1–12)	c. 1102	236 pp.	118	65	45	8	Psalms, John
Raymond of Aguilers, *Historia Francorum*	c. 1101	74 pp.	108	72	34	2	Psalms, Matthew
Baldric of Bourgueil, *Historia Ierosolimitana*	c. 1105–7	108 pp.	96	52	43	1	Psalms, Matthew
Gesta Francorum et aliorum...	c. 1099–1101	60 pp.	93[3]	32	58	3	Matthew, Luke, Acts
Monte Cassino Anon., *Hystoria de via et recuperatione...*	c. 1130	60 pp.	90	36	51	3	Matthew, Revelation
Peter Tudebode, *Historia de Hierosolimitano itinere*[4]	c. 1101	108 pp.	88	33	52	3	Matthew, Luke
Michelsburg Continuation (1095–99), incl. Ekkehard of Aura, *Hierosolimita* (c. 1114)	c. 1106	28 pp.	74	33	40	1	Matthew, Isaiah

Author	Date	Length[1]	Total references	Old Testament	New Testament	Ambiguous references[2]	Most-cited books
Ralph of Caen, *Tancredus*	bef. 1118	113 pp.	69	39	29	1	Psalms, Matthew
Fulcher of Chartres, *Historia Iherosolymitana* (book 1)	c. 1105 c. 1124	51 pp.	42	25	16	1	Psalms, Matthew
Orderic Vitalis, *Historia ecclesiastica* (book 9)	c. 1135	~45 pp.	37	14	21	2	Matthew, Revelation
Charleville Poet[5]	aft. 1120	23 pp.	30	9	20	1	Matthew, Genesis
Gilo of Paris, *Historia vie Hierosolimitane*	bef. 1120	72 pp.	22	7	12	3	Matthew
William of Malmesbury, *Gesta regum* (book 4.347–4.372)	c. 1125–35	~20 pp.	14	3	11	0	Matthew, Acts, Romans
Henry of Huntingdon, *Historia Anglorum* (book 7.5–7.18)	1129; 1154	5 pp.	12	9	2	1	Psalms

[1] Lengths of texts are given as page counts from editions of texts in RHC Oc. for all texts except William of Malmesbury and Orderic Vitalis; as these histories are not included in the RHC, I have provided estimated lengths based on the editions in the Oxford Medieval Texts series.

[2] References are to language repeated verbatim, or nearly so, in both the Old and New Testaments.

[3] Compare with the fourteen total citations documented in the text's most recent edition by Rosalind Hill (Oxford, 1962).

[4] On Ekkehard's relation to the Michelsberg material, see McCarthy, *Continuations*, 39–80. A much-needed complete scholarly edition of the *Hierosolimita* is in preparation by Thomas McCarthy and Benedikt Marxreiter.

[5] I.e., the anonymous continuator of Gilo of Paris' *Historia Vie Hierosolimitane*, to whom are attributed books 1–3, 6, and sections of books 4–5 of this work.

Appendix 2: List of Biblical References in the Texts

In the list below, allusions which could refer to multiple biblical passages are indicated by the abbreviation "cf.," as in Mat. 24:2 (cf. Mk. 13:2); I have resisted counting each possibility separately to avoid distorting the total number of references in the sources. Where multiple biblical passages are conflated this is indicated by "with" (abbreviated as "w/"), as in Gen. 18:3 w/33:10. Underlined references appear in the works of multiple authors. Asterisks (*) indicate ambiguous references which use language that appears verbatim in the Old and New Testaments.

Abbreviations of Sources

AA = Albert of Aachen
BB = Baldric of Bourgueil
CJ = "Capture of Jerusalem"
CP = Charleville Poet
EP = *Epistulae et chartae*
FC = Fulcher of Chartres
FE = Michelsberg Chronicle
GA = *Gesta Adhemari*
GF = *Gesta Francorum*
GN = Guibert of Nogent
GP = Gilo of Paris
HH = Henry of Huntingdon
MC = Monte Cassino Anonymous
OV = Orderic Vitalis
PT = Peter Tudebode
RA = Raymond of Aguilers
RC = Ralph of Caen
RR = Robert of Reims
SF = "Sermon on the Fall of Jerusalem"
WM = William of Malmesbury

Old Testament

Genesis

2:17	RA, p. 116
3:17–18	GN, p. 90
4:9f.	GN, p. 331
8:6–7	BB, p. 85; OV, p. 128
10:8–9	CP, p. 150
10:13–14	RR, p. 102
10:15	FC, p. 272
11:1–9	CP, p. 150
11:27–28	CP, p. 134
12:1–2	BB, p. 112; GN bis, pp. 88 and 312

<u>14:18</u>	BB, p. 112; RR, p. 109
16:6	GN, p. 93
18:3 (w/33:10)	AA bis, pp. 46 and 146
22:9–13	GF, p. 98
22:17	MC bis, pp. 5 and 8
<u>27:28</u> (cf. Hos. 13:3)	PT, p. 128; FC, p. 154
*27:40 (cf. Gal. 5:1)	AA, p. 400
28:12	RC, p. 112
28:16–17	RC, p. 112
31:2, 5 (cf. 4 Kgs. 13:5)	BB, p. 27
32:12	AA, p. 106
32:24	GF, p. 101
34:30	RC, p. 127
37:8	CP, p. 140
37:14	GF, p. 100
44:4	AA, p. 64
45:19	GN, p. 222
47:17	GN, p. 261
49:8	AA, p. 322
50:11	AA, p. 164

Exodus

3:1 (cf. Jer. 31:24)	GN, p. 296
3:2	GF, p. 100
<u>3:8</u> (cf. Num. 13:28)	EP, p. 148; RR bis, pp. 6 and 90
3:15	RC, p. 50
4:21 (w/7:3)	BB, p. 14
5:9	GN, p. 160
9:22	BB, p. 10
*10:21 (cf. Ez. 32:8, Mat. 27:45)	AA, p. 282
13:3	AA, p. 2
<u>13:9</u>	BB, p. 18; OV, p. 44
13:22	GN, p. 308
14 *passim*	RR, p. 62
14:11–12	GN, p. 308

Appendix 2: List of Biblical References in the Texts

14:14	AA, p. 192
<u>14:21</u>	BB, p. 8; GN, p. 308
14:22	BB, p. 8
15:6–13	RR, pp. 27–28
15:9	RR, p. 28
15:11	RR, p. 27
15:13	RR, p. 28
<u>17:6</u>	BB, p. 14; RC, p. 100
<u>17:13</u>	AA, p. 38; RC, p. 50
18:21	RC, p. 45
19:16	GN, p. 185
20 *passim*	CJ, p. 652
<u>20:11</u>	GF, p. 56; PT, p. 96
<u>23:13</u>	GF, p. 52; PT, p. 92
23:20–23	RR, p. 62
23:21–23	RR, p. 62
24:18 (cf. Deut. 9:9)	AA, p. 446
25 *passim*	FC, pp. 316–17
32:9	AA, p. 22
33:13	FE, p. 150
34:19	FE, p. 142

Leviticus

18:25	GN, p. 92

Numbers

10:35	GN, p. 159
16:14	GN, p. 118
<u>20:11f.</u>	GN, p. 340; RC, p. 100
20:17	AA, p. 390
21:4 with 19:20 (cf. Ez. 44:7)	BB, p. 108
21:5	GN, p. 308
21:6	BB, p. 25
21:21f.	RR bis, pp. 38 and 62
21:22	AA, p. 144

21:24	AA, p. 52
21:26	GN, p. 128
21:33–35	RR, p. 62
22:2f.	GN, p. 331
24:5	BB bis, pp. 25 and 26
24:10	GN, p. 277
25:6	BB, p. 25
<u>34:11</u>	FC, p. 216; CP, p. 96

Deuteronomy

2:26	AA, p. 390
2:27	AA, p. 258
3:22	FC, pp. 246–47
5:30	GN, p. 220
7:6 (w/14:2)	EP, p. 180
10:17	RR, p. 61
<u>11:24–25</u>	GF, p. 54; PT, p. 94; RR, p. 63; MC, p. 73
13:4	GN, p. 321
13:8	RR, p. 105
13:15	AA, p. 319
19:12	GN, p. 298
*19:15 (cf. Mat. 18:16, 2 Cor. 13:1)	GN, p. 339
20:11	GN, p. 92
26:11	AA, p. 336
28:7	AA, p. 190
28:34	GN, p. 146
28:35	RC, p. 37
28:47	AA, p. 470
28:51	AA, p. 386
32:11	RC, p. 61
32:12	RR, p. 94
32:29	RR, p. 61
<u>32:30</u>	EP, p. 178; GA, p. 355; RR bis, pp. 45 and 62; GN, p. 158; GP, p. 160

Appendix 2: List of Biblical References in the Texts

32:39–42	RR, p. 61
32:41–42	RR, p. 61
34:1–4	RC, p. 82

Joshua

2:20 (cf. Job 15:13)	GN, p. 322
6:1f.	GN, p. 276
6:5	GN, p. 203
6:9	RR, p. 17
10:12	FC, pp. 280–81
10:25	RR, p. 74
10:37	AA, p. 232
19:29 (cf. Ez. 26:2)	FC, p. 274
23:14 (cf. 3 Kgs. 2:2)	BB, p. 88; RC, p. 119; OV, p. 132

Judges

3:27 (cf. 2 Kgs. 2:28)	FE, p. 140
7:5–6	GN, p. 321
7:16	GN, p. 322
7:19 (cf. Ps. 98:6)	OV, p. 78
11:7	GN, p. 105
14:14	RR, p. 56
17:6	GN, p. 262
*19:24 (cf. Rom. 1:26)	GN, p. 341
21:6	GN, p. 267

Ruth

1:6	FE, p. 150
1:13 (cf. Ex. 17:16)	AA, p. 56
1:18	GN, p. 260
1:19	GN, p. 311
2:1	GN, p. 264

1 Kings (1 Samuel)

4:3 (cf. 1 Kgs. 12:10, 2 Kgs. 18:19, etc.)	AA, p. 266
4:18	AA, p. 110
5–7 *passim*	RR, p. 110
6:9, 12	MC, p. 131
10:11	CJ, p. 645
10:27	RR, p. 110
13:12 (cf. Dan. 14:2, Judith 11:7)	GN, p. 105
14:16	HH, p. 430
14:26, 27	AA, p. 388
14:39	GN, p. 281
15:22	GN, p. 282
15:32	MC, p. 107
*16:14 (cf. Acts 19:12,15)	GN, p. 324
16:17	BB, p. 9
<u>17:47</u>	CJ, p. 646; RR, p. 19
18:7	BB, p. 117
18:25	RC, p. 61
27:8	GN, p. 261

2 Kings (2 Samuel)

2:11	GF, p. 100
2:21	GF, p. 100
5:6, 8 (w/ Josh. 18:28)	RR, p. 109
5:8	BB, p. 8
7:13 (cf. 3 Kgs. 9:15, 2 Chron. 7:18)	GN, p. 115
7:22 (cf. Is. 33:5)	GN, p. 86
12:26	GN, p. 212
17:11	AA bis, pp. 12 and 454
<u>18:33</u>	GF, p. 64; PT, p. 106; MC, p. 83
22:3	GN, p. 259
24 *passim*	FC, p. 289

Appendix 2: List of Biblical References in the Texts

3 Kings (1 Kings)

8:46–50	RA, p. 155–56
10:25 (cf. 2 Chron. 9:24)	AA, p. 180
10:27	RR, p. 109
12:10	GN, p. 86
17:9	GN, p. 269
19:10, 14	FE, p. 132
20:1	GN, p. 269

4 Kings (2 Kings)

1:10–14	GF, p. 62; PT, p. 103; MC, p. 81; HH, p. 436
7:18	RA, p. 83
9:30	GN, p. 330
20:6	GF, p. 98
24 and 25 *passim*	AA, p. 432
25:2	GN, p. 276

1 Chronicles

7:40	GN, p. 207
15:16	HH, p. 432
29:2	AA, p. 434
*29:9 (cf. Tob. 11:21, Mat. 2:10)	AA, p. 238
29:13	RA, p. 141
36:20	MC, p. 105

2 Chronicles

10:10	GN, p. 86
14:11	BB, p. 68
18:14	GN, p. 192
24:13	GN, p. 220
35:3	FC, p. 288

1 Ezra

6:1–15	CP, p. 150

2 Ezra
*3:15 (cf. Jn. 9:7, 11)   GP, p. 238

4 Ezra
2:35   MC, p. 11

Nehemiah
1:10   BB, p. 115; OV, p. 178

Tobit
3:3   BB, p. 68
12:7   MC, p. 10

Judith
2:11   BB, p. 13, OV, p. 30
6:15   RC, p. 84; GN, p. 231
7:7   GN, p. 276
7:17   GN, p. 125
7:21   RA, p. 143
7:23   GF, p. 58; PT, p. 99; RA, p. 73
8:26 (cf. Ps. 30:3)   RA, p. 38
8:27   RA, p. 35
9:11   RC, p. 12
12:1   GN, p. 88
13:17   EP, p. 159; GN, p. 223
13:27   RA, p. 116
13:28   GN, p. 252
15:1   RR, p. 23
15:5–6   RR, p. 33

Esther
5:10   AA, p. 72
8:5   AA, p. 430
9:15   GN, p. 179
9:22   BB, p. 21

Appendix 2: List of Biblical References in the Texts

10:2	RA, p. 54
10:9 (cf. Ps. 30:3)	RA, p. 78

Job

1 *passim*	FC, p. 227
1:1,8	RA, p. 120
1:6	RA, p. 39
2:4	GN, p. 259
<u>3:11</u> (cf. 10:18)	GF, p. 64; PT, p. 106; MC, p. 83
3:19	GN, p. 312
5:9	GN, p. 151
5:18	RR, p. 110
7:1	RC, p. 47
7:2 (w/14:6)	BB, p. 103
15:2	GN, p. 112
26:11	GN, p. 326
30:14	GN, p. 93
40:28	RC, p. 56

Psalms (Vulgate numbering)

1:1	RA, p. 91
2:3	BB, p. 114
2:9	GN, p. 307
2:13	RA, p. 153
4:2	BB, p. 68
4:7	RR, p. 17
6:4	RA, p. 80
*8:3 (cf. Mat. 21:16)	CP, p. 4
8:6	GN, p. 230
<u>9:10</u>	GF, p. 58; PT, p. 99; RA, p. 60; GN, p. 307
9:21	GN, p. 93
10:2	RR, p. 45
12:7	FC, p. 226
*13:3 (cf. Prov. 6:18, Rom. 3:15)	AA, p. 184

227

14:1	RA, p. 72
16:2	RR, p. 48
17:35	RR, p. 48
17:43	RA, p. 155
<u>19:8</u>	AA, p. 234; GA, p. 355
20:13	GN, p. 214
21:7	BB, p. 8
21:30	GN, p. 270
22:5	AA, p. 436
22:28	RR, p. 19
<u>23:8</u> (cf. Ps. 63:3)	RA bis, pp. 57 and 73; RR, p. 36
24:7	RA, p. 86
25:6	CJ, p. 647
25:7 (cf. Ps. 39:6)	RA, p. 150
27:9	RR, p. 72
28:3	GN, p. 112
29:12	RA, p. 149
30:19	RR bis, pp. 61 and 62
<u>32:3</u> (cf. Ps. 95:1)	RA, p. 151; FC, p. 305
32:10	RA, p. 43
<u>32:12</u>	RA bis, pp. 79 and 103; RR, p. 4; FC, p. 318; GP, p. 104
32:18	RC, p. 60
33:12	FC, p. 118
33:16	RC, p. 60
34:2	GN, p. 260
36:8–9	CJ, p. 648
36:23	RR, p. 34
<u>39:13</u>	GN, p. 222; HH, p. 426
41:1 (cf. Num. 20:6, Jer. 2:13)	FE, p. 154
41:2	FE, p. 152
41:5	AA, p. 458
41:11	MC, p. 46
*43:22 (cf. Is. 53:7, Rom. 8:36)	FE, p. 330
43:26	RA, p. 60

Appendix 2: List of Biblical References in the Texts

44:3	RA, p. 69
44:4	BB, p. 9
44:11	BB, 112
45:8 (cf. Ps. 58:6)	GN, p. 304
45:9 (cf. Ps. 65:5)	RA, p. 80
47:4	MC, p. 77
47:6–7	RR, p. 45
47:8	GN, p. 118
47:11	AA, p. 360
48:13, 21	BB, p. 45
*48:16 (cf. Ps. 88:49, Rev. 20:13–14)	AA, p. 460
49:1 (cf. Ex. 23:13)	PT, p. 93; MC, p. 72
54:3	PT, p. 57
57:5	RC, p. 35
58:12	RR, p. 86; BB, p. 69
59:5	BB, p. 14
60:3	GN, p. 235
60:4	RR, p. 72
62:3 (cf. Ps. 74:7)	GF, p. 23; PT, p. 57; RA, p. 36; AA, p. 148; MC, p. 34
63:7	GN, p. 90
67:5	BB, p. 14; RR, p. 13
67:7	GN, p. 118
67:9	RA, p. 69
67:22	RR, p. 6
67:31 (cf. Ps. 78:6)	GF, p. 54; PT, p. 94; MC, p. 72; GN, p. 92
68:29 (cf. Ex. 32:32)	BB, p. 43; RA, p. 108
71:18	GN, p. 328
72:7	BB, p. 68
73:2 (cf. Ps. 88:51)	RA, p. 86
73:10	GN, p. 157
73:22	CJ, p. 648
73:23	RA, p. 60
75:3	RR, p. 85

75:5	RR, p. 108
76:14	RC, p. 100
76:20	RA, p. 130
77:1	RR, p. 68
77:8	RR, p. 5
77:12	GN, p. 305
77:24	GN, p. 308
77:27	HH, p. 434
77:38	RA, p. 143
77:44	AA, p. 430
*<u>78:1–3</u> (cf. Rev. 19:2)	BB, p. 8; RR, p. 99
78:4	BB, p. 8
<u>78:6</u>	GF, p. 54; RR, p. 86; MC, p. 72; GN, p. 214
79:7	BB, p. 8
79:6	GN, p. 282
79:10	CJ, p. 647
80:13	GN, p. 93
81:8	GN, p. 213
82:8	CJ, p. 648
85:9	FC, p. 162
87:2 (cf. Ps. 122:2)	EP, p. 164
88:11	RC, p. 12
90:7	RR, p. 41
92:4	GN, p. 298
93:1	AA, p. 58
93:11	RR, p. 102
93:19	FE, p. 332
94:9	CJ, p. 648
96:2	RA, p. 115
97:1–2	FE, p. 332
<u>98:6</u>	BB, p. 67; OV, p. 98
101:17–18	FE p. 328
103:32	CJ, pp. 643–44
<u>104:34</u> (cf. 146:5)	RA, p. 148; RR, p. 27

Appendix 2: List of Biblical References in the Texts

106:3	RR, p. 63; FE, p. 332
106:4	RR, p. 31
106:16	RR, p. 55
106:33–34	RA, p. 139; RR, p. 110
112:3–4	GN, p. 214
112:5	RC, p. 39
113:9	BB bis, pp. 38–39 and 74
113:13–14	RC, p. 41
115:15	AA, p. 152
117:15	RC, p. 101
*117:22 (cf. Mat. 21:42, Mk. 12:10, Lk. 20:17)	CJ, p. 652
*117:23 (cf. Mat. 21:42)	FC, p. 163
117:24	RA, p. 151
119:1	CJ, p. 647
121:1	GN, p. 289
121:4	FE bis, p. 332
123:6	FC, p. 318
124:3	GN, p. 230
125:6	BB, p. 103; OV, p. 156
131:7	FC, p. 162; FE, p. 330
131:13	RC, p. 112; FE, p. 328
135:13–14	RC, p. 104
136:8	AA, p. 432
137:6	RC, p. 39
138:18	AA, p. 268
138:21–22 (cf. Ps. 118:113)	RA, p. 115
143:1	RR, p. 98
144:5	GN, p. 112
146:10	RR, p. 41; FC, p. 197
147:20	GN, p. 98
148:8	RR, p. 37
148:13	HH, p. 438

Proverbs

1:7	RR, p. 72
*1:27 (cf. 1 Thess. 5:3)	AA, p. 286
8:15	RR bis, pp. 48 and 92
10:9	WM, p. 598
13:22	RR bis, pp. 37 and 90
16:9	GP, p. 192
17:3 (w/27:21)	CP, p. 46
17:13	AA, p. 26
20:17	GN, p. 342
21:1	RC, p. 93
22:15	OV, p. 120
22:28	GN, p. 93
25:23	RR, p. 106
26:11	GP, p. 192
30:8	GN, p. 160
30:27	GN, p. 88

Ecclesiastes

1:7	GN, p. 113
1:15	RR, p. 69
2:4	GN, p. 118
7:1	GN, p. 178
23:28	RC, p. 65
30:24	RC, p. 65

Song of Songs

1:4	BB, pp. 25–26
6:4	RR, p. 73

Wisdom

1:5	GN, p. 112
1:7	RR, p. 8
3:6	OV, p. 170
3:7	GN, p. 114

Appendix 2: List of Biblical References in the Texts

4:4	GN, p. 224
4:7	FC, p. 170
4:11	WM, p. 658
7:29	FE, p. 148
8:1	BB, p. 77
8:3	GN, p. 88
11:21	AA, p. 12
<u>13:17</u>	GF, p. 2; PT, p. 32; MC, p. 13
17:10	WM, p. 598

Sirach (Ecclesiasticus)

2:5	FC, p. 226
5:8	GN, p. 115
9:4	RA, p. 66
11:5	GN, p. 328
27:30	GN, p. 96
28:22	AA, p. 16
30:15	GN, p. 81
31:28	GN, p. 166
<u>32:22</u> (cf. 1 Macc. 2:65)	AA, p. 144; GN, p. 227
34:24	GN, p. 179
36:1–2 (cf. Ps. 58:12)	GN, p. 223
36:15	FE, p. 328
39:9	RA, p. 82
44:9	GN, p. 282
45:12	GN, p. 277

Isaiah

1:25	GN, p. 85
2:3	GN bis, pp. 113 and 301
3:8	GN, p. 212
5:1	FE, p. 332
5:20	FE, p. 130
<u>8:6</u>	GF, p. 100; FC, p. 282
10:2	GN, p. 179

10:4	FE, p. 330
10:20	GN, p. 338
<u>11:10</u>	RR, p. 100; GN, p. 112; FC, p. 305
12:1	FE, p. 150
13:19	GN, p. 85
14:12–17	RR bis, pp. 10 and 100
17:9	AA, p. 438
26:1–2	RR, p. 110
26:5 (cf. Ez. 38:20)	RA, p. 100
<u>30:23</u>	BB, p. 35; OV, p. 64
33:2	RR, p. 86
35:2	GN, p. 141
<u>35:10</u>	GF, p. 17; PT, p. 50; RA, p. 149; MC, p. 29
37:3	BB, p. 117
37:16	RC, p. 122
37:22	FE, p. 328
38:1f.	RA, p. 46
38:3	AA, p. 290
39:3	RA, p. 41
*<u>40:3</u> (cf. Mat. 3:3, Mk. 1:3)	RA, p. 86; GN, p. 312
40:11	GN, p. 328
40:24	RR, p. 106
41:10	FC, p. 263
42:2	AA, p. 160
42:8	GN, p. 328
<u>43:5–6</u>	RR, p. 13; GN bis, pp. 115 and 301
*43:10 (Lk. 24:39)	GN, p. 219
48:10	OV, p. 104
49:13	RR, p. 109
49:14–18	SF, p. 161
49:26	GN, p. 213
<u>52:2</u>	OV, p. 156; FE, p. 332
52:9 (cf. Tob. 13:19)	EP, p. 180
54:8	FE, p. 328

Appendix 2: List of Biblical References in the Texts

54:10	GN, p. 121
55:12	RR, p. 109
*56:7 (cf. Mat. 21:13, Mk. 11:17, Lk. 19:46)	RC, p. 112
56:10	RC, p. 86
59:3	AA, p. 174
60:1	FE bis, pp. 160 and 332
<u>60:4</u>	RC, p. 3; RR, p. 100
60:9–10	RR, p. 110
60:11	RR, p. 109
60:14	SF, p. 161
60:15–16	RR, pp. 28–29
61:5	RR, p. 109
63:3	BB, p. 109
65:17	RA, p. 151
66:6–9	SF, p. 162
<u>66:10</u>	SF, p. 162; FE tres, pp. 160, 328, and 332
66:11	FE bis, pp. 328 and 332

Jeremiah

2:13	RA, p. 139
4:16	RA, p. 41
8:22	GN, p. 287
9:8	RA, p. 38
9:10	GN, p. 152
10:2	RA, p. 74
14:15 (cf. Jer. 16:4, 44:12)	AA, p. 270
15:20 (cf. Is. 43:5)	RA, p. 46
<u>16:4</u>	AA bis, pp. 36 and 68; RA, p. 62
17:18	GN, p. 276
20:11	RR, p. 28
22:3 (w/23:5)	RA, p. 86
25:15, 17	RA, p. 101
<u>31:10</u>	GF, p. 53; PT, p. 94; MC, p. 72

32:24	AA, p. 230
34:20	CJ, p. 650
39:5–7 (w/52:9ff.)	GP, p. 96
52:19–27	CP, p. 150
50:13 (w/51:37)	CP, p. 150
51:6	RC, p. 88

Lamentations

1:2	MC, p. 133
1:8	SF, p. 161
1:16	RR, p. 96
2:15	EP, p. 180
2:17 (cf. Jer. 51:12)	SF, p. 161
3:12	PT, p. 35; MC, p. 16
3:27–28	GN bis, pp. 109 and 312
4:9	GN, p. 152

Ezekiel

1:8	GN, p. 298
3:20	GN, p. 92
5:5	GN bis, pp. 86 and 307
11:19	RR, p. 96
12:2 (cf. 4 Kgs. 13:11)	GF, p. 96; PT, p. 146
13:16	GN, p. 305
22:13	GN bis, pp. 112 and 277
23:12	GN, p. 225
23:32	GN, p. 142
25:6	GN, p. 296
28:13	RR, p. 6
29:7	BB, p. 43
29:18	GN, p. 302
33:11	MC, p. 109
47:15–18	GP, p. 96
47:17	FE, p. 132

Appendix 2: List of Biblical References in the Texts

Daniel

2:21	BB, p. 3
2:27 (cf. Dan. 4:7)	AA, p. 336
2:45	CJ, p. 652
<u>3:26</u>	GF, p. 17; PT, p. 50; MC, p. 30
3:32	GN, p. 189
3:36	RC, p. 116
4:1–18	CJ, p. 646
4:34 (cf. Is. 2:12)	AA, p. 82
7:24	GN, p. 114
8:27	RA, p. 72
9:24	RA, p. 143
11:28	GN, p. 165
13:42	GN, p. 156
13:46	AA, p. 480

Hosea

<u>1:7</u>	CJ, p. 646; RC, p. 12
2:18	RC, p. 12
<u>13:3</u>	BB, p. 79; GN, p. 345; OV, p. 110

Joel

1:5	GN, p. 226
1:17	BB, p. 14
<u>2:12</u>	PT, p. 39; MC, p. 18
<u>2:20</u> (cf. Is. 34:3)	GF, p. 58; PT, p. 99; MC, p. 77; HH, p. 436
<u>2:17</u>	BB, p. 68; CJ, p. 647
2:32 (cf. Is. 59:20)	FE, p. 332
*3:31 (cf. Acts 2:20)	AA, p. 398
3:3	RA, p. 130
*3:6 (cf. Mat. 23:37, Gal. 4:25)	OV, p. 18

Jonah

1:3–5	RA, p. 72

Micah

3:4	RC, p. 86
<u>5:8</u>	GF, p. 53; PT, p. 93; MC, p. 72

Habakkuk

2:19	GN, p. 204

Zechariah

<u>1:3</u>	GF, p. 58; PT, p. 99; RA, p. 73; MC, p. 77
3:3–5	RA, p. 95
7:12	GN, p. 118
12:1	GN, p. 301
12:2	GN bis, p. 301
12:3	GN bis, p. 302
12:4	GN bis, p. 303
12:5	GN, p. 303
12:6	GN, p. 304
12:7	GN, p. 305
12:8	GN bis, p. 306
12:9	GN, p. 306
12:10	GN, p. 307

Malachi

<u>3:3</u>	PT, p. 92; MC, p. 71
<u>3:7</u> (cf. Zech. 1:3)	GF, p. 58; PT, p. 70; MC, p. 45; HH, p. 438
3:10	GN, p. 243
3:17	BB, p. 68
<u>4:2</u>	AA, p. 450; GN, p. 88

1 Maccabees

1:3	RR, p. 32
1:20–40	AA, p. 432
<u>1:25</u>	PT, p. 109; MC, p. 85

Appendix 2: List of Biblical References in the Texts

1:63–64	GN, p. 240
2:41	PT, p. 44; MC, p. 23
4:38	GN, p. 280
5:31	GF, p. 34; PT, p. 72
5:62	AA, p. 448; GN, p. 216
6:6	GN, p. 273
6:39	RA, p. 57
6:40	AA, p. 196
9:71	PT, p. 69; MC, p. 45
10:68	GF, p. 61; PT, p. 102; MC, p. 80
10:74	GF, p. 46; PT, p. 86; MC, p. 65
12:44	RA, p. 40
13:25	FC, pp. 277–78
15:25	GN, p. 247

2 Maccabees

1:15	GN, p. 281
1:27	RA, p. 37
2:4–9	FC, p. 289
2:23	GN, p. 193
2:51	PT, p. 72
3:19	GN, p. 279
*4:11 (cf. 2 Cor. 5:20)	GN, p. 338
4:31	GF, p. 31; PT, p. 66
4:33	GP, p. 96
7:37	MC, p. 11
10:28	GN, p. 182
10:29–31	RA, p. 45
10:34	RA, p. 67
12:5	GN, p. 128
12:22	GN, p. 142
13:13	GN, p. 279
13:14	GN, p. 112
14:4	GN, p. 165
15:8	AA, p. 106; RA, p. 47

15:10	RA, p. 51
15:11	RA, p. 51
15:36	AA, p. 180

New Testament

Matthew

2:1–2	GN, p. 321
2:3	CP, p. 140
2:11	CP, p. 60
2:12	RC, p. 24
3:12	CP, p. 48; FE, p. 148
3:13–16 (cf. Mk. 1:9, Lk. 3:21)	GF, p. 100; BB, p. 8
3:17	PT, p. 93; RC, p. 82; MC, p. 72
4:4	GF, p. 34; PT, p. 69; MC, p. 45
5:8	CP, p. 44
5:9	FC, p. 132
5:26	CJ, p. 650
5:39–40 (cf. Lk. 6:29)	GF, p. 7; PT, p. 40; RC, p. 7; MC, p. 19
6:10	AA, p. 382
6:23	RA, p. 54
6:24 (cf. Lk. 16:13)	RC, p. 21
6:34	PT, p. 67
7:2 (cf. Lk. 6:38, Mk. 4:24)	RC, p. 39
7:7 (w/26:41)	CJ, p. 648
7:13–14 (cf. Lk. 13:24)	GF bis, pp. 18 and 31; PT bis, pp. 52 and 66; RA, p. 60; MC, p. 43; FE, p. 130; WM, p. 602
7:15	FE, p. 144
7:17	FE, p. 144
7:22	CJ, p. 646
8:9	GF, p. 9; PT, p. 42; MC, p. 21
8:12 (cf. Lk.13:28)	GN, p. 96
9:36	MC, p. 91
10:3 (cf. Mk. 3:18)	CP, p. 134

Appendix 2: List of Biblical References in the Texts

10:12	GN, p. 221
10:22	EP, p. 137
<u>10:28</u>	GF, p. 41; PT bis, pp. 35 and 76; MC bis, pp. 16 and 55
10:29	BB, p. 77
10:37	RR, p. 6
<u>10:38</u> (cf. Lk. 14:27)	FE, p. 136; RR, p. 8
11:5	CP, p. 28
<u>11:21</u> (cf. Lk. 10:13)	GF, p. 4; PT, p. 36; RA, p. 56; MC, p. 16
11:30	RC, p. 42
12:45 (cf. Lk. 11:26)	GN, p. 80
13:3	RC, p. 41
13:16, 17	EP, p. 138
13:25	FE, p. 144
13:30	RA, p. 52
13:35	RA, p. 37
13:47	GP, p. 202
13:52	RR, p. 101
14:21 (cf. Mk. 6:44)	GN, p. 336
15:16	GN, p. 213
15:21 (cf. Mk. 7:24)	FC, p. 274
<u>15:25</u>	GF, p. 58; PT, p. 99; MC, p. 77
15:31 (cf. Mk. 7:37)	CP, p. 4
16:17f. (cf. Mk. 14:12f., Lk. 22:7f., Jn. 13:1f.)	GF, p. 100
<u>16:19</u>	FC, p. 217; GN bis, pp. 219 and 246
<u>16:24</u> (cf. Mk. 8:34, Lk. 9:23)	GF, p. 1; PT, p. 31; MC, p. 12; GN, p. 178
16:26	GP, p. 68
17:1–9 (cf. Mk. 9:2–8, Lk. 9:28–36)	GF, p. 100
17:3	FC, p. 132
17:19 (cf. Lk. 17:7)	MC, p. 106
17:20, 22	CP, p. 48
18:18	FE, p. 138

18:20	RR, p. 7
19:19 (cf. Mat. 22:39)	PT, p. 122
19:26	GN, p. 182
19:27	MC, p. 11
19:29 (cf. Mk. 10:29, Lk. 18:29)	FE, p. 132; HH, p. 422; SF, p. 162; RR, p. 6; FC bis, pp. 115 and 163; BB, p. 3; MC, p. 10; GN quinquies, pp. 87–88, 132, 148, 156, 266; AA quater, pp. 2, 107, 236, 480; CP tres, pp. 12, 14, 16; CJ, p. 647; OV bis, pp. 16 and 34; WM, p. 609
20:1	RC, p. 111
20:1–16	EP, p. 176
20:16	BB, p. 9
20:22–23	FE, p. 330
20:26–27	RC, p. 22
21:10	GF, p. 7; PT, p. 40; MC, p. 19
21:13 (cf. Mk. 11:17, Lk. 19:46, Jn. 2:16)	BB bis, pp. 5 and 68; CJ, p. 648; RC, p. 112; CP, p. 8; WM, p. 604
22:5 (w/16:24)	GP, p. 70
*22:27 (cf. Mk. 12:30, Deut. 11:13)	RA, p. 118
22:29	OV, p. 186
*22:37 (cf. Jer. 32:41, Mk. 12:30, Lk.10:27)	GF, p. 34; PT, p. 69; MC, p. 45; AA, p. 2
23:11 (cf. Lk. 9:48, Mk. 9:34)	RC, p. 22
23:34 (cf. Mk. 13:2)	BB, p. 5
23:35 (cf. Lk. 11:51)	GF, p. 98
24:2 (cf. Mk. 13:2, Lk. 19:44, 21:6)	CJ, p. 644; GN, p. 283, AA, p. 432
24:7 (cf. Lk. 21:10, Mk. 18:8)	FE, p. 132
24:23, 26 (cf. Jn. 10:37)	GN, p. 338
24:24	FE, p. 144
24:29 (cf. Lk. 21:26)	BB, p. 11; GN, p. 304
24:31	FE, p. 132
25:21 (cf. Lk. 19:17)	RC, p. 37
25:33 (cf. Mk. 10:40)	EP, p. 173
25:34	EP, p. 148

Appendix 2: List of Biblical References in the Texts

25:35–40	RR, p. 33
<u>25:41</u>	PT, p. 76; MC, p. 55
<u>25:44</u>	GF, p. 25; PT, p. 60
<u>26:20f.</u> (cf. Mk. 14:16–26, Lk. 22:14–38)	BB, p. 104; GN, p. 270
26:28 (cf. Mk. 14:24)	BB, p. 6
26:29 (cf. Mk. 14:25)	RC, p. 129
26:31	FE, p. 146
26:36 (cf. Mk. 14:32)	GF, p. 99
26:39	GF, p. 99
26:47, 55 (cf. Lk. 22:52)	GN, p. 91
26:52	RR, p. 38
<u>26:53</u>	GP, p. 184, CJ, p. 653
26:64	RA, p. 114
26:66 (cf. Mk. 14:6)	RA, p. 114
<u>27:1</u>	RA, p. 56; GN, p. 140
27:2f. (cf. Mk. 15:1f., Lk. 23:13f., Jn. 19:29f.)	GF, p. 98
27:3	GN, p. 267
27:14	AA bis, pp. 266 and 312
<u>27:22–23</u>	BB, p. 109; OV, p. 168
27:27 (cf. Mk. 14:65, Jn. 19:1)	GF, p. 98
27:32	FE, p. 330
27:33 (cf. Mk. 15:22, Lk. 23:33, Jn. 19:17)	GF, p. 98
27:45 (cf. Mk. 15:33, Lk. 23:44)	GP, p. 244
<u>27:51–52</u>	RR, p. 110; GN, p. 112
27:55 (cf. Mk. 15:40, Lk. 23:49)	RA, p. 114
<u>27:57–60</u> (cf. Mk. 25:46, Lk. 23:50–53, Jn. 19:38)	GF, p. 98; BB, p. 108; GN, p. 104
<u>28:19</u>	GF, p. 99; GN, p. 92
28:20	BB, p. 102

Mark

1:45	AA, p. 148

4:11 (cf. Lk. 8:10)	BB, p. 11
4:40	AA, p. 148
6:3 (cf. Gal. 1:19)	BB, p. 112
<u>6:34</u>	GF, p. 33; PT, p. 67; MC, p. 44
7:14	RA, p. 118
8:18	RC, p. 41
9:49	RA, p. 87
10:21	RA, p. 74
11:23	CP, p. 48
12:1–9 (cf. Lk. 20:9–18)	CJ, p. 653
14:4	GN, p. 281
14:44	GN, p. 97
14:72	RC, p. 86
*15:24 (cf. Ps. 21:9)	RR, p. 15
15:25	GN, p. 277
16:14	OV, p. 38
16:19	RR, p. 96

Luke

1:37	AA, p. 308
1:52–53	RR, p. 28
1:53	RR, p. 38
1:58	EP, p. 168
1:66	FE, p. 152
1:68	EP, p. 180
2:4	GF, p. 101
<u>2:7</u>	GF, p. 101; RA, p. 155
2:9 (cf. Rev. 21:23)	GN, p. 343
2:12	GN, p. 97
2:14	EP bis, pp. 178 and 180
2:25	GF, p. 99
5:21	PT, p. 54
<u>6:1</u>	GF, p. 23; PT, p. 57; MC, p. 34; BB, p. 35; OV, p. 64; RR, p. 30
7:13 (cf. Lk. 10:33, 15:20)	AA ter, pp. 30, 44, 174

Appendix 2: List of Biblical References in the Texts

8:50	RA, p. 71
9:23	MC, p. 10
9:58	BB, p. 102
9:62	RC, p. 24
10:4	GF, p. 96; PT, p. 147
10:16	EP, p. 137
10:40	GN, p. 199
11:6–8	CJ, p. 648
11:32	RA, p. 91
12:32	GN bis, pp. 328 and 345
13:24	AA, p. 292
14:27 (cf. Mat. 16:24, 10:38; Mk. 8:34)	PT, p. 46; BB, p. 10; GN, p. 321; MC, p. 25
15:4	FE, p. 132
15:7	GN, p. 220
16:22	PT, p. 116; MC, p. 92
16:27	PT, p. 81; MC, p. 58
18:7	FE, p. 152
18:29	GN, p. 148
19:4	GF, p. 100
19:42–44	SF, p. 161; BB, p. 103
20:25	RC, p. 18
21:10–11	FE, p. 132
21:15	GF, p. 2; PT, p. 32; MC, p. 13
21:24	GN, p. 302
21:25 (cf. Acts 2:19–20)	FE, p. 140
23:23	GN, p. 205
23:46	FE, p. 312
23:48	RA bis, pp. 80 and 114
24:19	GN, p. 178
24:25	GN, p. 221

John

1:51	RC, p. 112
3:8	BB, p. 3; GN, p. 79

3:11	FE, p. 330
3:16	RR, p. 53
3:20	RC, p. 67
3:32	GN, p. 166
3:33	GN, p. 284
4:7f.	GF, p. 101
4:22	GN, p. 111
4:35	RA, p. 70
6:1f.	FC, p. 201
7:6	GN, p. 115
7:43 (cf. Acts 15:39, 23:10)	AA, p. 372
9:16	AA, p. 378
10:11	GN, p. 213
<u>10:12</u>	AA bis, pp. 56 and 222; FE, p. 146; GN, p. 176
11:4	RA, p. 119
11:33	AA, p. 4
11:49 (cf. Acts 4:6)	AA, p. 394
11:51	CJ, p. 646
12:36	CJ, p. 644
<u>13:16</u>	EP, p. 144; GN, p. 198
13:18	GN, p. 216
13:27	MC, p. 48
14:6	GN, p. 301
14:27	AA, p. 312
15:5	RR, p. 38
<u>15:13</u>	AA, p. 276; BB, p. 28; WM bis, pp. 600 and 604; OV, p. 56
15:14	FC, p. 137
16:20 (cf. Lk. 8:13)	CJ, p. 646
17:4	RC, p. 102
19:6 (cf. Lk. 23:21)	RA, p. 114
19:26–27	GF, p. 98

Appendix 2: List of Biblical References in the Texts

19:34	EP, p. 163; GF, p. 59; PT, p. 101; RA, p. 70; BB, p. 108; FC bis, pp. 236 and 263; MC, p. 78; GN, p. 221
20:24–29	CP, p. 134
20:29 (cf. 2 Cor. 4:18)	GN, p. 266
21:25	GF, p. 44

Acts of the Apostles

1:9	AA, p. 412
1:11 (w/2:7)	EP, p. 164
2 *passim*	GF, p. 100
2:3	GF, p. 2; PT, p. 32
2:4	RR, p. 68; MC, p. 113
2:9	CP, p. 6
*2:11 (cf. Deut. 11:2)	GP, p. 74, HH, p. 422
2:35	CP, p. 46
3:2–8	MC, p. 114
4:32	GF, p. 40; PT, p. 75; BB, p. 26; OV, p. 54
5:29	RR, p. 18
6:5	FE, p. 160
6:6 (cf. 8:17–19, 19:6)	GN, p. 117
7:3	AA bis, pp. 6 and 276
7:5	FE, p. 330
7:22	GN, p. 178
7:56–59	BB, p. 104; GN, p. 270; RC, p. 95; OV, p. 156
7:58	GF, p. 87; PT, p. 134; BB, p. 8; MC, p. 114
8:2	AA, p. 392
8:9–24	RC, p. 93
9:16	GF, p. 2; PT, p. 32; MC, p. 13
9:25 (cf. 2 Cor. 11:33)	GN, p. 217
10:1–33	RR, p. 94
10:41	AA, p. 448

11 *passim*	RR, p. 34; WM, p. 632
11:22f.	GN, p. 342
11:26	GP, p. 96
11:44	GF, p. 99
<u>12:9</u>	GF, p. 59; PT, p. 101; MC, p. 78
12:19, 23	RR, p. 94
13 *passim*	RR, p. 34
13:51f.	GN, p. 161
14:21	WM, p. 602
21:8–9	RR, p. 94
21:30	GN, p. 110
23:11	RC, p. 131
27:22–23	RA, p. 117
27:34	RC, p. 127

Romans

1:11	GN, p. 306
1:28	GN, p. 303
*<u>2:9</u> (cf. Is. 30:6)	GF, p. 74; PT, p. 117; MC, p. 92
5:1	GN, p. 195
5:9	BB, p. 9
6:3	RR, p. 74
6:8	AA, p. 276
6:10	EP, p. 148
<u>6:19</u>	GN, p. 97; AA, p. 228
<u>6:23</u>	CP, p. 2; WM, p. 598
7:18 (cf. Philip. 2:13)	EP, p. 179
<u>7:24</u>	PT, p. 56; MC, p. 33
8:14, 16 (cf. Gal. 3:26, Jn. 1:12)	EP, p. 176
8:15	GN, p. 214
<u>8:17</u>	GF, p. 54; PT, p. 94; BB, p. 10
8:18	WM, p. 604
8:27	GN, p. 110
8:28	RR, p. 41
8:30	FC, p. 227

Appendix 2: List of Biblical References in the Texts

8:35 (cf. 2 Cor. 11:27)	GF, p. 2; PT, p. 32; MC, p. 13; GN, p. 270
8:38	GN, p. 221
9:8 (cf. Gal. 4:5)	GF, p. 54; PT, p. 94; MC, p. 73
9:22	GF, p. 31
9:25	GN, p. 214
9:29	GN, p. 111
10:2	FE, p. 146; GN, p. 120
*10:8 (cf. Deut. 30:14)	OV, p. 128
10:11	GN, p. 85
11:17, 24	BB, p. 33
11:25–26	GN, p. 115
11:33	FC, p. 169
12:1	RR, p. 7
12:18 (cf. Heb. 12:14, 2 Tim. 2:22)	EP, p. 179
13:1	RR, p. 34
14:8	AA, p. 234
16:18	GN, p. 233

1 Corinthians

3:17	GN bis, pp. 112 and 242
4:6	GN, p. 267
6:5	BB, p. 6
6:6–10	FC, pp. 134–36
6:20	WM, p. 598
7:35	RA, p. 135
9:22	BB, p. 88; CP, p. 140; OV bis, pp. 134 and 186
9:24	OV, p. 78; FE, p. 330
10:11	FE, p. 328
10:13	GP, p. 186
11:19	GN, p. 322
13:1	GN, p. 240
13:8	RA, p. 108
13:12	RA, p. 121

15:18	GF, p. 74; PT, p. 116; MC, p. 92
15:33	GN, p. 109
15:57	HH, p. 434

2 Corinthians

1:6	GN, p. 161
1:10	GF, p. 68; PT, p. 110; RA, p. 47; MC, p. 87
1:12 (cf. Heb. 13:18)	RA, p. 77
3:8	GN, p. 97
4:7	GN, p. 322
4:10	FE, p. 142; GN, p. 322
4:16	GN, p. 238
6:16	EP, p. 178
7:1	AA bis, pp. 448 and 460
9:6	RC, p. 126
10:3	GF, p. 37
10:4	GN, p. 267
11:27	PT, p. 57; MC, p. 34; GN, p. 335; FE, p. 330
12:2,3	BB, p. 67
12:31 (cf. Philip. 1:10)	EP, p. 179

Galatians

2:1–2	GN, p. 301
2:4 (cf. 2 Cor. 11:26)	FE, p. 144
3:14	GN, p. 112
3:18	GF, p. 54; PT, p. 94
3:29	GN, p. 111
4:25	RR, pp. 6–7; OV, p. 18
4:26	SF, p. 161; BB, p. 103; OV, p. 156; AA, p. 410; FE, p. 328
4:30	SF, p. 160
5:15	RR, p. 6
6:14	FE, p. 330

Appendix 2: List of Biblical References in the Texts

6:17	GN, p. 117

Ephesians

5:3	GN, p. 98
5:17	PT, p. 93; MC, p. 72
5:27	GN, p. 90
5:30	GN, p. 350
6:10	AA, p. 64
6:11	GF bis, pp. 15 and 37; PT bis, pp. 49 and 72
6:12	BB, p. 108; GN bis, pp. 327 and 349
6:16	EP, p. 147; GP, p. 82

Philippians

1:6	EP, p. 178
1:9–11	EP, p. 178
1:14	FE, p. 132
2:7–8	RA, p. 116
2:9	EP, p. 165
2:13	BB, p. 111; OV, p. 146

Colossians

3:12	RR, p. 5
3:24	GF, p. 2; PT, p. 32; MC, p. 13

1 Thessalonians

1:9	GF, p. 75; PT, p. 117; MC, p. 93
3:12	OV, p. 154

2 Thessalonians

2:3	GN, p. 115
2:4	GN, p. 114

1 Timothy

1:5 (cf. 2 Tim. 2:22)	AA, p. 306

2:2	EP, p. 167
3:2, 12	GN, p. 93

2 Timothy

2:3	GF, p. 6; PT, p. 39; MC, p. 18; FC, p. 132
2:15	GN, p. 191
3:5	FE, p. 144
3:11	RR, p. 31
4:7	RC, p. 91
4:8 (cf. Rev. 2:10)	FE, p. 132; GP, p. 186

Philemon

1:14	MC, p. 105
2:9	CP, p. 10

Hebrews

2:9	AA, p. 308
7:19	GN, p. 182
9:4	AA, p. 434
10:26	GN, p. 92
10:35	AA, p. 108
11:9	FE, p. 134; EP, p. 180
11:39	GN, p. 191; BB, p. 15; OV, p. 38
11:40	GN, p. 268
12:6	BB, p. 73; EP, p. 157; GN, p. 233
12:22 (cf. Rev. 21:10)	EP, p. 180; BB bis, pp. 8 and 108
13:8	GN, p. 86
13:11–12	GN, p. 322

James

1:17	EP, p. 180; RC, p. 88
1:19 (w/ 5:7)	RA, p. 85
2:5	AA bis, pp. 196 and 270
2:13	GN, p. 246

Appendix 2: List of Biblical References in the Texts

4:1	RA, p. 100
4:4 (cf. 1 Jn. 2:15)	GP, p. 194
4:6 (cf. 1 Pet. 5:5)	CP, p. 46
5:4	GN, p. 93
5:20	RC, p. 89

1 Peter

1:18–19	AA, p. 58
<u>2:21</u>	EP, p. 148; GF, p. 2; PT, p. 32
3:14	MC, p. 11
3:18–20	RC, p. 94
<u>4:1</u>	PT, p. 43; MC, p. 23
4:10–11	EP, p. 175
5:2	FE, p. 148
<u>5:4</u>	BB, p. 9; RR, p. 7
<u>5:6</u>	RA, p. 76
<u>5:8–9</u>	GF, pp. 19–20; PT bis, pp. 53 and 79; RA, p. 38; CJ, p. 650; MC bis, pp. 31 and 58

2 Peter

<u>2:4</u>	GF, p. 2; PT, p. 32
2:22	GN, p. 102

1 John

2:1	FC, p. 220
2:13	GN, p. 325
3:10	HH, p. 436
5:4	GP, p. 116
5:6	AA, p. 234

3 John

1:13	BB, pp. 81–82

Jude
1:5 GN, p. 278

Revelation
1:8 RA, p. 109
1:14 MC, p. 48
<u>2:9</u> PT, p. 117; MC, p. 93
3:5 OV, p. 150
<u>3:18</u> (cf. 1 Pet. 1:7) CJ, p. 644; GP, p. 206
*3:21 (cf. Dan. 12:13) GP, p. 70
5:9 GN, p. 188
5:13 RR, p. 55
*<u>6:1–3</u> (cf. Zech. 6:1f.) GF, p. 69; PT, pp. 111–12; MC, p. 88
<u>6:10</u> GF, p. 40; PT, p. 75; MC bis, pp. 30 and 54
<u>7:9–17</u> MC, p. 59, PT, p. 81
8:2ff. FE, p. 132
8:4 WM, p. 650
13:13 FE, p. 132
<u>14:20</u> RA, p. 150; FE, p. 154
15:4 RR, p. 96
16:4 AA bis, pp. 224 and 244
17–18, *passim* RR, p. 107
<u>18:19</u> BB, p. 69; OV, p. 100
<u>19:14</u> BB, p. 81; OV, p. 112
20:2 RR, p. 102
<u>20:7</u> BB, p. 31; OV, p. 58
21:5 MC, p. 49
21:19–21 FC, p. 317
22:11 GN, p. 92

Bibliography

Manuscripts

Paris, Bibliothèque nationale de France:
Ms. latin 4892
Ms. latin 12056
Ms. latin 16481

Printed Sources

Achard of Arrouaise. "Poème sur le Templum Domini." In *Archives de l'Orient Latin*, 2 vols. Ed. Paul Riant, 1: 562–79. Paris, 1884.

Ademar of Chabannes. *Chronicon*. Ed. Richard A. Landes and Georges Pon. CCCM 129. Turnhout, 1999.

Alcuin. *Epistolae*. Ed. Ernst Dümmler. MGH Epp. 4: Epistolae Karolini aevi, 1–493.

Ambrose of Milan. *De excessu fratris sui Satyri*. PL 16: 1289–1317. Trans. H. De Romestin, E. De Romestin, and H. F. Duckworth, in *Ambrose: Selected Works and Letters*, 414–85. Edinburgh, 1986.

———. *Explanatio psalmorum XII*. Ed. Michael Petschenig and Michaela Zelzer. Vienna, 1999.

Augustine of Hippo. *De civitate Dei*. Ed. B. Dombart and A. Kalb. CCSL 47–48. Turnhout, 1955. Trans. R. W. Dyson as *The City of God against the Pagans*. Cambridge, 1998.

———. *Contra Faustum Manichaeum*. Ed. J. Zycha. Corpus Scriptorum Ecclesiasticorum Latinum 25/1. Vienna, 1891.

———. *De doctrina christiana*. Ed. R. P. H. Green. Oxford, 1995. Trans. D. W. Robertson as *On Christian Doctrine*. New York, 1958.

———. *Enarrationes in Psalmos*. Ed. Eligius Dekkers and Jean Fraipont. CCSL 38–40. Turnhout, 1956. Trans. Maria Boulding as *Expositions of the Psalms*. 6 vols. Hyde Park, NY, 1990–2004.

———. *Epistulae I–LV*. CCSL 31. Ed. Kl. D. Daur. CCSL 31. Turnhout, 2004.

———. *De Genesi ad litteram*. Ed. J. Zycha. Corpus Scriptorum Ecclesiasticorum Latinum 28/1. Vienna, 1894.

———. *In Iohannis Evangelium tractatus CXXIV*. Ed. Radbod Willems. CCCM 36. Turnhout, 1954.

———. *De libero arbitrio*. Ed. William M. Green. CCSL 29. Turnhout, 1970.

Bibliography

———. *The Rule of Saint Augustine*. Ed. Tarsicius J. Van Bavel. Trans. Raymond Canning. Cistercian Studies 138. Kalamazoo, MI, 1996.

———. *Sermones*. PL 38–39. Partial trans. John E. Rotelle and Edmund Hill as *Sermons 3/9 (306–340A): On the Saints, The Works of Saint Augustine: A Translation for the 21st Century*. Hyde Park, NY, 1994.

———. *Tractatus adversus Iudaeos*. PL 42: 51–64.

Baldric of Bourgueil. *Adelae Comitissae*. Ed. K. Hilbert in *Baldricus Burgulianus Carmina*, 149–89 (no. 134). Editiones Heidelbergenses 19. Heidelberg, 1979.

———. *Vita beati Roberti de Arbrisello*. PL 162: 1043–78.

Bartolf of Nangis. *Gesta francorum expugnantium Hierusalem*. RHC Occ. 3: 487–543.

Beati Gaufridi castaliensis prioris, dictamen de primordiis ecclesiae castaliensis. RHC Occ. 5: 348–49.

Bede. *Homiliarum evangelii libri II*. Ed. D. Hurst. CCSL 122. Turnhout, 1955.

———. *In Lucam Evangelium Expositio*. Ed. D. Hurst. CCSL 120. Turnhout, 1960.

———. *Libri Quatuor in principium Genesim ad Nativitatem Isaac et Eiectionem Ismahelis Adnotationum*. Ed. C. W. Jones. CSEL 118A. Turnhout, 1967. Trans. Calvin B. Kendall as *Bede, On Genesis*. Liverpool, 2008.

Beleth, Jean. *Summa de ecclesiasticis officiis*. Ed. Heribert Douteil. CCCM 41A. Turnhout, 1976.

Berger, David, ed. and trans. *The Jewish–Christian Debate in the High Middle Ages: A Critical Edition of the* Nizzahon Vetus. Philadelphia, 1979.

Bernard of Clairvaux. *De laude novae militiae*. In *Sancti Bernardi Opera*, 8 vols. Ed. Jean Leclercq, C. H. Talbot and Henri Rochais, 3: 212–39. Rome, 1957–77. Trans. M. Conrad Greenia as *In Praise of the New Knighthood*. Kalamazoo, MI, 2000.

Bernard of Hildesheim, *Liber canonum contra Heinricum quartum*. Ed. F. Thaner. MGH Lib. de lite 1: 471–516.

Bernard the Monk. *Itinerarium*. PL 121: 569–74.

Bernold of Constance. *De damnatione scismaticorum*. Ed. Friedrich Thaner. MGH Lib. de lite 2:27–58. Hannover, 1892.

Boca, M. L., ed. *Li romans de Baudouin de Sebourc, IIIe roy de Jhérusalem, poëme du XIVe siècle*. 2 vols. Valenciennes, 1841.

Brault, Gerard J., ed. *The Song of Roland: An Analytical Edition*. 2 vols. University Park, PA, 1978.

Bréhier, Louis, ed. *Gesta Francorum, Histoire anonyme de la première croisade*. Paris, 1924.

Bonizo of Sutri. *Liber ad amicum*. Ed. E. Dümmler. MGH Lib. de lite 1: 568–620.

(Pseudo-) Bruno of Chartreuse. *Expositio in Psalmos*, PL 152: 637–1419.

Bruno of Cologne. *Expositio in Epistolas Pauli*. PL 153: 11–568.

Bruno of Segni. *Commentaria in Lucam*. PL 165: 333–452.

———. *Commentaria in Matthaeum*. PL 165: 63–314.

———. *Expositio in Pentateuchum*. PL 164: 147–550.

Bibliography

———. *Expositio in Psalmos*. PL 164: 695–1128.
Bruno of Würzburg. *Commentarius in Cantica*, PL 142: 49–530.
Caffaro di Rustico da Caschifellone. *De liberatione civitatum orientis*. RHC Occ. 5: 41–73.
Caspar, Erich, ed. *Das Register Gregors VII*. MGH Epistolae selectae 2.1–2.2. Berlin, 1920–23.
Cassian. *Collationes*. Ed. Eugène Pichery. SC 42, 54, 64. Paris, 1955–59. Trans. Boniface Ramsey as *Conferences*. New York, 1987.
Cassiodorus. *Expositio psalmorum*. ed. M. Adriaen. CCSL 97–98. Turnhout, 1958.
———. *Institutiones divinarum et humanarum lectionum*. Ed. R. A. B. Mynors. Oxford, 1961. Trans. James W. Halporn as *Institutions of Divine and Secular Learning*. Liverpool, 2004.
Chronica Santa Maria of Ferraria. Ed. Umberto Caperna. Cassino, 2008.
Constable, Giles, and Bernard S. Smith, ed. and trans. *Three Treatises from the Abbey of Bec on the Nature of Monastic Life*. Toronto, 2008.
Cowdrey, H. E. J., ed. *The Register of Pope Gregory VII, 1073–1085*. Oxford, 2002.
De investigatione Antichristi. Ed. E. Sackur. MGH Lib. de lite 3: 304–95.
Epistola de vitanda missa uxoratorum sacerdotum. Ed. Ernst Sackur. MGH Lib. de lite 3: 2–11.
Fernández, Rodriguez, ed. *La pasión de S. Pelayo: edición crítica con traducción y comentarios*. Santiago de Compostela, 1991.
Fulbert of Chartres. *Tractatus contra Judaeos*. PL 141: 305–18.
Gervase of Canterbury. *Chronica*. In *The Chronicle of the Reigns of Stephen, Henry II and Richard I*, ed. William Stubbs. Rolls Series 73. London, 1879; repr. edn. Cambridge, 2012.
Gildemeister, J., ed. *De situ Terra Sanctae*. Bonn, 1882.
Geoffrey of Vendôme. *Sermo in festo S. Mariae Magdalenae*. PL 157: 273–74.
Gesta Adhemari, episcopi podiensis, hierosolymitana. RHC Occ. 5: 354–55.
Glossa Ordinaria. PL 113–114.
Godfrey of Babion (Ps.-Anselm of Laon). *Enarrationes in Matthaeum*. PL 162: 1227–500.
Gregory the Great. *Homiliarum in Evangelia*. Ed. R. Étaix, C. Morel, and B. Judic. SC 485. Paris, 2005.
———. *In Librum Primum Regum Expositionum Libri VI*. Ed. Pierre-Patrick Verbraken. CCSL 144. Turnhout, 1963.
———. *The Life of St. Benedict*. Ed. and trans. Terrence Kardong. Collegeville, MN, 2009.
———. *Registrum Epistularum*. Ed. Paul Ewald and Ludwig M. Hartmann. MGH Epistolae 1–2. Berlin, 1891–98.
Guibert of Nogent. *Contra iudaizantem et Iudeos*. In *Serta mediaevalia: textus varii saeculorum X–XIII in unum collecti*, CCSL 171, ed. R. B. C. Huygens, 310–73. Turnhout, 2000.

Bibliography

———. *Moralia in Genesin.* PL 156: 19–337.

———. *Petite chronique du règne de Baudouin Ier.* Ed. Huygens in *Dei gesta per Francos et cinq autres textes,* CCCM 127A, 361–66. Turnhout, 1966.

———. *Tropologiae in prophetas Osee et Amos ac Lamentationes Jeremiae.* PL 156: 341–488.

———. *De vita sua.* Ed. Edmond-René Labande. Paris, 1981. Trans. Paul J. Archambault as *A Monk's Confession: The Memoirs of Guibert of Nogent.* University Park, PA, 1996.

Guy of Amiens. *Carmen de Hastingae proelio of Guy, Bishop of Amiens.* Ed. Frank Barlow. Oxford, 1999.

(Pseudo-) Haimo of Auxerre. *Explanatio in Psalmos.* PL 116: 191–695.

Haimo of Halberstadt. *Homiliae de tempore.* PL 118: 11–746.

Henry of Marcy. *Tractatus de peregrinante civitate Dei.* PL 204: 251–402.

Hildebert of Lavardin. *De diversis.* PL 171: 339–964.

Hildemar of Corbie. *Expositio regulae.* Ed. Rupert Mittermüller. Ratisbon, 1880.

Hincmar of Reims. *Ad episcopos et procere provinciae Rhemensis.* PL 125: 961–84.

Honorius Augustodunensis. *De apostatis.* Ed. I. Dieterich. MGH Libelli de lite 3: 57–63.

Hrabanus Maurus. *Commentaria in libros Regum.* PL 109: 9–280.

———. *Enarratio super Deuteronomium libri quattuor.* PL 108: 837–998.

———. *Expositio in Matthaeum.* Ed. Bengt Löfstedt. CCCM 174A. Turnhout, 2000.

Hugh of Flavigny. *Chronicon Hugonis Monachi Virdunensis et Divionensis.* Ed. G. H. Pertz. MGH SS 8: 288–502.

Hugh of Fleury. *Historia Ecclesiastica.* PL 163: 821–54.

Hugh of St. Victor. *De sacramentis christianae fidei.* PL 176: 183–618.

Humbert of Silva Candida. *Libri tres adversus simoniacos.* Ed. Friedrich Thaner. MGH Lib. de lite 1: 100–253.

Huygens, R. B. C., ed. *Peregrinationes tres.* CCCM 139. Turnhout, 1994.

Isidore of Seville. *Etymologiae.* Ed. W. M. Lindsay. 2 vols. Oxford, 1911. Trans. Stephen A. Barney, W. J. Lewis, J. A. Beach, and Oliver Berghof as *Etymologies.* Cambridge, 2010.

———. *De fide catholica ex Veteri et Novo Testamento contra Judaeos.* PL 83: 449–538.

Itineraria et alia geographica. Ed. Ezio Franceschini and Robert Weber. CCSL 175. Turnhout, 1965.

Jerome. *Commentariorum in Matheum libri IV.* Ed. D. Hurst and M. Adriaen. CCSL 77. Turnhout, 1969. Trans. Thomas P. Scheck as *Jerome's Commentary on Matthew.* FC 117. Washington, D.C., 2008.

———. *Hebraicae quaestiones in libro Geneseos.* Ed. P. de Lagarde. CCSL 72. Turnhout, 1959.

———. *In Hieremiam libri VI.* Ed. S. Reiter. CCSL 74. Turnhout, 1960.

Liber de unitate ecclesiae conservanda. Ed. W. Schwenkenbecker. MGH Lib. de lite 2: 173–284.

Maier, Christoph T., ed. *Crusade Propaganda and Ideology: Model Sermons for the Preaching of the Cross.* Cambridge, 2004.

Marco Polo. *The Description of the World.* 2 vols. Ed. A. C. Moule and Paul Pelliot. London, 1938.

Olivar, Alejandro, ed. *El Sacramentario de Vich.* Barcelona, 1953.

Otto of Freising. *Chronica sive Historia de duabus civitatibus.* Ed. A. Hofmeister and Walther Larnmers. MGH Scriptores Rerum Germanicarum 45. Hannover, 1912.

Papias. *Elementariam doctrinae.* Venice, 1491.

Peter Damian. *Die Briefe des Petrus Damiani.* Ed. Kurt Reindel. MGH Briefe der deutschen Kaiserzeit 4.1–4. Munich, 1983–93.

Peter of Maillezais. *Qualiter fuit constructum Malliacense monasterium et corpus sancti Rigomeri translatum.* Ed. and trans. Yves Chauvin and Georges Pon as *La fondation de l'abbaye de Maillezais: Récit du moine Pierre.* La Roche-sur-Yon, 2001.

Peter the Venerable. "Sermo de laude Domini sepulchri." Ed. Giles Constable, in "Petri Venerabilis Sermones Tres." *Revue Bénédictine* 64 (1954): 232–65.

Peters, Edward, ed. *The First Crusade: The Chronicle of Fulcher of Chartres and Other Source Materials.* 2nd edn. Philadelphia, 1998.

Placidus of Nonantola. *Liber de honore ecclesiae.* Ed. L. de Heinemann and E. Sackur. MGH Lib. de lite 2: 566–639.

De proprietatibus gentium. Ed. T. Mommsen. MGH Auctores Antiquissimi 11: 389–90.

Radulfus Glaber. *Historiarum libri quinque.* Ed. Neithard Bulst. Trans. John France and Paul Reynolds. Oxford, 1989.

Rather of Verona. *Sermo de Ascensione Domini.* PL 136: 734–40.

Remigius of Auxerre. *Enarrationes in Psalmos.* PL 131: 149–844.

Rorgo Fretellus. *Descriptio de locis sanctis terre Jerusalem.* Ed. P. C. Boeren. Amsterdam, 1980.

Rupert of Deutz. *De Sancta Trinitate.* Ed. Hrabanus Haacke. CCCM 21. Turnhout, 1971.

Schaller, Hans Martin, ed. "Zur Zreuzzugsenzyklika Papst Sergius' IV." In *Papsttum, Kirche und Recht im Mittelalter: Feschschrift für Horst Fuhrmann zum 65. Geburtstag,* ed. Hubert Mordek, 150–53. Tübingen, 1991.

Scheiber, A., ed. "A Fragment from the Chronicle of Obadiah, the Norman Proselyte: From the Kaufmann Geniza." *Acta orientalia academice scientiarum Hungari* 4 (1954): 271–96.

Secunda pars historiae Hierosolimitanae. RHC Occ. 3: 549–85.

Sigebert of Gembloux. *Leodicensium epistola adversus Paschalem Papam.* Ed. E. Sackur. MGH Lib. de lite 2: 449–64.

Smaragdus of Saint-Mihiel. *Expositio in Regulam S. Benedicti*. Ed. Alfred Spannagel and Pius Engelbert. Corpus Consuetudinum Monasticarum 8. Siegburg, 1974.

Somerville, Robert, ed. *The Councils of Urban II, Vol. 1: Decreta Claromontensia*. Amsterdam, 1972.

Theodore Palidensis. *Narratio profectionis Godefridi ducis ad Jerusalem*. RHC Occ. 5: 189–98.

Thomas of Chobham. *Summa Confessorum*. Ed. F. Broomfield. Analecta mediaevalia Namurcensia 25. Louvain, 1968.

Urban II. *Epistulae, diplomata, sermones*. PL 151: 9–584.

Verdon, Jean, ed. *La Chronique de Saint-Maixent*. Paris, 1979.

Vogel, Cyrille and R. Elze, eds. *Le Pontificale Romano-Germanique du dixième siècle*. Studi e Testi 226–227, 266. Rome, 1963–72.

The Vulgate Bible. Ed. Swift Edgar and Angela M. Kinney. Dumbarton Oaks Medieval Library 1, 4, 5, 8, 13, 17, 21. Cambridge, MA, 2010–13.

Waddell, Helen, ed. and trans. *Mediaeval Latin Lyrics*. New York, 1929.

Wilkinson, John, trans. *Jerusalem Pilgrims Before the Crusades*. Warminster, 2002.

William of Jumièges et al. *Gesta Normannorum Ducum*. 2 vols. Ed. and trans. Elisabeth M. C. van Houts. Oxford, 1995.

William of Poitiers. *Gesta Guillelmi ducis Normannorum et regis Anglorum*. Ed. and trans. R. H. C. Davis and Marjorie Chibnall. Oxford, 1998.

William of Tyre. *Chronicon*. Ed. R. B. C. Huygens. CCCM 63–63A. Turnhout, 1986.

Secondary Works

Abulafia, Anna Sapir. *Christian–Jewish Relations, 1000–1300: Jews in the Service of Medieval Christendom*. Harlow, 2011.

———. *Christians and Jews in Dispute*. Aldershot, 1998.

———. *Christians and Jews in the Twelfth-Century Renaissance*. London, 1995.

Adler, William. "The Apocalyptic Survey of History Adapted by Christians: Daniel's Prophecy of 70 Weeks." In *The Jewish Apocalyptic Heritage in Early Christianity*, ed. James C. VanderKam and William Adler, 201–38. Minneapolis: Fortress Press, 1996.

Akbari, Suzanne Conklin. *Idols in the East: European Representations of Islam and the Orient, c.1100–1450*. Ithaca, NY, 2009.

Albu, Emily. *The Normans in Their Histories: Propaganda, Myth, and Subversion*. Woodbridge, 2001.

Alexis-Baker, Andy. "Violence, Nonviolence and the Temple Incident in John 2:13–15." *Biblical Interpretation* 20 (2012): 73–96.

Alford, John A. "The Scriptural Self." In *The Bible in the Middle Ages: Its Influence on Literature and Art*, ed. Bernard S. Levy, 1–21. Binghamton, NY, 1992.

Bibliography

Allen, Michael I. "Universal History, 300–1000: Origins and Western Developments." In *Medieval Historiography*, ed. Deborah Mauskopf Deliyannis, 17–42. Leiden, 2003.

Alphandéry, Paul. *La chrétienté et l'idée de croisade*. Ed. Auguste Dupront. Paris, 1954.

———. "Les citations bibliques chez les historiens de la première croisade." *Revue de l'histoire des religions* 99 (1929): 139–57.

Arjana, Sofia Rose. *Muslims in the Western Imagination*. Oxford, 2015.

Asbridge, Thomas. "The Holy Lance of Antioch: Power, Devotion and Memory on the First Crusade." *Reading Medieval Studies* 33 (2007): 3–36.

Babcock, William S. "*Caritas* and *Cupiditas*: The Early Augustine on Love and Human Fulfillment." In *Augustine Today*, ed. Richard Neuhaus, 1–34. Grand Rapids, MI, 1993.

Bachrach, Bernard S. *Early Medieval Jewish Policy in Western Europe*. Minneapolis, 1977.

Bachrach, David S. *Religion and the Conduct of War, c.300–1215*. Woodbridge, 2003.

Bagge, Sverre. *Kings, Politics, and the Right Order of the World in German Historiography, c.950–1150*. Leiden, 2009.

Bain, Emmanuel. *Église, richesse et pauvreté dans l'Occident médiéval: L'Exégèse des Évangiles aux XIIe–XIIIe siècles*. Turnhout, 2014.

———. "Les marchands chassés du Temple, entre commentaires et usages sociaux." *Médiévales* 55 (2008): 53–74.

Baraz, Daniel. *Medieval Cruelty: Changing Perceptions, Late Antiquity to the Early Modern Period*. Ithaca, NY, 2003.

Bartlett, Robert. "Medieval and Modern Conceptions of Race and Ethnicity." *Journal of Medieval and Early Modern Studies* 31, no. 1 (2001): 39–56.

Bates, David. *William the Conqueror*. New Haven, CT, 2017.

Beaune, Colette. *The Birth of an Ideology*. Trans. Fredric L. Cheyette. Berkeley, CA, 1991.

Becker, Alfons. *Papst Urban II (1088–1099)*. MGH Schriften 19, 1–3. Stuttgart, 1964–2012.

Beckett, Katharine Scarfe. *Anglo-Saxon Perceptions of the Islamic World*. Cambridge, 2003.

Bedos-Rezak, Brigitte Miriam. *When Ego Was Imago: Signs of Identity in the Middle Ages*. Leiden, 2010.

Beer, Jeanette. *In Their Own Words: Practices of Quotation in Early Medieval History-Writing*. Toronto, 2014.

Bennett, Matthew. *The Campaigns of the Norman Conquest*. London, 2001.

———. "First Crusaders' Images of Muslims: The Influence of Vernacular Poetry?" *Forum for Modern Language Studies* 22 (1986): 101–22.

Berger, Michael. "St. Peter Damian: His Attitude toward the Jews and the Old Testament." *Yavneh Review* 4 (1965): 80–112. Repr. in *Persecution, Polemic and Dialogue: Essays in Jewish-Christian Relations*, 261–83. Boston, 2010.

Bibliography

Bernstein, David J. *The Mystery of the Bayeux Tapestry.* Chicago, 1987.

Biddlecombe, Steven. "Baldric of Bourgueil and the *Familia Christi*." In *Writing the Early Crusades: Text, Transmission, and Memory,* ed. Marcus Bull and Damien Kempf, 9–23. Woodbridge, 2014.

———. "Baudri of Bourgueil and the Flawed Hero." *Anglo-Norman Studies* 35 (2014): 79–94.

Bloomfield, Morton W. *The Seven Deadly Sins: An Introduction to the History of a Religious Concept, with Special Reference to Medieval English Literature.* East Lansing, MI, 1952.

Blumenkranz, Bernhard. *Juifs et chrétiens dans le monde occidental, 430–1096.* Paris, 1960.

———. "*Perfidia.*" *Bulletin du Cange* 22 (1952): 157–70.

Bogaert, Pierre-Maurice. "The Latin Bible, c.600 to c.900." In *The Cambridge History of the Bible, Vol. 2: From 600 to 1450,* ed. Richard Marsden and E. Ann Matter, 69–92. Cambridge, 2012.

Bord, Lucien-Jean Bord. *Maillezais: Histoire d'une abbaye et d'un evêché.* Paris, 2007.

Bouchard, Constance Brittain. "The Carolingian Creation of a Model of Patrilineage." In *Paradigms and Methods in Early Medieval Studies,* ed. Celia Chazelle and Felice Lifshitz, 135–52. New York, 2007.

———. *"Every Valley Shall Be Exalted": The Discourse of Opposites in Twelfth-Century Thought.* Ithaca, NY, 2003.

Boyarin, Adrienne Williams. *Miracles of the Virgin in Medieval England: Law and Jewishness in Marian Legends.* Cambridge, 2010.

Boynton, Susan. "Prayer as Liturgical Performance in Eleventh- and Twelfth-Century Medieval Psalters." *Speculum* 82 (2007): 896–931.

Bredero, Adriaan H. "Jerusalem in the West." In *Christendom and Christianity in the Middle Ages: The Relations between Religion, the Church, and Society,* trans. Reinder Bruisma, 79–104. Grand Rapids, MI, 1994.

———. "Jérusalem dans l'Occident médiévale." In *Mélanges offerts à Réné Crozet,* 2 vols. Ed. Pierre Gallais and Yves-Jean Riou, 1: 259–71. Poitiers, 1966.

Breisach, Ernst. *Historiography: Ancient, Medieval and Modern.* Chicago, 1983.

Bresc, Henri. "Les historiens de la croisade: Guerre sainte, justice et paix." *Mélanges de l'Ecole française de Rome, Moyen Age* 115 (2003): 727–53.

Brown, Elizabeth A. R. and Michael W. Cothren. "The Twelfth-Century Crusading Window at the Abbey of Saint-Denis: *Praeteritorum Enim Recordatio Futurum est Exhibitio.*" *Journal of the Warburg and Courtauld Institutes* 49 (1986): 1–40.

Brown, Peter. "Pagan." In *Late Antiquity: A Guide to the Postclassical World,* ed. G. W. Bowersock, Peter Brown, and Oleg Grabar, 625. Cambridge, MA, 1999.

Brown, R. Allen. *The Normans and the Norman Conquest.* 2nd edn. Dover, NH, 1994.

Brown, Shirley Ann and Michael W. Herren. "The '*Adelae Comitissae*' of Baudri of Bourgueuil and the Bayeux Tapestry." *Anglo-Norman Studies* 16 (1993): 55–73.

Bibliography

Bruce, Scott G. *Cluny and the Muslims of La Garde-Freinet: Hagiography and the Problem of Islam in Medieval Europe.* Ithaca, NY, 2015.

Buc, Philippe. *Holy War, Martyrdom, and Terror: Christianity, Violence, and the West.* Philadelphia, 2015.

———. "La vengeance de Dieu: De l'exégèse patristique à la Réforme ecclésiastique et à la première croisade." In *La vengeance, 400–1200,* ed. Dominique Barthélemy, François Bougard and Régine Le Jan, 451–86. Rome, 2006.

———. *L'ambiguïté du livre. Prince, pouvoir et peuple dans les commentaires de la Bible au Moyen Age.* Paris, 1994.

———. "David's Adultery with Bathsheba and the Healing Power of the Capetian Kings." *Viator* 24 (1993): 101–20.

Buck, Andrew D. *The Principality of Antioch and its Frontiers in the Twelfth Century.* Woodbridge, 2017.

Bull, Marcus. *Eyewitness and Crusade Narrative: Perception and Narration in Accounts of the Second, Third, and Fourth Crusades.* Woodbridge, 2018.

———. "Robert the Monk and His Source(s)." In *Writing the Early Crusades: Text, Transmission, and Memory,* ed. Marcus Bull and Damien Kempf, 127–39. Woodbridge, 2014.

———. "The Historiographical Construction of a Northern French First Crusade." *Haskins Society Journal* 25 (2013): 35–56.

———. "The Pilgrimage Origins of the First Crusade." *History Today* 47 (1997): 10–15.

———. *The Knightly Response to the First Crusade: The Limousin and Gascony, c.970–c.1130.* Oxford, 1993.

Cahn, Walter. *Romanesque Bible Illumination.* Ithaca, NY, 1982.

Callahan, Daniel F. *Jerusalem and the Cross in the Life and Writings of Ademar of Chabannes.* Leiden, 2016.

Cameron, Averil. "Eusebius' *Vita Constantini* and the Construction of Constantine." In *Portraits: Biographical Representation in the Greek and Latin Literature of the Roman Empire,* ed. M. J. Edwards and Simon Swain, 145–74. Oxford, 1997.

Capitani, Ovidio. "La Riforma gregoriana." In *Le Bibbie atlantiche,* ed. Marilena Maniaci and Giulia Orofino, 7–14. Milan, 2000.

Carter, P. N. "The Historical Content of William of Malmesbury's Miracles of the Virgin." In *The Writing of History in the Middle Ages: Essays Presented to Richard William Southern,* ed. R. H. C. Davis and J. M. Wallace-Hadrill, 146–54. Oxford, 1981.

Cartwright, Steven R., ed. *A Companion to St. Paul in the Middle Ages.* Leiden, 2013.

Caspary, Gerard E. *Politics and Exegesis: Origen and the Two Swords.* Berkeley, 1979.

Cassel, J. David. "Patristic Interpretation of Isaiah." In *"As Those who are Taught": The Reception of Isaiah from the LXX to the SBL,* ed. Claire Matthews McGinnis and Patricia K. Tull, 145–70. Atlanta, 2006.

Cassidy-Welch, Megan, ed. *Remembering the Crusades and Crusading*. London, 2016.
Cassidy-Welch, Megan and Anne E. Lester. "Memory and Interpretation: New Approaches to the Study of the Crusades." *Journal of Medieval History* 40 (2014): 1–12.
Chasson, Robert Timothy. "Prophetic Imagery and Lections at Passiontide: The Jeremiah Illustrations in a Tuscan Romanesque Bible." *Gesta* 42 (2003): 89–114.
Châtillon, Jean. "La Bible dans les écoles au XIIe siècle." In *Le Moyen Age et la Bible,* ed. Pierre Riché and Guy Lobrichon, 178–83. Paris, 1984.
Chazan, Robert. *Fashioning Jewish Identity in Medieval Western Christendom.* Cambridge, 2004.
———. *In the Year 1096: The First Crusade and the Jews.* Philadelphia, 1996.
———. "Daniel 9: 23–27: Exegesis and Polemics." In *Adversus Iudaeos: Ancient and Medieval Polemics between Christians and Jews,* ed. Ora Limor, 143–60. Tübingen, 1996.
Chenu, M.-D. *Nature, Man, and Society in the Twelfth-Century.* Ed. and trans. Jerome Taylor and Lester Little. Chicago, 1968.
———. *Toward Understanding St. Thomas*. Trans. A.-M. Landry. Chicago, 1964.
Chevedden, Paul. "A Crusade from the First: The Norman Conquest of Islamic Sicily, 1060–1091." *Al-Masāq: Journal of the Medieval Mediterranean* 22 (2010): 191–225.
Chibnall, Marjorie. *The Debate on the Norman Conquest.* Manchester, 1999.
———. "Orderic Vitalis on Castles." In *Studies in Medieval History Presented to R. Allen Brown,* ed. Christoper Harper-Bill, Christopher J. Holdsworth, and Janet Nelson. Woodbridge, 1989.
———. *The World of Orderic Vitalis: Norman Monks and Norman Knights.* Oxford, 1984.
Choy, Renie S. *Intercessory Prayer and the Monastic Ideal in the Time of the Carolingian Reforms.* Oxford, 2016.
Chydenius, Johan. *Medieval Institutions and the Old Testament.* Helsinki, 1965.
Ciggaar, Krijnie. "Antioche: Les sources croisées et le plan de la ville." In *Les sources de l'histoire du paysage urbain d'Antioche sur l'Oronte: Actes des journées d'études des 20 et 21 setembre 2010 à l'Université de Paris-8,* 223–34. Paris, 2010.
Clark, Elizabeth. *Reading Renunciation: Asceticism and Scripture in Early Christianity.* Princeton, 1999.
Classen, Peter. "*Res gestae*, Universal History, Apocalypse: Visions of Past and Future." In *Renaissance and Renewal in the Twelfth Century,* ed. Robert L. Benson and Giles Constable, 386–417. Cambridge, MA, 1982.
Cluse, Christoph. "Stories of Breaking and Taking the Cross: A Possible Context for the Oxford Incident of 1268." *Revue d'histoire ecclésiastique* 90 (1995): 396–442.

Bibliography

Cochelin, Isabelle. "When Monks Were the Book: The Bible and Monasticism (6th–11th Centuries)." In *The Practice of the Bible in the Middle Ages,* ed. Susan Boynton and Diane J. Reilly, 61–83. New York, 2011.

Cohen, Jeremy. *Sanctifying the Name of God: Jewish Martyrs and Jewish Memories of the First Crusade.* Philadelphia, 2004.

———. *Living Letters of the Law: Ideas of the Jew in Medieval Christianity.* Berkeley, 1999.

———. "The Muslim Connection, or On the Changing Role of the Jew in High Medieval Theology." In *From Witness to Witchcraft: Jews and Judaism in Medieval Christian Thought,* ed. Jeremy Cohen, Wolfenbiitteler Mittelalter-Studien 11, 141–62. Wiesbaden, 1996.

———. *"Be Fertile and Increase, Fill the Earth and Master It": The Ancient and Medieval Career of a Biblical Text.* Ithaca, NY, 1989.

———. "The Jews as Killers of Christ in the Latin Tradition, from Augustine to the Friars." *Traditio* 39 (1983): 1–27.

Cole, Penny J. "'O God, the Heathens Have Come into Your Inheritance' (Ps. 78:1): The Theme of Religious Pollution in Crusade Documents, 1095–1188." In *Crusaders and Muslims in Twelfth-Century Syria,* ed. Maya Shatzmiller, 84–111. Leiden, 1993.

———. *The Preaching of the Crusades to the Holy Land, 1095–1270.* Cambridge, MA, 1991.

Coleman, Janet. *Ancient and Medieval Memories: Studies in the Reconstruction of the Past.* Cambridge, 1992.

Colish, Marcia L. *Ambrose's Patriarchs: Ethics for the Common Man.* Notre Dame, IN, 2005.

———. *Medieval Foundations of the Western Intellectual Tradition, 400–1400.* New Haven, CT, 1997.

Collins, Ann. *Teacher in Faith and Virtue: Lanfranc of Bec's Commentary on Saint Paul.* Leiden, 2014.

Collins, Samuel W. *The Carolingian Debate over Sacred Space.* New York, 2012.

Connolly, Daniel K. *The Maps of Matthew Paris: Medieval Journeys through Space, Time, and Liturgy.* Woodbridge, 2009.

Constable, Giles. *Crusaders and Crusading in the Twelfth Century.* Burlington, VT, 2008.

———. "The Three Lives of Odo Arpinus: Viscount of Bourges, Crusader, Monk of Cluny." In *Religion, Text, and Society in Medieval Spain and Northern Europe: Essays in Honor of J. N. Hillgarth,* ed. Thomas E. Burman, Mark D. Meyerson, and Leah Shopkow, 183–99. Toronto, 2002.

———. *The Reformation of the Twelfth Century.* Cambridge, 1996.

———. "A Living Past: The Historical Environment in the Middle Ages." *Harvard Library Bulletin,* n.s. 1/3 (1990): 49–70.

———. "Monachisme et pèlerinage au moyen âge." *Revue historique* 258 (1977): 3–27.

———. "A Report of a Lost Sermon by St Bernard on the Failure of the Second Crusade." In *Studies in Medieval Cistercian History*, ed. Joseph F. O'Callaghan, 49–54. Shannon, 1971.

Contreni, John J. "The Patristic Legacy to c.1000." In *The New Cambridge History of the Bible*, ed. Marsden and Matter, 527–532.

Courtenay, William J. "The Bible in Medieval Universities." In *The New Cambridge History of the Bible*, ed. Marsden and Matter, 555–78.

Cowdrey, H. E. J. "New Dimensions of Reform: War as a Path to Salvation." In *Jerusalem the Golden: The Origins and Impact of the First Crusade*, ed. Susan B. Edgington and Luis García-Guijarro Ramos, 11–24. Turnhout, 2014.

———. *Pope Gregory VII, 1073–1085*. Oxford, 1998.

———. "Pope Urban II and the Idea of Crusade." *Studi Medievali* 36 (1995): 721–42.

———. *Popes, Monks, and Crusaders*. London, 1984.

———. *The Age of Abbot Desiderius: Montecassino, the Papacy, and the Normans in the Eleventh and Early Twelfth Centuries*. Oxford, 1983.

———. "Pope Urban II's Preaching of the First Crusade." *History* 55 (1970): 177–88.

Cruz, Jo Ann Hoeppner Moran. "Popular Attitudes Toward Islam in Medieval Europe." In *Western Views of Islam in Medieval and Early Modern Europe*, ed. David R. Blanks and Michael Frassetto, 55–81. Basingstoke, 1999.

Cushing, Kathleen. *Reform and the Papacy in the Eleventh Century*. Manchester, 2005.

Dahan, Gilbert. *Lire la Bible au Moyen Âge: Essais d'herméneutique médiévale*. Geneva, 2009.

———. "Innovation et tradition dans l'exégèse chrétienne de la Bible en occident (XIIe–XIVe siècle)." In *Auctor et Auctoritas: invention et conformisme dans l'écriture médiévale: actes du colloque tenu à l'Université de Versailles-Saint-Quentin-en-Yvelines (14–16 juin 1999)*, ed. Michel Zimmerman, 255–66. Paris, 2001.

———. "Genres, Forms and Various Methods in Christian Exegesis of the Middle Ages." In *Hebrew Bible, Old Testament: The History of Its Interpretation*, 2 vols. Ed. Magne Saebo, 196–236. Göttingen, 2000.

———. *L'Exégèse chrétienne de la Bible en Occident médiévale, XIIe–XIVe siècles*. Paris, 1999.

———. *Les intellectuels chrétiens et les juifs au moyen âge*. Paris, 1990.

———. *The Christian Polemic against the Jews in the Middle Ages*. Trans. Jody Gladding. Notre Dame, IN, 1988.

Dalché, Patrick Gautier. "Notes sur la tradition du '*De rebus in oriente mirabilibus*.'" In *Amicorum societas: Mélanges offerts à François Dolbeau*, ed. Jacques Elfassi, Cécile Lanéry, and Anne-Marie Turan-Verkerk, 237–70. Florence, 2013.

Bibliography

———. "Cartes et enseignement de la 'géographie' durant le haut Moyen Âge: l'exemple d'un manuel inédit." In *Du copiste au collectionneur: Mélanges d'histoire des textes et des bibliothèques en l'honneur d'André Vernet,* ed. Donatella Nebbiai-Dalla Guarda and Jean-François Genest, 49–56. Turnhout, 1998.

Daniélou, Jean. *From Shadows to Reality: Studies in the Biblical Typology of the Fathers.* Trans. Wulstan Hibberd. London, 1960.

———. *The Bible and the Liturgy.* Trans. Anon. Ann Arbor, MI, 1956.

Darby, Peter. *Bede and the End of Time.* London, 2012.

Davis, James. *Medieval Market Morality: Life, Law and Ethics in the English Marketplace, 1200–1500.* Cambridge, 2012.

Davis, R. H. C. *From Alfred the Great to Stephen.* London, 1991.

Davis, R. H. C. and J. M. Wallace-Hadrill, eds. *The Writing of History in the Middle Ages: Essays Presented to Richard W. Southern.* Oxford, 1981.

D'Avray, D. L. *The Preaching of the Friars: Sermons Diffused from Paris before 1300.* Oxford, 1985.

de Hamel, Christopher. *The Book: A History of the Bible.* London, 2001.

de Jong, Mayke. "The Empire as *Ecclesia*: Hrabanus Maurus and Biblical *Historia* for Rulers." In *Uses of the Past in the Early Middle Ages,* ed. Yitzhak Hen and Matthew Innes. 191–226. Cambridge, 2000.

———. "Old Law and New-Found Power: Hrabanus Maurus and the Old Testament." In *Centres of Learning: Learning and Location in Pre-Modern Europe and the Near East,* ed. Hendrick Jan van Drijvers and Alastair A. MacDonald, 161–76. Leiden, 1995.

Delahaye, Philippe. "L'Organization scholaire au XIIe siècle." *Traditio* 5 (1947): 211–68.

Delaruelle, Étienne. "La vie commune des clercs et la spiritualité populaire au XI siècle." In *La vita commune del clero nei secoli XI e XII,* Atti della Settimana di Studio, 2 vols, 1:142–85. Milan, 1962.

Delisle, Léopold, ed. *Cabinet des manuscrits de la Bibliothèque nationale,* 4 vols. Paris, 1868–81.

———. "Recherches sur l'ancienne bibliothèque du Puy." *Annales de la Société Académique du Puy* 28 (1866–67): 1–21.

de Lubac, Henri. *Medieval Exegesis: The Four Senses of Scripture.* 3 vols. Trans. Mark Sebanc and E. M. Macierowski. Grand Rapids, MI, 1998–2009.

Derbes, Anne. "A Crusading Fresco Cycle at the Cathedral of Le Puy." *Art Bulletin* 73 (1991): 561–76.

Dereine, Charles. "Le problème de la vie commune chez les canonistes: d'Anselme de Lucques à Gratian." *Studi Gregoriani per la storia di Gregorio VII e della riforma gregoriana* 3 (1948): 287–98.

Derolez, Albert. *The Autograph Manuscript of the* Liber Floridus*: A Key to the Encyclopedia of Lambert of Saint-Omer.* Corpus Christianorum, Autographa Medii Aevi 4. Turnhout, 1998.

Bibliography

Diehl, Jay. "Harmony between Word and World: Anselm of Canterbury, Aelred of Rievaulx, and Approaches to Language in Twelfth-Century Monasticism." In *Saint Anselm of Canterbury and His Legacy,* ed. Giles E. M. Gasper and Ian Logan, 95–113. Toronto, 2012.

Dodwell, Charles Reginald. *The Pictorial Arts of the West, 800–1200.* New Haven, CT, 1993.

Dondi, Cristina. *The Liturgy of the Canons Regular of the Holy Sepulchre: A Study and a Catalogue of the Manuscript Sources.* Turnhout, 2004.

Donnini, Mauro. "Bibbia e storiografia." In *La bibbia nel medioevo,* ed. Giovanni Cremascoli and Claudio Leonardi, 313–26. Bologna, 1996.

Douglas, David C. *The Norman Achievement.* Berkeley, 1969.

Duchet-Suchaux, M. and Y. Lefèvre, Y. "Les noms de la Bible." In *Le Moyen Age et la Bible,* ed. Riché and Lobrichon, 13–23.

Dunbabin, Jean. "Geoffrey of Chaumont, Thibaud of Blois and William the Conqueror." *Anglo-Norman Studies* 16 (1993): 101–16.

Dupront, Alphonese. "La spiritualité des croisés et des pèlerins d'après les sources de la première croisade." In *Pellegrinaggi e culto del santi in Europa fino alla I^a crociata,* Convegni del centro di studi sulla spiritualità medievale 4, 449–83. Todi, 1963.

Dyer, Joseph. "The Psalms in Monastic Prayer." In *The Place of the Psalms in the Intellectual Culture of the Middle Ages,* ed. Nancy Van Deusen, 59–89. Albany, NY, 1999.

Edbury, Peter W. and John Gordon Rowe. *William of Tyre: Historian of the Latin East.* Cambridge, 1988.

Edgington, Susan B. "The *Gesta Francorum Iherusalem expugnantium* of 'Bartolf of Nangis.'" *Crusades* 13 (2014): 21–35.

———. "Romance and Reality in the Sources for the Sieges of Antioch, 1097–1098." In *Porphyrogenita: Essays on the History and Literature of Byzantium and the Latin East in Honour of Julian Chrysostomides,* ed. Charalambos Dendrinos et al., 33–35. Aldershot, 2003.

———. "Albert of Aachen and the *chansons de geste.*" *The Crusades and Their Sources: Essays Presented to Bernard Hamilton,* ed. John France and William G. Zajac, 23–37. Aldershot, 1998.

Elm, Kaspar. "Die Eroberung Jerusalems im Jahre 1099: Ihre Darstellung, Beurteilung und Deutung in den Quellen des Ersten Kreuzzugs." In *Jerusalem im Hoch- und Spätmittelalter: Konflikte und Konfliktbewältigung – Vorstellungen und Vergegenwärtigungen,* ed. Dieter R. Bauer and Nikolas Jaspert, 31–54. Frankfurt, 2001.

Emmerson, Richard Kenneth. *Antichrist in the Middle Ages: A Study of Medieval Apocalypticism, Art, and Literature.* Seattle, 1981.

Epp, Veronica. *Fulcher von Chartres.* Düffeldorf, 1990.

Bibliography

Erdmann, Carl. *The Origin of the Idea of Crusade.* Trans. Marshall W. Baldwin and Walter Goffart. Princeton, NJ, 1977.

Evans, G. R. *The Language and Logic of the Bible: The Earlier Middle Ages.* Cambridge, 1984.

———. *Anselm and a New Generation.* Oxford, 1980.

———. *Old Arts and New Theology: The Beginnings of Theology as an Academic Discipline.* Oxford, 1980.

———. "St Anselm and Sacred History." In *The Writing of History in the Middle Ages,* ed. Davis and Wallace-Hadrill, 187–210.

Farmer, Hugh. "William of Malmesbury's Commentary on Lamentations." *Studia monastica* 4 (1962): 283–311.

Figuet, Jean. "La Bible de Saint Bernard: Données et ouvertures." In *Bernard de Clairvaux: Histoire, mentalités, spiritualité: colloque de Lyon-Cîteaux-Dijon,* SC 380, 237–69. Paris, 1992.

Firey, Abigail. "The Letter of the Law: Carolingian Exegetes and the Old Testament." In *With Reverence for the Word: Medieval Scriptural Exegesis in Judaism, Christianity, and Islam,* ed. Jane Dammen McAuliffe, Barry D. Walfish, and Joseph W. Goering, 204–24. Oxford, 2003.

Fitzgerald, Allan D. and John C. Cavadini, eds. *Augustine through the Ages: An Encyclopedia,* Grand Rapids, MI, 1999.

Flierman, Robert. "Religious Saxons: Paganism, Infidelity and Biblical Punishment in the *Capitulatio de partibus Saxoniae.*" In *Religious Franks: Religion and Power in the Frankish Kingdoms in Honour of Mayke de Jong,* ed. Rob Meens, Dorine van Espelo, Bram van den Hoven van Genderen, Janneke Raaijmakers, Irene van Renswoude, and Carine van Rhijn, 172–92. Manchester, 2016.

Flori, Jean. "Jérusalem terrestre, céleste, et spirituelle: Trois facteurs de sacralisation de la première croisade." In *Jerusalem the Golden,* ed. Edgington and Ramos, 25–50.

———. *Chroniqeurs et propagandistes: Introduction critique aux sources de la Première Croisade.* Geneva, 2010.

———. *L'Islam et la fin des temps: l'interprétation prophétiques des invasions musulmanes dans la chrétienté médiévale.* Paris, 2007.

———. "Première croisade et conversion des 'païens.'" In *Migrations et diasporas méditerranéens (Xe–XVI siècles): Actes du colloque de Conques (octobre 1999),* ed. Michel Balard and Alain Ducellier, 449–57. Paris, 2002.

———. "La caricature de l'Islam dans l'Occident médiéval: origine et signification de quelques stéréotypes concernant l'Islam." *Aevum* 2 (1992): 245–56.

Fornasari, Giuseppe. "L'esegesi gregoriana." In *La bibbia nel medioevo,* ed. Cremascoli and Leonardi, 199–214.

France, John. "The Use of the Anonymous *Gesta Francorum* in the Early Twelfth-Century Sources for the First Crusade." In *From Clermont to Jerusalem: The Crusades and Crusader Societies, 1095–1500,* ed. Alan V. Murray, 29–42. Turnhout, 1998.

———. "The Election of and Title of Godrey of Bouillon." *Canadian Journal of History* 18 (1983): 321–29.
Frank, Robert Worth Jr. "*Meditationes Vitae Christi:* The Logistics of Access to Divinity." In *Hermeneutics and Medieval Culture,* ed. Patrick J. Gallagher and Helen Damico, 39–50. Albany, NY, 1989.
Frederiksen, Paula. *Augustine and the Jews.* New Haven, CT, 2008.
Frenkel, Yehoshua. "Crusaders, Muslims and Biblical Stories: Saladin and Joseph." In *The Crusader World,* ed. Adrian Boas, 362–77. London, 2016.
Froehlich, Karlfried. "Saint Peter, Papacy Primacy, and the Exegetical Tradition, 1150–1300." In *The Religious Role of the Papacy: Ideals and Realities,* ed. Christopher Ryan, 3–44. Toronto, 1989.
Funkenstein, Amos. *Theology and the Scientific Imagination from the Middle Ages to the Seventeenth Century.* Princeton, NJ, 1986.
Gabriele, Matthew. "From Prophecy to Apocalypse: The Verb Tenses of Jerusalem in Robert the Monk's *Historia* of the First Crusade." *Journal of Medieval History* 42 (2016): 304–16.
———. "The Last Carolingian Exegete: Pope Urban II, the Weight of Tradition, and Christian Reconquest." *Church History* 81 (2012): 796–814.
———. *An Empire of Memory: The Legend of Charlemagne, the Franks, and Jerusalem before the First Crusade.* Oxford, 2011.
Gaposchkin, M. Cecilia. *Invisible Weapons: Liturgy and the Making of Crusade Ideology.* Ithaca, NY, 2017.
———. "Louis IX, Crusade, and the Promise of Joshua in the Holy Land." *Journal of Medieval History* 34 (2008): 245–74.
Garipzanov, Ildar H. *The Symbolic Language of Royal Authority in the Carolingian World (c.751–877).* Leiden, 2008.
Garnett, George. *Conquered England: Kingship, Succession, and Tenure, 1066–1166.* Oxford, 2007.
Garrison, Mary. "The Franks as the New Israel? Education for an Identity from Pippin to Charlemagne." In *Uses of the Past,* ed. Hen and Innes, 114–61.
Gibson, Margaret T. "The Place of the *Glossa Ordinaria* in Medieval Exegesis." In *Ad Litteram: Authoritative Texts and Their Medieval Readers,* ed. Mark D. Jordan and Kent Emery, Jr., 5–27. Notre Dame, IN, 1992.
———. "Lanfranc's Notes on Patristic Texts." *The Journal of Theological Studies*, new ser. 22 (1971): 435–50.
———. "The *Artes* in the Eleventh Century." In *Arts libéraux et philosophie au moyen âge, Actes du IVe Congrès international de Philosophie médiévale.* Montreal, 1967.
Given-Wilson, Chris. *Chronicles: The Writing of History in Medieval England.* London, 2004.
Goetz, Hans-Werner. "The Concept of Time in the Historiography of the Eleventh and Twelfth Centuries." In *Medieval Concepts of the Past: Ritual, Memory, Historiography,* ed. Gerd Althoff, Johannes Fried and Patrick J. Geary, 139–65. Cambridge, 2002.

———. "Die 'Geschichte' im Wissenschaftssystem des Mittelalters." In Franz-Josef Schmale, *Funktion und Formen mittelalterlicher Geschichtsschreibung: eine Einführung*, 165–213. Darmstadt, 1985.
Goffart, Walter. *The Narrators of Barbarian History (A.D. 550–800): Jordanes, Gregory of Tours, Bede, and Paul the Deacon*. Princeton, NJ, 1988.
Gorman, Michael M. "A Survey of the Oldest Manuscripts of St. Augustine's *De Civitate Dei*." *Journal of Theological Studies* n.s. 33, pt. 2 (1982): 398–410.
Gransden, Antonia. *Legends, Traditions, and History in Medieval England*. London, 2004.
Green, D. H. *The Millstätter Exodus: A Crusading Epic*. Cambridge, 1966.
Griffiths, Fiona J. "The Trouble with Churchmen: Warning against Avarice in the 'Garden of Delights.'" In *Frauen – Kloster – Kunst: Neue Forschungen zur Kulturgeschichte des Mittelalters*, ed. Jeffrey Hamburger, Carola Jäggi, Susan Marti, and Hedwig Röckelein, 147–54. Turnhout, 2007.
Gross-Diaz, Theresa. *The Psalms Commentary of Gilbert of Poitiers: From* Lectio Divina *to the Lecture Room*. Leiden, 1996.
Guenée, Bernard. *Histoire et culture historique dans l'Occident médiéval*. Paris, 1980.
———. "L'Historien par les mots." In *Études sur l'historiographie médiévale*. Paris, 1977.
Hamilton, Bernard. "The Growth of the Latin Church of Antioch and the Recruitment of Its Clergy." In *East and West in the Medieval Mediterranean, Vol. 1: Antioch from the Byzantine Reconquest Until the End of the Crusader Principality*, Orientalia Lovaniensia Analecta 147, ed. K. Ciggaar and M. Metcalf. 171–84. Leuven, 2006.
———. *The Latin Church in the Crusader States: The Secular Church*. London, 1980.
Hamilton, Louis I. "Sexual Purity, 'the Faithful,' and Religious Reform in Eleventh-Century Italy: Donatism Revisited." In *Augustine and Politics*, ed. John Doody, Kevin L. Hughes, and Kim Paffenroth, 237–60. Lanham, MD, 2005.
Hanning, Robert W. *The Vision of History in Early Britain from Gildas to Geoffrey of Monmouth*. New York, 1966.
Harkins, Franklin T. *History and the Work of Restoration: History and Scripture in the Theology of Hugh of St Victor*. Toronto, 2009.
Harris, Jennifer A. "The Bible and the Meaning of History in the Middle Ages." In *The Practice of the Bible*, ed. Boynton and Reilly, 84–104.
———. "The Body as Temple in the High Middle Ages." In *Sacrifice in Religious Experience*, ed. Albert I. Baumgarten, 233–56. Leiden, 2002.
Hartmann, Florian. "'*Quid nobis cum allegoria?*' The Literal Reading of the Bible in the Era of the Investiture Conflict." In *Reading the Bible in the Middle Ages*, ed. Jinty Nelson and Damien Kempf, 101–18. London, 2015.

Bibliography

Hartmann, Wilfried. "Die karolingische Reform und die Bibel." *Annuarium Historiae Conciliorum* 18 (1986): 57–74.

Head, Thomas. "The Marriages of Christina of Marykate." In *Christina of Markyate: A Twelfth-Century Holy Woman,* ed. Samuel Fanous and Henrietta Leyser, 116–37. London, 2005.

Healy, Patrick. *The Chronicle of Hugh of Flavigny: Reform and the Investiture Contest in the Late Eleventh Century.* Aldershot, 2006.

Hen, Yitzak. "The Uses of the Bible and the Perception of Kingship in Merovingian Gaul." *Early Medieval Europe* 7 (1998): 277–90.

Heng, Geraldine. *The Invention of Race in the European Middle Ages.* Cambridge, 2018.

Hiestand, Rudolf. "Gaufridus abbas Templi Domini: An Underestimated Figure in the Early History of the Kingdom of Jerusalem." In *The Experience of Crusading, Vol. 2: Defining the Crusader Kingdom,* ed. Peter Edbury and Jonathan Phillips, 48–59. Cambridge, 2003.

Hillgarth, J. N. "L'Influence de la *Cité de Dieu* de saint Augustin au Haut Moyen Age." *Sacris Erudiri* 28 (1985): 5–34.

Hodgson, Natasha R. "The Role of Kerbogha's Mother in the *Gesta Francorum* and Selected Chronicles of the First Crusade." In *Gendering the Crusades*, eds. Susan B. Edgington and Sarah Lambert, 163–76. New York, 2002.

Hofreiter, Christian. *Making Sense of Old Testament Genocide: Christian Interpretations of* Herem *Passages.* Oxford, 2018.

Horowitz, Elliott S. *Reckless Rites: Purim and the Legacy of Jewish Violence.* Princeton, NJ, 2006.

Housley, Norman. *Fighting for the Cross.* New Haven, CT, 2008.

———. "Jerusalem and the Crusade Idea." In *The Horns of Hattin,* ed. Benjamin Z. Kedar, 27–40. London, 1992.

Ihnat, Kati. "Getting the Punchline: Deciphering Anti-Jewish Humor in Anglo-Norman England." *Journal of Medieval History* 38 (2012): 408–23.

Jaeger, C. Stephen. "Pessimism in the Twelfth Century Renaissance." *Speculum* 78 (2003): 1151–83.

James, Dominic. "The World and its Past as Christian Allegory in the Early Middle Ages." In *The Uses of the Past in the Early Middle Ages,* ed. Hen and Innes, 102–13.

Jensen, Janus Møller. "*Peregrinatio sive expeditio*: Why the First Crusade Was Not a Pilgrimage." *Al-Masaq: Journal of the Medieval Mediterranean* 15 (2003): 119–37.

Jestice, Phyllis G. *Wayward Monks and the Religious Revolution of the Eleventh Century.* Leiden, 1997.

Joslyn-Siemiatkoski, Daniel. *Christian Memories of the Maccabean Martyrs.* New York, 2009.

Jotischky, Andrew. "The Christians of Jerusalem, the Holy Sepulchre and the Origins of the First Crusade." *Crusades* 7 (2008): 35–57.

Kannengiesser, Charles, ed. *Handbook of Patristic Exegesis: The Bible in Ancient Christianity*, 2 vols. Leiden, 2004.

Kedar, Benjamin Z. "The Jerusalem Massacre of July 1099 in the Western Historiography of the Crusades." *Crusades* 3 (2004): 15–75.

Kedar, Benjamin Z. and Denys Pringle. "1099–1187: The Lord's Temple (*Templum Domini*) and Solomon's Palace (*Palatium Salomonis*)." In *Where Heaven and Earth Meet*, ed. Oleg Grabar and Benjamin Z. Kedar, 132–49. Jerusalem, 2009.

Kempf, Damien. "Towards a Textual Archaeology of the First Crusade." In *Writing the Early Crusades*, ed. Bull and Kempf, 116–26.

Kempshall, Matthew. *Rhetoric and the Writing of History, 400–1500*. Oxford, 2011.

Kenaan-Kedar, Nurith. "The Figurative Western Lintel of the Church of the Holy Sepulcher in Jerusalem." In *The Meeting of Two Worlds*, ed. Vladimir P. Goss, 123–31. Kalamazoo, MI, 1986.

Kerr, Julie. *Monastic Hospitality: The Benedictines in England, c.1070–c.1250*. Woodbridge, 2007.

Keskiaho, Jesse. "The Transmission of Peter Tudebode's *De Hierosolymitano itinere* and Related Chronicles, with a Critical Edition of *Descriptio sanctorum locorum Hierusalem*." *Revue d'histoire des textes*, n.s. 10 (2015): 69–102.

Kjær, Lars. "Conquests, Family Traditions, and the First Crusade." *Journal of Medieval History* 45 (2019): 553–579.

Klepper, Deeana Copeland. *The Insight of Unbelievers: Nicholas of Lyra and Christian Reading of Jewish Text in the Later Middle Ages*. Philadelphia, 2007.

Kletter, Karen M. "Christian Reception of Josephus in Late Antiquity and the Middle Ages." In *A Companion to Josephus*, ed. Honora Howell Chapman and Zuleika Rodgers, 368–81. Malden, MA, 2016.

Köhler, Michael. *Allianzen und Verträge zwischen fränkischen und islamischen Herrschern im Vorderen Orient*. Berlin, 1991.

———. "Al-Afdal und Jerusalem – was versprach sich Äegypten von ersten Kreuzzug?" *Saeculum: Jahrbuch für Universalgeschichte* 37 (1986): 228–39.

Kostick, Conor. "A Further Discussion on the Authorship of the *Gesta Francorum*." *Reading Medieval Studies* 35 (2009): 1–14.

Krey, August C. "A Neglected Passage in the *Gesta* and its Bearing on the Literature of the First Crusade." In *The Crusades and Other Historical Essays Presented to Dana C. Munro*, ed. Louis J. Paetow, 57–78. Freeport, NY, 1928.

Kühnel, Bianca. "Virtual Pilgrimages to Real Places: The Holy Landscapes." In *Imagining Jerusalem in the Medieval West*, ed. Lucy Donkin and Hanna Vorholt, 243–64. Oxford, 2012.

———. *Crusader Art of the Twelfth Century: A Geographical, an Historical, or an Art Historical Notion*. Berlin, 1994.

Bibliography

———. *From the Earthly to the Heavenly Jerusalem: Representations of the Holy City in Christian Art of the First Millennium.* Rome, 1987.

Lacroix, Benoît. *L'Historien au moyen âge.* Montreal, 1971.

Landgraf, Artur Michael. *Introduction à l'histoire de la littérature théologique de la scolastique naissante.* Montréal, 1973.

Lapina, Elizabeth. *Warfare and the Miraculous in the Chronicles of the First Crusade.* University Park, PA, 2015.

———. "The Maccabees and the Battle of Antioch." In *Dying for the Faith, Killing for the Faith: Old-Testament Faith- Warriors (Maccabees 1 and 2) in Cultural Perspective,* ed. Gabriela Signori, 147–59. Leiden, 2012.

———. "Anti-Jewish Rhetoric in Guibert of Nogent's *Dei gesta per Francos.*" *Journal of Medieval History* 35 (2009): 239–53.

———. "The Problem of Eyewitnesses in the Chronicles of the First Crusade." *Viator* 38 (2007): 117–39.

Lauwers, Michel. "Usages de la Bible et institution du sens dans l'Occident médiéval." *Médiévales* 55 (2008): 5–18.

Lecaque, Thomas. "Reading Raymond: The Bible of Le Puy, the Cathedral Library and the Literary Background of Raymond of Aguilers." In *The Uses of the Bible in Crusader Sources,* ed. Elizabeth Lapina and Nicholas Morton, 105–32. Leiden, 2017.

Leclercq, Jean. "Usage et abus de la Bible au temps de la réforme grégorienne." In *The Bible and Medieval Culture,* ed. W. Lourdaux and D. Verhelst, 89–108. Leuven, 1979.

———. "The Exposition and Exegesis of Scripture: From Gregory the Great to Saint Bernard." In *The Cambridge History of the Bible, Vol. 2: The West from the Fathers to the Reformation,* ed. G. W. H. Lampe, 183–97. Cambridge, 1969.

———. *The Love of Learning and Desire for God.* Trans. C. Misrahi. New York, 1961.

———. "Monachisme et pérégrination du IXe au XII siècle." *Studia Monastica* 3 (1961): 33–52.

Lees, Jay Terry. *Anselm of Havelberg: Deeds into Words in the Twelfth Century.* Leiden, 1998.

Le Goff, Jacques. *The Medieval Imagination.* Trans. Arthur Goldhammer. Chicago, 1988.

Lesne, Emile. *Histoire propriété ecclésiastique en France, Vol. 5: Les Écoles de la fin du VIIIe siècle à la fin du XIIe.* Lille, 1940.

Lester, Anne E. "What Remains: Women, Relics, and Remembrance in the Aftermath of the Fourth Crusade." *Journal of Medieval History* 40 (2014): 311–28.

Lev, Yaacov. *State and Society in Fatimid Egypt.* Leiden, 1991.

Levine, Robert. "The Pious Traitor: Rhetorical Reinventions of the Fall of Antioch." *Mitellateinisches Jahrbuch* 33 (1998): 59–80.

Lifshitz, Felice. "Gender and Exemplarity East of the Middle Rhine: Jesus, Mary and the Saints in Manuscript Context." *Early Medieval Europe* 9 (2000): 325–44.

Limor, Ora. "Early Pilgrimage Itineraries (333–1099)." In *The Encyclopedia of Medieval Pilgrimage*, ed. Larissa J. Taylor, Leigh Ann Craig, John B. Friedman, Kathy Gower, Thomas Izbicki, and Rita Tekippe, 170–73. Leiden, 2010.

Linder, Amnon. "The Liturgy of the Liberation of Jerusalem." *Mediaeval Studies* 52 (1990): 110–31.

Lipton, Sara. "Christianity and Its Others: Jews, Muslims, and Pagans." In *The Oxford Handbook of Medieval Christianity*, ed. John H. Arnold, 413–35. Oxford, 2014.

Little, Lester K. "Pride Goes Before Avarice: Social Change and the Vices in Latin Christendom." *American Historical Review* 76 (1971): 16–49.

Lobrichon, Guy. "The Early Schools, c.900–1100." In *The New Cambridge History of the Bible, Vol. 2: From 600 to 1450*, ed. Richard Marsden and E. Ann Matter, 536–54. Cambridge, 2012.

———. "La Bible de la réforme ecclésiastique: Aspects textuels." In *La Bible au Moyen Age*, ed. Lobrichon, 94–108. Paris, 2003.

———. "Stalking the Signs: The Apocalyptic Commentaries." In *The Apocalyptic Year 1000: Religious Expectation and Social Change, 950–1050*, ed. Richard Landes, Andrew Gow, and David C. van Meter, 67–79. Oxford, 2003.

———. "Riforma ecclesiastica e testo della Bibbia." *Le Bibbie atlantiche. Il libro delle Scritture tra monumentalità e rappresentazione*, ed. Marilena Maniaci and Giulia Orofino, 15–26. Milan, 2000.

———. "Une nouveauté: les gloses de la Bible." In *Le Moyen Age et la Bible*, ed. Riché and G. Lobrichon, 95–114. Paris, 1984.

Loutchitskaja, Svetlana. "L'Image des musulmans dans les chroniques des croisades." *Le Moyen Age* 105 (1999): 717–35.

———. "*Barbarae Nationes*: Les peuples musulmans dans les chroniques de la Première Croisade." In *Autour de la Première Croisade, Actes du Colloque de la Society for the Study of the Crusades and the Latin East (Clermont-Ferrand, 22–25 juin 1995)*, ed. Michel Balard, 99–107. Paris, 1996.

Lozovsky, Natalia. *"The Earth is Our Book": Geographical Knowledge in the Latin West, ca. 400–1000*. Ann Arbor, MI, 2000.

Lynch, Joseph H. *Simoniacal Entry into the Religious Life from 1000 to 1260*. Columbus, OH, 1976.

Madigan, Kevin. *Olivi and the Interpretation of Matthew in the High Middle Ages*. Notre Dame, IN, 2003.

———. "Nicholas of Lyra on the Gospel of Matthew." In *Nicholas of Lyra: The Senses of Scripture*, ed. Philip D. Krey and Lesley Janette Smith, 195–221. Leiden, 2000.

Mähl, Sibylle. "Jerusalem in mittelalterlicher Sicht." *Die Welt als Geschichte* 22 (1962): 11–26.

Bibliography

Malegam, Jehangir Yezdi. *The Sleep of Behemoth: Disputing Peace and Violence in Medieval Europe, 1000–1200.* Ithaca, NY, 2013.

Marenbon, John. *Pagans and Philosophers: The Problem of Paganism from Augustine to Leibnitz.* Princeton, 2015.

Markus, R. A. *The End of Ancient Christianity.* Cambridge, 1990.

———. *Saeculum: History and Society in the Theology of St. Augustine.* Cambridge, 1970.

Matter, E. Ann. "The Church Fathers and the *Glossa Ordinaria*." In *The Reception of the Church Fathers in the West,* ed. Irena Dorota Backus, 83–112. Leiden, 1997.

———. "The Apocalypse in Early Medieval Exegesis." In *The Apocalypse in the Middle Ages,* ed. Richard K. Emmerson and Bernard McGinn, 38–50. Ithaca, NY, 1992.

Mayer, Cornelius Petrus, gen. ed. *Augustinus-Lexikon.* 4 vols. Basel, 1986–.

McCarthy, Thomas J. H. *The Continuations of Frutolf of Michelsberg's Chronicle.* Wiesbaden, 2018.

———. "Scriptural Allusion in the Crusading Accounts of Frutolf of Michelsberg and his Continuators." In *The Uses of the Bible,* ed. Lapina and Morton, 152–75.

McCormick, Michael. "Liturgie et guerre des Carolingiens à la première croisade." In *'Militia Christi' e Crociata nei secoli XI–XIII: Atti della undecima Settimana internazionale di studio, Mendola, 28 agosto – 1 settembre 1989,* 209–38. Milan, 1989.

McDonnell, Ernest W. The *Vita apostolica*: Diversity or Dissent." *Church History* 24 (1955): 15–31.

McGinn, Bernard. "From Admirable Tabernacle to House of God: Some Theological Reflections on Medieval Architectural Integration." In *Artistic Integration in Gothic Buildings,* ed. Virginia Chieffo Raguin, Kathryn Brush, and Peter Draper, 41–56. Toronto, 1995.

———. "*Iter Sancti Sepulchri*: The Piety of the First Crusaders." In *Essays on Medieval Civilization: The Walter Prescott Webb Memorial Lectures,* ed. Bede Karl Lackner and Kenneth Roy Philp, 33–71. Austin, TX, 1978.

McKitterick, Rosamund. *The Frankish Church and the Carolingian Reforms.* London, 1977.

Meens, Rob. "The Uses of the Old Testament in Early Medieval Canon Law." In *The Uses of the Past,* ed. Hen and Innes, 67–77.

Mégier, Elisabeth. "Christian Historical Fulfilments of Old Testament Prophecies in Latin Commentaries on the Book of Isaiah (ca. 400 to ca. 1150)." *Journal of Medieval Latin* 17 (2007): 87–100.

———. "Divina Pagina and the Narration of History in Orderic Vitalis' *Historia Ecclesiastica*." *Revue Bénédictine* 110 (2000): 106–23.

Meiser, Martin. *Galater.* Novum Testamentum Patristicum 9. Göttingen, 2007.

Mellinkoff, Ruth. *The Horned Moses in Medieval Life and Thought.* Berkeley, 1970.

Merlet, Lucien. "Catalogue des livres de l'abbaye de Saint-Père de Chartres, au XIe siècle." *Bibliothèque de l'Ecole des Chartes* 3rd ser., vol. 5 (1854): 263–70.

Mews, Constant J. and Micha J. Perry. "Peter Abelard, Heloise, and Jewish Biblical Exegesis in the Twelfth Century." *Journal of Ecclesiastical History* 62 (2011): 3–19.

Meyer, Ann R. *Medieval Allegory and the Building of the New Jerusalem.* Cambridge, 2003.

Miccoli, Giovanni. *Chiesa Gregoriana: Ricerche sulla riforma del secolo XI.* 2nd edn. Rome, 1999.

———. *Povertà e ricchezza nella spiritualità dei secoli XI e XII.* Todi, 1969.

Minnis, Alastair J. *Medieval Theory of Authorship: Scholastic Literary Attitudes in the Later Middle Ages.* 2nd edn. Aldershot, 1988.

Mirbt, C. *Die Stellung Augustins in der Publicistik des gregorianischen Kirchenstreits.* Leipzig, 1888.

Moore, Michael E. "Prologue: Teaching and Learning History in the School of Reims, c.800–950." In *Teaching and Learning in Northern Europe, 1000–1200,* ed. Sally N. Vaughn and Jay Rubenstein, 19–49. Turnhout, 2006.

Morgan, Edward. *The Incarnation of the Word: The Theology of Language of Augustine of Hippo.* London, 2010.

Morris, Colin. *The Sepulchre of Christ and the Medieval West: From the Beginning to 1600.* Oxford, 2005.

———. "The *Gesta Francorum* as Narrative History." *Reading Medieval Studies* 19 (1993): 55–71.

Morris, David. "The Servile Mother: Jerusalem as Woman in the Era of the Crusades." In *Remembering the Crusades: Myth, Image, and Identity,* eds. Nicholas Paul and Suzanne Yeager, 174–94. Baltimore, 2012.

Morrison, Karl. *History as a Visual Art in the Twelfth-Century Renaissance.* Princeton, NJ, 1990.

Morton, Catherine. "Pope Alexander II and the Norman Conquest." *Latomus* 34 (1975): 362–82.

Morton, Nicholas. *Encountering Islam on the First Crusade.* Cambridge, 2016.

———. "The Defence of the Holy Land and the Memory of the Maccabees." *Journal of Medieval History* 36 (2010): 275–93.

Munro Dana, Carleton. "The Speech of Urban II at Clermont, 1095." *The American Historical Review* 11 (1906): 231–42.

Münsch, Oliver. "Hate Preachers and Religious Warriors: Violence in the *Libelli de Lite* of the Late Eleventh Century." In *Dying for the Faith,* ed. Signori, 161–76.

Murray, Alan V. "Biblical Quotations and Formulaic Language in the Chronicle of William of Tyre." In *Deeds Done Beyond the Sea: Essays on William of Tyre, Cyprus, and the Military Orders Presented to Peter Edbury,* ed. Susan B. Edgington and Helen J. Nicholson, 25–34. Farnham, 2014.

———. "The Siege and Capture of Jerusalem in Western Narrative Sources of the First Crusade." In *Jerusalem the Golden,* ed. Edgington and Ramos, 191–215.

Naus, James. *Constructing Kingship: The Capetian Kings of France and the Early Crusades.* Manchester, 2016.

Newman, Barbara. *God and the Goddesses: Vision, Poetry, and Belief in the Middle Ages.* Philadelphia, 2005.

Newman, Martha G. *The Boundaries of Charity: Cistercian Culture and Ecclesiastical Reform, 1098–1180.* Stanford, CA, 1996.

Ní Chléirigh, Léan. "*Nova Peregrinatio*: The First Crusade as a Pilgrimage in Contemporary Latin Narratives." In *Writing the Early Crusades,* ed. Bull and Kempf, 63–74.

Nichols, Stephen G. *Romanesque Signs: Early Medieval Narrative and Iconography.* New Haven, CT, 1983.

Niermeyer, J. F. *Mediae Latinitatis lexicon minus.* Leiden, 1976.

Niskansen, Samu. "The Origins of the *Gesta Francorum* and Two Related Texts: Their Textual and Literary Character." *Sacris Erudiri* 51 (2012): 287–316.

Noble, Thomas F. X. *Images, Iconoclasm, and the Carolingians.* Philadelphia, 2009.

———. "The Bible in the Codex Carolinus." In *Biblical Studies in the Early Middle Ages: Proceedings of the Conference on Biblical Studies in the Early Middle Ages,* ed. Claudio Leonardi and Giovanni Orlandi, 61–74. Florence, 2005.

Noonan, J. T. *The Scholastic Analysis of Usury.* Cambridge, MA, 1957.

North, William L. "St. Anselm's Forgotten Student: Richard of Préaux and the Interpretation of Scripture in Early Twelfth-Century Normandy." In *Teaching and Learning in Northern Europe,* ed. Vaughn and Rubenstein, 171–215.

———. "Polemic, Apathy, and Authorial Initiative in Gregorian Rome." *Haskins Society Journal* 10 (2001): 113–25.

O'Brien, Conor. *Bede's Temple: An Image and Its Interpretation.* Oxford, 2015.

Olsen, Derek A. *Reading Matthew with Monks: Liturgical Interpretation in Anglo-Saxon England.* Collegeville, MN, 2015.

Olsen, Glenn W. "The Idea of the *Ecclesia Primitiva* in the Writings of the Twelfth-Century Canonists." *Traditio* 25 (1969): 61–86.

Omont, Henri, Auguste Molinier, and Ernest Coyecque. *Catalogue générale des manuscrits des bibliothèques publiques de France: Départements, 11: Chartres.* Paris, 1890.

Otten, Willemien. "The Reception of Augustine in the Early Middle Ages (c.700–c.1200)." In *The Oxford Guide to the Historical Reception of Augustine, Vol. 1,* ed. Karla Pollman and Willemien Otten, 22–39. Oxford, 2013.

Partner, Nancy F. *Serious Entertainments: The Writing of History in Twelfth-Century England.* Chicago, 1977.

Paterson, Linda. "Occitan Literature and the Holy Land." In *The World of Eleanor of Aquitaine: Literature and Society in Southern France between the Eleventh and Thirteenth Centuries,* ed. Marcus Bull and Catherine Léglu, 73–98. Woodbridge, 2005.

Bibliography

———. "Syria, Poitou, and the Reconquista (or Tales of the Undead): Who was the Count in Marcabru's *Vers del Lavador?*" In *The Second Crusade: Scope and Consequences,* ed. Jonathan Phillips and Martin Hoch, 133–49. Manchester, 2001.

Paul, Nicholas. *To Follow in Their Footsteps: The Crusades and Family Memory in the High Middle Ages.* Ithaca, NY, 2012.

Peters, Edward. "Transgressing the Limits Set by the Fathers: Authority and Impious Exegesis in Medieval Thought." In *Christendom and Its Discontents: Exclusion, Persecution, and Rebellion, 1000–1500,* ed. Scott L. Waugh and Peter D. Diehl, 338–62. Cambridge, 1996.

Phillips, Jonathan. *The Second Crusade: Extending the Frontiers of Christendom.* New Haven, CT, 2007.

———. *Defenders of the Holy Land: Relations between the Latin East and the West, 1119–1187.* Oxford, 1996.

Piazzoni, Ambrogio M. "L'esegesi neomonastica." In *La bibbia nel medioeveo,* ed. Cremascoli and Leonardi, 217–37. Bologna, 1996.

Poleg, Eyal. *Approaching the Bible in Medieval England.* Manchester, 2013.

Poole, Kevin. "The Western Apocalypse Commentary Tradition of the Early Middle Ages." In *A Companion to the Premodern Apocalypse,* ed. Michael A. Ryan, 103–43. Leiden, 2016.

Powell, James M. "Myth, Legend, Propaganda, History: The First Crusade, 1140–ca.1300." In *Autour de la Première Croisade,* ed. Michel Balard, 127–41. Paris, 1996.

Prawer, Joshua. "Christian Attitudes Towards Jerusalem in the Early Middle Ages." In *The History of Jerusalem: The Early Muslim Period,* ed. Joshua Prawer and Haggai Ben-Shammai, 311–48. New York, 1996.

Price, Merrall Llewelyn. "Medieval Antisemitism and Excremental Libel." In *Jews in Medieval Christendom: Slay Them Not,* ed. Kristine T. Utterback and Merrall L. Price, 177–88. Leiden, 2013.

Pringle, Denys. *The Churches of the Crusader Kingdom of Jerusalem, a Corpus, Vol. 3: The City of Jerusalem.* Cambridge, 2010.

Purkis, William J. "'Zealous imitation:' The Materiality of the Crusader's Marked Body." *Material Religion* 14, no. 4 (2018): 438–53.

———. *Crusading Spirituality in the Holy Land and Iberia, c.1095–c.1187.* Woodbridge, 2008.

Raby, F. J. E. *A History of Secular Latin Poetry in the Middle Ages.* Oxford, 1967.

Ray, Roger D. "Bede, the Exegete, as Historian." In *Famulus Christi: Essays in Commemoration of the Thirteenth Centenary of the Birth of the Venerable Bede,* ed. Gerald Bonner, 125–40. London, 1976.

———. "Medieval Historiography through the Twelfth Century: Problems and Progress of Research." *Viator* 5 (1974): 33–60.

———. "Orderic Vitalis and William of Poitiers: A Monastic Reinterpretation of William the Conqueror." *Revue belge de philologie et d'histoire* 50, fasc. 4 (1972): 1116–27.

Reilly, Diane J. "The Bible as Bellwether: Manuscript Bibles in the Context of Spiritual, Liturgical and Educational Reform, 1000–1200." In *Form and Function in the Late Medieval Bible,* ed. Diane Reilly, 9–30. Leiden, 2013.

———. *The Art of Reform in Eleventh-Century Flanders: Gerard of Cambrai, Richard of Saint-Vanne and the Saint-Vaast Bible.* Leiden, 2006.

Renna, Thomas J.. "Zion and Jerusalem in the Psalms." In *Augustine: Biblical Exegete,* ed. Frederick Van Fleteren and Joseph C. Schnaubelt, 279–98. New York, 2001.

———. "Bernard of Clairvaux and the Temple of Solomon." In *Law, Custom, and the Social Fabric in Medieval Europe: Essays in Honor of Bryce Lyon,* ed. Bernard S. Bachrach and David Nicholas, 73–88. Kalamazoo, MI, 1990.

———. "The Idea of Jerusalem: Monastic to Scholastic." In *From Cloister to Classroom: Monastic and Scholastic Approaches to Truth,* ed. E. Rozanne Elder, 96–109. Kalamazoo, MI, 1986.

Resnick, Irven M. "Attitudes towards Philosophy and Dialectic during the Gregorian Reform." *The Journal of Religious History* 16 (1990): 115–25.

Richard, Jean. *Les récits de voyages et de pèlerinages.* Typologie des sources du Moyen Age occidental 38. Turnout: Brepols, 1981.

Riché, Pierre. *Les écoles et l'enseignement dans l'Occident chrétien de la fin du Ve siècle au milieu du XIe siècle.* Paris, 1979.

———. "Le psautier, livre de lecture elementaire d'après les vies des saints mérovingiens." In *Études mérovingiennes: Actes des Journées de Poitiers,* 253–56. Paris, 1953.

Rietbergen, Peter. *Europe: A Cultural History.* 3rd edn. London, 2015.

Riley-Smith, Jonathan. *The First Crusade and the Idea of Crusading.* 2nd edn. Philadelphia, 2009.

———. *The First Crusaders, 1095–1131.* Cambridge, 1997.

———. "Death on the First Crusade." In *The End of Strife,* ed. David Loades, 14–31. Edinburgh, 1984.

———. "The First Crusade and Saint Peter." In *Outremer: Studies in the History of the Crusader Kingdom of Jerusalem Presented to Joshua Prawer,* ed. Benjamin Z. Kedar, H. E. Meyer, and R. C. Smail, 41–63. Jerusalem, 1982.

———. "Crusading as an Act of Love." *History* 65 (1980): 177–92. Repr. in *The Crusades: Essential Readings,* ed. Thomas Madden, 32–50. Malden, MA, 2002.

Rist, Rebecca. *Popes and Jews, 1095–1291.* Oxford, 2016.

Rivard, Derek A. *Blessing the World: Liturgy and Lay Piety in Medieval Religion.* Washington, D.C., 2009.

Roach, Daniel. "Orderic Vitalis and the First Crusade." *Journal of Medieval History* 42 (2016): 177–201.

Roberts, Kathleen Glenister. *Alterity and Narrative: Stories and the Negotiation of Western Identities.* Albany, NY, 2007.

Bibliography

Robinson, I. S. "Church and Papacy." In *The Cambridge History of Medieval Political Thought, c.350–1450,* ed. J. H. Burns, 252–305. Cambridge, 1988.

———. "The Bible in the Investiture Contest: The South German Gregorian Circle." In *The Bible in the Medieval World: Essays in Memory of Beryl Smalley,* Studies in Church History, Subsidia 4, ed. Katherine Walsh and Diana Wood, 61–84. Oxford, 1985.

———. "'Political Allegory' in the Biblical Exegesis of Bruno of Segni." *Recherches de Théologie ancienne et médiévale* 50 (1983): 69–98.

———. *Authority and Resistance in the Investiture Contest.* Manchester, 1978.

———. "Gregory VII and the Soldiers of Christ." *History* 58 (1973): 169–92.

Rotter, Ekkehart. *Abendland und Sarazenen: Das okzidentale Araberbild und seine Entstehunt im Frühmittelalter.* Berlin, 1986.

Rough, Robert H. *The Reformist Illuminations in the Gospels of Matilda, Countess of Tuscany.* The Hague, 1973.

Rousset, Paul. "L'idée de croisade chez les chroniqueurs d'Occident." In *Storia del medioevo: Relazioni del X congresso internazionale di scienze storiche iii,* 547–63. Florence, 1955.

———. *Les origines et les caractères de la première croisade.* Neuchâtel, 1945.

Rubenstein, Jay. *Nebuchadnezzar's Dream: The Crusades, Apocalyptic Prophecy, and the End of History.* Oxford, 2019.

———. "Holy Fire and Sacral Kingship in Post-Conquest Jerusalem." *Journal of Medieval History* 43 (2017): 470–84.

———. "Miracles and the Crusading Mind: Monastic Meditations on Jerusalem's Conquest." In *Prayer and Thought in Monastic Tradition: Essays in Honour of Benedicta Ward SLG,* ed. Santha Bhattacharji, Rowan Williams, and Dominic Mattos, 197–210. London, 2014.

———. "Lambert of Saint-Omer and the Apocalyptic First Crusade." In *Remembering the Crusades,* ed. Paul and Yeager, 69–95. Baltimore, 2012.

———. *Armies of Heaven: The First Crusade and the Quest for Apocalypse.* New York, 2011.

———. "Godfrey of Bouillon versus Raymond of Saint-Gilles: How Carolingian Kingship Trumped Millenarianism at the End of the First Crusade." In *The Legend of Charlemagne in the Middle Ages: Power, Faith, and Crusade,* ed. Matthew Gabriele and Jace Stuckey, 59–76. New York, 2008.

———. "What is the *Gesta Francorum,* and Who Was Peter Tudebode?" *Revue Mabillon* n.s. 16 (2005): 179–204.

———. "How, or How Much, to Reevaluate Peter the Hermit?" In *The Medieval Crusade,* ed. Susan J. Ridyard, 53–70. Woodbridge, 2004.

———. "Putting History to Use: Three Crusade Chronicles in Context." *Viator* 35 (2004): 131–68.

———. *Guibert of Nogent: Portrait of a Medieval Mind.* New York, 2002.

Bibliography

Rudy, Kathryn M., *Virtual Pilgrimages in the Convent: Imagining Jerusalem in the Late Middle Ages.* Turnhout, 2011.

Ruether, Rosemary Radford. "The *Adversus Judaeos* Tradition in the Church Fathers: The Exegesis of Christian Anti-Judaism." In *Essential Papers on Judaism and Christianity in Conflict: From Late Antiquity to the Reformation,* ed. Jeremy Cohen, 174–89. New York, 1991.

Russo, Luigi. "The Sack of Jerusalem in 1099 and Crusader Violence Viewed by Contemporary Chroniclers." In *The Uses of the Bible in Crusader Sources,* ed. Elizabeth Lapina and Nicholas Morton, 63–73. Leiden, 2017.

———. "The Monte Cassino Tradition of the First Crusade: From the *Chronica Monasterii Casinensis* to the *Hystoria de via et recuperatione Antiochae atque Ierusolymarum.*" In *Writing the Early Crusades,* ed. Bull and Kempf, 53–62.

Saak, Eric L. "Augustine in the Western Middle Ages to the Reformation." In *A Companion to Augustine,* ed. Mark Vessey, 465–77. London, 2009.

Salomon, David A. *An Introduction to the* Glossa Ordinaria *as Medieval Hypertext.* Cardiff, 2012.

Sawyer, John F. A. *The Fifth Gospel: Isaiah in the History of Christianity.* Cambridge, 1996.

Scheil, Andrew. *Babylon under Western Eyes: A Study of Allusion and Myth.* Toronto, 2016.

Schein, Sylvia. *Gateway to the Heavenly City: Crusader Jerusalem and the Catholic West (1099–1187).* Aldershot, 2005.

———. "Babylon and Jerusalem: The Fall of Acre, 1291–1996." In *From Clermont to Jerusalem: The Crusades and Crusader Societies 1095–1500,* ed. Alan V. Murray, 141–50. Turnhout, 1998.

———. "Between Mount Moriah and the Holy Sepulchre: The Changing Traditions of the Temple Mount in the Middle Ages." *Traditio* 40 (1984): 175–95.

Schenk, Jochen. *Templar Families: Landowning Families and the Order of the Temple in France, c.1120–1307.* Cambridge, 2012.

Schmeck, H. "*Infidelis*: Ein Beitrag zur Wortgeschichte." *Vigiliae Christianae* 5 (1951):129–47.

Schreckenberg, Heinz. *Die christlichen Adversus-Judaeos-Texte und ihr literarisches und historisches Umfeld (1.–11. Jh.).* Frankfurt, 1999.

Shadle, Matthew A. *The Origins of War: A Catholic Perspective.* Washington, D.C., 2011.

Shimahara, Sumi. "Exégèse et politique dans l'oeuvre d'Haymon d'Auxerre." *Revue de l'histoire des religions* 225 (2008): 471–86.

Siberry, Elizabeth. *Criticism of Crusading, 1095–1274.* New York, 1985.

Signer, Michael. "Peshat, Sensus Literalis, and Sequential Narrative: Jewish Exegesis and the School of St. Victor in the Twelfth Century." In *The Frank Talmage Memorial Volume,* ed. Barry Walfish, 203–16. Haifa, 1993.

Bibliography

Signer, Michael A. and John Van Engen, eds. *Jews and Christians in Twelfth-Century Europe.* Notre Dame, IN, 2001.

Silvestre, Hubert. "Le 'plus grand miracle' de Jésus." *Analecta Bollandiana* 100 (1982): 1–15.

Simon, Denis. *Supplément à l'histoire du Beauvaisis.* Paris, 1704.

Skottki, Kristin. *Christen, Muslime und der Erste Kreuzzug: Die Macht der Beschreibung in der mittelalterlichen und modernen Historiographie.* Münster, 2015.

Smalley, Beryl. *The Gospels in the Schools, c.1100–1280.* London, 1985.

———. *Historians in the Middle Ages.* London, 1974.

———. *The Becket Conflict and the Schools: A Study of Intellectuals in Politics.* London, 1973.

———. *The Study of the Bible in the Middle Ages.* New York, 1941; paperback edn.; Notre Dame, IN, 1964.

———. "L'Exégèse biblique dans la littérature latine." In *La Bibbia nell'Alto Medioevo*, Settimane di studio del Centra Italiano di Studi sull'Alto Medioevo 10, 631–55. Spoleto, 1963.

———. "Quelques prédecesseurs d'Anselm de Laon." *Recherches de théologie ancienne et médiévale* 9 (1937): 365–401.

Smith, Katherine Allen. "The Crusader Conquest of Jerusalem and Christ's Cleansing of the Temple." In *The Uses of the Bible in Crusader Sources,* ed. Lapina and Morton, 19–41. Leiden, 2017.

———. "Monastic Memories of the Early Crusading Movement." In *Remembering the Crusades and Crusading,* ed. Megan Cassidy-Welch, 131–44. New York, 2016.

———. "Glossing the Holy War: Exegetical Constructions of the First Crusade, c.1099–c.1146." *Studies in Medieval and Renaissance History*, 3rd series, vol. 10 (2013): 1–39.

———. *War and the Making of Medieval Monastic Culture.* Woodbridge, 2011.

Smith, Lesley. *The Glossa Ordinaria: The Making of a Medieval Bible Commentary.* Leiden, 2009.

Smith, Mary Frances. "Archbishop Stigand and the Eye of the Needle." *Anglo-Norman Studies* 16 (1994): 199–220.

Smith, Thomas W. "First Crusade Letters and Medieval Monastic Scribal Cultures." *Journal of Ecclesiastical History* (forthcoming).

———. "The Use of the Bible in the *Arengae* of Pope Gregory IX's Crusade Calls." In *The Uses of the Bible,* ed. Lapina and Morton, 206–35.

———. "Scribal Crusading: Three New Manuscript Witnesses to the Reception and Transmission of First Crusade Letters." *Traditio* 72 (2017): 133–69.

Southern, R. W. "Aspects of the European Tradition of Historical Writing: 4. The Sense of the Past." *Transactions of the Royal Historical Society* 23 (1973): 243–63.

Spiegel, Gabrielle M. *The Past as Text: The Theory and Practice of Medieval Historiography.* Baltimore, 1997.

———. "History as Enlightenment." In *Abbot Suger and Saint-Denis,* ed. Paula Gerson, 151–58. New York, 1986.

Stein, Robert M. "Literary Criticism and the Evidence for History." In *Writing Medieval History,* ed. Nancy Partner, 67–86. London, 2005.

Stella, Francesco. "La trasmissione nella letteratura: la poesia." *La bibbia nel medioevo,* ed. Cremascoli and Leonardi, 47–63.

Stoclet, Alain J. "Le '*De civitate Dei*' de saint Augustin: Sa diffusion avant 900 d'après les caractères externes des manuscrits antérieur à cette date et les catalogues contemporains." *Recherches Augustiniennes et Patristiques* 19 (1984): 185–209.

Stegmüller, Friedrich. *Repertorium Biblicum Medii Aevi.* 11 vols. Madrid, 1950–80.

Strack, Georg. "The Sermon of Urban II in Clermont and the Tradition of Papal Oratory." *Medieval Sermon Studies* 56 (2012): 30–45.

Strickland, Debra Higgs. "Looking Back: the Westminster Psalter, the Added Drawings, and the Idea of 'Retrospective Crusade.'" In *The Crusades and Visual Culture,* ed. Elizabeth Lapina, April Jehan Morris, Susanna A. Throop, and Elizabeth Whatley, 157–84. Farnham, 2015.

———. *Saracens, Demons and Jews: Making Monsters in Medieval Art.* Princeton, NJ, 2003.

Sweetenham, Carole. "Robert the Monk's Use of the Bible in the *Historia Iherosolimitana.*" In *The Uses of the Bible in Crusader Sources,* ed. Elizabeth Lapina and Nicholas Morton, 133–51. Leiden, 2017.

Symes, Carol. "Popular Literacies and the First Historians of the First Crusade." *Past & Present* 235 (2017): 37–67.

Szpiech, Ryan. *Conversion and Narrative: Reading and Religious Authority in Medieval Polemic.* Philadelphia, 2012.

Tanner, Heather J. *Families, Friends and Allies: Boulogne and Politics in Northern France and England, c. 879–1160.* Leiden, 2004.

Tessera, Miriam Rita. "The Use of the Bible in Twelfth-Century Papal Letters to Outremer." In *The Uses of the Bible in Crusader Sources,* ed. Lapina and Morton, 179–205.

Thomas, David and Alex Mallett, eds. *Christian–Muslim Relations: A Biographical Dictionary, Vol. 3: 1050–1200.* Leiden, 2009.

Thomas, Hugh M. *The Norman Conquest: England after William the Conqueror.* Lanham, MD, 2008.

Thomson, Rodney M. "William of Malmesbury, Historian of Crusade." *Reading Medieval Studies* 23 (1997): 121–34.

———. *William of Malmesbury.* Woodbridge, 1987.

Throop, Susanna A. *Crusading as an Act of Vengeance, 1095–1216.* Farnham, 2011.

Timmer, David. "Biblical Exegesis and the Jewish-Christian Controversy in the Early Twelfth Century." *Church History* 58 (1989): 309–21.

Tinkle, Theresa. *Gender and Power in Medieval Exegesis.* New York, 2010.

Bibliography

Tolan, John V. *Sons of Ishmael: Muslims through European Eyes in the Middle Ages.* Gainesville, FL, 2008.

———. *Saracens: Islam in the Medieval European Imagination.* New York, 2002.

———. "Muslims as Pagan Idolaters in Chronicles of the First Crusade." In *Western Views of Islam in Medieval and Early Modern Europe: Perception of Other,* ed. Michael Frassetto and David R. Blanks, 97–117. New York, 1999.

Tranchant, Mathias and Cécile Treffort, eds. *L'Abbaye de Maillezais: des moines du marais aux soldats huguenots.* Rennes, 2005.

Traver, Andrew Garrett. "The Identification of the '*vita apostolica*' with a Life of Itinerant Preaching and Mendicancy: Its Origins, Adherents, and Critics ca. 1050–1266." Unpublished PhD diss. University of Toronto, 1996.

Trick, Bradley. *Abrahamic Descent, Testamentary Adoption, and the Law in Galatians.* Leiden, 2016.

Tyerman, Christopher. "Were There Any Crusades in the Twelfth Century?" *English Historical Review* 110, no. 437 (1995): 553–77.

van der Elst, Stefan. *The Knight, the Cross, and the Song: Crusade Propaganda and Chivalric Literature, 1100–1400.* Philadelphia, 2017.

Vanderputten, Steven. "Benedictine Local Historiography From the Middle Ages and Its Written Sources: Some Structural Observations." *Revue Mabillon,* n.s. 15 (2004): 107–29.

Van Deusen, Nancy and Marcia L. Colish. "*Ex utroque et in utroque: Promissa mundo gaudia, Electrum,* and the Sequence." In *The Place of the Psalms,* ed. Van Deusen, 105–38.

Van Engen, John. *Rupert of Deutz.* Berkeley, 1983.

van Houts, Elisabeth. "The Memory of 1066 in Written and Oral Traditions." *Anglo-Norman Studies* 19 (1996): 169–79.

———. "The Norman Conquest through European Eyes." *English Historical Review* 110 (1995): 832–53.

van Liere, Frans. "Biblical Exegesis Through the Twelfth Century." In *The Practice of the Bible,* ed. Boynton and Reilly, 157–78.

Van Oort, Johannes. *Jerusalem and Babylon: A Study into Augustine's* City of God *and the Sources of His Doctrine of the Two Cities.* Leiden, 1991.

Vitz, Evelyn Birge. "Liturgy as Education in the Middle Ages." In *Medieval Education,* ed. Ronald B. Begley and Joseph W. Koterski, 20–34. New York, 2005.

Ward, Benedicta. *The Venerable Bede.* Kalamazoo, MI, 1990.

———. *Miracles and the Medieval Mind: Theory, Record, and Event, 1000–1215.* 2nd edn. Philadelphia, 1987.

Ward, John O. "Some Principles of Rhetorical Historiography in the Twelfth Century." In *Classical Rhetoric and Medieval Historiography,* ed. Ernst Breisach, 127–48. Kalamazoo, MI, 1985.

Weeda, Claire. "Violence, Control, Prophecy and Power in Twelfth-Century France and Germany." In *Reading the Bible in the Middle Ages,* ed. Nelson and Kempf, 147–66.

Weiss, Daniel H. "Biblical History and Medieval Historiography: Rationalizing Strategies in Crusader Art." *Modern Language Notes* 108 (1993): 710–37.

Wells, David. "The Medieval Nebuchadnezzar: The Exegetical Tradition of Daniel IV and Its Significance for the *Ywain* Romances and for German Vernacular Literature." *Frühmittelalterliche Studien* 16 (2010): 398–405.

Whalen, Brett. *Dominion of God: Christendom and Apocalypse in the Middle Ages.* Cambridge, MA, 2009.

———. "The Discovery of the Holy Patriarchs: Relics, Ecclesiastical Politics, and Sacred History in Twelfth-Century Crusader Palestine." *Historical Reflections / Réflections Historiques* 27 (2001): 139–76.

Wilken, Robert L. *The Land Called Holy: Palestine in Christian History and Thought.* New Haven, CT, 1992.

Wolf, Kenneth Baxter. "Crusade and Narrative: Bohemond and the *Gesta Francorum.*" *Journal of Medieval History* 17 (1991): 207–16.

Wolff, Anne. *How Many Miles to Babylon? Travels and Adventures to Egypt and Beyond, 1300 to 1640.* Liverpool, 2003.

Wood, Diana. *Medieval Economic Thought.* Cambridge, 2002.

Wood, Ian. "Who Are the Philistines? Bede's Readings of Old Testament Peoples." In *The Resources of the Past in Early Medieval Europe,* ed. Clemens Gantner, Rosamund McKitterick, and Sven Meeder, 172–87. Cambridge, 2015.

Wright, Neil. "Epic and Romance in the Chronicles of Anjou." *Anglo-Norman Studies* 26 (2004): 177–89.

Yawn, Lila. "The Italian Giant Bibles." In *The Practice of the Bible,* ed. Boynton and Reilly, 126–56.

Yeager, Suzanne M. "*The Siege of Jerusalem* and Biblical Exegesis: Writing About Romans in Fourteenth-Century England." *The Chaucer Review* 39 (2004): 70–102.

Zacher, Samantha. *Rewriting the Old Testament in Anglo-Saxon Verse: Becoming the Chosen People.* London, 2013.

Zemler-Cizewski, Wanda. "The Literal Sense of Scripture According to Rupert of Deutz." In *The Multiple Meanings of Scripture: The Role of Exegesis in Early Christian and Medieval Culture,* ed. Ineke van 't Spijker, 203–24. Leiden, 2009.

Index

1 Corinthians 37, 72
1 Peter 77–78

Aaron 122
Abiathar 116
Abraham 65, 73, 117, 125–27, 129, 131, 153
Adam 148
Acre 103
Acts of the Apostles 46, 57, 59–60, 63–64, 69, 70, 105, 160–61
Adela, countess of Blois 42
Ademar of Chabannes 144 n.233, 173
Adhemar, bishop of Le Puy 117, 122–23, 123 n.135, 138
Adversus Judaeos see polemic, anti-Jewish
Agabus 108
Agag 133–34
ages of the world 21, 29
al-Afḍal Shāhanshāh 176
Albert of Aachen 3–4, 25, 53 n.20, 63, 68, 68–69 n.90, 82 n.153, 106 n.58, 122, 122 n. 133, 134, 139, 143, 169 n.60, 170, 177, 189
Alcuin of York 120
Aleppo 82, 121
Alexander II, pope 39–40
Alexander the Great 51
Alexius I, emperor 166, 176
Al-Aqsa Mosque 111, 197, 205
Al-Ḥākim 173–74
Alpert of Metz 142–43
Amalek, Amalekites 73, 128, 133–34, 136, 153, 191
Ambrose of Milan 20, 50
Amorites 86, 116
Anatolia 101
Andreas, bishop of Bari 183
Anselm of Canterbury 62
Anselm of Havelberg 29
Anselm of Laon 17
Anselm of Lucca 37, 196
Antichrist 37, 65–66 n.76, 74, 171, 173, 196
Antioch 81–83, 95, 102–03, 108–110, 112, 119, 121, 122, 123 n.136, 124, 127, 132, 134, 138, 139–40, 140 n.214, 141, 148, 176, 176 n.98, 203

Antiochus 79
apostles, apostolic life 13, 34, 37, 38, 63, 102, 103, 108, 109, 162–63, 185–87, 195, 205–06
  See also crusaders, first, as apostles
Aracaeus 103
Arius 101
Arnulf of Chocques 24, 120, 189, 199
ʻArqa, siege of 103, 176
Ascalon, battle of 53, 121, 175, 176, 178–80
Augustine 1, 19, 20, 28, 50, 60, 118 n.109, 128, 146–47, 149–50, 155–71, 172, 175, 179, 180, 190–91, 194, 199, 200, 208, 212
  avarice 4, 72, 135, 159, 163–64, 165, 166, 175, 178, 192, 193–202, 206
  De civitate Dei 50, 156, 157, 159, 160 n.21, 163–65
  Enarrationes in Psalmos 156, 157, 180
  See also two cities, concept of

Avars 115

Baal 152
Babylon, Babylonians 79, 134, 145, 153, 155, 156, 159, 160, 171–88, 189, 190–91, 192, 197, 201, 202–03, 208
  See also Muslims, Egyptians, Fatimids, two cities, concept of
Babylonian Captivity 172, 179, 185
Baghdad 134
Balaam 135
Baldric of Bourgueil (Baldric of Dol) 15–16, 24, 26, 42, 46, 56, 72, 74, 77, 82, 85, 89, 90, 97–98 n.18, 100, 105, 106 n.59, 118–19
Baldwin, count of Boulogne (later King Baldwin I) 102, 133
Baligant 173
Banias 108, n 64
baptism 62, 140, 144
Barnabas 102
Bartolf of Nangis 133–34
Bede 30, 50, 63 n.64, 100 n.21, 107, 108, 130, 131, 157, 171, 186, 194–95
bellum publicum 41
Benedict, Saint 187
Berengar of Tours 64

287

Index

Bernard of Clairvaux 61, 205–06
Bernard the Monk 105
Bertrand of Scabrica 176
Bible *see* Scriptures
biblical exegesis
  as political commentary 33–38
  Carolingian 20, 25, 27, 34, 36, 50, 64, 114–15, 130, 138, 195
  patristic 19, 20, 21, 27, 28, 34, 36, 50, 62, 64, 114, 120, 138, 200
  revival of in eleventh and twelfth centuries 2, 9–10, 21, 22–23, 28
  techniques and traditions of 2–4, 17–22, 28–29, 30–31
Bruno of Cologne 17, 26, 64
Bruno of Segni 116, 186–87, 196
Bruno of Würzburg 127 n.157
Byzantines 69, 101, 110

Cairo 173, 174, 177, 181, 184
  See also Babylon
Caen 24, 40
Caesarea 103, 108
Caffaro di Rustico da Caschifellone 103 n.44
Cain 152
Calvary 104
Canaan, Canaanites 58, 86, 103, 107, 108, 122, 125, 127, 152
Canterbury 24
caritas 159, 163–64, 166–67, 170, 199–200, 206
Carolingian exegetes *see* biblical exegesis, Carolingian
Cassian 63
Cassiodorus 19, 20, 50, 118 n.109, 120, 131, 157
catena 20, 78
Cecilia, daughter of William I 40
celibacy, clerical 37–38, 41
Chaldeans 130 n.168, 131
Chanson de Roland 173
chansons de geste 82 n.153, 173
Charlemagne 115
Charleville Poet 24, 68 n.87, 71 n.101, 77, 106 n.58, 109–10, 177, 181, 201
Chartres 23, 138 n.205
Les Chétifs 184
Christ 2, 3, 21, 37, 45, 58, 59, 60, 64, 71, 73, 77, 78, 79, 80 n.145, 81, 102, 103, 110, 113, 114, 117, 119, 122–23, 125–26, 139–40, 143, 144, 150, 151, 152, 153, 159, 163, 165, 166, 167, 168, 169, 170, 179, 180, 181, 182, 182 n.128, 186, 188, 190, 192–93, 194, 195, 196, 198, 201, 202, 203, 204, 205, 208
  crucifixion of 105, 140–42
  imitation of 51, 56, 59, 62, 64, 104, 117, 120, 161, 203, 206
  passion of 104–05, 114, 117, 147, 190
  resurrection of 51, 88, 198
christology 12, 21, 59, 98, 114, 136, 137, 145–50
  See also prophecy, typology
Chronicle of Saint-Maixent 93 nn.1 and 3, 94 n.4, 95, 96
Cilicia 101
city of god *see* Augustine, *De civitate Dei*; two cities, concept of
classical literature, as model 8, 43, 44, 89
cleansing of the Temple 13, 77, 188–207
Clermont, Council of 12, 39, 52, 55, 68–78, 79, 100 n.23, 113 n.86, 119, 125, 164 n.36, 168, 170, 196–97, 201
  See also Urban II
Cluny, Cluniacs 24, 26, 69, 130 n.170, 151–52
commemoration 5, 9
Constance of Antioch 95
conversion, converts 66, 136 n.197, 138, 139–141, 177, 181–82, 183
Cornelius 108
confusion 155, 159, 171, 172–73, 174, 175, 178, 181
  See also Babylon
cornerstone, parable of 152
crusaders, first
  as apostles 22, 51, 56, 59–60, 63–64, 71, 72, 73, 76, 77, 109, 160–71, 175, 178, 180, 187–88, 189–90, 191, 207–08
  as captives 123 n.136, 181–88
  as Israelites 12, 55, 58, 65, 72, 80, 87, 98, 107, 112–28, 133–36, 138–39, 152–53, 161, 165, 191, 212
  as martyrs 57, 62, 71, 78, 100, 134, 180–81
  as *milites Christi* 71–72, 74
  as monks 57, 163, 170, 187
  as pilgrims 65, 101, 104, 105–112, 117, 159, 163, 164–66
  See also Christ, imitation of
cupiditas see avarice
Cyrus 175

Dagon 133

288

Index

Damascus 3, 121
Daniel, Book of 134, 145, 147–48, 172, 185,
David 34, 79, 114, 119, 132, 133, 138,
  147–48
De excidio urbis Hierosolymitanae 109
Descriptio sanctorum locorum
  Hierusalem 97–98, 110–11
Deuteronomy 68, 85–87, 118, 124, 127
devil 13, 45, 81, 116, 130, 167, 171, 173,
  174, 180, 186–87
divine office *see* liturgy
divisio apostolorum 189
Dome of the Rock 94 n.5, 111, 197, 198
  n.200, 199, 204
Dorylaeum 82, n.153, 127

Edessa 105
Edom, Edomites 124, 128, 132, 133
education 12, 15–26, 54, 61, 67, 160 n.21, 212
Edward the Confessor 39
Egypt, Egyptians 58, 80, 86, 117, 121, 128,
  132, 133, 134, 173, 174–80, 183–84
  See also Babylon, Fatimids, pharaoh
Ekkehard of Aura 25, 55 n.29, 105
Ekron 103
Elijah 103, 116
Elisha 107, 108, 116
Encyclical of Sergius IV 125 n.146
Epistles 36, 37–38, 56, 57, 59–60, 64, 83
  See also 1 Corinthians, 1 Peter, 2
  Thessalonians, Galatians, Romans
Erkembert of Corvey 105
eschatology 5, 31, 34, 45, 54, 66, 72, 74,
  87, 89, 101, 148, 191, 198
Eucharist 62, 64, 195
Eusebius 29
exegesis *see* biblical exegesis; Scriptures
exempla 50, 83, 84, 183, 185
exile *see* crusaders, first, as pilgrims
Exodus 4, 57, 65, 87, 114, 118, 121–22,
  125, 132, 135
Ezekiel, Book of 62, 78, 81

familia Christi 72, 142
fasting 122, 123, 181, 186, 187
Fatimids 12, 80, 105, 142, 171, 173–83,
  192, 197, 201
  See also Egypt, Babylon, Babylonians
figurae see typology
First Crusade
  apocalyptic significance of 31, 65–66,
  72, 74, 81, 87, 89, 178, 191, 198

as act of vengeance 45, 47, 54, 74, 86,
  144, 199
as moral performance 158–59, 165–67,
  177, 181–83
as text 4, 71, 111, 191, 207, 212
as part of sacred history 3, 4, 46, 51, 96,
  101, 102, 104, 155, 174, 191
historiography of 4–9
letters associated with 52, 55–56, 80 n.145,
  113, 125
liturgical commemorations of 50,
  116–17, 128, 198, 204–05
preaching of 67, 68–78, 104, 112–13,
  120, 138, 161, 196–97
  See also crusaders, first
florilegia 27, 157, 159 n.17
Fontevrauld 161 n.23
Franks 34, 69, 73, 87, 93, 95, 96, 114–115,
  120, 127, 143, 176
as new Israelites 34, 114–115, 120, 126
  n.153
Fulbert of Chartres 151 n.258
Fulcher of Chartres 23, 45, 53 n.20, 61,
  71–72, 74, 75, 80, 100, 102, 103, 106
  n.58, 109, 110, 113 n.86, 121, 126 n.151,
  131–32, 133 n.186, 134 n.188, 150, 166,
  179, 196

Galatians, Epistle to 77, 81, 126
Galilee 37, 111
Genesis 16 n.6, 57, 65, 100 n.21, 114,
  125–26, 128, 151–52
geographical knowledge 64, 96–98
Gervase of Canterbury 27
Gesta Adhemari 127
Gesta Francorum 45, 49, 50, 57, 67, 68,
  70–71, 74, 75, 76, 79, 82, 83–90, 96,
  102–03, 106, 110, 119, 128, 139, 148
  authorship of 53–54 n.23, 84–85, 91
giant bibles 35
Gibeon 133 n.186
Gilbert Crispin 59, 137
Gilo of Paris 24, 26, 68 n.87, 75 n.123,
  103, 106 n.58, 121, 127, 132, 139, 140
  n.214, 144 n.232
Glossa Ordinaria 61 n.52, 63 n.64, 149
  n.251, 168 n.54
Godfrey, duke of Bouillon 3–4, 122, 132,
  147, 180
Godfrey of Babion 187
Goliath 132, 132 n.180
Gospels 21–22, 30 n.74, 36, 51, 56, 57–58,

Index

59, 60–61, 68, 71, 77, 78, 103, 105, 162, 163, 193, 194
  See also John, Gospel of; Luke, Gospel of; Mark, Gospel of; Matthew, Gospel of
greed *see* avarice
Gregorian reform *see* reform, ecclesiastical
Gregory I (the Great), pope   19, 20, 50, 138 n.203, 157, 187 n.152, 194
Gregory VII, pope   35–38, 60, 64, 116
Gregory of Tours   30
Guibert of Nogent   16 n.6, 23, 26, 44, 56, 63, 68, 72, 73, 74, 80, 82, 85, 87–89, 100 n.24, 101, 103, 104–05, 119, 123 n.136, 124, 125–26, 127, 128, 133, 137, 138–39, 140, 146, 148, 169, 175, 196, 200
Guy of Amiens   43

Hagar, Hagarenes   131, 133, 135
hagiography   8, 27, 35, 47, 63, 184, 200
Haifa   143
Haimo of Auxerre   25
Haimo of Halberstadt   186
Harold, king of England   40–41
hell   74, 132
Henry IV   35, 116, 172
Henry of Huntingdon   24, 42, 43–44, 46
Henry of Marcy   208
heresy, heretics   34, 101, 102, 130, 131, 162, 171, 173, 194, 195, 196, 199, 201
hermits   162
Herod, king   108, 142
Hincmar of Reims   156
Historia Nicaena vel Antiochena   127
history
  composition and study of   1–3, 7, 8–10, 15–17, 19, 26–34, 39, 44, 46
  in relation to theology   16, 31, 32, 47
  medieval definitions of   2, 27
Holofernes   58
Holy Lance   109, 178
Holy Land   43, 50, 58–59, 66, 74, 96, 97, 98–112, 164, 208
Holy Mandylion   102
Holy Sepulcher   3, 45 n.151, 70, 110 n.76, 112, 124, 127, 144 n.234, 147, 150, 151, 173, 182–83, 184, 188, 198, 199, 202, 204
Honorius Augustodunensis   66
Hrabanus Maurus   20, 25, 50, 63 n.64, 124 n.139, 127, 130 n.170, 157, 168 n.54, 186
Hugh of Bellefaire   176
Hugh of Flavigny   116, 156 n.6
Hugh of Fleury   158

Hugh of Saint Victor   29
Humbert of Silva Candida   131
humility   4, 40, 59, 81, 117, 139, 159, 163, 177, 188

Iconium   101
idolatry   58, 72, 87, 112, 113, 127, 131, 134, 135, 140, 148, 152, 161, 171, 173, 177, 192, 195, 199, 200–01, 202, 206, 207
imitatio Christi see Christ, imitation of
Incarnation   21, 51, 62, 88, 137, 146, 148, 150
Investiture Contest   35–36, 116, 158–59 n.17, 172
  See also reform, ecclesiastical
Isaac   21, 114
Isaiah, Book of   3, 57, 62, 74, 78, 81, 145, 146–47
Ishmael, Ishmaelites   131, 135
Isidore of Seville   2 n.5, 19, 27, 93 n.3, 94 n.4, 147, 171 n.71, 172 n.76
Israel, Israelites   2, 12, 31, 34, 51, 55, 58, 65, 72, 73, 80, 81, 86–87, 98, 100, 102, 107, 112–128, 130, 132–36, 138–39, 146–47, 152–53, 156, 161, 165, 167, 191, 200, 212
  See also Holy Land; crusaders, first, as Israelites
Ivo of Chartres   23

Jacob   3, 4, 79
James, apostle   79
Jarento of Saint–Bénigne   116
Jebusites   73, 129, 133
Jeremiah, Book of   57, 62
Jericho   107
Jerome   20, 29, 50, 60. 62, 100 n.21, 125 n.146, 131, 155 n.3, 167–68, 185–86, 193–94
Jerusalem   2, 3–4, 15, 57, 59, 62, 74, 77, 78, 100, 101, 103–05, 107, 110–11, 119, 121, 122, 132, 135, 146, 148, 166, 168, 171, 176, 182–83, 184 n.144, 188–207
  as heavenly city   13, 120, 155–56, 159–60, 172–73, 179–80, 208
    See also two cities, concept of
  as mother   77, 179
  Christ's entry into   84 n.145
  crusader conquest of   1, 12, 45, 51, 52, 68, 78–81, 91, 103–05, 132–34, 141–43, 144, 150, 152, 177–78, 188–207

Index

pilgrimage to   71, 72, 73, 96–97, 106, 151, 173–74, 175, 176 n.100
Jerusalemites *see* crusaders, first
Jews, Judaism   12, 20–21, 34, 55, 58, 59, 66, 73, 84, 88, 98, 104, 125–26, 131, 136–153, 183, 197, 201
See also polemic, anti-Jewish
Joachim of Fiore   65–66
John, Gospel of   37, 49, 57, 67, 192–93, 194
John of Würzburg   204 n.234
Jordan, river   104, 107
Joseph of Arimathea   105, 142
Josephus   43 n.142, 97–98 n.18, 191
Josiah   114
Joshua   80, 107, 108, 122, 133 n.186
Joshua, Book of   85
Judah Maccabee   58
Judith   58

Kerbogha, atabeg of Mosul   81–90, 121, 124, 132, 139–40, 149
  mother of   81–90, 128, 134 n.191
Kings, Books of   30 n.74, 116, 134,

Lambert of Hersefeld   35
Lambert of Saint-Omer   39 n.121
Lamentations, Book of   16 n.6, 81
Lanfranc of Bec   18 n.12, 24, 64, 158 n.13
Laon, school of   23, 64
Last Emperor   66
Last Judgment *see* First Crusade, apocalyptic significance of
Le Puy, abbey   24, 117, 123 n.135, 138 n. 203
Leviticus   127
Liber de unitate ecclesiae conservanda   172–73
Lincoln   24
liturgy   6, 13, 27, 46, 49, 50, 61, 62, 67, 91, 114, 116–118, 119, 128, 136, 148, 172, 184, 189 n.158, 204–05
Lombards   115
Longinus   142
Louis VII, king   31
Luca of Bitonto   183
Luke, Gospel of   57, 67, 74, 76 n.129, 78, 196

Ma'arat (Ma'arra)   128, 148, 149
Maccabees   51, 57, 62–63, 100, 114 n.90, 116 n.100, 118, 153, 203
See also Judah Maccabee, Mattathias
Maillezais *see* Saint–Pierre de Maillezais
Marbod of Rennes   24

Marco Polo   183
Mark, Gospel of   60 n.45, 140
Mars   43, 89
martyrdom   57, 62, 71, 78, 100, 114 n.90, 134, 180
See also crusaders, first, as martyrs
Mass   61, 63 n.64
Mattathias   203
Matthew, Gospel of   13, 36, 45, 57–58, 58 n.42, 61–61, 63, 66, 67, 69, 71, 73, 76, 77, 78, 81, 162, 167–71, 181–82, 185–88, 193, 202, 204–05
Medes   131
Melchizedek   104, 116
memory   9, 20, 49, 91
Michelsberg Continuator   25, 69 nn.90 and 93, 119–20, 124, 125 n.150, 175, 177
Midian, Midianites   131, 132, 135–36
milites Christi see crusaders, first, as *milites Christi*
monks   13, 17, 18, 25–26, 33, 35, 37, 39, 41 n.132, 49, 57, 59, 60, 61, 62–63, 66, 75 n.124, 76, 78, 85, 86, 91, 93–97, 112, 116, 130, 145, 152, 158, 159, 162, 163, 164, 168, 169, 170, 183, 187, 190, 200 n.211, 206, 212
Monte Cassino, abbey   157 n.11, 183, 184 n.144
Monte Cassino Anonymous   25, 63, 67, 68, 76, 82, 84, 85, 106 n.58, 106, n.59, 128, 169, 176, 181–83, 184, 184 n.142
Moses   27, 29, 58, 65, 80, 110, 113, 114, 122–23, 124, 125, 127, 147
Mount of Olives   104, 111
Muslims   2, 4, 73, 77, 82–90, 109 n.72, 111, 121, 127, 163, 167, 192, 197–202, 206–07
  as Babylonians   177–88
  as descendants of Ishmael   131, 135
  as pagans   12, 58, 72, 83, 86, 88, 89, 98, 108, 113, 118, 128–36, 212
  compared with Jews   98, 137, 139–46, 148, 150–52
  conversion of   66, 139–40, 177, 181–82
See also Fatimids, Hagarenes, Ishmaelites, Turks

Nathan, prophet   116
Nebuchadnezzar   79, 150, 172, 173, 177, 185
New Fire, miracle of   173, 182–83, 184
New Testament   4, 5, 12, 20, 21–22, 36–37, 55–56, 57–58, 59–60, 62, 66, 67, 69, 71,

291

Index

76, 79–80, 101, 114, 160, 161, 162, 163, 191
  See also 1 Corinthians, 1 Peter, 2 Thessalonians, Acts of the Apostles, Galatians, John, Luke, Mark, Matthew, Romans
Nicaea   100–01, 102, 135, 175
Noah   103
Norman Conquest   12, 17, 38–41, 212
  compared to First Crusade   39, 46
  Latin narratives of   41–46
Numbers, Book of   118

Obadiah, priest   183
Odo Arpin, viscount of Bourges   184 n.143
Old Testament   3, 12, 20–21, 45, 55–59, 63, 66, 67, 69, 79–80, 83–84, 86, 87, 98, 105, 113–118, 122–23, 127, 129–33, 135–37, 145–51, 171, 198, 201, 212
  See also Genesis, Exodus, Leviticus, Numbers, Deuteronomy, Joshua, Kings, Psalms, Isaiah, Jeremiah, Lamentations, Ezekiel, Daniel, Zechariah
Orderic Vitalis   16, 25, 40 n.125, 42–46, 60–61, 69 n.93, 74–75, 77, 82, 102, 123 n.136, 126 n.151, 132, 137, 144
Origen   193
Orosius   29, 50, 157, 171 n.74
Otbert of Liège   116
Otto of Friesing   208

pagans, paganism   58, 66, 73, 116, 129–31, 132, 134
  See also Muslims, as pagans
papacy   22 n.32, 38, 40, 162, 196
  See also Alexander II, Gregory I, Gregory VII, Pascal II, Urban II
Paris   24, 157 n.11
Pascal II, pope   127
patristic exegetes *see* biblical exegesis, patristic
Paul, Saint   37–38, 57, 64, 71, 72, 102, 103, 108, 126, 190, 193
  See also Epistles
Peace of God   69, 72
Pentecost   103, 146–47
Peter, Saint   37, 102–03, 109, 110, 139–40
  banner of   39–40
Peter Abelard   155
Peter Alfonsi   138
Peter Bartholomew   141

Peter Damian   59, 131 n.172, 147 n.243, 152 n.258, 196
Peter of Maillezais   15–16, 94
Peter of Picca   176
Peter the Hermit   139–40
Peter the Venerable   151–52
Peter Tudebode   61, 63, 67, 68, 76, 79, 82, 84, 85, 95, 106, 109, 110, 119, 143
Pharaoh   58, 86, 116, 132
Philip, apostle   103, 108
Philistines   103, 130, 132, 133, 134, 138, 153
Phineas   135
Phoebus   43
pilgrimage *see* Jerusalem, pilgrimage to
pilgrimage guides   8, 33, 47, 98, 152
  crusade chronicles as   96–97, 105–12
  See also Holy Land
Poitou   94–95
polemic, anti–Jewish   12, 20, 98, 136–152, 211
poverty   59, 70, 178, 205
preaching *see* First Crusade, preaching of
pride   4, 81, 155, 159, 164, 165, 174, 177, 178, 186, 188
Promised Land *see* Holy Land
prophecy   57, 58–59, 62, 66, 72, 74, 78, 80–81, 83, 86–87, 88, 114, 116, 126, 129, 136, 137, 143–51, 152, 171, 175, 191, 208
Proverbs, book of   18, 57, 124
Psalms   30 n.74, 36, 57, 58, 60, 61–62, 63, 64, 66, 68, 69, 73, 74, 78, 80, 83, 84 n.166, 85, 87, 88, 114, 118–20, 145, 149–50
Pseudo-Bruno of Chartreuse   120, 128
Psychomachia   159

quadrivium   17

Ralph Glaber   173–74, 184 n.144
Ralph of Caen   24, 68, 79, 104, 110, 112, 122–23, 132, 138, 139–40, 189, 198 n.200, 199
Ramleh, second battle of   184
Raphidim   133
Raymond of Aguilers   24, 44, 50, 55, 56, 63, 67, 80, 104, 109 n.68, 110, 117, 119, 121, 122, 124, 127, 138 n.203, 138–39 n.206, 141, 143, 147–48, 166, 189, 199
Raymond of Poitiers   95
Raymond of Saint–Gilles, count of Toulouse   104–05, 122, 166 n.48

Index

Red Sea, parting of 80, 86, 121, 132, 191
reform, ecclesiastical 4, 9–10, 21–22, 23, 32, 33–38, 40, 41, 47, 54, 60, 63, 64, 66, 69, 72, 116, 122 n.132, 130–31, 136, 156, 161, 162–63, 168, 169, 172, 192, 195–97, 206–07, 211
regular canons 13, 17, 18, 24, 26 n.53, 49, 63, 110 n.76, 117, 153, 162
Reims 24, 26, 157 n.11, 181, 184
relics 40–41, 100, 109, 144 n.228, 178, 188
 See also Holy Lance, True Cross
Remigius of Auxerre 63 n.64, 120
Revelation, book of 45, 57, 63 n.64, 65–66, 171, 179, 202–03
Rhineland massacres 136, 141 n.218, 144
Ripoll Anonymous 133, 144
Robert of Normandy, duke 104
Robert of Reims (Robert the Monk) 23–24, 44, 51, 56, 67–68, 72, 74 n.122, 75 n.123, 77, 80, 81, 82, 86, 96–97, 101, 104, 106 nn.58 and 59, 108, 118 n.108, 132–33, 121 n.122, 124, 125, 127, 128, 132, 133, 134, 139 n.208, 148, 166, 168, 178–79, 180, 200–01
Roger II, bishop of Beauvais 184
Romans, Epistle to 37, 56, 69, 88
Rome 171, 172, 200
Rorgo Fretellus 106 n.59, 153
Rothard 3
Rule of Augustine 63
Rule of Benedict 168 n.56
Rupert of Deutz 23, 28–29, 66, 158

Saewulf 204 n.234
Saint-Bertin, abbey 111
Saint-Evroul, abbey 60–61, 75 n.124, 137
Saint-Martial, abbey 133
Saint-Pierre de Maillezais, abbey 15–16, 93–97, 152
Saladin 96 n.12
Samaria 124, 130 n.170
Samuel, prophet 37
Santa Maria of Ferraria, abbey 183
Saracen, origin of term 131
Sarah 131
Sarepta 103
Saul 37, 79, 133–34, 191
Scriptures
 allegorical sense 3, 16, 20, 23, 28, 30, 32, 33, 34, 36, 37, 38, 54, 58, 59, 62, 87 n.178, 113, 114, 116, 120, 124 n.139, 127, 130, 130 n.170, 135, 139, 152, 155, 156, 160 n.21, 162, 169, 170–71, 174, 175, 187, 190, 193, 195, 204, 205–06, 213
 as a mirror 31
 Latin style 29–30, 49–50, 53
 literal (or historical) sense 10–11, 20, 24–25, 28–29, 34, 36, 65, 87, 113, 125, 132, 139, 193, 194 n.180
 moral sense 3, 4, 20, 21, 25, 28, 30, 34, 36, 52, 55, 71, 72, 73–74, 79, 80, 156, 160 n.21, 162, 190, 191, 192, 199, 201
 study of 15–26, 30–31
 See also biblical exegesis, prophecy, typology
Second Crusade 1, 7, 12, 49, 52, 151
Second Crusade Cycle 183
Seon, king 86
Sermon on the Mount 71, 76
schools *see* education
Shaizar 121
Sidon 103
Sigebert of Gembloux 172
simony 37, 38, 41, 72, 130, 194, 195–97, 199, 200, 201, 206, 207
Sodom and Gomorrah 125
Soissons 24
Solomon 75, 114, 116, 153
Stabelo 3
Stephen, priest 119
Stephen, Saint 104
Suleiman 82 n.153

Tancred of Hauteville 102, 104, 122, 199, 201
Tarsus 102
Temple at Jerusalem 13, 38, 73, 77, 77, 79, 111, 126, 143–44, 188–207, 212
 See also cleansing of the Temple
Templars 205–06
Third Crusade 95
Titus, Roman emperor 79, 144 n.229
Tower of Babel 178
Tripoli 103
trivium 17
Troy, siege of 43, 51
True Cross 127, 144 n.228, 178
Turks 64, 73, 83, 87, 88, 102, 109–110, 112, 124, 126 n.151, 128, 132, 133, 139, 176, 201
 See also Muslims
two cities, concept of 12–13, 155–60, 165–66, 170, 171–75, 178–80, 188–90, 192, 199–200, 204

293

See also Augustine, Babylon, Jerusalem
typology   3, 4, 16, 21, 30, 37, 52, 55, 57, 58, 59, 62, 65, 71, 72, 77, 79–80, 87, 100, 101, 103–06, 111, 113, 115, 116, 119, 123 n.135, 126, 128–29, 133, 134, 135, 153, 156, 160, 161, 174, 175, 178, 179, 187, 189, 191, 192, 198, 203–04, 207, 211, 212
See also biblical exegesis, christology, Scriptures, allegorical sense of
Tyre   103

Urban II, pope   12, 26, 40, 45, 53, 68–78, 100 n.23, 102, 116, 119, 123, 125, 133, 146, 156, 164 n.36, 166, 168, 170, 196–97, 201–02
See also Clermont, Council of
usury   195, 200, 201, 207

Valéry, Saint   40
Virgin Mary   21, 105, 109
virtues and vices *see* First Crusade, as moral performance; Psychomachia
vita apostolica see apostolic life

W. Grassegals, crusader   31
William I, king of England   39–41, 43
William IX, duke of Aquitaine   15 n.1, 94, 95, 184 n.142
William of Malmesbury   16 n.6, 24, 25, 40 n.125, 42, 43–45, 45 n.152, 74–75, 77, 102, 105, 109 n.70, 125 n.147, 137, 156 n.4, 164 n.36, 168, 170, 175, 196–97, 201
William of Poitiers   40–41, 43
William of Tyre   192, 202–03
witnesses, witnessing 7, 68–69, 84, 91, 109, 149–50

Xerxes   43

Zechariah, Book of   57, 62, 68, 81

www.ingramcontent.com/pod-product-compliance
Lightning Source LLC
Chambersburg PA
CBHW051602230426
43668CB00013B/1945